THE

# DETROIT

# SYMPHONY

# ORCHESTRA

# THE DETROIT SYMPHONY ORCHESTRA

## Grace, Grit, and Glory

LAURIE LANZEN HARRIS

with Paul Ganson

A Painted Turtle book

Detroit, Michigan

20  19  18  17  16          5  4  3  2  1

ISBN 978-0-8143-3136-1 (jacketed cloth)
ISBN 978-0-8143-4062-2 (e-book)

Library of Congress Control Number:
2016932279

*Designed and typeset by Bryce Schimanski*
*Composed in Adobe Garamond Pro*

Painted Turtle is an imprint of
Wayne State University Press

Wayne State University Press
Leonard N. Simons Building
4809 Woodward Avenue
Detroit, Michigan 48201-1309

Visit us online at wsupress.wayne.edu

We gratefully acknowledge Gwen and Richard Bowlby, longtime patrons and tireless supporters of the Detroit Symphony Orchestra and Wayne State University Press, whose generous gift has made possible both the publication of this volume and a partial matching gift from the Community Foundation of Southeast Michigan.

# Contents

# Preface

THE DETROIT SYMPHONY ORCHESTRA BEGAN IN 1887 AS A RATHER small ensemble of around thirty-five players in a city that was just emerging as an industrial power. From that time to the present, the two entities—the city and its orchestra—have grown and prospered, making their mark on a national scale, in musical artistry for the symphony, and in economic might for the city. But they have each faced crises as well—financial, social, and cultural—that have forced the DSO out of existence three times, and the city to the brink of dissolution.

Yet in the face of adversity, they have revived, and thrived. How did it happen, and what does it mean for the future of the orchestra and the city?

*The Detroit Symphony Orchestra: Grace, Grit, and Glory* offers a perspective on this shared story. It describes and documents the history of the DSO through the prism of the history of the city it has called home for nearly 130 years. It details the orchestra's cycle of growth, glory, collapse, and renewal in light of the city's own dynamic economic, demographic, and cultural changes.

This book also provides a perspective on the DSO in the context of the history of the American symphony orchestra, from the nineteenth century to the present, from the "Make America Musical" movement and Theodore Thomas in the 1870s to the current economic and cultural crises that have threatened the viability of many modern symphony orchestras today, including the DSO.

It is a story that builds on the work of others, most importantly the history of the symphony that was written in 1964 by Edith Rhetts Tilton. The former

Educational Director for the DSO, and the first person to hold that title for an American orchestra, she had been brought to Detroit in the 1920s by Ossip Gabrilowitsch, one of the finest and most important music directors in the orchestra's history, who led the DSO during its first "Golden Age."

Tilton's importance to the DSO and Detroit cannot be overemphasized. She forged relationships first with the public and parochial schools of the city, then with the state of Michigan that established music education in curriculums statewide. She brought classical music, played by the DSO, into classrooms throughout Detroit, introducing students—and their parents—to music, helping to realize Gabrilowitsch's mission to reach out to the community, share the beauty of classical music, and build knowledgeable listeners and supporters for the orchestra.

Yet Tilton's history, published in 1964, was written to celebrate the fiftieth anniversary of the DSO's founding, which at that time was acknowledged as the ensemble that began in 1914 under the baton of Weston Gales. And while that date was long accepted as the establishment of the first Detroit Symphony, subsequent research suggests a longer, richer history.

For the purposes of this book, we suggest that the history of the orchestra begins twenty-seven years earlier, with the first ensemble to call itself the "Detroit Symphony Orchestra," in 1887. Thus the history of the founding of that first

DSO, and the history of what led up to its creation, needed to be documented and explored, and that is how we begin this study. So, too, did the subsequent fifty years, from 1964 to the present, need to be examined to fully understand the context of the changing fortunes of the DSO. Throughout, our purpose has been to chart the full history of the DSO—the musicians, the music directors, the management, and the boards—as they sought for musical excellence, and the consistent funding and leadership to achieve it, in the changing economic and cultural landscape of Detroit.

We envision that the audience for this history is made up of the general reading public, non-professionals who nonetheless are current and past supporters of the DSO, as well as people interested in Michigan history, music, and the background of one of the oldest cultural institutions in Detroit. That means that the language used throughout the book to describe the music and the workings of the orchestra has been chosen with a general audience in mind.

A work such as this could never have been accomplished without the help of many individuals, and I will try to list them all here, and to acknowledge their contributions to the project.

First, I would like to thank Paul Ganson, longtime Assistant Principal Bassoon with the DSO, who was an integral part of launching this project, who worked tirelessly to save Orchestra Hall, and whose wit and wisdom inform this book.

Next, I would like to thank the librarians of the Detroit Public Library Main Branch, especially Jo Ann Poske and Cully Sommers of the Music, Art, and Literature Department. They provided me with original programs from the earliest DSO to the present, as well as scrapbooks containing some of the only surviving copies of the earliest reviews of that first ensemble. They also gave me access to the unpublished master's thesis of Lynne Marie Mattson, which, along with Tilton's history, represents only the second history of the DSO covering the period from 1914 to 1964. Additionally, they made available the online databases of the DPL that contain some newspaper holdings dating back to the nineteenth century, which, while incomplete due to lack of funding, offered at least a place to start for this research.

Also at the Main Branch, the staff of the Burton Historical Collection was of crucial importance to the research for this book, including Mark Bowden, Coordinator of Special Collections, as well as Assistant Manager for Special Collections Romie Minor and Archivist Dawn Eurich. Through them, I was able to read the earliest physical evidence of the DSO, the ledgers of Fritz Kalsow, and to hold in my hand the documents establishing the Symphony Society and Orchestra Hall.

A portion of the DSO Archive is now housed at the Walter Reuther Library at Wayne State University, and the staff of the Reading Room, especially Reference Archivist Kristen Chinery, was always helpful to me as I researched the collection, which offers resources especially pertinent to the study of labor relations and financial information from the period 1950 to 1986.

The DSO Archive, containing thousands of pieces and compiled from over 100 years of materials donated to or purchased by the orchestra, was for many years under the superb direction of Archivist Cynthia Korolov. Although Cynthia is no longer part of the organization, she was my sure and unfailingly helpful guide to the contents of the Archive, and was especially important in finding the many photos that illustrate the text. Her contributions were crucial to making this book what it is.

During the tenure of Paul Paray, in what is known as the "Second Golden Age" of the DSO, the orchestra made a series of recordings for the Mercury label that are still prized by collectors. I would like to thank the staff of Mercury Classics and the Universal Music Group for their generosity in allowing us to use the Paray album covers in the book, and to Tom Fine, son of producer Wilma Cozart Fine, whose production expertise shaped these timeless classics of recording. Universal also granted us permission to use album covers from several London recordings made by Antal Dorati and the DSO, and for this we are most grateful. Similarly, I would like to thank the staff of Chandos Records for granting permission to use album covers from the "Third Golden Age" of the DSO, under Neeme Järvi.

And speaking of libraries and recordings, I would be remiss if I did not thank the staff of my own local library, the Huntington Woods Public Library, especially Director Anne Hage and staff member Sally Kohlenberg, as well as the resources of the Library Network, through whose combined collections I was able to borrow and listen to most of the DSO recordings that are described in the text. They are, like the DSO, "a source of civic pride."

The actual writing of the book was improved greatly by three individuals, each of whom read the book as it was written. First, Art Woodford, a colleague and friend of many years, read each chapter in draft and then in final form, offering the kind of advice that only someone with his experience as an historian, author, and editor could bring. Next, another friend, Laurence Liberson, Assistant Principal Clarinet with the DSO for thirty-five years, brought a lifetime of experience as a symphony musician as well as a razor sharp understanding of English grammar and usage, to his reading of each chapter.

Finally, Kathy Wildfong, Editor-in-Chief and Associate Director of Wayne State University Press, was the most patient and helpful guide any author could have wished for, offering advice and commentary at every stage of development. I would

like to thank her, and the entire staff of the Press, especially Emily Nowak, Carrie Teefey, and Bryce Schimanski, and Director Jane Hoehner for presenting me with this wonderful project. It's been a pleasure working with you all.

And to my husband, Dan Harris, who read every chapter and every revision, and who listened to every piece on every recording cited here, and whose insights into the music inspired my own understanding, grateful thanks.

—Laurie Lanzen Harris

THE DETROIT SYMPHONY ORCHEStra, despite all its virtues and all its graces, has not worn its history on its sleeve. Until now the closest thing to an official history of the DSO was a series of articles that appeared in the program books of the 1964–65 season. The primary author was Edith Rhetts (Mrs. Arthur) Tilton, the first, most renowned, most beloved, and longest serving Director of Education; J. Dorsey Callaghan, the Music Writer of the *Detroit Free Press*, and Harvey Taylor, a music critic with the Detroit Times, among others, also contributed. The occasion was styled as the Orchestra's Fiftieth Anniversary Season, hearkening to its rebirth in 1914. When a few members of the public approached the powers-that-were in an effort to recognize the Orchestra's founding in 1887, they were threatened with bodily harm if they tried to present the case for 1887 and thereby blemish the party-planning for 1964.

Fortunately, the Detroit Symphony Orchestra has not been able to long tolerate any attempt to shorten or embellish its history. Its very richness resides in its full length and diversity. True, it has gone out of business more times than any other major American orchestra but that very fact implies that the DSO has also come into business more times than any of its peer orchestras. And throughout and even between all its incarnations there lives an inextinguishable musical pulse that survives when every other reason for establishing and promoting an orchestra succumbs to the ceaseless ebb and flow of human caprice.

Beneath every silent season of the DSO there lurks a business failure—or, perhaps more aptly, a failure of business to come to sustain a marriage between the spirit of music and the intended and agreed purposes of the Detroit Symphony Orchestra. Calvin Coolidge once remarked from the bully pulpit of the US Presidency: "The business of America is business."Alfred P. Sloan, renowned for his business acumen in assembling the General Motors Corporation from an inchoate host of smaller car companies during the early years of the American automobile industry, later went even further. He famously intoned: "The business of business is business." But it took Sol Hurok, the irrepressible impresario who graced America's platforms with the cream of talent from around the globe,

to put his finger on the oft-distempered relationship between business and the arts of music and musical performance: "If I was in this business for the business, I wouldn't be in this business."

Throughout the many booms and busts of Detroit's rapid industrialization and even during the great demographic changes wrought by the promise of the Five Dollar Day, the unequalled sufferings of the Great Depression and the need to staff the Arsenal of Democracy during World War II, the DSO still managed to make the world's first radio broadcast of a program of symphonic music, win the first-ever Grand Prix du Disque for a compact disc, and provide the first regular series of live webcasts worldwide.

These events and more are recounted in this history of the Detroit Symphony Orchestra. May they satisfy, and increase, your curiosity and your interest in the ineffable, overpowering beauties of the music of the Detroit Symphony Orchestra in Orchestra Hall.

I would like to provide special mention of the following institutions and individuals for their work in preserving and making available materials essential to telling the story of the DSO:

The Archives of the Detroit Symphony Orchestra: Stephanie Chantos Lucas and Cynthia Porter Korolov. Thanks, too, to Paul Marotta, formerly of the Pubic Relations Department of the DSO, who rescued some DSO records from an impending flood in the old Winkelman Building.

————————

The Library of the Detroit Symphony Orchestra: Arthur Luck, Albert Steger, Elkhonon Yoffe, Robert Stiles, and Ethan Allen

————————

The Detroit Public Library, Music and Performing Arts Division: E. Kurtz Myers, Jeanne Salathiel, Joanne Poske, and Cully Sommers

————————

The Burton Historical Collection: David Poremba, Mark Bowden, Romie Minor, and Dawn Eurich

————————

Wayne State University Department of Music: Valter Poole, Theresa Volk, and Professor Dennis Tini

————————

The Walter P. Reuther Library of Labor and Urban Affairs: Founding Director Dr. Philip P. Mason, Alberta Asmar, Director Erik Nordberg, and Louis Jones

————————

The University of Michigan: Professors Mark Clague, Lewis Hugh Cooper, and John Mohler

————————

The University of Michigan Musical Society: Gail Rector and Kenneth Fischer

————————

The Bentley Historical Library: Dr. Francis Blouin and William Wallich

————————

The Benson Ford Research Center at The Henry Ford: Terry Hoover

————————

The State of Michigan History Division: James M. Bryant and Sandra Clark

————————

The Harmonie Club: Eugene Strobel

————————

The Historical Society of Detroit: Solan Weeks and Robert Bury

————————

Maureen Murphy, Jeffrey Montgomery, Robert Warsham, Jill Woodward, Caroline Goldstein, John Lucas, Natalie Gottfreund, Jacob Kellman, Martha Volpe, Jian Desjardins, Norman Schweikert, and Donald McDonald Dickinson Thurber

————————

And my star, Astrid, who possesses a keener ear, a larger spirit, and is still pointing upward.

—Paul Ganson
Historian, Detroit Symphony Orchestra

THE

**DETROIT**

**SYMPHONY**

**ORCHESTRA**

# An Emerging City and Its Music, 1701–1887

HOW DID SYMPHONIC MUSIC COME TO MICHIGAN?

And how did the organization now known as the Detroit Symphony Orchestra develop from a group of musicians made up mainly of European immigrants in the nineteenth century into one of the finest professional ensembles in the country in the twenty-first? And what were the challenges and triumphs along the way?

In many ways, the rise and fall of the Detroit Symphony parallels the financial and social fortunes of the city itself. This book was written shortly after the city of Detroit filed for bankruptcy in 2013. It was the largest municipal bankruptcy in the nation's history. The DSO has also failed financially, and gone out of business, more often than any other major ensemble in the country. But it has also come *back* more times than any other symphonic organization.

It is in this spirit that this book seeks to chronicle the history of the Detroit Symphony Orchestra: how it began, how it flourished and failed, only to come back to life again. It is the story of the musicians, organizations, boards, patrons, management, and audiences, from the early days of Detroit as an emerging industrial center, through the boom and bust economic cycles of the last century, to the present day, in which the musical, financial, and cultural forces that have shaped the ensemble and the city continue to play out.

In 1805, most of the city of Detroit was destroyed in a devastating fire. One of the city's leaders, Father Gabriel Richard, famously vowed, "We hope for better things; it will arise from the ashes."[1] So, too, has the DSO come back time and again, tempered by time and change, and determined to survive. Here is its story, entwined throughout history with the city of its founding.

## DETROIT'S BEGINNINGS

The earliest inhabitants of what is now Detroit were Native Americans, who lived along what is now the Detroit River and used the area as a trading site. When the first Europeans arrived in the region in the 1600s, they encountered several main tribal groups: the Huron (or Wyandotte), the Ottawa (Odawa), the Chippewa (or Ojibwa), the Fox, the Sac (or Sauk), the Miami, and Potawatomi.[2] Some of the paths used by these early tribes became the highways and streets of Detroit still used today, including Woodward Avenue, home to the DSO's Orchestra Hall.

The first Europeans to reach the Detroit region were most likely French fur trappers and traders. Like the Native Americans, they made their living along the river, and traded their furs throughout the Great Lakes region by way of its interconnected lakes and rivers. They referred to the river that linked Lake Erie and Lake St. Clair as "the strait," or "le détroit," in French.

On July 24, 1701, French explorer Antoine Laument de Lamothe Cadillac landed on the shore of the river. Along with soldiers, traders, farmers, and priests, Cadillac founded a French fortress, which he called "Fort Pontchartrain du Detroit."[3] Cadillac thus established French control over the fur trade, the region, and the waterway of Detroit, which lasted until 1760. That year, the British took over the settlement during the French and Indian War. The British remained in control of the region for almost three decades, even after their surrender to the new United States in 1781, and the signing of the Treaty of Paris in 1783, which ended the Revolutionary War and granted the lands, including Michigan, to the United States. When the British finally ceased their occupation of Detroit in 1796, they moved across the river to Fort Malden, in Amherstberg, Ontario, Canada.[4]

It is at this historical juncture that we read one of the first mentions of instrumental music in Michigan. In 1798, Father Gabriel Richard brought the first organ to Detroit, which was installed at the city's first church, Ste. Anne's. One year later, in 1799, Dr. William Harffy, a British surgeon with the garrison in Detroit, mentioned having a harpsichord, albeit one that never seemed to play in tune.[5] In 1804, Sarah Whipple Sproat married Judge Solomon Sibley and brought what is thought to be the first piano to their new home in Detroit.[6]

In 1805, the Michigan Territory was established, and Detroit, by then a settlement of about 500 people, was named its capital. But the new capital was destroyed by fire in June of 1805. When it was time to rebuild, the regional leadership, under the governorship of William Hull and vision of

Judge Augustus Woodward, chose to adopt a plan similar to that used by Charles L'Enfant in designing the layout for the nation's capital in Washington, DC.

So the new city of Detroit emerged from the ruins of the fire, and after the War of 1812 ended in 1815, the city and its population began to grow. Lewis Cass had been named governor in 1813, and he oversaw the growth and prosperity of Detroit and Michigan for the next two decades. He negotiated with the Indian tribes for the purchase of land, which brought many migrants from New England to Michigan to establish farms throughout the state. Steamboats began bringing people and goods to Michigan, and the opening of the Erie Canal in 1825 brought an ever-increasing stream of new settlers to the region.[7]

The city's population reached 2,222 in 1830, as Detroit became a stopping point for migrants to gather supplies as they pushed into the interior of the region to establish their homesteads. Soon, ships were bringing people to the territory and shipping back produce and other agricultural products from Michigan to the eastern United States. Commercial fishing, too, began to flourish in the region, with seven ships carrying salted fish east from Detroit every day.

## IMMIGRANTS AND THE DEMAND FOR MUSIC

As the population of Detroit grew, tripling to 9,124 in 1840 and reaching 21,019 in 1850, the demand for consumer goods, and for culture, grew as well. The study and performance of music became part of a growing interest in defining a cultural sensibility in the city. New churches sprang up for the growing population, and church choirs became among the first amateur musical groups in the region. Music education was considered important enough that it was part of the curriculum of such private schools as the Detroit Female Seminary, where it was taught for its religious and "humanizing" effect. As the principal of the school, George Willson, wrote to C. C. Trowbridge:

> The cultivation of *sacred music* ought in my judgment to be a regular branch of instruction in all our principal schools, and the singing of a verse or two of some appropriate hymn, should be part of the stated religious exercises of the school. The softening, harmonizing, and *humanizing* influence of music has ever been admitted.[8]

Immigrant groups continued to arrive in Detroit, many from New England, and, beginning in the 1830s, from Germany. Soon, the Germans became the largest immigrant group in the region. They came for many reasons, seeking opportunities away from the political unrest in their own country, and the chance to establish their own businesses in the growing city. They were largely an educated group, and had capital to invest as well. They settled in an area between Jefferson and Gratiot that became known as "Germantown." There, they started small businesses, worked in the tobacco, brewing, and stone and marble works industries, and also established St. Mary's Catholic Church.[9]

## THE GERMANIA MUSICAL SOCIETY

In the late 1840s, the continuing political unrest in Germany brought a group of musicians to the United States that would have a defining impact on the development of professional musical ensembles in Detroit and the country. The Germania Musical Society, made up of twenty-four young professional musicians, most of them educated and conservatory-trained, left Germany in 1848 for the New World. They played their first concert in New York on October 5, 1848, and spent the next six years traveling the country, bringing performances of nineteenth-century European classical music, including Beethoven and Schubert, to the cities of the East Coast and the Midwest. They played over 900 concerts, and it is estimated that over one million people heard them from 1848 to 1854, when the group disbanded.[10]

The Germania performed in Detroit in 1853 and 1854 to much acclaim, providing programming that became something of a standard for orchestras into the late nineteenth century. Their concerts included excerpts from classical symphonies by Beethoven and other European composers, arias and overtures from popular operas by Rossini, and well-known folk tunes, such as "The Old Folks at Home."[11] Detroit proved to be so receptive to the Germania's music that two of its members, violinist Charles F. Stein and violist William Buchheister, decided to settle in the city when the ensemble broke up. They formed their own orchestra and also began a successful music business, selling pianos and other instruments as well as sheet music from their store in Detroit.[12]

## THE HARMONIE SOCIETY

The influence of German immigrants on the musical vitality of Detroit continued for decades, as more German musicians settled in the area and, often under the auspices of the Harmonie Society, which had been founded in 1849, gave concerts that featured vocal as well as instrumental music. In 1857, Harmonie also hosted the annual Saengerbund, a national vocal festival, with groups coming from German communities across the Midwest.[13]

Detroit was one of many American cities whose musical life was influenced by the influx of German immigrants. Germany had a history of strong monetary support for musical education and performance that dated back several centuries and included both royal and civic patronage. Most cities and towns in Germany have opera houses and orchestras that were established in the nineteenth century. But even smaller cities had music

## THE HARMONIE CLUB

Harmonie Hall was built in 1874 at the corner of Lafayette Avenue and Beaubien Street in the section of Detroit known as "Germantown." It was the first home of the popular German singing association, the Harmonie Society, the oldest musical group in the state, and was a center of social and musical life for the local German community. After the hall burned in 1893, the current Harmonie Club was built nearby on East Grand River, designed by architect Richard E. Raseman and completed in 1895.

The Harmonie Club is a four-story, buff-colored brick building, and contains such classical architectural motifs as Corinthian columns as well as elements of Beaux Arts design. Eric J. Hill notes that its round-corner design "is wonderfully shaped to its site geometry," and that Harmonie Park's "Manhattan feel is largely attributed to the sophisticated character of this landmark building."

Sources: Eric J. Hill and John Gallagher, *AIA Detroit: The American Institute of Architects Guide to Detroit Architects* (Detroit: Wayne State University Press, 2003), 48.

a significant reorientation of American orchestras."[15] The colonial orchestras of the eighteenth century were small ensembles, usually under twenty men, and they played English compositions. The German immigrants brought a different type of ensemble and music to America. "Immigrant German musicians made up an increasing proportion of the instrumentalists in American theaters and concert halls. German immigrants also constituted a growing proportion of audiences for orchestras." Their influence had far-reaching effects. "Immigrant performers and listeners brought many aspects of German musical life to the United States: a repertory of overtures and symphonies, concerts in restaurants and beer gardens, choral societies and orchestral accompaniment."[16]

### STEIN AND BUCHHEISTER

On Jefferson Avenue, the music store of the former Germania musicians Stein and Buchheister flourished. Its success was due to the expanding role that music study and amateur music performance were playing among the citizens of Detroit. The company provided eager new students with sheet music and musical instruments of all kinds, including pianos made by Steinway and Sons.

Stein and Buchheister were also both accomplished musicians, and their performances with their own small orchestra, sometimes playing their own music, made them a popular ensemble. They, in

ensembles, including brass bands, which produced music for civic and religious events.[14] This was the background of the middle-class German immigrants who were part of the migration to Detroit and other cities.

These Germans brought important changes to the American orchestral scene. According to John Spitzer, "The wave of German immigration that began in the 1840s and continued into the 1880s brought

Title page of music for Buchheister's "Bell Polka," 1855. (Courtesy Library of Congress)

turn, paid tribute to their adopted city. In 1855, Buchheister published his "Bell Polka," subtitled "Remembrance of the Germania Musical Society," and dedicated "to the Ladies of Detroit."[17]

Like their earlier programs with the Germania, Stein and Buchheister's ensemble played a variety of music, including classical European symphonies, opera arias, excerpts from ballet music, and, with a smaller ensemble, the chamber music of Beethoven and Mozart. Their concerts were popular with Detroit audiences from the 1850s until 1865, when Stein returned to Germany.

The quality of their performances was credited with lifting the quality of music performed in the city, and for "elevating public taste," according to musicologist Mary Teal. In addition, professional musicians looking for a permanent home, as well as those touring the country in search of receptive audiences, considered Detroit as a destination.

Stein and Buchheister also helped nurture the development of a discerning audience in Detroit. Schools began to teach music and private teachers also trained a young generation to play and to appreciate classical music. Similarly, amateur organizations, from choirs to instrumental ensembles, performed for the public, and the "ranks of concert-goers began to swell," according to Teal.[18]

## THE LIGHT GUARD BAND

Another popular form of ensemble music in Detroit dating from the 1850s was the military band. There were several in the region, and one of the most popular was the Light Guard Band, under the direction of Heinrich Kern. They played concerts throughout the city, and one such performance, on Campus Martius in 1859, was praised by the *Detroit Free Press* as an "instructive and useful" form of entertainment.[19]

In 1861, the band performed at the White House, accompanying the Michigan Light Guard as they were called at the beginning of the Civil War. Their performance was lauded by none other than the Commander in Chief himself, President Abraham Lincoln, who thanked the Men of Michigan for their service and praised the musical performance of the band.[20]

Kern led the band in Detroit throughout the war era, playing public concerts and even providing the music for steamboat cruises on the Detroit River. After the war, Kern played with the German Veterans' Orchestra in Detroit.

## THE DETROIT OPERA HOUSE

On March 29, 1869, the Detroit Opera House opened to much fanfare. Situ-

Photo of the Michigan Light Guard and Band, Campus Martius, circa 1860. (Courtesy DSO Archives)

ated on Campus Martius, the five-story building was designed by the Detroit architectural firm of Sheldon Smith and Son, with interior decoration by Robert Hopkin. With 1,700 seats, it was a gracious and awe-inspiring setting, called a "luxurious temple of art" by the *Detroit Free Press*. On its ground floor was the very first clothing store opened by J. L. Hudson, whose name would be synonymous with Detroit for more than a hundred years.[21]

The Opera House became one of the city's most important cultural and architectural landmarks, and also hosted what is considered Detroit's first professional symphony orchestra concert: the November 1869 performance of the Theodore Thomas Orchestra.

The German Veterans' Orchestra, from an 1870 photo. Heinrich Kern is in the back row, at the far right.

## HEINRICH KERN

In May of 1861, the Michigan Light Guard assembled on Detroit's Campus Martius for a photograph before departing for Washington, DC. That photograph was taken only a month after Major Robert Anderson, the Commander of US Army at Fort Sumter, surrendered to the Confederate forces bombarding the fort. The Michigan Light Guard "became the first company or Company A of the First Michigan Infantry"—first responders to President Lincoln's call for troops.

They traveled by ship to Cleveland and from there to Washington by rail via Pittsburgh. In Washington, they "were complimented as having the best band in the city, considering the number of pieces." And, after an impromptu concert on the White House Lawn, President Lincoln invited the officers and men and the first citizens of Michigan into the East Room for a reception. "The President then expressed a desire that the band should be presented." He "had a word of welcome for each, and for 'Mr. Kern, the leader,' whom he facetiously styled the 'biggest blower' in the service, as Mr. Kern weighed 375 pounds."

Sources: James D. Elderkin, *Biographical Sketches and Anecdotes of a Soldier of Three Wars* (self-published, Detroit: 1899).

## THEODORE THOMAS

Theodore Thomas, born in Germany in 1835, moved with his family to New York in 1845 and began a musical career that had a great influence on the history of the symphony orchestra in the US. He conducted traveling musical ensembles, including the American Opera Company, which toured the country in 1866, performing music of such celebrated composers as Leo Delibes, Jules Massenet, and Richard Wagner, who, in an interesting bit of musical history, were all alive at the time.

In 1869, Thomas began touring with his own ensemble, the Theodore Thomas Orchestra, which brought a high caliber of music and music performance to Midwestern cities like Detroit and Cleveland, traveling, in the words of his wife, Rose, "the great musical highway" of America. Thomas toured with his orchestra until 1888, visiting Detroit nearly every year, to full houses and much acclaim. He also took time to serve as the conductor of the New York Philharmonic from 1877 to 1891, then as music director and founding conductor of the Chicago Symphony Orchestra from 1891 to 1905.[22]

## CREATING A PUBLIC FOR SYMPHONIC MUSIC

According to musicologist John Spitzer, Thomas and other symphony conduc-

A photo of the Detroit Opera House, built in 1869. The first J. L. Hudson's was opened on the main floor in 1881. (Courtesy Burton Historical Collection, Detroit Public Library)

tors of the later nineteenth century were *creating* demand for their music in their programming. The symphonies, concertos, and chamber pieces in their repertoire were the kind of music they had been trained to play in European conservatories and were standard fare for European audiences. But to tempt the new American listeners, they added opera arias, which were widely popular with general audiences, as well as popular dance melodies and solos by individual musicians.[23]

So, in addition to traveling that great musical highway, Thomas also was *educating* audiences about classical music. Audi-

ences learned about music: who the major composers were, what type of music they created, and, in a certain way, what "good music," and good music performance, truly were.

## FREDERICK ABEL

One of the most important aspects of Thomas's impact on Detroit was the high quality of the musicianship of his ensemble, which inspired local musicians and raised expectations of audiences. In 1872, the newly formed Detroit Musical Society brought conductor Frederick Abel to continue the production and appreciation of good music to Detroit.

**FREDERICK ABEL**

One of the most important figures in establishing classical music in Detroit in the late 1800s was Frederick Abel. He had been born in Landau, Bavaria, on December 22, 1824. During the political upheaval of the late 1840s, Abel left Bavaria for Paris, then moved to the United States. He found work in New York as both a singer and a pianist, performing as part of an opera company for several years, then moving to the Midwest.

In Cleveland, Abel founded a successful German singing ensemble, the Gesangverein, then moved on to Milwaukee, where he founded and directed the Milwaukee Musikverein, the largest musical society in the country at that time. He spent fifteen years in Milwaukee, founding an American chorus, and serving as organist and choir director of the First Presbyterian Church.

Abel moved to Chicago in 1870, where he again founded a German singing society and directed music at a local church until the Chicago Fire of 1871 brought him to Detroit. Over the next several decades, Abel directed both the Detroit Musical Society orchestral performances and those of the Harmonie Society, and also served as choirmaster at Christ Church in Detroit.

Although Abel retired from directing in 1895, he continued to be involved in music, establishing himself as a musical arranger and providing manuscripts to the professional and amateur ensembles of Detroit. At the time of his death in 1904, he also had collected one of the largest and most complete musical libraries in the country.

Source: *Detroit Free Press*, March 19, 1904.

Abel was born in 1824 in Landau, Germany, where he studied piano and voice and began to perform and teach. In 1849, he moved to the United States, where he pursued a career in music as a teacher and performer. He spent eleven years in Cleveland, where he taught piano and voice and helped form and lead a German singing society. He moved on to Milwaukee, where he again taught singing and directed the Milwaukee Musikverein, at that time the largest musical society in the country.

In 1872, Abel moved to Detroit, whose population had grown to more than 80,000, many of them part of the continuing wave of German immigrants. Over the next twenty-three years, Abel directed a variety of ensembles in Detroit, including the Detroit Musical Society and the Harmonie Society, which often contained musicians who would figure in what is considered the first "official" Detroit Symphony Orchestra.[24]

On October 20, 1874, an article by "A Frequent Reader" in the *Detroit Free Press* noted that Abel had announced a symphony concert series, with subscriptions available. The anonymous author encouraged Detroiters to subscribe, noting that the city's audiences had "repeatedly shown their appreciation of high musical art," and that Detroit could "boast of artists who compare favorably with the members of [Theodore] Thomas's orchestra and the best orchestras of our largest cities."[25]

These first concerts were well attended and well received, according to the *Detroit*

Theodore Thomas, conducting his orchestra in 1890. They first performed in Detroit in 1869. (Courtesy Library of Congress)

*Free Press.* A concert on December 30, 1874, showed a blend of orchestral music similar to that popularized by Thomas. It featured a symphony by Franz Josef Haydn, an excerpt from a symphony of Hector Berlioz, an opera aria by Rossini (featuring Abel's daughter, Mrs. K. Green, as soprano soloist), and a Beethoven piano trio featuring Rudolph Speil, who would become the first conductor of the "first" DSO.[26]

## LOOKING FOR SUBSCRIBERS— AND TO EDUCATE THE PUBLIC

On October 31, 1875, an article in the *Free Press* outlined the plan by Abel's orchestra to present a series of concerts, as well as open rehearsals, to subscribers, with three concerts and eighteen rehearsals in all, for a price of $5, which provided tickets for two people. These concerts would, according to the author, be both "interesting and valuable," a nod to the idea that classical music was "good for you," and added to a level of cultivation and taste to the discerning listener.[27]

But this effort proved to be less successful than Abel and his group had hoped. In January 1876, an article in the *Free Press* noted that the concerts had been delayed, due to "unlooked for apathy on the part of our music-loving people." The article takes the would-be Detroit audiences to task, noting that, "this enterprise had been undertaken for the purpose of improving home talents and giving Detroit an orchestra of which it may be proud."[28]

The call went out, and the audience responded. On February 26, 1876, Abel's orchestra performed at the Opera House in a concert attended by "a magnificent audience," according to the *Free Press*. It was a great success: "there is nothing hazarded in saying that it was one of the most delightful concerts with which local artists have ever favored Detroit." The program contained Beethoven's Symphony no. 6 in F Major, the Pastoral, much praised by the newspaper and appreciated by the audience: "As interpreted by the orchestra, it was rich in beautiful thoughts expressed with consummate art and feeling and with a degree of mechanical excellence that enlisted the enthusiastic admiration of the critical hundreds who listened to it with undisguised delight."[29]

The final concert of the series was given on May 31, 1876. Once again the *Free Press* covered the event, promoting the quality of the performance, but also of the *audience*, suggesting the idea of a cultural elite and its role in the success of a local orchestra, and furthering the idea of a symphony orchestra as necessary to cultivate taste and the musical education of the people of Detroit: "The third and last concert was given at the Opera House before an unusually brilliant audience,

distinguished alike for its beauty, wealth, and intelligence. The origin and inception of these concerts are not new . . . but the influence they continue to exercise on the education of public taste is only now beginning to be felt and appreciated."

The music critic also praised Abel's choice of programming: "an apt and well-reasoned program, therefore, becomes a matter of no Minor importance." He praised "the intellectual beauty of those tone-poems, symphonies, as they emanate from the head of the great master [Beethoven]," and how the "study of the musical treatment . . . becomes a source of infinite profit and delight."[30]

The theme of a "quality" audience continued in the *Free Press* review of May 26, 1880, which critiqued the thirty-fourth concert of the Detroit Musical Society and praised "an audience remarkable for numbers and social standing." The review also praised the new system of "reserved seating."[31]

Abel continued to enlarge his orchestra's reach into the Detroit community through a subscription program, announcing the formation of a "Symphony Society" in the *Free Press* on October 18, 1882, and stating that a subscriber base of 300 would "insure the success of the undertaking." As of October 27, 1882, the Society had 230 subscribers, with only seventy needed to fully fund the symphony, according to the paper. Also, a partial listing of the officers of the Detroit Symphony Society appeared, including Walter Crane, Charles Moore, and George Wiley.[32]

The program for the first concert of the series, dated January 8, 1883, stated that the personnel of the orchestra "contains the complete Opera House Orchestra, augmented by the best instrumental talent of the city."[33] The season's second concert, given on March 8, 1883, featured Rudolph Speil as a flute soloist. In terms of programming, Abel's ensembles continued to play a variety of music that had become familiar to Detroit audiences, from the time of the Germania and Theodore Thomas Orchestras: symphony excerpts, concertos, as well as excerpts from ballets and operas, from well-known composers, as well as those—Joachim Raff, Antonín Dvořák, and Anton Rubinstein—in the middle of their musical careers.

Abel's orchestra presented its third concert on May 11, 1883. The program featured a cello solo by a "Mr. F. Abel Jr.," Abel's son, Frederick, who went on to play with the Detroit Philharmonic Club and the first DSO. The *Free Press* declared the concert series "an unqualified success" and the audience "large, cultured, and appreciative."[34]

By 1884, the population of Detroit had grown to 132,956, and the city was emerging as an industrial giant in the Midwest, with booming manufacturing in industries relating to transportation, especially railroad equipment. The growing population included more German immigrants, who

WILLIAM YUNCK    FREDERIC L. ABEL    HUGO KALSOW    HERMAN BRUECKNER

DETROIT, MICHIGAN

Cover of a brochure for the Detroit Philharmonic Club, with, from left to right, William Yunck, Frederic L. Abel, Hugo Kalsow, and Herman Brueckner.

made up more than twenty percent of the city's population at the time.[35] They enjoyed the local music offerings, taking part in amateur vocal societies, and attending concerts where they heard classical music, much of it from the German masters they were already familiar with.

As director of both his own orchestra and the Harmonie Society, Abel provided the German population, and all of Detroit,

Rudolph Speil in an undated photo, probably from the early 1880s. (Courtesy Burton Historical Collection, Detroit Public Library)

chorus: an overture, opera arias, ballet music, and, in the second half, Max Bruch's "Scenes from E. Tegner's Legend of Frithjof," featuring Juch and the entire male chorus. According to the *Free Press*, the concert was a great success, attended by "a very numerous and very musical audience."[36]

## THE DETROIT PHILHARMONIC CLUB

While Abel was building his orchestra and his audience, a younger generation of musicians was coming to the fore in the city. Made up of musicians from German and German-American backgrounds, these players formed the Detroit Philharmonic Club, a string quartet that became one of the most famous chamber ensembles in the country and played a key role in the development of the first Detroit Symphony Orchestra. There were a number of personnel changes over the years, but four of its members in particular—William Yunck, Frederick Abel Jr., Herman Brueckner, and Hugo Kalsow—forged an ensemble that gained a national reputation for the quality of their musicianship. They toured the country, impressing music lovers from east to west.

William Yunck, violinist, was born in 1853 in Cassel, Germany. Like all of the members of the quartet, Yunck was educated at a music conservatory in Europe, the Vienna Conservatory, where he graduated first in his class. He spent eight years as first violin and soloist at the Vienna Court Orchestra, touring Europe

with a Music Festival on March 10 and 11, 1884, billed as "Two Grand Concerts, Under the Auspices of the Harmonie Society." The concert boasted 200 male choristers, including members from the following German singing societies: Harmonie, Constatter, Detroit-Maennerchor, Germania, Lyra, Schweizer-Maennerchor, Socialistischer-Maennerchor, and St. Joseph Casino, all accompanied by "36 of Our Best Musicians," and featuring Miss Emma Juch, "the celebrated New York Prima Donna."

The program, written in both German and English, outlined a mix of music that highlighted Juch and the combined male and developing his reputation as a soloist. Yunck was also a gifted tenor and sang with opera companies in Prague and Berlin, while continuing his violin playing.

Yunck moved to the United States in the early 1880s, where he sang at the Metropolitan Opera, moving on to Detroit several years later. There, he met Frederick Abel Jr., Herman Brueckner, and later Hugo Kalsow, and joined the Philharmonic Club, also serving for years as director of the ever-important Harmonie Society.

Frederick Abel Jr., cellist, was born in Detroit in 1856 into a very musical family: his father was the director of the Detroit Musical Society, where the elder Abel also performed, and his mother and sister were also professional singers. He studied music in Germany, graduating from the Raff Conservatory of Music in Frankfurt, where he studied cello, piano, and theory. Returning to the United States, he played with the Philharmonic Club and other local orchestras.

Herman Brueckner, violinist, was born in 1864 in Erfurt, Germany. His father was the director of music at the Royal Court in Erfurt, and Brueckner studied with his father as well as with a famous violinist, E. Rappoldi. After he graduated, Brueckner became first violinist and soloist for the Gewerbehaus Orchestra in Dresden, then moved on to orchestras in Ems, Arnheim, and Amsterdam. He came to Detroit and joined the Philharmonic Club in the 1880s, played in several different ensembles, and also served as a conductor of the Harmonie Society.

Hugo Kalsow, violinist, was born in Detroit in 1876, also into a musical family: his father, Fritz, a cornetist, had come to the United States with a Prussian army band and made Detroit his home. In 1887, he became the first manager of the first DSO, and he made sure his son received an excellent musical education. Like Brueckner, Hugo Kalsow also studied with Rappoldi and graduated from the Dresden Conservatory. [37, 38]

## RUDOLPH SPEIL

Another key figure in the development of symphonic music from this second generation of musicians was Rudolph Speil. Born in 1846, Speil is first mentioned in the Detroit newspapers in 1874, when he appears as a flute soloist with Abel's orchestra. He was a multitalented—and incredibly hardworking—musician, who played both the flute and cello, composed, and conducted a number of different types of ensembles in Detroit, as well as teaching flute, cello, and brass instruments at the Detroit Conservatory of Music.[39]

In 1880 alone, Speil led the orchestra at St. Aloysius Church, conducted a band and orchestra at the Detroit Opera House in a concert that featured excerpts from Gilbert and Sullivan's *Pirates of Penzance*, led a promenade concert on Belle Isle, and conducted a series of subscription concerts at

Arbeiter Hall, featuring the Detroit Opera House orchestra. The *Free Press* noted that the popular orchestra was having "a handsome new uniform made, which is very tasty in design."[40]

Throughout the 1880s, Speil was similarly engaged and busy: in 1882, he led a band to First Prize in the State Band competition, and his Opera House Military Band performed concerts on Belle Isle. In 1883, he and his orchestra gave concerts for visiting travel agents aboard an excursion boat on the Detroit River, and he also played solo flute concerts at the Whitney Opera House.

Not only does this give some idea of the indefatigable Speil himself, but also of the wide variety of music that was being enjoyed by Detroit audiences at the time: band concerts, popular operettas, and more "traditional" symphonic music.

Speil's name appears in an intriguing listing of local music on December 28, 1884: "A movement is on foot looking to the giving of a series of symphony concerts in this city during March and April, which, if carried out according to the proposed plan, will give a number of musical entertainments of a much better character than ever given before by local talent. Rudolph Speil is at the head of the enterprise."[41]

What was this ensemble? A listing of "Amusements" in the *Free Press* on March 15, 1885, includes the announcement of "The First Symphony Concert, Detroit Symphony Orchestra, Harmonie Hall, March 18, Orchestra of 40, R. Speil, Director." The concert was reviewed in the paper on March 19, and the critic praised the musicians, the audience, and the program, and opined that "it is probable that less than one-sixth of the appreciative patrons of music in Detroit heard the concert." But the critic also predicted a "profitable permanency" for the ensemble should a larger audience appear for the next concert.[42]

That next concert, on May 14, 1885, did indeed have a larger audience, and according to the *Free Press*, "it was such a concert as could command the interest and approval of the most exacting music lovers." The critic made a prediction that proved, at last, to be prophetic: "the time is not far distant when they may again announce a series of symphonic concerts" that would "prove a success financially as well as in an artistic sense."[43]

At this point, newspaper reporting on the progress toward that goal falls silent for two years. Yet the stage was set for something new in professional music-making in Detroit. After decades of small chamber orchestras appearing and then disappearing, a permanent symphonic ensemble, with steady funding and management from some of the leading families of the city, was about to emerge: the first Detroit Symphony Orchestra.

# The Founding and the Founders, 1887–1910: Rudolph Speil, Fritz and Hugo Kalsow, and the First DSO

ON DECEMBER 18, 1887, THE FOLLOWING ANNOUNCEMENT APPEARED in the *Detroit Free Press*:

> The concert which is to be given at the Detroit Opera House Monday evening will be the first of a series proposed by the Detroit Symphony Orchestra, an organization which is managed by an executive committee composed of John N. Bagley, John R. Russel, Louis P. Campau, Charles T. Wilkins, Sidney T. Miller, J. H. Hahn, and C. A. Ducharme. These and J. Harrington Walker, W. E. Jarvis, W. C. McMillan, N. G. William Jr., C. L. Freer, and Clarence Carpenter have raised by subscription the large sum necessary to carry out the liberal and progressive idea which finds expression in a whole season of high class symphony concerts. This heroic effort to advance the standard of orchestral music in Detroit already celebrated for its achievements in vocal music should command the quick sympathy and the cordial support of every cultured person in the community.[1]

This laudatory and optimistic announcement introduced the very first Detroit Symphony Orchestra to the people of Detroit. It had come about due to the efforts of a prominent group of Detroiters, members of the "executive committee" and the other men listed above, whose last names read like a roster of the "captains of industry" of Detroit and who were then riding a wave of unprecedented economic success in the booming city. But a closer look indicates something more intriguing. Most of these were not the "captains" themselves, but their *sons*.

For example, Sidney T. Miller was not the founder of the famed Miller, Canfield, Paddock, and Stone law firm; his father, John Davy Miller, was. John N. Bagley had not made a fortune in tobacco; that was his father, John J. Bagley, who also served as governor of the state of Michigan. Similarly, Louis P. Campau was the descendent of Joseph Campau, who had built a family fortune in real estate. W. C. McMillan was the son of railroad car magnate and US Senator James McMillan. John R. Russel's grandfather had founded one of the most successful railroad car manufacturing companies in the city. And J. Harrington Walker was the son of Hiram Walker, founder of a whiskey distillery across the Detroit River in Walkerville, Ontario, still flourishing today.[2]

These young men, most of them in their twenties when they signed on to become the benefactors of the fledgling Detroit Symphony Orchestra, were all wealthy, educated, and had money to invest. But they were also coming of age during an important historical era in American culture: the establishment of the first permanent professional orchestras in the country. In 1887, Detroit became only the fourth city in the country to establish a permanent symphony orchestra. The first, the New York Philharmonic, was founded in 1842. The next, the St. Louis Symphony, was founded in 1880. The next year, 1881, marked the establishment of the Boston Symphony Orchestra.

## "MAKE AMERICA MUSICAL" MOVEMENT

These first professional orchestras were in part an outgrowth of a movement known as "Make America Musical." The movement promoted the idea that a permanent professional orchestra was good for society: it was a sign of a city's progress, a reflection of its industrial stature and wealth, and a measure of its cultural and social achievement. According to John Spitzer in *American Orchestras in the Nineteenth Century*, "the 'permanent' orchestra immediately became the most prestigious of the city's ubiquitous and diverse orchestras." These early permanent ensembles, like the early DSO, "hired the best players; it programmed the greatest number of 'composers of the highest order'; it was patronized by the social elites."[3]

Between 1887 and 1918, many other American cities, flush with wealth from a booming economy, followed New York, St. Louis, Boston, and Detroit, as permanent orchestras were established in Chicago, Cincinnati, Pittsburgh, Dallas,

Philadelphia, Minneapolis, Seattle, San Francisco, Denver, Houston, Baltimore, and Cleveland.

In Detroit, as in many of these cities, the development of a permanent symphony orchestra was funded in part by a wealthy elite, with almost a sense of noblesse oblige. As the *Free Press* announcement indicates, they saw it as their responsibility to provide money ("large sum"), vision ("the liberal and progressive idea"), and audience (the "support of every cultured person in the community"). However, the funding levels provided by the wealthy elite of Detroit never came close to matching the amounts spent in other major cities. That financial fact did much to determine the fate of the first Detroit Symphony Orchestra, from its first concert in 1887 to its last, in 1910.

## THE RUDOLF SPEIL YEARS: 1887–94

The first concert of the newly formed Detroit Symphony Orchestra took place on December 19, 1887, at the Detroit Opera House. With Rudolph Speil again at the helm, the ensemble played works by Peter Josef von Lindpaintner (overture to *Faust*), Beethoven (Symphony no. 2), Charles Gounod (an opera aria), Berlioz (two excerpts from *The Damnation of Faust*), Louis Moreau Gottschalk ("Last Hope"), Giuseppe Verdi ("Bolero" from *The Sicilian Vespers*), and Franz Liszt (Hungarian Rhapsody no. 2). The programming for the season provided what audiences had

Rudolph Speil, conductor of the DSO from 1887 to 1894. (Courtesy Burton Historical Collection, Detroit Public Library)

become used to, with some newer works as well. And from the first season to the last, nearly every concert included a soloist singing popular opera arias.

The *Detroit Evening News* reviewed the concert, in terms and tone that echoed the *Free Press*, noting the culture and wealth of the audience: "the concert . . . afforded the means of demonstrating the fact that this city contains a sufficient number of people who possess the culture necessary to proper appreciation of symphony concerts, and who have enough wealth to purchase this form of entertainment."[4]

The second concert of the first season, given on January 25, 1888, elicited the same kind of praise from the *Free Press* critic, who noted that the new symphony's audience displayed a "marked advance in musical intelligence" for Detroit. So, too, does the critic praise the new Board of the symphony for its "enlightened encouragement." The review also includes some of the earliest true music criticism pertaining to the ensemble. Of Felix Mendelssohn's Symphony no. 4 (the "Italian"), the writer praised the playing of the *Allegro vivace* and *Saltarello* sections as "strong and musicianly." And while liking, for the most part, the DSO's rendering of "Siegfried's Death" from the opera by Wagner, the critic noted that the horn section was guilty of "some painful self-assertions."[5]

A review of the third concert in the series, of March 16, 1888, from the *Free Press* notes the "large and delighted audience" for the program. The final concert of the first season, given on May 8, 1888, was praised in the *Free Press* as "a delightful study in musical progression."[6]

An announcement made just prior to that last concert, in the *Free Press* of May 6, 1888, offers some insight into the economic status of the new ensemble. It states that the season had not been as financially successful as the "committee would have wished," and that to sustain the symphony, the committee needed "better financial support," an "increased number of subscribers,"[7] and an idea of how many subscriptions could in fact be sold to insure a second season. It would seem that the young businessmen who

had served as the founders of the first DSO were not relying on large amounts of their own capital to keep the symphony running; they wanted a show of *community* support, quantifiable in money and in audience numbers.

The first concert of the second season, on December 20, 1888, was heralded two days before by the *Detroit Free Press*, which noted that the original orchestra had been infused with "new blood," and had been hard at work practicing for their new season. The critic promised that the ensemble was ready to dazzle the city with "as good music as has ever been heard in Detroit." The writer goes on to remind patrons to be "in their seats promptly by 8 o'clock," and to praise the committee for providing excellent music at a price "within the reach of all": $10 for three tickets to four concerts.[8]

The placement of the review of the second concert offers an important insight into the musical world of Detroit in the late 1880s: it appears after the reviews of three opera companies who were performing in Detroit in the same week: the J. C. Duff Opera Company, the American Opera Company, and the MacCollin Opera Company. These listings indicate the popularity of opera, the variety of music available, and the competition for audiences and dollars, too.

The *Tribune* review of the final concert of the second season, given on May 15, 1889, quotes Sidney T. Miller of the executive committee, who stated that there would be a third season, with "contributions solicited" to continue the symphony, but no "further definite plans" for its longevity.[9] The concert also received a brief paragraph in the *Free Press*, and was followed by a listing of six concerts also taking place that week in Detroit. Of special notice was the appearance of the Boston Symphony Orchestra, which played regularly in Detroit.

Also listed among the performing ensembles was the Detroit Philharmonic Club, led by William Yunck, which gave eleven concerts during the season, and whose members also played regularly with the DSO. It was another indication that the early Detroit Symphony, with a schedule of just four concerts per season, was only one of many ensembles vying for the attention of the public, and that symphony musicians needed to play a variety of music—symphonic, operatic, and popular—to make a living.[10]

## "THE MUSICAL TASTE OF DETROIT: WHAT IS IT?"

Trying to discern just what the audiences of Detroit wanted in their musical entertainment provided a question not just for the fledgling DSO, but for all the purveyors of music in the city. It provided the headline, above, to an October 1889 article in the *Free Press* that described a series of concerts to be presented in Detroit by the popular and influential Theodore Thomas. In a pre-

scient move right out of modern marketing, Thomas had sent out questionnaires to "the leading society and musical people" of Detroit, asking what they wanted to hear his orchestra play. These "quality" listeners were given a choice of three programs, all quite similar, and all including the well-known mix of classical pieces by Beethoven, Wagner, and Weber, with more "popular" works, such as Liszt's "Les Preludes," and songs by Grieg. But it was in using the "data" he collected that Thomas showed his marketing savvy: he listed the programs in the paper, including the names of the socialites who voted for each.

The last names were those of the well known, wealthy, and connected, including Trowbridge, Lothrop, Moran, Neff, and many others. And their "good taste" was rewarded, as Thomas gave a two-concert series, providing their choices to an audience that was, of course, "large and fashionable."[11]

The first concert of the DSO's third season took place on January 12, 1891—there were no concerts given in 1890—and was announced in the *Free Press* with a note that tickets were much in demand. The second, given on February 9, 1891, was reportedly well attended.[12] The third concert of the season was announced by an ad in the *Free Press*, but not reviewed in the paper. Instead, there were two articles in the paper, both interviews with noted musicians performing in Detroit, and both focusing on the continued viability of a

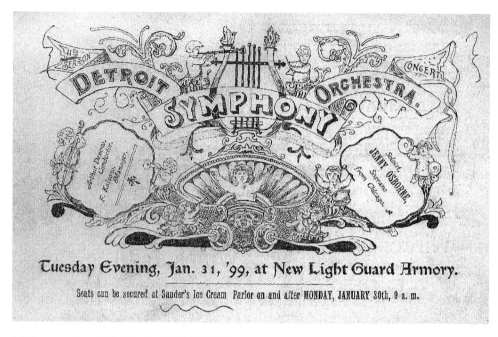

A DSO program from 1899. (Courtesy Detroit Public Library)

permanent symphony orchestra in the city. Constantin Sternberg, a noted pianist, was performing in Detroit at the time, and during an interview stated that what Detroit needed was a financial and management plan similar to that enacted in Boston.[13]

The Boston Symphony Orchestra had been created by businessman and philanthropist Henry Lee Higginson, who invested $120,000 of his own money to fund the symphony during its first year. He lost that sum but continued to fund the orchestra, and within several years had turned a profit. That, stated Sternberg, was the model for Detroit to follow, and he predicted a "handsome profit" for the enterprise should it come to pass.

The other musician who weighed in on the financial situation of the symphony was Charles Heydler, a cellist from Cleveland, who played with the DSO on several occasions. He believed that the monetary commitment needed for a symphony in Detroit was less than that required in Boston, stating that $100,000, put up by a group of subscribers, would produce an ensemble that would be financially successful "from the start."[14]

The review in the *Detroit Tribune* of the third concert of the third season provides additional insight into the issue. The critic calls the comparison of the DSO to the Boston Symphony Orchestra "unjust." He notes that the BSO is a much larger organization, and plays a much longer season. A look into the BSO archives reinforces the point: in 1892, the Boston

Symphony Orchestra was playing twenty-one concerts a year in Boston alone, along with touring concerts around the country. They were a well-paid, well-rehearsed organization, and it was reflected in their playing.[15]

The theme of the financial plight and future viability of the symphony was the focus of the review of the final concert of the season, given on April 24, 1891. The *Free Press* noted that the musicians played well, "taking all the circumstances into consideration." The critic then went on to state that the musicians were woefully underpaid, listing their compensation at $10 per concert, and $2.50 per rehearsal, which, the writer noted, is not even union scale. The musicians needed more money, the critic claimed, to make better music.[16]

In contrast, Theodore Thomas was able to pay his musicians a regular salary, according to John Spitzer. And even though professional musicians in New York often had to play in a number of different ensembles (i.e., the New York Philharmonic and the Brooklyn Philharmonic, as well as vaudeville and popular orchestras), there were numerous other opportunities to make a living, too. For example, the going rate for a Broadway musician was $12 per week in 1863; compared to the wages paid to DSO musicians nearly thirty years later, it is no wonder that the performances were neither well rehearsed nor polished.[17]

## OF MONEY AND MUSIC: THE FINANCIAL SITUATION OF THE EARLY DSO

The 1891 season is the first for which there are financial records: the ledgers of Fritz Kalsow, the DSO's manager for its first twenty-three years, lists subscribers, amounts paid, as well as a record for expenditures for each concert of the season. According to these sources, there were 420 subscribers that year, with some subscribing at the $5 level and some at the $10 level, with a total income of $2,505. The subscribers, who signed Kalsow's ledger in their own hand, included such well-known supporters (and executive committee members) as C. A. Ducharme, John Russel, Charles Wilkins, Dexter Ferry, W. C. McMillan, J. Hahn, and William H. Murphy.

Fritz Kalsow, manager of the first DSO, 1887 to 1910. (Courtesy DSO Archives)

F. KALSOW, Manager.

## FRITZ KALSOW

Fritz Kalsow was born in Stolp, Germany, around 1846, and moved with his wife to the United States around 1869. He played a variety of instruments, including the cornet, and performed in the United States with the Prussian Army Bugle Band. He and his wife moved to Detroit around 1870, and Kalsow became an established musician and music teacher, playing cello and double bass in a variety of ensembles, and teaching privately and at the Michigan Conservatory of Music.

Kalsow became the first manager of the first DSO in 1887, and for twenty-two years hired musicians, conductors, and soloists, arranged for performances, and handled all details, large and small, recording expenditures in his ledgers, which are available in part in the Burton Historical Collection of the Main Branch of the Detroit Public Library.

These remarkable notes detail the ewxpenses of the fledgling orchestra, and include, for example, the following items, for the "First Symphony Concert, January 12th 1891":

| | |
|---|---|
| House Rent | $150 |
| Prima donna | $125 |
| [this was Mrs. Julie E. Wyman] | |
| Orchestra | $267 |

| | |
|---|---|
| Press | $12.25 |
| Tickets | $4 |
| Stamps | $4.10 |
| Weiss Music | $3.00 |
| Weiss Extras | $5.00 |

Other entries note varying payments to conductors (Rudolph Speil got $40 per concert; Johann Beck received $100), payments to ushers, for sundries, and even for flowers, kept in Kalsow's meticulous hand.

Yet despite his decades of hard work, including his tireless attempts to raise funds by going door to door to businesses, that early DSO never managed to make enough money to survive. When it went out of business in 1910, an exhausted Fritz Kalsow went back to Germany to recuperate; while his name is not associated with the revival of the DSO in 1914, Kalsow appears in the news once again in 1919, when he and his wife celebrated their fiftieth wedding anniversary, surrounded by family. He died in Detroit on November 10, 1930.

Sources: *DAC News*, May 2013, 31–32; Fritz Kalsow, ledgers for the Detroit Symphony Orchestra, unprocessed collection of documents, Burton Historical Collection, Detroit Public Library, Detroit, Michigan; George W. Stark, *City of Destiny: The Story of Detroit* (Detroit: Arnold-Powers, Inc., 1943), 478; *Detroit Free Press*, September 15, 1919; *Detroit News*, November 11, 1930.

Expenditures for the year, according to Kalsow's records, totaled $2,096.35. That amount covered rent of the Opera House, salaries paid to soloists and the orchestra, ads placed in newspapers, tickets, stamps, and music. It would appear that at this point in its history, the Detroit Symphony Orchestra was barely breaking even, and their budget was a small fraction of the symphonies of Boston and New York.[18]

The DSO fared slightly better in the 1891–92 season, with a total of $2,870 in revenue (there are no figures for expenditures). That season's ledger indicates businesses giving at the $10 level, including the Stroh's Brewing Company and the Bagley Tobacco company. John Russel is listed twice: once for his company, at the $10 level, and once as an individual, at the $5 level.[19]

Kalsow's ledgers indicate continuing improvement for the 1892–93 season, with $3,165 in revenue. There are only expenditure listings for two concerts, which total $1,367. The programs for the Detroit Symphony Orchestra that season offered several pieces of information pointing to changes in the organization and income, too. There were new members of the management committee, including Frank J. Hecker, Edwin S. Barbour II, Henry B. Joy, and Homer Warren. And, for the very first time, there were advertisements in the program, including one for the C. J. Whitney and Company music store.[20] It is possible that payment for the program ad may be linked to Kalsow's ledger, which notes that Whitney had paid $200 for the year as a subscriber, substantially above the other $10 subscriptions.[21]

How was the DSO faring in the eyes of the critics? In its final review of the season the *Free Press* published a scorching condemnation of conductor Rudolph Speil, who fired back in a letter to the editor of the *Free Press* published on May 22, 1893.[22] Speil claims that rumors about any "reorganization" of the symphony, and of his dismissal, are "clearly imaginary." He claims that the musicians are committed to working hard, under his direction, in the coming year.[23]

In 1893–94, revenue was down again for the orchestra, to $3,125.[24] The DSO had a new concertmaster, William Yunck, who had played in Detroit since the 1880s, and was a well-known and respected violinist and member of the Detroit Philharmonic Club. The final concert of the season, given on April 28, 1894, was reviewed in the *Free Press*, which continued its harsh criticism of Speil. The brief review ends with a striking announcement: "Next season the orchestra will be under the direction of Mr. Yunck."[25]

So Speil left the DSO, but not Detroit, or music-making. He continued to direct other ensembles, including the Detroit Society Orchestra and Professor Speil's Orchestra. Just three months after losing his position with the DSO, he had founded another new group: the Speil and Keintz Orchestra and Band, which performed in Detroit for several years, before Speil moved to Toledo, where he lived and conducted until his retirement.[26]

## WILLIAM YUNCK: 1894–95

The revenue for Yunck's only season as conductor, 1894–95, showed a small uptick, to $3,665, but the orchestra was still struggling to compete with a wide array of other music.[27] The second concert of the season was announced in the January 20, 1895, edition of the *Free Press*, along with a listing of eight other classical music concerts given in the same week in Detroit. Among them were concerts by the Philharmonic Club, the Detroit Institute of Music, and the Tuesday Musicale, an influential organization created in 1885 by a group of women musicians who sponsored local and national musicians,

William Yunck,
conductor of
the DSO from
1894 to 1895.
(Courtesy DSO
Archives)

CHAPTER TWO

MR. WILLIAM YUNCK,
DIRECTOR DETROIT SYMPHONY ORCHESTRA.

season, which included advertisements far beyond the music-oriented ads of previous years. Now, perhaps indicating a new (and not as "fashionable") audience, the ads offered everyday merchandise, including shoes, trousers, flour, wines and liquors, insurance and loans, and "Wonderful Dream Salve," for the treatment of "Piles, Chilblains, Corns, Bunyons, and Ingrowing Toenails."[30] It is also interesting to note that by 1895, according to Kalsow's ledger, the $5 subscription level, with 420 subscribers, was much more popular than the $10 level, with just 142 subscribers.[31]

A letter to the editor of the *Free Press* that appeared on May 5, 1895, includes some interesting information on the relationship between the orchestra and its patrons at the time. The letter writer (Frederic Irland) claimed that the music critic of the *Detroit Tribune* had been unduly harsh to the Detroit Symphony, and had even been caught reviewing pieces in the paper that the orchestra had not played. He stated that "every intelligent listener" had noted the profound improvement of the group under Yunck. He also quoted the noted New York music critic Henry Krehbiel, who said, "Do not let the newspaper critic think for you." In noting the difference between Detroit and such great orchestras as Boston, Irland claimed that Boston was supported by "millions in expenditure," while Detroit received only "hundreds." In a rebuke of both the *Tribune* and *Free Press* critic, he stated, "Let us, music

including Theodore Thomas in the 1880s, and Ossip Gabrilowitsch in 1901.[28]

The *Free Press* remained dismissive of the DSO, even with a new director. In a review of the season's third concert, the critic notes that the orchestra's playing of a waltz by Johann Strauss was "acceptable," but that its inclusion indicated a "common" quality of both the selection and the audience's taste. A Strauss waltz indicated that the city needed a "good popular orchestra," not a "bad symphony orchestra."[29]

This bit of snobbery could also have been prompted by the programs of the lovers of Detroit, stand up for what we like, and applaud what pleases us."[32]

## JOHANN BECK: 1895–96

William Yunck's tenure as conductor lasted only one season. In the fall of 1895, Johann Beck, a well-known conductor, composer, and violinist from Cleveland, Ohio, took over as director. Beck had been born in Cleveland in 1856 and studied at the Leipzig Conservatory, premiering his own String Quartet in C Minor at the world-famous Gewandhaus before returning to Cleveland in 1882. There he composed, taught, and conducted ensembles, including his own, the Beck String Quartet.[33]

The second concert of Beck's first season was given in celebration of Mozart's 140th birthday, and the music he programmed showed signs of innovation never before seen in Detroit. He included three pieces by Mozart: the Overtures to both *The Marriage of Figaro* and *The Magic Flute* and portions of the Symphony no. 40 in G Minor. But he also chose a piece he had arranged for strings, played for the first time in Detroit, as well as the "Fest Marsch" by H. Huss, which, according to the program, was "New. First Time. Manuscript." To a city used to repetition of old favorites, this was new indeed.[34]

From the program for April 11, 1896, it is clear that Beck was committed to bringing new music to Detroit. In addition to well-known works by Rossini, Beethoven, and Weber, Beck presented a piece by Carl Busch, played from manuscript. This piece, as well as Borodin's *In the Steppes of Central Asia*, Heberlein's Overture to *Robinson Crusoe*, and Grieg's "Spring," were all designated as being performed for the "First Time in Detroit."[35]

An announcement in the final program by manager Fritz Kalsow thanked subscribers for their patronage and promised another season. But a look at Kalsow's ledger indicates that bringing in Beck had not helped out the orchestra financially. Total revenues for the season were $3,118.50, which, according to an entry in the ledger, resulted in concert expenses of $2,511.23, and a loss of $319 for the year. For the season, Kalsow detailed the payments made for three concerts, which showed that Beck was paid $100 and $125 as conductor, considerably higher than the $40 conductor's fee paid to Rudolph Speil during his tenure.[36]

Whether the decision was financial or artistic, Johann Beck left the DSO after one season. He returned to Cleveland, where, with Emil Ring, he helped found and conduct the Cleveland Symphony Orchestra, an early incarnation of what would become one of America's finest orchestras, the Cleveland Orchestra. The next season, the DSO would be conducted by G. Arthur Depew, a well-known local organist and choir director.

## G. ARTHUR DEPEW: 1896–1900

The ninth season opened, with Depew as conductor and Yunck as concertmaster. There were also several new members of the "supervising committee," including R. A. Alger Jr., W. A. Dwyer, R. H. Fyfe, C. Hecker, W. A. Livingstone, and H. Schellenerg. Gone from the listing were the following names: Bagley, Russel, Shaw, Campau, Jarvis, Wilkins, Hahn, Carpenter, and Ducharme. Some had given their support to other musical organizations; others had found other places to invest their money.[37]

This shifting of financial backing can be seen in the season's programs, which by the ninth year had grown to eighteen pages, most of them ads, for everything from musical instruction to a variety of everyday household products, including a "microbe killer," gas and electric fixtures, lace curtains, shirtwaists, hair dressing, beer, eggs, and butter, as well as services as varied as massage, laundry, lending companies, funeral parlors, and real estate. It would seem that the management was trying to draw in a more modest, middle-class audience, and selling ads that would appeal to them.[38] That tendency is reflected in looking at the revenues during Depew's first year, which totaled $3,320, with only ninety-nine subscribers at the $10 level, but a whopping 466 pledging $5 per year.[39]

On October 7, 1897, the Detroit Opera House was destroyed by fire. So the tenth season's concerts had to be rescheduled and were given at the Auditorium in Detroit, which was located at the corner of Larned and Woodward. Depew's second season was praised by the *Free Press*, which claimed that he was "deserving of warm praise," especially for the "fire, enthusiasm, and vim" of the orchestra's playing.[40] The concerts of the tenth season included several newer pieces, including works by Burmeister, Dudley Buck, Otto Langey, and Eva Dell A'cqua, and continued to offer other established classical works, as well as opera arias by soprano soloists. The DSO increased its revenues during the season, to $3,567, with expenditures of $2,092.[41]

The next season, the DSO moved to the New Light Guard Armory, at the corner of Brush and Larned, which would be their home for the next ten years. Subscriptions for that season, 1898–99, totaled $3,635 in revenue, with expenditures of $2,180.[42] It would appear that, despite the herculean efforts of Fritz Kalsow, the DSO was not making progress toward a solid financial footing. This was the topic of the *Free Press*'s review of the third concert, of March 14, 1899. The critic compared Detroit's orchestra to those established in Boston, Chicago, Cincinnati, and other major American cities, noting that they were supported by a "large endowment fund, subsidized by the leading citizens to pay the deficits," while in Detroit, the orchestra was maintained by the "tireless efforts of one man, Mr. Kalsow."[43]

Interestingly, that is the same conclusion drawn by musicologist John Spitzer, in *American Orchestras in the Nineteenth Century*. Like some musicologists, he recognizes the "official" Detroit Symphony as beginning in 1914, largely because of its precarious financial status during its first incarnation. Spitzer notes that by the end of the nineteenth century, Boston, Chicago, St. Louis, Cincinnati, Pittsburgh, and Philadelphia all had orchestras that "enjoyed generous financial support from local patrons, who guaranteed yearly contributions to cover deficits."[44]

In Spitzer's analysis, it was not until the twentieth century that Detroit and other cities developed any kind of self-sustaining ensemble, organized according to what he refers to as the "corporate" model: "local symphony orchestras . . . with a board of guarantors and a large base of subscribers, [which] proved successful and durable."[45]

## THE CHICAGO SYMPHONY ORCHESTRA

In his essay in Spitzer's book, musicologist Mark Clague describes the Chicago Symphony Orchestra as the first to be established on this "corporate model."[46] In 1890, businessman Charles Norman Fay asked Theodore Thomas if he would move to Chicago to help establish a permanent symphony orchestra. Fay organized a guaranteed fund of $50,000 a year

**LIGHT GUARD ARMORY**

After the Detroit Opera House burned, the fledgling DSO had to find another place to perform, and they chose to play most of their concerts, from 1899 to 1910, at the new Light Guard Armory, which had been completed in April 1898, to much acclaim. The original Armory had been built on Jefferson in the 1860s, and was replaced by the new structure, which was 15,000-square-feet in size and boasted an auditorium that could seat more than 2,000.

Built at the corner of Brush and Larned downtown, the new Armory was described as "castle-like," made of brick with arched windows and crenelated towers. At its grand opening in April 1898, the guard marched from the old Armory to the new, and John Philip Sousa's "Trooping of the Colors" was played, by the Sousa Band, at its dedication.

Although they played an occasional concert at the Arcadia, the DSO played almost all of their concerts at the Light Guard Armory, from 1899 to their final concert, in April 1910. The building was destroyed by fire in 1940.

Sources: *Detroit Free Press*, April 26, 1898, Detroit Public Library, http://digitalcollections.detroitpubliclibrary.org/islandora/object/islandora%3A160140.

for three years to pay for the orchestra, which allowed it to begin without debt. Fay initially planned to raise the money by seeking contributions of $5,000 each from ten wealthy local businessmen, including Marshall Field, George Pullman, and himself. Then, he was encouraged to instead seek contributions of $1,000 each from a larger group of potential donors. The reaction was swift and generous: soon, he had the funding he needed to begin, and more.

Three years in, the plan was a success: a popular orchestra with a secure, solid base of support. Then, the symphony's sales manager, Anna Miller, expanded the donation pool even further. She offered patronage at ever more affordable levels, of $50 to $1,000, to the people of Chicago. This brought even more money into the organization's coffers. Then, Theodore Thomas demanded that a new performance space be built for the symphony, and threatened to leave if it was not. The city responded with overwhelming support for what became Chicago's Orchestra Hall: there were more than 8,000 contributors, some of whom gave only 10 cents, but all of whom saw the Hall as a source of citywide pride.[47]

The contrast with the DSO, which, with total income hovering between $3,000 to $3,500, could barely support an ensemble playing four concerts a year, is vivid and provocative. Why didn't one individual, or a group of individuals, step forward with a similar plan?

### FRANK BRISCOE

Still, the early DSO soldiered on. In October 1899, a new conductor, Frank Briscoe, was named to lead the orchestra. He was a Detroit-born, European-educated composer and musician, of whom much was expected. At his first concert, on December 12, 1899, an audience estimated at 1,500 was on hand to hear Briscoe's debut. The program for the concert contained, for the first time, lengthy notes on the pieces played to help "educate" the audience, written by Briscoe himself. The *Free Press* found much to be wanting in the performance, however, blaming, again, the lack of rehearsal, but neither the musicians nor the conductor.[48]

Briscoe's tenure with the DSO was very short-lived: on December 31, 1899, it was announced that, due to lack of a permanent contract, he was leaving. Once again, Arthur Depew stepped in as director. The season's revenues totaled $4,149, with the addition of a new level of subscription, at $3.[49]

### HUGO KALSOW: 1900–1910

The next season was one of great expectations for the ensemble, as Fritz Kalsow's son, Hugo, was named the next conductor of the Detroit Symphony. He had been studying violin and conducting in Europe with the noted violinist Rappoldi, the concertmaster of the Dresden Royal Opera House, when he returned to his hometown.

An article in the *Free Press* of November 25, 1900, signed by Walter Boynton, noted that Kalsow had great ambitions for the orchestra in the coming season, including expanding the number of musicians to forty, adding a zither, and performing Tchaikovsky's *1812 Overture* for the first time in Detroit.[50]

Kalsow's first concert, given on December 11, 1900, received a glowing review in the *Free Press*. The concert featured

Kalsow not only conducting, but playing Max Bruch's first Concerto for Violin, already a well-known and well-loved piece. Directly following the review in the paper was a fascinating piece about the Cincinnati Symphony, noting that one "Cincinnati capitalist" had offered $5,000 to keep the current conductor, Van de Stucken, from leaving the symphony for another position. Also, a society in that city announced the beginning of a fundraising campaign, aiming for $20,000 a year for six years, to pay for the entire orchestra. Compared to the meager pay of DSO musicians at the time, it would seem the article and its placement were a further inducement to the people of Detroit to fund their orchestra.[51]

The second and third concerts of Kalsow's first season as conductor were both well attended, and also featured several pieces that had never been performed in Detroit, including the Overture to Smetana's *Bartered Bride*, Bizet's *Jeux d'enfants*, and, "By Request," the maestro playing his own "Pizzicato Gavotte."[52] Finally, on March 14, 1901, the *1812 Overture* made its Detroit debut, applauded by the audience, which numbered over 2,000, according to the *Free Press*.[53]

Although it was not directly related to the symphony, a notice in the paper, dated January 13, 1901, described the program "for the Gabrilowitsch recital," sponsored by the Tuesday Musicale, where the future, and famed, conductor of the DSO

Hugo Kalsow, conductor of the DSO from 1900 to 1910. (Courtesy DSO Archives)

performed works by Bach, Schumann, Chopin, Rubinstein, Glinka, and a piece of his own composition.[54]

Unfortunately, Fritz Kalsow's ledgers for the period 1900 to 1910 are not available, and without that financial information, it is difficult to get an "insider's" understanding of how the orchestra was fairing economically. Relying on the newspaper record, we learn that the audience for the opening concert of the 1901–02 season was neither as large nor as appreciative as in the past, according to the *Free Press*. The critic listed a litany of complaints that followed Hugo Kalsow throughout his tenure as conductor: the orchestra's playing was not polished, the concert was overlong, and, in a comment that was repeated well into the late twentieth century, the writer took the audience to task for getting up and rushing to the exits before the final number was finished. That final piece, a waltz by Johann Strauss, began a tradition for the orchestra, as Kalsow closed every concert with a piece by the "Waltz King" for the next nine years.[55]

The *Free Press* continued to review some, but not all, of the DSO's concerts. Most criticism focused on Kalsow, taking him to task for his programming decisions. Also by this point, the concerts had not been covered in the *Detroit Tribune* regularly for years. Unfortunately, this means that modern readers know even less about audience size, response, and attitude toward the symphony in its early years.

The 1904–05 season began on December 13, 1904, and the *Free Press* was there to witness it, with the following weary commentary: "This organization has been long among us, and has suffered many vicissitudes; it still exists as a monument to the energy of its management."[56]

## DETROIT ORCHESTRAL ASSOCIATION

Beginning in 1905, a major shift occurred on the orchestral music scene in Detroit. In May 1905, F. K. Stearns, a successful businessman, collector of art, lover of music, one-time owner of a Detroit baseball team, and son of the founder of a major pharmaceutical company, announced the formation of the Detroit Orchestral Association. Its purpose was to bring a series of orchestral concerts to Detroit within the year that would "eclipse anything of the kind that has been heard in years."[57]

The Association was funded by Stearns and approximately 100 other guarantors, who pledged money to support a series of six concerts to be given, not by the local orchestra, but by those that were considered the best in the country at the time: Boston, Chicago, Pittsburgh, Cincinnati, and New York. The initial concerts in the series were given in the Fall of 1905, and the series flourished. N. J. Corey, manager of the organization, announced that Stearns had raised $15,000 in 1905, with 150 guarantors giving $100 each. By 1906, the group had raised $25,000, with 250 guarantors, which allowed the visiting orchestras to bring larger groups of musicians, as well as soloists.[58]

The DSO continued, with its familiar number of concerts and format, seeing first a decline in the size of its audience, but finally, on March 6, 1907, scoring a triumph. The soloist for that concert was the Russian pianist and composer Alexander Scriabin, making his debut in the city. The audience adored him, even if the *Free Press* critic did not. While noting his facility as a player, the critic found his compositions distasteful, claiming that his Concerto in F Major was "inconsequential, and a

## FREDERICK KIMBALL STEARNS

Wealthy pharmaceutical executive and music enthusiast Frederick Kimball Stearns was born in Buffalo, New York, on December 6, 1924, to Frederick and Eliza Stearns, and moved with his family to Detroit as an infant. He attended the University of Michigan from 1873 to 1875, but left in his junior year to join the family business. At Frederick Stearns and Company, he worked in every division, rising through the ranks and becoming the president of the company in 1887.

Under his direction, the company became an international success, with offices around the world; in Detroit, Stearns built a laboratory on Jefferson near Belle Isle in 1900, designed by William Stratton with an addition by Albert Kahn, which still stands today, now converted to residential apartments.

Stearns had many interests, including sports: he owned the Detroit Baseball Club from 1885 to 1887, during which time it won the world championship, and was also one of the founders and president of the Detroit Athletic Club. But Stearns also had a deep love of the arts: he served as a trustee for the Detroit Museum of Art, a forerunner of the DIA, and one of his great passions was music. His father had given his collection of musical instruments to the University of Michigan in 1899, where it formed the basis of the renowned Stearns Collection, and Stearns followed in his footsteps, donating 1,600 items to the library's music collection in 1905, which doubled the size of the music library.

In Detroit, Stearns gave money and organizational skills to several groups, including the Detroit Musical Society and the Detroit Orchestral Association, which he founded in 1905 and which brought the leading orchestras of the country to Detroit to perform, including the Boston Symphony, Cincinnati Symphony, Pittsburgh Symphony, New York Philharmonic, and Chicago Symphony.

It appears that Stearns did not lend financial support to the foundering DSO during its last decade; in fact, his concert series may have led potential patrons away from their local orchestra. But when Stearns resigned as president of the Detroit Orchestral Association in 1910, he was replaced by William T. Murphy, whose vision incorporated what Stearns desired—music of the highest caliber played in Detroit—with his own desire to make it a product of Detroit. Murphy would go on to oversee the establishment and great success of the reborn DSO under Ossip Gabrilowitsch, as well as the quiet demise of the Detroit Orchestral Association. It is perhaps for this reason that Stearns's biography in Clarence Burton's *History of Wayne County and the City of Detroit* claims that "The present Detroit Symphony Orchestra is an outgrowth of the Detroit Orchestral Association."

Stearns retired from his company and moved to California, where he became involved in music once again, as a supporter of the nascent Los Angeles Philharmonic; he died there in 1924.

Sources: *DAC News*, May 2013, 32; Clarence Burton, *History of Wayne County and the City of Detroit*, Vol. 3 (Chicago: S. J. Clarke), 403–05.

rabid example of the most ultra-modern Russian school."[59]

The symphony's next season opened in December 1907, with the *Free Press* commenting that Kalsow still had the "rare secret" of getting a crowd to show up, even though the program contained "old war-horses," presented with only "fair ability."[60] The review of the final concert ended on a strange note: there were "disquieting rumors" that the current season would be the DSO's last.[61]

Yet things appeared to be looking up for the ensemble in the summer of 1908.

That year, the Wayne Casino opened downtown. Located on the Detroit River, between Second and Third, it was attached to the Wayne Hotel and covered an entire block. In the summer, its wide pavilion, built to resemble the rooftop gardens of New York, offered a place where city dwellers could go and seek relief from the heat—the *Free Press* called it an "Ideal Place to Keep Cool."

It was a structure of brick and steel, built for "amusement lovers of Detroit," and contained spaces for performances, conventions, and banquets, including an auditorium large enough to accommodate 3,000 people. There was free entertainment every night, including both popular and classical music, and the DSO played there throughout the summer.[62]

In the fall of 1908, the Boston Symphony Orchestra played in Detroit, under the auspices of the Detroit Orchestral Society. An article in the *Free Press* made several pointed comments regarding the distinct differences between the DSO's concerts and those of the Orchestral Society:

> People should not confound these concerts with those of the Detroit Symphony Orchestra, for it is in the Orchestral Association concerts that the Boston Symphony appears, together with the New York, Chicago, and Pittsburgh Orchestras.
>
> Patrons of the concerts will hear the greatest compositions of the greatest composers played by the greatest orchestral players and led by the greatest conductors in the world.

And if that were not enough to influence ticket buyers, the writer ended with a comment on the goodwill and sense of civic duty behind the entire endeavor:

> There is no financial profit to anyone in this association, but it is a civic enterprise organized by F. K. Stearns, and maintained by the public-spirited citizens of Detroit, in order that all might have the advantage of hearing great orchestral music at reasonable prices.[63]

The Orchestral Association's success did not bode well for the DSO. Any positive public feeling brought about by the summer concert series at the Wayne Casino did not translate into full crowds for the regular season. Instead, the symphony, which relocated their concerts to the Casino for the season, drew some of the smallest audiences in its history. The *Free Press* noted the meager numbers who attended the opening concert in December 1908, and again for the second concert and third concerts.[64]

## THE LAST SEASON OF THE FIRST DETROIT SYMPHONY: 1909–10

The DSO's twenty-second season began on December 14, 1909, with all four concerts given again at the Light Guard Armory. That week, five other concerts also were presented in the city, including grand opera and a string quartet. That first concert drew a crowd of around 1,500 people, according to the *Free Press* critic, who also found the orchestra's playing "uneven." The review of the second concert descended to mocking the ensemble, claiming that "the orchestra at times seemed to have some knowledge of score," and describing the playing as a "melee" and "chaos."[65]

It was the last word from the paper on the first DSO; neither the third nor fourth concerts even received a review. The orchestra went out of business, and its demise did not even warrant a column in the paper.

Yet a poignant portrait of its passing was given by George Washington Stark, in his 1943 book *City of Destiny: The Story of Detroit*:

Beyond the memories of many of the patrons of the present orchestra would be the orchestra that was fostered by Fritz Kalsow. His season consisted of three or four concerts and all the players were local musicians, with purely local reputations. Starting in the early spring, Mr. Kalsow toiled early and late for eight months out of the year to make his dream of a great symphony orchestra in Detroit a reality. He called from door to door, walked from one office building to another, explaining the desperate need for subscribers and presenting his well-worn subscription book for the signatures of those whose regard for music would prompt them to disgorge $5, the price of two tickets for each of the concerts.[66]

What had happened to an ensemble that had begun with such promise? Why had the wealthy businessmen of Detroit not followed the lead of those in Boston or Chicago, and found a way to fund a local orchestra at a sustainable level? Perhaps some of the problem lay with the stasis of that early group: over twenty-two seasons, the number of the concerts and the repertoire varied little, especially in its last decade. And when the prosperous industrialists led by F. K. Stearns put their money and support behind the Detroit Orchestral Association, that money fed the growth of outside orchestras, not the local ensemble. It would be four years before the Detroit Symphony would rise again, and know its first days of glory.

# A Glorious Rebirth, 1914–36:
# Weston Gales, Ossip Gabrilowitsch,
# Orchestra Hall, and the First "Golden Age"

Weston Gales came to Detroit in December 1913, and came to see me introduced by Miss Mary Trowbridge, who had met him in Munich. He had been studying conducting in Europe and had been led to come to Detroit by some press publicity in a New York newspaper pointing out the need and opportunity for an orchestra in this city.[1]

THUS BEGINS THE STORY OF THE REBIRTH OF THE DETROIT SYM-phony Orchestra. The quotation is from the diary of Miss Frances Sibley. A descendent of Alexander Sibley, she grew up in the Sibley House, where one of the first pianos to reach Detroit had arrived in 1804. When she met Gales in 1913, she had just returned from musical study and travel in Europe, and was a wealthy, well-connected patroness of the arts, especially music.[2]

Weston Gales, thirty-six years old, was a graduate of Yale, where he studied theory, piano, and organ. After college, he worked for a decade as an organist and choir director in the United States, then moved to Paris in 1908 to study conducting. In 1913, he turned his attention back to the United States in general and Detroit in particular, and returned to America and the possibilities of becoming a conductor in Detroit.[3]

Gales encouraged Sibley to put together a committee of women who were willing to raise $100 each to pay for rehearsals for an orchestra made up of local musicians, after which a concert would be given, to gauge interest in a new symphony for Detroit.[4]

N. J. Corey, organist at Detroit's Fort Street Presbyterian Church, also encouraged the enterprise. Corey had for years been associated with the Detroit Orchestral Association, and when F. K. Stearns decided to retire from the organization in 1910, Corey took a leading role in the association. The new management of the Society also included a man who became a pivotal figure in the rebirth of the DSO: William H. Murphy.[5]

Murphy had made his fortune in the lumber industry and was also the first major financial backer of Henry Ford. He took over the Orchestral Association in 1910, just months after the first DSO had ceased operations. From 1910 to 1914, he led the organization, which continued to bring the major symphonic orchestras to Detroit, including Boston, Philadelphia, Chicago, and Pittsburgh. The Orchestral Association had by that time also become supported by many of the former benefactors of the first DSO, including Fred M. Alger, Charles Freer, J. Harrington Walker, and Ralph M. Dyar.[6]

Members of Frances Sibley's "committee of women" were in large part the spouses and children of the early patrons of classical music in Detroit, and like her,

Weston Gales, conductor of the DSO from 1914 to 1917. (Courtesy DSO Archives)

were wealthy and socially prominent. They included Mrs. F. M. Alger, Mrs. N. J. Corey, Miss Clara E. Dyar, Mrs. Charles H. Hodges, Mrs. H. B. Joy, Mrs. S. Olin Johnson, Mrs. Sidney T. Miller, Mrs. F. B. Stevens, Miss Jennie M. Stoddard, Miss Stella D. Ford, Mrs. Abner E. Larned, and Mrs. George Stillman.[7]

With the funding they provided, Gales gathered sixty-five musicians "from the theatres, restaurants, and studios" of Detroit, according to Edith Tilton, and they rehearsed for four weeks. Then, in January 1914, the new Detroit Symphony Orchestra played for an audience for the first time, presenting a private concert in the ballroom of the Hotel Pontchartrain for 150 subscribers and potential donors. According to Sibley, "some of the ladies who had worked very hard were quite emotional on hearing our orchestra for the first time." The audience liked what they heard, and more subscribers came forward, with 100 patrons paying $10 each to produce a Demonstration Concert for the public at large.[8]

Given on February 26, 1914, at 4 p.m. at the Opera House, the concert included two movements from Dvořák's "New World" Symphony, an overture by Mendelssohn, and preludes by Wagner. The Demonstration Concert was a major cultural event, featuring a speech by the mayor and members of the Common Council in the audience. It was also a great success, and led to the creation of one of the most important organizations in the orchestra's history: the Detroit Symphony Society.[9]

## THE DETROIT SYMPHONY SOCIETY

Otto Kirchner, noted lawyer and former Attorney General of Michigan, called the first meeting of the Society one week after the concert. Kirchner was named the Society's first president, with Sidney T. Miller and Frances Sibley as vice presidents, Paul Gray as treasurer, N. J. Corey as business manager, and Weston Gales as musical director. The structure and donor levels were established as well, with active members contributing $100 or more per year, and associate members contributing

up to $100. This group raised $16,000 for a first season of ten concerts, which ran from November 1914 to April 1915.[10]

That this figure was about five times that of the annual budget of the former DSO under Fritz Kalsow indicated an important change in Detroit: for the first time, the city had grown in size and economic might to become one of the top industrial regions in the country. Detroit had not experienced the tremendous industrial growth and wealth achieved by Chicago and Cleveland in the later nineteenth century, but from 1910 to 1920, the city was transformed into an industrial behemoth.

The size and scope of the growth of Detroit was staggering. Between 1910 and 1920, the population of the city grew from 465,766 to 993,078. In area, it expanded from 40.8 square miles in 1910 to 77.9 square miles in 1920; these statistics changed Detroit's place in the national rankings, as it grew from the country's ninth largest city to its fourth.

The city's tremendous growth was fueled by the meteoric rise of the auto industry. In 1910, as the first DSO faded away, Detroit's automotive factories produced 181,000 cars and 6,000 trucks; just five years later, in 1915, as the DSO was reborn, those figures had risen to 895,930 cars and 74,000 trucks. And by 1920, the Motor City produced 1,905,560 cars and 321,789 trucks.[11]

This explosion of wealth created a class of philanthropists in Detroit who funded the city's arts and cultural organizations, and allowed the most significant patrons of the new DSO, especially William H. Murphy, Jerome Remick, and Horace Dodge, to provide the funding necessary to bring about a symphony of the first rank.

Murphy was one of the most significant financial backers of the symphony from its rebirth in 1914 to his death in 1929. He was one of the most successful businessmen of his era. His family had made their fortune in lumber, which Murphy enhanced through early investments in the booming auto industry and in commercial real estate: he was responsible for building the original section of the Penobscot Building. Murphy was also a great music lover, and owned several valuable instruments, including a viola that had once belonged to Felix Mendelssohn. Such a music lover was Murphy that in the days before the DSO, he had a performance space built on the top of the Penobscot Building, where, under the direction of violinist (and later concertmaster) William G. King, a small orchestra made up of local musicians performed private concerts for him.[12]

Jerome Remick was also from a family who had made their money in lumber, but he made his money in music publishing. Remick was the world's largest music publisher, specializing in popular songs in sheet music form, at a time when popular music was being played in private homes,

## CONCERTMASTER: WILLIAM GRAFING KING (1914–19)

"William Grafing King, the first DSO concertmaster, was a good-looking man with receding, slicked-down hair, a long nose, and a dimple on his chin." That is how Anne Mischakoff Heiles describes the first concertmaster of the "reborn" DSO, who served in that capacity from 1914 to 1919. He was born in Florida and, according to a brief profile of him in a program, "had studiously and successfully worked under the greatest teachers this country afforded."

King was named concertmaster by Weston Gales, and he also continued to teach and perform during his years with the orchestra. He was the head of the Detroit Conservatory of Music's violin department and taught at the Detroit Institute of Musical Arts. He was also the leader of the Detroit Symphony String Quartet, which performed chamber music around Detroit and also with the DSO. King also played as a soloist with the orchestra during Gales's tenure, in such standard favorites as the Bruch Concerto in G Minor.

When Gabrilowitsch took over as music director in 1918, he kept King on as concertmaster, and considered him, according to Clara Clemens, as one of "only three or four men of first-rate caliber." After King had served one year in the position, Gabrilowitsch replaced him with Ilya Schkolnik; still, King was highly valued by Gabrilowitsch, whom he considered "an indispensable member of the orchestra from its very beginning," and who shared the first desk with Schkolnik until 1939; from 1939 to 1946, King played in the first violin section.

After Gabrilowitsch's death, it was King, then the oldest member of the orchestra, who drew aside the veil revealing the Brenda Putman bust of the conductor, at the dedication concert given at Orchestra Hall on November 11, 1937.

Sources: Anne Mischakoff Heiles, *America's Concertmasters* (Sterling Heights: Harmonie Park Press, 2007), 214–16; Clara Clemens, *My Husband, Gabrilowitsch* (New York: Harper and Brothers, 1938), 104, 110, 329.

on pianos, at an ever-growing pace. His company sold millions of copies of some of the most popular music hits of the early twentieth century, including such standards as "Oh, You Beautiful Doll" and "In the Shade of the Old Apple Tree." Although he remained at the helm of his company for years, he also became active in philanthropy in Detroit, especially as a patron of the DSO.[13]

Horace Dodge did not come from either money or a musical background. He had, however, loved music since he was a child growing up in Niles, Michigan. Though he was too poor to afford an instrument, a wealthy businessman who owned a piano became a friend to him and let him play the piano in his home. When he was still a young boy, Horace spent his savings on a violin, which he also learned to play. And when he met the woman who would become his wife, Anna Thomson, one of her special charms for him was her ability as a pianist. After he had made his fortune in the auto industry, Dodge had an organ built at his mansion, Rose Terrace, in Grosse Pointe, as well as in several of his yachts.[14]

## WESTON GALES: 1914–17

These and other patrons hopeful for a symphony of stature in Detroit attended the inaugural concert of the revitalized Detroit Symphony Orchestra, which took place on November 19, 1914, at 4 p.m., at the Opera House, with Weston Gales on the podium. The performance time of the regular concerts was necessary because so many of the musicians were playing in other ensembles in the evening. It also reflected the fact that so many of the orchestra's patrons were women, who could attend a weekday afternoon concert in sufficient numbers. The program for this first concert included Beethoven's Symphony no. 1 in C Major, Wagner's "Siegfried Idyll," and Weber's "Invitation to the Dance." This first concert of the season was followed by five more afternoon concerts, as well as two "popular" concerts (with programs that were nearly identical to the afternoon concerts), given on Sunday evenings at the Opera House, and a Young People's Concert, performed at Central High School in February 1915. And in its first act of "outreach" concerts, the DSO also performed out of town, at the Atheneum in Jackson, Michigan, in March, 1915.[15]

It is interesting to note the activities of the Detroit Orchestral Association during this time period. In January 1914, just as the new DSO was getting on its feet, the DOA reduced the number of concerts in its season, as a "concession to the Detroit Symphony Orchestra."[16] In 1915, the Association made further changes in deference to the DSO, renaming its series the "Great Orchestras" to "avoid confusion" with the symphony's offerings. Although it is nowhere stated in the press, it appears that the Orchestral Association, which shared so many patrons with the new DSO, wanted to give it the best chance possible of surviving.[17]

During the 1915–16 season, the number of concerts expanded: there were ten regular concerts on Friday afternoons at the Opera House, and ten popular concerts on Sunday evenings at the Arcadia. The programs for these concerts contain extensive "Program Notes," by Arthur Prescott Lothrop, which, in addition to placing a piece within its historical context, also included excerpts from the symphonic works in musical notation, with explications of specific phrases, rhythms, voicings, and themes. It wasn't "spoon-feeding" for an audience; rather, it was sophisticated, insightful commentary on the composers and the pieces for the layperson, a "first" for patrons of the orchestra. As part of its second season of concerts, the DSO also presented a concert out of town in Ypsilanti, Michigan, and a Young People's Concert, both in April 1916.[18]

In an article published in the *Free Press* in 1915, Gales commented on several familiar concerns regarding the ensemble. First, he claimed that the orchestra needed to be put on secure financial footing. "What do we need for the Orchestra most of all? Money," he claimed in an article dated January 3, 1915.[19] As Lynne Marie Mattson explained in her 1968 master's thesis, at that point in history no American symphony existed on income from ticket sales alone. "Even if a symphony orchestra were to sell every ticket to all of its concerts, it would still lack

approximately one-half of the funds necessary for its yearly operations."[20] Instead, the major orchestras of the era ran large deficits, often between $50,000 and $75,000 each year. To pay off the deficits, the DSO had to rely on donations, which, according to Mattson, "came almost exclusively from a few wealthy citizens." It was an unfortunate, persistent problem: "this narrow base of support perpetuated itself, causing the orchestra much trouble later."[21]

Gales also outlined two other concerns reiterated throughout the DSO's history: the need for a hall of its own, and the need to develop a solid base of support among all of the people of Detroit, not just the wealthy elite. One of the reasons the orchestra had to play its concerts in the afternoons was because the other locales, such as the Opera House and the Armory, were booked most evenings. According to Gales, a successful orchestra, in its own hall, would be viewed as an important "civic asset," and be more likely to draw in the popular support of the people, than the current system of financial support and performance. He even likened it to a positive "advertisement" for the city, just like the Detroit Tigers, then as now another beloved "civic asset."[22]

Gales's third season, of 1916–17, included several major visiting guest artists, including Percy Grainger and Ossip Gabrilowitsch. Gabrilowitsch had performed several times in Detroit since 1901, and always drew an enraptured audience. Calling him a "pianist of the first grade," the *Free Press* claimed he was a "serious minded musician who combines intellectual interpretation with fire and enthusiasm."[23]

The programs for the third season included the variety of advertisements seen over the previous years for music lessons with local musicians, dairy products, corsets, hats, and jewelry, but also something new, a technology soon to be enjoyed by musical audiences worldwide, which would have a great effect on classical music, too. Thomas Edison had invented the first record player in 1877, and by 1916 the technology had improved to the point that the first phonographs for home use were widely available and affordable. Ads in the DSO's programs showed famous opera stars singing next to the record players, noting that audiences could not tell the difference between the recording and the live performance. The Edison Shop, on Woodward, offered demonstrations daily.[24]

The 1916–17 season ended under the specter of war. World War I had begun in 1914 in Europe, and the United States entered the conflict in April 1917. As the nation's industrial centers, including Detroit, geared up to help the war effort, there were food and fuel shortages in the region.[25] It is no wonder that money became an issue for cultural organizations in Detroit and nationwide.

Programs announcing the 1917–18 season contained pleas to Detroiters to give financial support to the orchestra and outlined the Symphony Society's goals: an ensemble of sixty to seventy musicians on a regular salary basis for a period of thirty weeks, with fourteen pairs of subscription concerts, fourteen popular concerts, outstanding soloists, and tours of twenty to thirty cities.

The program announcement stated that such a schedule would require an estimated $40,000 to $60,000, which was their fundraising goal. The plea ended with the following: "It is for you to decide whether or not Detroit is to keep pace in this respect with the important cities of America." Lending their names to the request for funds was a separate message in the program from Sidney T. Miller, Truman Newberry, Jerome Remick, Frances Sibley, and Charles Warren. Appealing to the "civic pride and musical interests" of the public, they called for more contributions to the Society, to help give the city "an orchestra capable of taking its place among the greatest organizations of its kind in this country." Pledges of support were requested to be made to a Guaranty Fund, with monies due July 1, 1917, and included an agreement to be signed by the donor to help pay any deficit incurred by the symphony during the following season.[26]

Clearly, the DSO was facing financial difficulties. According to Edith Rhetts Tilton, in the fall of 1917 the musicians were supposed to be on salary, but when payday rolled around, the orchestra's business manager, Harry Cyphers, "would

Ossip Gabrilowitsch, conductor of the DSO from 1918 to 1936. (Courtesy DSO Archives)

open his desk drawers in a payday gesture of saying, 'If you can find any money take it.'" When there was no money to be found, someone was "sent to borrow payroll again, from Horace Dodge."[27]

In December 1917, just as the new season was getting under way, Weston Gales resigned abruptly. Although the reasons behind his leaving were never publicized by the DSO, the following appeared in the *Free Press* in an article announcing his resignation: "In resigning he took the stand that the substitution of a new personality in the conductor's box will give the orchestra its best chance for renewed prosperity and permanence."[28] But Gales's departure had a distinct silver lining. As the DSO's management began a search for his replacement, one name emerged above all others: the esteemed Russian pianist and conductor Ossip Gabrilowitsch.

## OSSIP GABRILOWITSCH: THE DETROIT SYMPHONY'S GOLDEN AGE, 1918–36

By the time he joined the DSO in 1918, Gabrilowitsch had an international reputation as an outstanding pianist and conductor. He was born in St. Petersburg in 1878 and began studying piano with his brother at the age of six. At the age of ten, he played for the great Russian pianist and composer Anton Rubinstein, who was mightily impressed with the young prodigy. On his recommendation, Gabrilowitsch attended St. Petersburg's Imperial Conservatory, studying piano with Victor Tolstov and composition with Alexander Glazunov. An outstanding student, Gabrilowitsch graduated in 1894 with highest honors and the Rubinstein Prize in piano.[29]

He moved to Vienna, where he began studying piano with the legendary Theodor Leschetizky. While in Vienna, he met another of Leschetizky's students, Clara Clemens, daughter of Samuel Clemens, the famous author Mark Twain, who was then living in Vienna, and was as popular in Austria as he was in America. Gabrilowitsch and Clara Clemens were immediately drawn to one another, and continued an on-again, off-again romance for more than a decade.[30]

After two years of study with Leschetizky, Gabrilowitsch made his formal

Gabrilowitsch and
Clara Clemens.
(Courtesy Library
of Congress)

debut in Berlin in 1896, and was an immediate success. He began a storied career as a piano soloist, traveling, concertizing, and gaining accolades as one of the leading virtuosos of the era. His style "was one of great finish, delicacy, and restraint," according to the *New Grove Dictionary of Music and Musicians*.[31]

Gabrilowitsch shared these gifts with thousands of concertgoers in Europe and the United States. Modern listeners can glean insights into his style of playing on the small portion of his concert work available on recently reengineered recordings. A review of these recordings by critic Alexander Morin claims: "His technique was superb and he could launch bravura displays on a par with the other keyboard giants of the 1920s." Yet Gabrilowitsch

"preferred to play the gentler and more lyrical parts of the piano repertoire, including much chamber music and two-piano works (usually with Harold Bauer)." Of his recording of the Schumann Quintet and the Gluck-Brahms Gavotte, Morin claims, "His playing is simple and unaffected, his phrasing exquisite, and his control of tone and color in these small gems make them luminous and moving. The Quintet is tender and warmly romantic; the liquid legato of the Gluck-Brahms Gavotte is remarkable."[32]

Gabrilowitsch was also a composer of several piano pieces. He had studied with Alexander Glazunov in St. Petersburg, and most of his piano compositions, including his "Melodie in E Minor," "Caprice Burlesque," and "Fantasie Nocturne," date from early in his career and show the influence of the German Romantic music he loved.

By 1905, Gabrilowitsch was ready for a new challenge. He began to study conducting in Leipzig with Artur Nikisch, who was considered the finest orchestral conductor of his time. After making his directorial debut in Paris in 1906, Gabrilowitsch began a dual career as piano soloist and conductor, which he would continue throughout his life.[33]

In 1909, Gabrilowitsch and Clara Clemens met again. This time, the great virtuoso was gravely ill, and as Clara nursed him back to health at her family's home, the romance between the two rekindled.

They married in October 1909. In 1910, the couple moved to Europe, where Gabrilowitsch became conductor of the Munich Philharmonic, a position he held until 1914. With the outbreak of war, the family, which now included a daughter, Nina, was forced to flee, as Gabrilowitsch was named an enemy alien in Germany. They settled in the United States, which became their permanent home.[34]

For the next four years, Gabrilowitsch continued his dual career as a concert pianist and conductor, performing all over the country. One of his greatest accomplishments during this era was a series of concerts representing "The Development of Piano Music from the Days of the Clavichord to the Present Time." Presented in major cities around the United States, Gabrilowitsch performed the works of English, German, Italian, French, and Russian composers. It was a wildly successful series, yet he never let fame affect him or his playing, and instead performed with characteristic humility. As Clara Clemens wrote of him, "I doubt whether Gabrilowitsch was ever inclined to adulterate the purity of his art with egotistical efforts to satisfy his vanity." Rather, he displayed "the characteristic qualities of the composers; but never for the purpose of exciting personal enthusiasm for the performer, himself."[35]

From the time he was a student, Gabrilowitsch had forged close professional and personal relationships with several of the outstanding musicians of his era. They included pianist Harold Bauer, conductor Bruno Walter, violinist Fritz Kreisler, conductor Leopold Stokowski and his wife, pianist Olga Samaroff, conductor Walter Damrosch, and many other "stars" of the classical world. They would become an important source of talent and further the "allure" of Gabrilowitsch, as he took on the role of conductor of the Detroit Symphony.

## TAKING OVER FOR GALES

In December 1917, Gabrilowitsch was preparing to appear in Detroit as a soloist with the symphony when Harry Cyphers, the DSO's business manager, asked him to take over as guest conductor of the orchestra following Gales's sudden departure. Gabrilowitsch agreed, and gave an interview as he prepared the orchestra for its first concert under his baton. He was full of praise for the members of the symphony, expressing his admiration for their musicianship and dedication. Knowing that the financial future of the ensemble was less than secure, he spoke fervently of the need for music in Detroit, especially in time of war. "Art is not a luxury, it is a necessity," he claimed, "and it is time people began to realize it. The two most potent agencies in maintaining the courage of the people in these war times are religion and music. . . . In this period of national stress it is especially important that music be fostered and protected against dissolution. War stuns the morale and blunts the enthusiasm of the people and they absolutely need music to lift them."[36]

Gabrilowitsch made his debut as conductor of the Detroit Symphony on December 28, 1917. With Efrem Zimbalist as violin soloist, the DSO under their new guest conductor was a smashing success, establishing Gabrilowitsch as both a consummate artist as well as the leading candidate for the position of permanent conductor. In a program that included Tchaikovsky's Symphony no. 4 in F Minor, Beethoven's Violin Concerto in D Major, and Wagner's Overture to *Tannhäuser*, Gabrilowitsch displayed his particular genius, according to the *Free Press*, drawing a musical performance from the orchestra that was characterized by "power, balance, depth of background and constant poetic undertone."[37]

Praise for Gabrilowitsch continued throughout the season. He cut quite a figure from the podium: he was tall, slender, and favored high collars (supposedly to hide his thin neck), his head crowned with a large pompadour of wavy hair. For the final concert of the season in March 1918, Gabrilowitsch chose an all-Russian program, in which he performed as both pianist and conductor. His conducting of Tchaikovsky's Symphony no. 5 in E Minor was praised for drawing "every bit of power and tonal resource" from the musicians. And in the Tchaikovsky Concerto no. 1 for Piano in B-flat Minor, his solo work

revealed "perfect rhythm, poetry, delicacy, fire, passion, digital facility and adroit pedaling,"[38] according to the *Free Press*. The superlatives didn't stop with praise for the DSO, but added a comparison, too. Victor Herbert, at that point the conductor of the Cincinnati Orchestra, had performed Tchaikovsky's Fifth Symphony in Detroit two weeks prior to Detroit's performance. And whose interpretation was preferred? Gabrilowitsch's, hands down: "Mr. Gabrilowitsch imbued the players with some of his own sympathetic insight into the composition, and the result was an inspiring and beautiful achievement."[39]

The comparison with Herbert was apt for another reason: both he and Gabrilowitsch were being considered for the position of permanent conductor of the DSO. Horace Dodge helped fund the search for the new maestro, and, according to Dodge biographers Jean Maddern Pitrone and Joan Potter Elwart, Gabrilowitsch had the edge because both Horace and Anna favored pianists.[40]

MAKING DETROIT HOME

In May 1918, Gabrilowitsch was offered the position as permanent conductor of the Detroit Symphony. He accepted, for "one single determining reason," according to Clara Clemens. The offer, created especially for him, allowed Gabrilowitsch to continue his career as a concert pianist. The schedule in Detroit was for fourteen pairs of concerts, given at two-week intervals, over a season lasting from late October to early April. Not only was the number of concerts in the season fewer than in any other major city, the contract stipulated that Gabrilowitsch could conduct every other week, allowing him to accept outside engagements every other week as well. It also allowed for an assistant conductor to take over the directorial duties when Gabrilowitsch was out of town.[41]

Detroit was generous in its offer to Gabrilowitsch for a good reason: it wasn't the only city eager to engage him as its maestro. He had conducted a series of concerts in New York, which led to rumors that an offer for a director's position was forthcoming. Boston, too, wanted the brilliant musician, and public and private reports began to circulate that he would be offered the directorship of the Boston Symphony Orchestra.[42]

But Gabrilowitsch chose Detroit, and things began to look up for the symphony and its fortunes. The precarious nature of the DSO's finances seemed closer to being resolved, thanks to new donations. Several wealthy patrons, notably William H. Murphy and Horace Dodge, who pledged $25,000 per year for three years, were among the most generous contributors, and Murphy lent his business expertise to the organization as well, serving as president of the Detroit Symphony Society for ten years.[43]

Gabrilowitsch embraced his new responsibilities eagerly. He was especially interested in building a new ensemble from the small core of first-rate musicians then currently playing with the orchestra. According to Clemens, Gabrilowitsch thought the ensemble at that time contained only "three or four men of first-rate caliber, the chief one being William G. King, the concertmaster."[44]

But trying to fill those positions brought about Gabrilowitsch's first management crisis as conductor. He held auditions to fill the seventy-six positions in the orchestra, and of the nearly 100 musicians who tried out, he selected only twenty, stating that if the Detroit Symphony was to be among the nation's best, he would need to find musicians up to his standards elsewhere.

It caused a firestorm: "A tiger-hunt in the jungle is a tango by comparison," wrote Clemens. The members of the American Federation of Musicians objected to Gabrilowitsch's plans, wanting to keep as many jobs as possible for Detroit musicians. The new maestro resigned in protest.[45] Only after the intervention of Harry Cyphers, members of the board, and the president of the musician's union was a compromise reached that was acceptable to all parties: "Of the 76 players in the orchestra, 40 will be Detroit musicians, the remainder to be chosen by Mr. Gabrilowitsch, one representative of the union, and one representative of the management of the orchestra," stated Cyphers.[46]

At last, Gabrilowitsch was free to plan his first full season as conductor. Among the most important new musi-

## CONCERTMASTER: ILYA SCHKOLNIK (1919–44)

Ilya Schkolnik was born in Odessa, Russia (now Ukraine), on February 24, 1890. He first studied violin with his father, then moved to Berlin in 1903, where he won a scholarship to study with Gustav Hollanader. Schkolnik graduated from the Leipzig Conservatory in 1905, and was a student of Hans Stitt. He toured as a soloist in Europe, and then, when war broke out in 1914, moved to the United States.

Schkolnik played in several ensembles in New York, including the Symphony Society and the Russian Symphony Orchestra, and was the assistant concertmaster of the New York Symphony. In 1919, he joined the DSO as concertmaster, chosen by Gabrilowitsch to replace William Grafing King, who continued as his standmate for many years.

Gabrilowitsch often featured Schkolnik in concerts as violin soloist, in well-known concertos by Tartini, Brahms, and Paganini, as well as more recent works by Christian Sinding and Saint-Saëns. He also performed the concertmaster solos in such works as Rimsky-Korsakov's *Scheherazade* and Richard Strauss's *Ein Heldenleben*. As concertmaster, he led his section to produce a sound praised by the *New York Herald* as "solid, brilliant, and muscular."

Clara Clemens recounts in her book on Gabrilowitsch a remarkable story about one of Schkolnik's violin students, Beatrice Griffin, who had been chosen to appear with the DSO, but had a poor-quality instrument. Gabrilowitsch learned that Henry Ford had a collection of valuable violins, including one made by the world-renown Stradavarius, and one day, out of the blue, he received a call from Ford, asking him to come to his home, where he produced the instruments and asked the conductor to choose one for Griffin.

Gabrilowitsch said he thought the young violinist should choose for herself, and when Griffin visited Ford in person, she played on all the instruments. When she was asked to choose among them, she selected the Stradavarius; that evening, Ford's secretary delivered not only the Strad, but another of the student's favorite violins, and was told "she need not hurry about returning them."

Schkolnik and the maestro also enjoyed a great friendship, and when Gabrilowitsch was in his final days, the violinist played for him, a violin transcription of one of his own piano pieces, Melody in E Minor. The music deeply moved Gabrilowitsch, who asked to have the work performed twice.

After Gabrilowitsch's death, Schkolnik stayed on with the DSO, playing under both Franco Ghione and Victor Kolar. After the DSO went out of business in 1942, Schkolnik stayed on in Detroit, and was once again concertmaster during the early years of the Reichhold era, under Karl Krueger. He left Detroit in 1944, moving to Baltimore, where he taught at the Peabody Conservatory and served as concertmaster for the Baltimore Symphony Orchestra. Schkolnik retired to California, where he died in 1963.

Sources: Anne Mischakoff Heiles, *America's Concertmasters* (Sterling Heights: Harmonie Park Press, 2007), 217–19; Clara Clemens, *My Husband, Gabrilowitsch* (New York: Harper and Brothers, 1938), 110, 184, 245, 291–92.

cians were violinists Ilya Schkolnik as concertmaster, and Victor Kolar, who became Gabrilowitsch's right-hand man and reliable assistant conductor throughout his tenure with the orchestra. Among the soloists performing in that first season were pianist Olga Samaroff and singer Clara Clemens, who by that point had gained a reputation as an accomplished soprano soloist. Here is how she describes the first concert of that first year:

When in the fall of 1918 ninety men were seated upon the stage of the Arcadia Auditorium, my husband felt great happiness in the thought of what might come to pass in the musical life of Detroit. The mammoth hall was filled and the atmosphere of expectancy was charged with electric feeling.[47]

And how did the musicians feel about their new conductor?

He fires us. When we sit under his baton he makes us into artists. When we are away from him we know that many of us are only ordinary musicians, but under his dominating artistry he transforms us into something greater than we know ourselves to be. He actually draws the music from us; we *must* play it as he wants it.[48]

For his part, Gabrilowitsch was only willing to sign a one-year contract, a practice he continued for all his years in Detroit. He wanted the freedom and flexibility to make a change, if he felt that one was needed. "How stupid," he said, "to remain in a place just because you have promised to. A year is long enough. It may seem like ten!"[49]

The 1918–19 season's concerts were well attended and rapturously reviewed. Even the specter of Spanish influenza, which closed the concert halls temporarily, could not dim the enthusiasm for the orchestra and its new director. The season ended with an announcement marked "Important" in the program:

Through the generosity, broad vision, and public spirit of a small group of men who have substantially supported the Detroit Symphony Orchestra during the past season, a new home will be provided for the organization with the erection of a building especially designed to meet the orchestra's purposes.

Orchestra Hall, as the new structure probably will be known, will be located at Woodward Avenue and Parsons Street on the present site of Westminster Church. Its completion by October first of this year has been guaranteed.[50]

The symphony would finally get its own hall, largely due to the demands of its new maestro: while negotiating his annual contract, Gabrilowitsch informed the Symphony Society "that unless a new hall could be built suitable to the needs of the orchestra, he would have to resign his post as conductor. More than that, the hall must be built and ready for use for the opening concert in the fall."[51]

## THE BUILDING OF ORCHESTRA HALL

A Herculean task, and a Herculean effort: that is what it took to realize Gabrilowitsch's dream. The Symphony Society selected three people—William H. Murphy, Paul Gray, and famed architect Albert Kahn—to serve as the building committee. They in turn chose architect C. Howard Crane to design the hall, with general contracting to be provided by the firm of Walbridge and Aldinger.[52]

Crane was born in Hartford, Connecticut, in 1885, where he became an apprentice draftsman. He moved to Detroit in 1904, and worked for a brief time for Albert Kahn's architectural firm. In 1905, he became the chief draftsman for Field, Hinchman, and Smith (later Smith, Hinchman, and Grylls).

Crane next worked for Gustave A. Mueller as chief draftsman, then opened his own firm in 1909. After designing smaller projects, including offices and residences, he began the work for which he became famous, as the designer of more than 250 movie houses, especially the ornate "movie palaces" that were popular throughout the country at the time. His chief client, John Kunsky, was Detroit's major theater owner, especially of movie houses. In Detroit, Crane designed more than fifty movie the-

Blueprints for Orchestra Hall, 1919. (Courtesy Library of Congress)

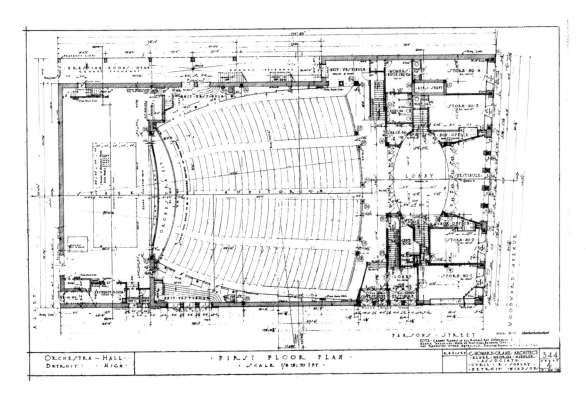

First floor plan, Orchestra Hall, 1919. (Courtesy Library of Congress)

aters, most of them for Kunsky. The most famous of these "palaces" was the opulent Fox Theater, fashioned, in the words of a contemporary reporter, "after the Hindoo Mosques of Old India, bewildering in their richness and dazzling in their appointments."[53] In addition to the Fox, Crane designed the Capitol Theater, which later housed the Detroit Opera House, as well as the Madison, the Adams, the State, the Majestic, the Palace, the Rialto, and the Riviera Theaters, and also Olympia Stadium, home of the Detroit Red Wings from 1927 to 1979.[54]

After Crane was hired, the Hall needed to be financed. A new organi-

zation, the Orchestra Hall Association, was incorporated on May 5, 1919, to achieve that task, with the stated purpose of "the erection, maintenance, and operation of a building for musical and theatrical purposes." Its stockholders included William H. Murphy, Paul Gray, David Gray, Horace Dodge, Alice Gray Kale, Jerome Remick, Charles H. Hodges, David A. Brown, Sidney T. Miller, Ossip Gabrilowitsch, Roy D. Chapin, and Julius Haas.[55]

It was estimated that it would cost $800,000 to build the Hall, and half of it was raised within days, thanks to the largesse of, once again, William H. Mur-

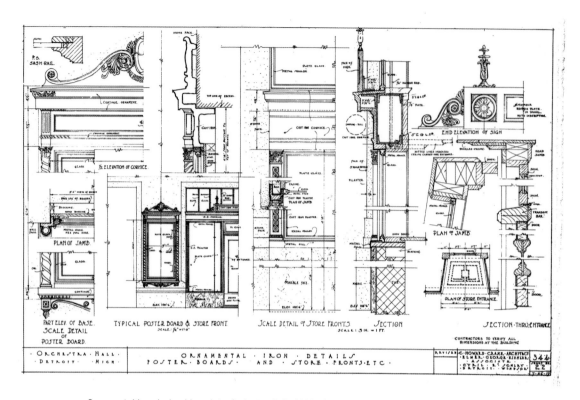

Ornamental iron design blueprints, Orchestra Hall, 1919. (Courtesy Library of Congress)

phy, Horace Dodge, and Jerome Remick. Bond buyers provided the rest of the funds. Gabrilowitsch, who contributed $5,000 to the project, declared the successful fundraising a "miracle."[56]

Then it was time to build the hall, and with lightning speed. The first thing to be done was the demolition of the existing structure on the corner of Woodward and Parsons, Old Westminster Church. According to one story, the destruction began as a wedding was still underway inside. In all it took only four months and twenty-three days to build Orchestra Hall, from then until now considered one of the most acoustically perfect performance halls in America.[57]

The plan of the building's exterior was unlike Crane's movie theater designs. With its combination of Beaux Arts and Art Deco elements, Orchestra Hall's exterior followed classical, elegant lines, very much unlike the "bold colors, wildly eclectic references, and shoot-the-moon ornamentation" of the Fox Theater.[58] Built of limestone, the exterior was decorated with ornamental relief and cornices outlined in gold.

But it was Orchestra Hall's interior, especially its acoustical properties, which made it extraordinary. No one is exactly sure how Crane was able to create such an acoustical gem, especially in just under five months, but a brief history of concert hall construction of the time gives some clues. During the nineteenth century, most European concert halls were built in what is called the "shoe box" shape: a rectangle that was long, tall, and narrow. Such masterpieces of acoustics as the Musikverein in Vienna, completed in 1870, are examples of this design.

A central concept of the acoustics of concert hall design is reverberation. Sound traveling in an enclosed space needs proper reflection and diffusion to create the reverberation needed for the music to be heard properly by as many audience members as possible. Irregular and uneven surfaces of a theater all contribute to the proper diffusion of sound. So concert halls like the Musikverein were designed with heavy use of ornamentation, coffered ceilings, and irregular surfaces on back walls and side walls, all of which help to scatter sound.[59]

Crane's design was not a true a "shoe box," but also incorporated dimensions similar to a fan-shape design to the hall, which was in keeping with the structure of the early movie houses he designed. This shape sent the sound out from the stage to tiers of 2,200 seats, which were set at angles so that each one commanded an unobstructed view of the stage. The Hall's interior features heavily ornamented de-

signs, with ornate plaster work. There are also chandeliers, curtains, convex fronts to the balconies, and even ceiling "cameos," completed in 1990, which feature portraits of some of the most important "angels" who helped the Hall come to fruition, including Horace Dodge, Anna Dodge, Crane himself, William H. Murphy, as well as Ossip Gabrilowitsch and Clara Clemens.[60]

The Hall is also asymmetrical in shape and design, as can be seen in examining the blueprints for the first floor. The asymmetry extends to many details of the Hall's construction. During the renovation of Orchestra Hall in the 1970s, it was discovered that the plaster on the right side of the Hall is one-half inch thicker than on the left. Even the walls vary in width by as much as two or three feet.[61] The ornamentation and the asymmetry all add to the enhanced acoustics of the Hall, as did the materials used to build the stage, which is hard maple in front and soft pine in back, to add to the "scattering" of the sound as it reverberates out from the stage.

Another element of the design involved limiting the noise from the outside. It was necessary to block as much of the noise from the busy thoroughfare of Woodward Avenue as possible. This Crane accomplished with three sets of doors from the street to the interior of the performance space. Outside noise was also tempered by the use of cement flooring in the exterior portions surrounding the performance space. Ornamental materials, like terrazzo and marble, were used for the flooring in the entry way, as well as additional rooms, such as the vestibule, lobby, smoking room, and foyer.[62]

The color scheme used for the interior of the Hall, as well as the rooms outside the concert space—the Mezzanine foyer, "retiring rooms," dressing rooms, executive offices, even the ladies' lounges—was chosen for its understated elegance and flair. According to Edith Rhetts Tilton, "The interior was a soft cream tint relieved by touches of gold and old blue. It offered a restful atmosphere and an unobtrusive air of quiet elegance."[63]

It is part of the lore of the building of Orchestra Hall that the construction crews worked round the clock to meet the deadline, often under the glare of night lighting. Still, they cut no corners in constructing this "Temple consecrated to the holiest Muse."[64] Not all of the ornamental elements were finished in time for Opening Night in October 1919, and the crews were walking out the back door as the first audience was walking in the front, but what they had accomplished was monumental; it left those early patrons dazzled, and continues to inspire today.

## OPENING NIGHT

Orchestra Hall was completed, as promised, in time for the opening of the 1919–20 season. On October 23, 1919, Detroiters experienced "what was undoubtedly the most splendid, the most widely appreciated, the most significant event in the musical history of Detroit."[65] As Gabrilowitsch walked on stage, the audience broke into applause, then leapt to its feet, giving him a standing ovation. They were joined by the orchestra, and the conductor acknowledged it all with a sweep of his arm, in a gesture of exuberant joy shared by all.

The concert began with the "Star-Spangled Banner," then the formal program opened with Weber's Overture to *Oberon*. Gabrilowitsch next joined his friend and fellow pianist Harold Bauer in performing Mozart's Concerto in E flat for Two Pianos and Orchestra, with Victor Kolar conducting. After intermission, Gabrilowitsch again took the stage with Bauer and Olga Samaroff, where they played, for the first time in Detroit, Bach's Concerto in C Major for Three Pianos and Orchestra. The concert closed with Beethoven's Symphony no. 5 in C Minor, with Gabrilowitsch back on the podium. When it was finished, the audience again rose to its feet, flooding the space with grateful applause.[66]

It was an exciting moment, and marked another new beginning for Gabrilowitsch, the symphony, and Detroit. Over the next two decades, Orchestra Hall would play host to a gallery of stars of the artistic world, not just classical musicians, but also dancers and opera stars.

Their names read like a Who's Who of artists of the early twentieth century.

Orchestra Hall, completed, 1919. (Courtesy Library of Congress)

Over the course of Gabrilowitsch's tenure, such famous classical musicians as Richard Strauss, Igor Stravinsky, Sergei Prokofieff, Bruno Walter, and Alexander Glazunov served as guest conductors, and often conducted their own work. Among the many guest artists who performed with the DSO were Fritz Kresiler, Jascha Heifitz, Vladimir Horowitz, Sergei Rachmaninoff, Artur Rubinstein, Pablo Casals, Artur Schnabel, Wanda Landowska, Percy Grainger, Gregor Piatigorsky, Yehudi Menuhin, and Efrem Zimbalist.

From the world of opera, Enrico Caruso and Marianne Anderson, Lotte Lehmann and Kirsten Flagstad brought their talents to Detroit, under the auspices of Gabrilowitsch and the Symphony Society.

The world of dance was well represented, too. Anna Pavlova and the Ballet Russe performed in the hall, accompanied by the DSO, as did the famous—and somewhat notorious—Isadora Duncan, who, as outlined in a headline from the local news, disappointed at least some of her audience by "keeping her clothes on" during her performance.[67]

Under Gabrilowitsch, the Detroit Symphony Orchestra became one of the most prominent ensembles in the country. He brought prestige and fame—and revenue—to his new orchestra. The budget, and the income, for the DSO grew substantially under his conductorship. The entire budget for the 1919–20 season was $238,500; by 1920–21, that had grown

To Mrs. James Duval
The faithful friend
of the Detroit Sym-
phony Orchestra
Most cordially
[signature]
April 1922

Mary Dale Clarke

Gabrilowitsch, 1922. (Courtesy DSO Archives)

to $378,113, with a profit of $702 for the Symphony Society.[68] Over the course of the 1920s, the budget total varied between $355,000 and $394,000; it was clear that the Detroit Symphony under Gabrilowitsch was an artistic and financial success.

The maestro wanted to expand its capabilities and its reach even further. In 1922, the DSO became the first orchestra to perform a symphonic concert for a radio audience, in a performance that featured noted pianist Artur Schnabel and was broadcast on Detroit's radio station WWJ.[69]

The DSO's programs from this era were wonders of artistry and information. Each one was graced with prints of famous

masterpieces from the Detroit Institute of Arts. Each also contained articles on music written by the staff of the Detroit Public Library. In addition to these articles, the programs contained explanatory notes pertaining to each concert, written by several fine musicologists of the time, including James Huneker and composer Daniel Gregory Mason.

The programs were full of advertisements, but, unlike the programs of the first DSO, there was nary a mention of butter, eggs, or bug spray. Instead, the ads, drawn in Art Deco fashion, promoted goods to an audience flush with cash, including furs, jewelry, oriental rugs, high-end automobiles, fine china, cruises to Europe, estate and trust planning, and musical instruction from the academies of Detroit.[70]

In October 1927, the DSO performed at the dedication of the new Detroit Institute of Arts building. The DIA's Board of Commissioners contained many of the same names as long-time patrons of the DSO, including Edsel Ford, William Gray, and Albert Kahn. The program for the event was reprinted as part of the program for the DSO's season. So, even in the symphony's programs, Gabrilowitsch sought to unite the cultural resources of the city—its orchestra, its museum, and its public library—and showcase them to the people of Detroit and the country.[71]

In 1924, Gabrilowitsch brought famed organist Marcel Dupré of Notre Dame

Cathedral in Paris to inaugurate the Murphy Organ, donated by the ever-generous DSO board member and philanthropist, William H. Murphy.

Sadly, Horace Dodge, one of the greatest benefactors of the orchestra, did not live to see many of its glory years under Gabrilowitsch. The DSO, which had played at the wedding of Horace's daughter Delphine in June 1920, played at his funeral months later. His contribution to the symphony was commemorated in a program note: "Whenever you think of the great miracle which has arisen in the midst of Detroit's super industrial development—the miracle of this superb orchestra and its inspired conductor—let your hearts grow warm at the remembrance of Horace Dodge, who has, in a larger measure than any other citizen, made it possible."[72]

## REACHING OUT TO THE YOUTH OF DETROIT: EDITH RHETTS TILTON

Gabrilowitsch had another goal for his orchestra: he wanted to develop stronger ties to members of the Detroit community. "Thousands have not the slightest idea of our symphony," he said. "They could be interested if properly approached."[73] Gabrilowitsch thought that one way to build a future audience was to reach out to and educate the school children of Detroit. If they were taught to understand classical music, to learn about it, appreciate it, and enjoy it as part of everyday life, they would become lifelong listeners, supporters, and knowledgeable audience members of the DSO. It would also be an important step away from relying solely on the generosity of the small handful of wealthy supporters who had, up to that point, been the sole source of donations for the symphony.

In 1922, he contacted an individual who proved to be essential in helping him accomplish his goal: Edith Rhetts (later Edith Tilton), who became the Educational Director of the DSO, and the first person named to that role for an American orchestra. "We need a wedding in our city," he told her, "a wedding of our orchestra and our community. I believe you could help us work out some fundamental plan for extending our orchestra into our city life. Will you come?" She did.[74]

Edith Rhetts came to Detroit from Kansas City, where she was a concert pianist and accompanist and then became involved in music education. She worked on the educational programs of the Victor Recording Company and had also helped develop music education programs in the Kansas City schools for the St. Louis Symphony. She was also known for her inspiring talks on classical music, which she gave to women's clubs, men's clubs, Rotary clubs, and similar organizations, educating them while encouraging them to support their local symphony.

In Detroit, Rhetts began a program that reached out to civic groups, church groups, and especially the schools. She began an ambitious program of youth education that included Educational Concerts, Young People's Concerts, and Children's Concerts at Orchestra Hall. She worked with both the public and parochial schools of Detroit on the educational series, developing a special program for the study of music. It was called "a far-reaching and deliberate process of public relations," that linked the people of Detroit to their orchestra, in which "the classroom became the immediate point of contact, reaching through it, to the home, and the neighborhood."[75]

There were ten Educational Concerts given by the DSO each year, which students attended for free. Prior to each concert, students studied the works to be performed, and then took quizzes based on what they had learned. Those who scored the highest were chosen to attend the concerts. Yet even those not chosen were "winners" in a sense, as they were able to listen to the concerts on special radio broadcasts.

At each concert, Edith Rhetts gave a lecture introducing the orchestral pieces on the program, and then hosted a contest based on "Music Memory." This was followed by the concert itself, conducted by Victor Kolar. The concerts were a great success; it is estimated that during the 1920s and 1930s, more than 20,000 children attended them, with thousands more listening in their schools all over the state, extending the richness and beauty of classical music from urban to rural communities. They were also serious enough in their design and content that they became part of the curriculum for the schools of Michigan, and were shared with a generation of students. Tilton also hosted the Young People's Concerts for twenty years, as well as a series of Children's Concerts for the youngest listeners. For her contribution to the musical education of the people of Detroit, she was awarded an honorary doctorate by Wayne State University, which stated: "Through her work with the children's concerts in cooperation with the music department of the Detroit Public Schools, and her many lectures throughout the community, she had helped to develop widespread interest in the forms and significance of music."[76]

In 1926, the musical outreach of the Detroit Symphony extended from the young people of the state to aspiring musicians of the nation, as Orchestra Hall played host to the National High School Youth Orchestra. The ensemble, which numbered 275 young people, was conducted by Victor Kolar. Though Gabrilowitsch did not at first conduct the group himself, he did at one point listen to them rehearse. What he heard astounded him. It was clear that these young players were capable of incredible musicianship.

Gabrilowitsch met the young instrumentalists and agreed to conduct a portion of their program. Through the Youth Orchestra, Gabrilowitsch met Joseph Maddy, who was then a professor of music at the University of Michigan and would go on to found the Interlochen Arts Academy in northern Michigan. From that first hearing, Gabrilowitsch became an enthusiastic supporter of Maddy's program, and in later years often served as a guest conductor for the summer program at Interlochen.[77]

The conductor's outreach to the community continued with a series of lectures he began in 1927. The talks covered five topics on "The Development of the Symphony from the Eighteenth to the Twentieth Century," and included "Early Masters of the Symphony," "The Classic Symphony at its Zenith," "The Romantic Composers," "The Advent of Descriptive Music," and "Modern Composers." The lectures included excerpts played by the orchestra, and were intended, according to manager Jefferson B. Webb, to provide a "liberal education in the masterpieces of music." Webb enjoined concertgoers to "Learn from Mr. Gabrilowitsch how to listen to a symphony, how to get out of it what the composer put into it, how to get one hundred percent of enjoyment from a symphony concert!"[78]

## SUMMER CONCERTS ON BELLE ISLE

Gabrilowitsch's desire to reach the greater Detroit community did not end with stu-

Richard Strauss with Ossip Gabrilowitsch, 1924. (Walter P. Reuther Library, Archives of Labor and Urban Affairs, Wayne State University)

dents and the education programs. Still in search of new listeners, he was very receptive to the suggestion of Mayor John Smith that the DSO play concerts on Belle Isle in the summer. Conducted by Victor Kolar, the concerts were free for the audience, and paid for by the City of Detroit. They began in the summer of 1925, and were thoroughly enjoyed by the citizens of the city for years.[79]

To commemorate the series, Kolar wrote a march entitled "Belle Isle" in 1925 and dedicated it to Mayor Smith, which was performed on the island and as part of the regular program for the DSO in 1927. In another outreach gesture, Kolar asked the 250,000 Belle Isle concertgoers to select their favorite pieces, which he then conducted during the series of the Sunday Popular Concerts.[80]

## BACH'S *ST. MATTHEW PASSION*

Gabrilowitsch's greatest musical achievement in Detroit is widely considered to be his production of the Bach *St. Matthew Passion*, first performed in March 1926. The work, regarded as one of the finest masterpieces of music, was not well known to American audiences at the time, especially in the Midwest, and had never been performed in Detroit.

Gabrilowitsch began planning for the production years before its first performance. He had developed a Detroit Symphony Chorus in the early 1920s, so that the DSO could produce choral masterworks, especially oratorios, on a regular basis. Among these, Mendelssohn's *Elijah* and Handel's *Messiah* were the most popular and frequently performed in Detroit. The chorus was ably trained and conducted by Victor Kolar, and its performances provided "small steps on the ascent to Gabrilowitsch's grandest artistic achievement," according to Clara Clemens.[81]

Gabrilowitsch poured himself into the work, attending to every detail, and they were legion. He said in the late 1920s that he had been studying the work for twenty years, and still had more to learn. "I know that to my dying day I shall still be studying this score and searching for new and finer possibilities, because the depth and beauty of this music is inexhaustible. Happy conductor who is permitted to work at such a masterpiece! I truly believe there can be no greater or more lasting joy for the musician."[82]

The *St. Matthew Passion* presents a formidable challenge musically and also logistically. It requires two main choirs as well as a children's choir, two orchestras, five soloists, an organ, and a harpsichord. And, in addition to the two main choirs, Gabrilowitsch added another chorus to sing the chorales, which, during Bach's time were sung by the congregation, but in a modern performance required a separate choir. For his first performance in Detroit in 1926, Gabrilowitsch assembled about 400 people in all. The conductor had to determine where to place the choirs for the greatest musical effect, and even whether they would sit or stand, for that, too, affected the ultimate blend of sound.

The two orchestras were conducted by Gabrilowitsch from a harpsichord that had been handmade from a piano for the performance (at that time, harpsichords were rare). He had also written out parts for organ and harpsichord, which was necessary because, while they were an integral part of the orchestra in Bach's time, he had not written parts for them in his score. So Gabrilowitsch, basing his scoring "strictly on Bach's indication of a figured bass," wrote out the parts for himself and the organist. He also conducted the massive work completely from memory.[83]

Gabrilowitsch's care in preparing the work extended to all aspects of interpretation. Musically, he saw the great-est challenge in Bach's intricate use of polyphony and counterpoint, in which multiple voices and parts, in both the chorus and the orchestra, are juxta-posed in harmonic lines. "Sometimes, when both choruses and both orchestras are employed, we find sixteen-part and even twenty-four part counterpoint," he wrote. "Each voice or part must be given its due and yet the listener must never get the impression of a score overladen with polyphony. Dynamic clarity and trans-parency must be obtained."[84]

But it was in bringing to life the dra-matic aspects of the work that Gabrilow-itsch saw the greatest challenge. The *St. Matthew Passion* is a multilayered work, at once an act of faith and of the dramatic possibilities of music. It tells the story of the Passion of Jesus, of his betrayal and death, but the way in which Bach presents the story marks a stunning development in music. It is presented as a dramatic narra-tive that has its own surging momentum, enacted by the biblical characters drawn from Matthew's gospel during Jesus's final days. Yet the narrative is interrupted con-stantly, by soloists and by the chorus, who comment on and lament the suffering of a very human Christ.

As the great Bach conductor John Eliot Gardner has written, "It would be hard to better [the *St. Matthew Passion*] as an essentially *human* drama—one involv-ing immense struggle and challenge, be-

trayal and forgiveness, love and sacrifice, compassion and pity—the raw material with which most people can instantly identify. At times Bach's music suggests an almost physical engagement with the bones and the blood of the story that gives life both to Matthew's account and to the horrified commentators, so that 'we tremble, we grow cold, we shed tears, our hearts race, we can barely breathe.'"[85]

Gabrilowitsch sought just such a re-action from his own listeners. "If he is deeply in love with Bach's score and has an ardent desire to see it produce on the hearers the greatest and profoundest im-pression, he must decide to be more than a rehearser of orchestra, choir, and soloists," he wrote. "He must become something of a dramatic director as well as musical. He must have the drama clearly before his eye," yet never let the dramatic overpower the "religious sincerity and simplicity" of Bach's score.[86]

According to all accounts, Gabri-lowitsch succeeded in every way. The au-dience in Detroit that first night, March 30, 1926, openly wept during the per-formance, then stood in stunned silence when it was over. Gabrilowitsch had pre-pared listeners with explanatory notes on the piece, and requested that there be no applause, and that women wear dark and somber clothing to maintain the work's "dignity and simplicity." Instead "a mo-tionless audience vibrated in awe to the impressive scenes," according to Clemens,

## GABRILOWITSCH: "WITH THE EMPHASIS ON LOVE"

With his high collars, upright bearing, reputation, and aristocratic demeanor, Gabrilowitsch, though only about 5'7" or 5'8", was an imposing, even an awe-inspiring figure. And those characteristics, as well as the Germanic, rather than Russian, spelling of his last name that he adopted and preferred, could cause confusion, even intimidation, for those who wished to pronounce his name properly.

Yet when one of them would pronounce his name with the accent on the second—and incorrect—syllable of his last name, as "Mr. Ga-BRILL-owitsch," he would lovingly and gently correct them: "No, no, no. It is Gabril-LOVE-itsch, with the emphasis on 'love.'"

## THE WORLD'S FIRST LIVE SYMPHONIC RADIO BROADCAST

The following paragraphs are from a 1922 publication written by the staff of the *Detroit News* that outlined the historic achievements of radio station "WWJ The Detroit News," which began broadcasting in Detroit in 1920. They carried the first broadcast of an entire symphony concert in history, on February 10, 1922, which featured Gabrilowitsch conducting the DSO and the pianist Arthur Schnabel, and also broadcast performances of the Detroit News Orchestra, a small ensemble made up mostly of DSO musicians, another "first" for the orchestra and the station.

In February, 1922, The News first broadcast a concert by the Detroit Symphony Orchestra. Thereafter every program presented by that splendid organization was sent to music lovers, not only in Detroit but over half of the North American continent. Expressions of enthusiastic appreciation from persons in all walks of life have followed this development of The News' radio service. Contributions for the support of the orchestra have come from grateful people in a score of states, and even in Cuba, who have thus been enabled to hear finer music and better played than could ever be heard in the small towns where they make their residences. The radio-phone has opened new worlds of appreciation to music-hungry folk.

On May 28, 1922, The Detroit News Orchestra appeared for the first time in the studio. This, the first radio orchestra ever organized, is a 16-piece symphonic ensemble, composed of soloists of note. Its members were drawn almost exclusively from the Detroit Symphony Orchestra, but are representative of a dozen of the greatest orchestras of the United States, with which they have been connected.

Source: *"WWJ The Detroit News: The History of Radiophone Broadcasting by the Earliest and Foremost of Newspaper Stations; Together with Information on Radio for Amateur and Expert"* by The Radio Staff of The Detroit News. Published by *The Evening 1 News Association*, Detroit, Michigan, 1922, http://archive.org/stream/thedetroitnews00detriala/thedetroitnews00detriala_djvu.txt.

then, when it was over "sat some minutes in emotional stress, unable to loosen the bonds of tragic consciousness that held them."[87]

Gabrilowitsch conducted the *St. Matthew Passion* for three years in De-troit, and in April 1928, the entire ensemble went to New York, where they performed the piece twice at Carnegie Hall. They were enthusiastically received, by public and press alike. Olin Downes, music critic for the *New York Times*, praised all aspects of the performance, from the chorus to the orchestra, saving special praise for the conductor, who, he claimed, achieved a faithful, nuanced reading of the work of the "giant," Bach. It was, of course, an enormously expensive venture, but the bill was paid by the always-generous William H. Murphy, Mrs. John Newberry, Mrs. Hugh Dillman (the former Mrs. Horace Dodge), and Jerome Remick.

During the 1928–29 season, Gabrilowitsch took a sabbatical from his symphony duties. According to Clara Clemens, he was supposed to rest, but instead traveled the United States and Europe as a guest conductor and soloist. In Detroit, several guest conductors led the symphony, including Leopold Stokowski, Eugene Goossens, Emil Overhoffer, and Victor Kolar.

## THE DETROIT SYMPHONY UNDER GABRILOWITSCH

Commentators describing the Detroit Symphony under Gabrilowitsch often mention the distinct sound he was able to elicit from the ensemble. The famed conductor Bruno Walter described his experience as a guest conductor of the orchestra in 1923: they were, he wrote, a "superbly trained orchestra; in intonation, rhythm, dynamic, precision, tonal beauty—finally and above all an ideal surrender to the music itself," which, he said, revealed "the constructive work sustained through many years, of a true conductor and musician."[88]

Gabrilowitsch himself described what he aimed for in tonal quality this way:

Just as the voices of individuals identify them as they speak, so do the individual tones or voices of instrumental players identify them in performance. The writer has listened to flute quartets played in an adjoining room and easily distinguished the individual players by the voices of their instruments as they played.

Treating the orchestra as an ensemble instrument and the conductor as the player, the tone of the orchestra reflects the physical and mental characteristics of the conductor. The goal of tone production in the orchestra, as with the individual instrumentalist, is the singing tone. Particularly is this achievement the test of the strings. When the violins impress listeners with a sense of the singing tone, an orchestra may be said to have arrived.[89]

## GABRILOWITSCH AS ADMINISTRATOR

The administrative aspects of his position as conductor were scarcely Gabrilowitsch's favorite tasks, but they were responsibilities he took very seriously, though they

Gabrilowitsch, 1933. (Courtesy DSO Archives)

were both time-consuming and draining for him. According to Clara Clemens, "It was often a puzzle to me at first, how so many hours of Ossip's time could go into dictating letters and telegrams. How could there be that many things to say and that many people to say them to?"[90]

The Gabrilowitsch correspondence relating to the DSO held in the Detroit Public Library fills forty-nine boxes. A review of the contents reveals a careful, courteous, consummately professional musical administrator, devoted to his ensemble and its future, aware of the delicate balance needed between donors and audience, and striving for artistic success in uncertain financial times.

There is a letter of support for a young musician, Joseph Knitzer, who was starting out in the professional world, and who had competed in the Schubert Me-

morial violin competition and not been selected. His cause was championed by Frederick M. Alger, a major contributor to the symphony and a personal friend of Gabrilowitsch, who asked if the conductor could intervene on the young violinist's behalf.

Gabrilowitsch carefully states that, while he was an officer of the Schubert organization, he was not a judge of the competition, and that "it would not be proper for me, or anyone else, to try and influence the decisions of the jury one way or the other." He does, however, offer to help:

Of course I shall be glad to hear young Knitzer someday when I am in New York. . . . Will you ask him to write me a letter sometime after January? I will then arrange an appointment.[91]

In a more playful mood, Gabrilowitsch responds to a request from Alger's wife, Mignon, to attend a rehearsal:

When you and Harriet Atterbury spoke to me on Sunday about coming to rehearsals I said jokingly you may not be admitted. I hope you thoroughly understand that you both are most welcome whenever you wish to come. . . . If you or Harriet or both wish to come, give me a ring and I will see that you are properly taken care of. I dare not even suggest Fred's joining you as I know his ardent love of Brahms.[92]

Another chronicles his problems with a tuba player, who left the symphony to take a position with another orchestra in 1932, breaking his contract. In a series of telegrams and letters between Gabrilowitsch and Joseph Weber, President of the American Federation of Musicians, we read the efforts of Gabrilowitsch to find suitable replacements for the tuba player and to fill other openings as well, illustrating the continuing battle between the conductor and national musician's union over hiring only local musicians. Although the tone remains invariably polite, one can almost see the steam coming out of his ears as the dispute drags on for over a year.

The correspondence begins in October 1932, with Gabrilowitsch outlining his concerns for maintaining the high quality of the DSO, as well as the financial constraints brought about by the Depression:

I believe that the gentleman of the Detroit Board do not fully realize in what serious difficulties I have been working these last two or three years and how much personal work I have done in approaching contributors to give financial support to our orchestra, without which efforts of mine, the organization might have gone to smash long before this.

Yet, he stresses, even in times of financial duress, "the *quality* of a symphony orchestra must not be impaired." Gabrilowitsch states that he is ultimately responsible to the symphony Board, and the "public of Detroit." In light of this responsibility, "my judgment should be final."[93]

However, Gabrilowitsch remained committed to using local musicians for the DSO concerts. In the following letter to the DSO manager, quoted in Clara Clemens biography, he outlines his reasons:

If it should become the policy of our Society to bar local talent from a chance to appear in public, then I for one will not be a party to such a policy. If you have occasion again to discuss this matter with the Board of Directors, I wish you would state my views as I am giving them here to you plainly. We are running this orchestra with funds furnished by Detroit people. Therefore, it is only fair that we should give Detroit artists an equal chance with others. Do you mean to infer that if a man plays the piano well or sings well or fiddles well he should be barred from our concerts just because he had the misfortune to be born in Detroit or of being a resident of this city? . . . The first requisite of a truly musical city is that there should be some good musicians in it and we never *will* have good musicians if it becomes known that we are not giving them a fair chance.[94]

Another side of Gabrilowitsch, this time the pianist and artist, is revealed in a letter to conductor Walter Damrosch, which accompanied an annotated score of a Brahms's concerto, containing several pages of notes that outline his interpretation:

> You will find in [my orchestra score] several annotations and even a few changes of scoring, some of which may please you and some not. . . .
>
> Second movement: I think it is a good idea to double the woodwinds in several places as indicated. The doubling of the horns, p. 88, before no. 7 is also desirable. . . .
>
> Third movement: p. 116, the use of sordines [mutes] on the first and second violins makes a beautiful effect.[95]

### THE GREAT DEPRESSION

Perhaps the greatest test of all of Gabrilowitsch's abilities came with the crash of the stock market in 1929, and the Great Depression that followed.

Because of its dependence on automobile manufacturing, Detroit was one of the first cities in the nation to suffer the effects of the Depression. A look at the total number of cars produced from 1929 to 1931 tells the story: in 1929, 5,337,000 were manufactured by the industry; in 1930, the number fell to 3,363,000, and in 1931 to 1,332,000. That number translated into huge job losses: at General Motors, 100,000 of 260,000 employees were laid off between 1929 and 1930; at Ford, two thirds of the employees were laid off in 1932. There were some 223,000 people out of work in the city by 1931–32.[96]

Many of the city's wealthy elite had lost substantial amounts of money during the Depression, and its effect was felt among the ranks of the donors to the Detroit Symphony as well. In 1931–32, the budget for the DSO was $360,000; in 1932–33, it had fallen to $260,000. By 1933–34, the budget was a mere $141,000. The season was reduced to twenty-one weeks from twenty-eight, the number of concerts reduced from sixteen to fourteen, and the salaries of everyone on the payroll, from the musicians to the manager, were cut by at least forty percent.[97]

It affected Gabrilowitsch's livelihood, too. According to Clara Clemens, "The funds of the Detroit Symphony Society were so greatly reduced that it would be impossible to offer a salary acceptable to any conductor of superior reputation." And by the worst days of the Depression, Gabrilowitsch's health had begun to fail. His wife urged him to consider giving up his post as conductor, and in 1932, he resigned.

Mrs. John Newberry, president of the Society, urged him to reconsider. She,

DSO manager Murray Paterson, and others were convinced that if Gabrilowitsch left, "it would mean the destruction of the orchestra." In a decision that revealed at once his consummate devotion to the orchestra and his art, as well as his innate humility, Gabrilowitsch agreed to return as conductor, but insisted that he work without pay for the entire 1933–34 season. He also requested that the decision remain a secret; it didn't remain a secret, but it did speak volumes about the man.[98]

Gabrilowitsch was not alone in making personal financial sacrifices to benefit his orchestra. Victor Kolar, too, conducted fifty-six concerts during the 1933–34 season without pay.

So the Detroit Symphony soldiered on, with the musicians taking half-pay, and their director taking nothing. Yet despite all the sacrifices, the orchestra's fortunes continued to decline. The programs of the era reflect this austerity. The bound programs for the 1927–28 season number just under 1,000 pages; in 1932–33, they total sixty-two pages. There are no advertisements in the season's programs, and the opening pages begin with this announcement:

This simplified program is offered to you without apology. For many years Mr. Richard Cohn published our complete program without expense to the Detroit Symphony Society. We wish at this time to thank those who in past seasons supported the program.[99]

Times were so dire that at one point, according to an old anecdote, Mrs. Hugh Dillman stood outside the stage door and handed the musicians potatoes to take home after performances. Mrs. Dillman later proved to be the "miracle" that saved the DSO. In 1934, she stepped forward with a donation of $100,000, in the name of Horace Dodge, that both paid the entire deficit of the orchestra and provided money for the future of the organization.[100]

## THE CENTURY OF PROGRESS CONCERTS AND FORD RADIO CONCERTS

There were other bright spots in the gloom. In 1934, the DSO was invited to play at the Century of Progress Exhibition in Chicago. With Victor Kolar on the podium, the orchestra played a whopping 160 concerts, all but four conducted by Kolar, during a twelve-week summer season. With only fifteen rehearsals, the orchestra presented an incredible 500 compositions under the baton of their associate conductor, earning Kolar the moniker "The Iron Man of Music" from the Chicago press.[101]

The sponsor of the program was the Ford Motor Company, and the concerts, two per day, were performed next to the Ford exhibit. They were broadcast over the radio around the country, reaching an estimated ten to fifteen million people over the summer months.

The DSO's radio concerts were incredibly popular. In September 1934, the Ford Motor Company received a petition signed by thousands of listeners, praising the orchestra's broadcasts and Ford's support of them. The company decided to make a permanent arrangement with the orchestra. The result was the Ford Sunday Evening Hour, featuring the Detroit Symphony, renamed the Ford Symphony Orchestra for the radio concerts. They were broadcast weekly from 1934 until the Second World War, from the stages of Orchestra Hall and Masonic Temple. The DSO was delighted with the arrangement, because the contract paid them to perform, bringing much-needed revenue to the symphony during the Depression.[102]

## VICTOR KOLAR

Kolar was the conductor of most of the Ford Symphony Orchestra concerts, and as Gabrilowitsch's health failed, he took on more of the directorial responsibilities for the DSO as well. Born in Budapest in 1888, Kolar was a consummate musician, a violinist and a composer, who had been conservatory-trained and studied violin with Jan Kubelik and composition with Antonín Dvořák. He had come to America as a teenager, and played with the Pittsburgh Orchestra as an assistant to Emil Pauer and under the baton of Victor Herbert, who became a close friend. He next worked as the assistant of Walter Damrosch at the New York Symphony, then moved to Detroit in 1918, becoming first the assistant, then the associate conductor of Gabrilowitsch.

The two worked well together, and had a cordial and collegial relationship. The schedules for the symphony used to be marked with their initials, "O. G." and "V. K.," indicating when each was slotted to rehearse and conduct the orchestra. Soon, they began to call one another by those initials, and the musicians adopted the nicknames, too.

They complemented each other musically, too. Gabrilowitsch had little taste for most modern composers. Clara Clemens recalled that they once heard Prokofieff playing a concert of his own compositions, and Gabrilowitsch could barely stand it: "He plays mighty well," he said, "but if that is good music, then it is time for me to die."[103]

Kolar, on the other hand, embraced the modernist movement in music. During his years as Associate Conductor, he introduced the music of many of the giants of modern music to the audiences in Detroit. Among the works that received their first performances in the city under his baton are the Symphonies 1, 2, 4, and 7 by Jean Sibelius; the *Symphonia Domestica* by Richard Strauss; the *Firebird Suite* and *Rite of Spring* by Igor Stravinsky; *La Valse*, *Daphnis et Chloe*, and *Bolero* by Maurice Ravel; Concerto no. 2 for Violin in G Minor by Sergei Prokofiev; and Rhapsody on a Theme of Paganini by Sergei Rachmaninoff, which premiered with Rachmaninoff playing the piano.[104]

## GABRILOWITSCH'S FINAL SEASON

The 1934–35 concert season was one of the busiest of Gabrilowitsch's life; it also proved to be his last. As he took on more conducting and solo work, he began to suffer from neuritis in his arm, which had plagued him for years and was probably due to overuse when he was young. He was also often very fatigued. Still, he kept up a nearly impossible schedule, conducting the DSO, performing as a guest soloist, and presenting a new program of his own design: sixteen concertos in five concerts, which traced the development of the piano concerto from Bach to the present.

In addition to all his other work, Gabrilowitsch also conducted an opera for the first time: Wagner's *Tristan and Isolde*, which was performed to positive reviews at the Detroit Masonic Temple in November 1934.[105]

On March 14, 1935, Gabrilowitsch conducted his final concert with the Detroit Symphony Orchestra. In a coincidence one can only call uncanny, the program's two main works were the same as those he had conducted in his first concert: Tchaikovsky's Symphony no. 6 in B Minor, the "Pathetique," and, as soloist, Chopin's Concerto for Piano and Orchestra in E Minor. The audience gave their beloved maestro a long ovation, with no one, neither musician nor avid listener,

realizing it would be the last time they would hear him.[106]

Feeling weak, but dedicated to completing the final leg of the concerto series, Gabrilowitsch left for New York immediately. On March 22, he suffered an intestinal hemorrhage, but performed his final concert on March 23 in New York, once again receiving accolades from the people and the press.[107]

When he and Clara returned to Detroit, he was admitted to Henry Ford Hospital, where he remained for six months. He required five blood transfusions and two operations; the last revealed that he had stomach cancer. For reasons known only to Clara and the medical professionals at that time, Gabrilowitsch was never told the true nature of his illness. He was treated at home, with a combination of traditional and faith healing, and died on September 14, 1936.[108]

He was mourned around the world, and a special service was held at Orchestra Hall on September 16, where Victor Kolar conducted two pieces Gabrilowitsch had selected, Schubert's Symphony no. 8 in B Minor, the "Unfinished," and the "Liebestod" from Wagner's *Tristan and Isolde*.[109]

Tributes poured in from all over the globe, perhaps none more touching than that given by his devoted colleague and friend Bruno Walter:

His body is no more, his music silenced; but the light of that descended star still brightens the horizon; his noble, soulful tone sings in our hearts. To those who knew the man, or heard the musician—and both mean the same—he is alive with the fruitful, ever creative immortality of the good and beautiful.[110]

With their charismatic maestro gone, and the country, especially Detroit, still mired in the worst Depression in history, the future looked bleak for the Detroit Symphony. But in many ways the worst was yet to come, as the organization tried to find its way forward in the years after Gabrilowitsch's death.

Silhouette of Gabrilow-itsch, 1935. (Courtesy DSO Archives)

CHAPTER FOUR

# A City and an Orchestra Struggle, 1936–42: Victor Kolar, Franco Ghione, Depression, and War

As Manager of the Detroit Symphony Orchestra I wish to express to the Board of Directors my deep personal loss in the death of our beloved leader, Mr. Ossip Gabrilowitsch. . . . Mr. Gabrilowitsch's death is the definitive end of a period in the life and development of the Detroit Symphony Orchestra in Detroit.

Murray Paterson, Letter to the Board of Directors[1]

THE DEATH OF GABRILOWITSCH AND THE CONTINUING FINANCIAL DIF-ficulties of Detroit during the Depression cast a pall over the late 1930s for the symphony. Gone, too, were donors like William H. Murphy, with both the money and management skills to provide guidance and funding during tumultuous times. The DSO still played its seasons, but was plagued with financial worries, deficits, and labor struggles from one season to the next, then by global political turmoil. In just six years, from 1936 to 1942, a combination of diverse events changed the fortunes of the DSO dramatically: Orchestra Hall was foreclosed, the DSO moved to Masonic Temple, the management hired and let go a new director, World War II transformed the city and the economy, Ford canceled its radio contract with the DSO, and a contentious labor

Victor Kolar, conductor of the DSO from 1936 to 1942. (Courtesy DSO Archives)

the famous director who later became the revered—and often feared—conductor of the Chicago Symphony.

These noted directors also brought innovative programming to DSO audiences that season. Iturbi conducted a program that included significant new music from such contemporary composers as Howard Hanson, José André, and Paul White. He also led the orchestra in the music of established composers that had their first hearing in Detroit under his baton, including "La Mer" by Claude Debussy. Reiner introduced Detroit audiences to the music of the young British composer William Walton, conducting the DSO in a performance of his "Façade." And Kolar also brought solo artists of international renown, including cellist Gregor Piatigorsky and violinist Nathan Milstein, during the season.[2]

Kolar kept other DSO initiatives alive, too. In addition to conducting the symphony, he continued to direct all the Young People's Concerts and the Belle Isle summer concert series. Edith Rhetts Tilton continued her educational programs for young people, and, with Kolar, taught an adult education course at Wayne University in Music Literature. It included five concerts by the DSO and one by the Wayne Orchestra, with lectures given by Tilton covering such topics as "Suite and Symphony," "Dance Forms and Rhapsody," "Classicism and Romanticism," and "Overture, Prelude, and Symphonic Poem."[3] The Ford

dispute, in conjunction with the threat of war rationing, led to the DSO going out of business, silencing the symphony for the second time in its history.

It was, of course, hard to imagine this cataclysmic string of events in 1936, when the direction of the DSO fell to former Associate Conductor Victor Kolar. Though lacking the charisma and international stature of Gabrilowitsch, Kolar brought a calming, knowledgeable hand to the helm of the orchestra. During his first season as conductor, 1936–37, he brought to Detroit such major figures from the classical music world as conductor and pianist Jose Iturbi and conductor Fritz Reiner,

A large audience of children attending a Young People's Concert at Orchestra Hall, conducted by Kolar with commentary by Edith Rhetts Tilton. (Courtesy DSO Archives)

Sunday Evening Hour radio programs also continued, with Kolar and other conductors leading the DSO. The Ford broadcasts represented an important source of much-needed income for the orchestra, providing $30,000 for the season.[4]

The 1936–37 DSO season also included exciting new programming from the world of dance: performances by the Ballet Russe, one of the most famous dance companies in the world. Founded by the famed impresario Serge Diaghilev in 1909, in 1936 the company was under the direction of Colonel W. de Basil and included such outstanding dancers as Alexandra Danilova and works by such legendary choreographers and dancers as Leonide Massine, Michel Fokine, and Vaslav Nijinsky. The DSO accompanied the Ballet Russe, under the baton of a young Hungarian conductor named Antal Dorati, who would become the conductor of the DSO forty years later.

The selections performed by the company included works that became classics of the ballet stage, including *Petrouchka*, set to music by Stravinksy; *Swan Lake*, with music by Tchaikovsky; *Les Sylphides*, with music by Chopin; and *Afternoon of a Faun*, with music by Debussy.[5]

The 1936–37 season proved to be a good one for the DSO. The budget had risen from $230,000 the previous year to $258,000, and included an important new source of revenue for the orchestra. According to Manager Murray Paterson, the year's solicitation for funds had included an appeal to Detroit companies for money to fund the free Belle Isle summer concert series, and it had succeeded admirably. Paterson recorded that $25,000 had been donated by General Motors, Chrysler, Briggs Manufacturing Company, the Detroit City Gas Company, Fisher Brothers, and Detroit's Common Council.[6]

## THE FORD RADIO BROADCASTS

The Ford-sponsored radio broadcasts, known as the "Ford Sunday Evening Hour," helped to make the DSO a nationally known ensemble, and a cherished one, too. The series began in 1934, after the broadcasts of the orchestra from the Chicago World's Fair under Victor Kolar had made the DSO such a popular draw that thousands wrote letters to the Ford Motor Company asking that they continue.

Edsel Ford saw it as a positive move for the company, telling his father, Henry Ford, "this thing is too good to pass up." Henry agreed, and encouraged his son to develop a program. The Ford Hour was financed by the company itself, not by the dealer organization, which sponsored other popular radio shows, including Fred Waring and his Pennsylvanians. According to automotive historian David L. Lewis, many of the dealers "looked askance at sponsorship of a symphony orchestra"; he also notes that while the music presented during the Ford Hour "although regarded as 'light' by the sophisticated listener, probably was considered 'heavy' by the average American and buyer of Ford cars."

The Sunday Evening Hour was broadcast over all eighty-eight stations in the CBS network, and over the eight years of its run, the concerts were directed by the DSO's Victor Kolar, as well as a roster of some of the best-known conductors of the era, including Eugene Ormandy, George Szell, Fritz Reiner, and Sir Thomas Beecham.

The show's philosophy—"music of familiar theme, with majestic rendition"—was evident in its format and programming: the shows opened and closed with the sentimental strains of the "Children's Prayer" from *Hansel and Gretel* by Humperdinck. The selections reflected the musical tastes of its founder, too. In addition to well-known works from the classical repertoire, there were always selections like "Turkey in the Straw" and "Home Sweet Home," favorites of Henry Ford.

The list of guest stars who performed over the years is astonishing—including Jascha Heifetz, Yehudi Menuhin, Nelson Eddy, Kirsten Flagstad, Marian Anderson, Oscar Levant, and Risë Stevens—as was their pay. Heifitz and Eddy commanded $6,000 for their performances, and Ormandy received $1,500 to conduct (although Victor Kolar was only paid $600).

The concerts were broadcast from Orchestra Hall from 1934 through the first half of 1936, and then from Masonic Temple until the series ended in 1942. The broadcast concerts were free of charge and played to full houses: it is estimated that 1.3 million people attended them over the years, and that ten to thirteen million more listened in every week. While by no means the most popular radio broadcasts of their era, they were still a beloved staple for many listeners, and paid dividends for their sponsor, too.

According to David L. Lewis, "The average annual cost of the Sunday Evening Hour was $918,000, of which from $500,000 to $600,000 was paid annually to CBS, and a yearly average of $327,000 for talent, exclusive of conductors. In return for its $7,344,000 outlay, the Ford Company reached radio audiences totaling more than 500,000,000,000 and entertained studio audiences aggregating 1,300,000. Unquestionably the company looked upon the investment as sound."

Source: David L. Lewis, *The Public Image of Henry Ford: An American Folk Hero and His Company* (Detroit: Wayne State University Press, 1976), 315–29.

## FRANCO GHIONE

In January 1937, the DSO announced that Victor Kolar would begin the 1937–38 season with a new "co-conductor," Franco Ghione. Expectations were high for the new conductor, who was born in Italy in 1886 and trained at the Parma Conservatory. Ghione was a respected opera conductor and violinist, who had been an assistant of Arturo Toscanini and had directed at the famous La Scala opera house in Milan before coming to Detroit.

According to Herman Wise, publicity director of the DSO in the 1930s, Ghione had been "discovered" in Europe in 1935 by Thaddeus Wronski, the artistic director of the Detroit Civic Opera. After attending a performance of Verdi's *Otello* conducted by Ghione, Wronski wanted to bring him to Detroit to direct the Civic Opera orchestra. The ensemble offered Ghione a contract to conduct the English world premiere of *The Dybbuk* by Ludovico Rocca, and he accepted.[7]

The opera was first performed in Detroit in May 1936 to broad acclaim. The production next moved to Carnegie Hall in New York, where it was scheduled to run for three performances. The critics, however, savaged the production, with Olin Downes of the *New York Times* faulting the orchestra for overplaying, the singers for oversinging, the translation as incomprehensible, and the music itself as lacking in any merit. It closed after only one performance.[8]

Ghione returned to Detroit, where he was still a popular musician, and in late 1936 was offered a one-year contract as co-conductor of the DSO. His first season, 1937–38, was announced with much fanfare. There were to be fourteen Thursday night subscription concerts, ten Saturday night concerts, five Young People's concerts, ten afterschool concerts, and thirty-nine radio broadcast concerts. In addition, Kolar continued his ambitious program of summer concerts on Belle Isle, leading the DSO

Franco Ghione, co-conductor of the DSO from 1937 to 1940. (Courtesy DSO Archives)

in six weeks of performances and presenting an astonishingly wide variety of music, from nineteenth-century classical symphonies to modern tone poems. The audience for the series numbered over 200,000 that summer, and was again funded from Detroit businesses and the city, with 156 companies giving $23,000 and the City contributing $13,000, which paid for the entire series and left no deficit.

The DSO as a whole, however, was not as fortunate. The deficit at the end of the season was $18,000, which had to be carried over to the following year. But the Symphony Society was encouraged by the positive response to the new director, and offered Ghione a three-year contract, with Kolar continuing his role as co-conductor.[9]

## CARMINE COPPOLA

Carmine Coppola, principal flutist with the DSO during the 1930s, named his second son, famed moviemaker Francis Ford Coppola, in honor of his birthplace, Henry Ford Hospital in Detroit, as well as to honor the automaker for funding the radio broadcasts that helped to keep the orchestra alive during the Depression.

Coppola was born in 1910 in New York to Italian immigrants who had come to the United States earlier in the century. He soon showed talent playing the flute and attended Julliard on a scholarship. After playing with the DSO for several years, Coppola was hired by Arturo Toscanini to play for the NBC Symphony Orchestra, where he was principal flute for a decade.

Coppola had always wanted to be a composer, and he did indeed achieve fame, as the composer of music for his famous son's movies, especially *The Godfather Part II*, for which he received an Academy Award in 1975. He also composed film scores for his son's other films, including *Apocalypse Now*, *The Black Stallion*, and *The Outsiders*. In 1981, Coppola wrote the film score for Abel Gance's iconic silent film *Napolean*, whose original score had been composed by Arthur Honegger, but had been lost. Coppola himself conducted a performance at New York's Radio City Music Hall in 1981. He died in California in 1991.

Sources: *New York Times*, April 28, 1991; December 12, 1999.

## TWENTY-FIFTH ANNIVERSARY— AND CONTINUING FINANCIAL PROBLEMS

The 1938–39 season was celebrated as the DSO's twenty-fifth (the orchestra's management did not acknowledge the earlier DSO, which had existed from 1887 to 1910, until much later). And for the first time since the Depression, the ads returned to the concert programs, aimed decidedly at the wealthier patron of the symphony. Ball gowns and formal eveningwear by Walton-Pierce, Edith Brown, B. Siegel, and other clothiers featured photos and drawings of stylish ladies ready for an evening at the symphony. In addition to ads for private music instruction, of special note were full-page ads for Victor Records, which listed recordings of the pieces to be played by the symphony that night, placed facing the DSO's evening's program.[10]

In celebration of the DSO's silver anniversary, the program for the first concert of 1938–39 season, dated November 3, 1938, opened with the following list of highlights of the previous twenty-five years:

Total concerts and broadcasts played—3,632. (An average of over 150 per year for 24 years.)

Over 1,000,000 persons have heard the 608 subscription concerts.

Forty-three of the world's greatest conductors have appeared as guests on this series.

More than 200 of the world's greatest soloists have appeared with the orchestra.

More than 750,000 persons have attended the popular-priced concerts.

More than 400,000 school children have been the guests of the symphony in Orchestra Hall.

More than 2,000,000 persons have heard the free summer series at Belle Isle.

More than 1,000,000 were present at the Century of Progress concerts, in Chicago.

More than 800,000 persons in eighty-three cities have heard the orchestra on tour.[11]

But these highlights were followed by grim news regarding the financial situation of the DSO and the Detroit Symphony Society that supported it. On the facing page was a message from Manager Murray Paterson. Titled "Plain Facts from the Office of the Manager," it was a very open letter to the audience regarding the financial predicament the Detroit Symphony Society was facing. He stated that the total cost of maintaining the orchestra for the season was $293,000; that earnings from ticket sales, radio, tours, and endowment funds was estimated at $101,000; that the balance of $192,000 would have to

come from contributions, which to that point had only amounted to $162,000, leaving $30,000 to raise to maintain the orchestra. Paterson further stated that the amount required would be needed to be raised in sixty days, and that he would update the DSO's patrons in upcoming programs.

But perhaps the most startling piece of information to come out of Paterson's "Plain Facts" was that the DSO was paying higher rent because a Bondholders' Committee now owned Orchestra Hall. This news shocked many readers, so much so that Paterson devoted the next "Facts" page in the program to explaining just what had happened.[12]

## LOSING CONTROL
## OF ORCHESTRA HALL

As Paterson explained, Orchestra Hall did not belong to the DSO. It had been built by the Orchestra Hall Corporation as a home for the DSO, which since 1919 had been supported by the Symphony Society. The total cost of completing the Hall, including the land ($214,000), all building costs ($763,000), and furnishings ($23,000), totaled $1 million. The Orchestra Hall Corporation financed the amount with a first mortgage, a bond issue, of $400,000, and a stock issue of $600,000; the stock issue was eventually retired as a gift, by generous patrons of the previous era, including William T. Murphy and Horace Dodge.[13]

## PARADISE THEATRE

When the DSO left Orchestra Hall in 1939 for Masonic Temple, the great performance space stood vacant for two years. Then, on the day after Christmas in 1941, it reopened, as the Paradise Theatre. The building had been purchased by two brothers, Ben and Lou Cohen, who wanted to present the best of jazz and Big Band music in their new venue.

They did just that: over the years, some of the finest performers in the history of American jazz took the stage, including instrumentalists Louis Armstrong, Count Basie, Duke Ellington, Lionel Hampton, Cab Calloway, Billy Eckstine, Jimmy Lunsford, Earl Hines, and Charlie Parker, as well as famed jazz singers Ella Fitzgerald, Billie Holiday, Sarah Vaughan, and Lena Horne.

The Paradise took its name from the area in which it stood: Paradise Valley, the name of the largely African American neighborhood bounded by Vernor in the north, Madison on the south, Hastings on the east, John R. on the west, and with Gratiot running right through it. It was home to many black-owned businesses, from grocery stores, shops, bowling alleys, hotels, restaurants—and seventeen nightclubs.

Soon, the Paradise was drawing in overflowing crowds, eager to see the top headliners at the theater, which now boasted a movie palace–style marquee, and a movie-style box office, too, for the regular feature films that rotated with music performances at the Paradise.

One audience member from the early years at the theater recalls a particularly memorable night: "I remember that I was here when Count Basie and his Orchestra were on stage. The place was really jumpin'! People got out

The marquee of the Paradise Theater, announcing Duke Ellington's performance, September 15, 1944. (Courtesy DSO Archives)

of their seats and rushed the stage and began dancing. More people got up and filled the aisles—dancing. They were even dancing on top of the seats! I thought the place was going to come down that night."

The Paradise continued to host the finest in jazz and Big Band music until 1951, when it, too, went out of business. The building was sold to the Church of Our Prayer, which became the site for the earliest recordings of the DSO under Paul Paray, laying the groundwork for the triumphant return of the orchestra in 1989.

Sources: Arthur M. Woodford, *This Is Detroit* (Detroit: Wayne State University Press, 2001), 170–71; Paul Ganson, "Count on Paradise," DSO Program notes, 1992–99; *Stages: 75 Years with the Detroit Symphony Orchestra and Orchestra Hall* (Detroit: Detroit Symphony Orchestra Hall, 1994), 37.

At first, Orchestra Hall earned more than it owed through rental income, as the premiere showcase for musical and theatrical performances in the city. In its first year, revenues for the Hall were $69,000, with $20,000 of that coming in

Masonic Temple, which became the DSO's home in 1939. (Courtesy Library of Congress)

the form of rent paid by the Symphony Society for use of the Hall by the DSO, $40,000 from other concert rentals, and $9,000 in rent paid by the Hall's four retail stores. That season, 1919–20, revenues were high enough to pay bond interest of $24,000 and taxes of $9,000, leaving a profit of $11,000.[14]

For several seasons, the profits allowed for regular payments on the bonds and taxes to be paid out of earnings. But soon there were two other performance halls in Detroit: Masonic Temple, which opened in 1926, and the auditorium at the new Detroit Institute of Arts, completed in 1927. That, and the ensuing Depression, prompted a precipitous drop in revenue from the Hall, from $68,000 in 1919–20 to $25,800 in 1937–

38. Previously wealthy patrons no longer had access to funds that might have helped to save the Hall. Thus, beginning in the early 1930s, there was not enough revenue to pay the bond interest and the taxes owed; for five years, the payments were in default, and on October 20, 1937, Orchestra Hall was foreclosed to the Bondholders' Protective Committee. It was sold to them for $137,000, with back taxes owed of $30,000.[15]

The Bondholders' Committee tried to work out a rental arrangement with the Symphony Society to keep the DSO in the Hall. It proposed a rent of $10,800 per year, with the DSO turning over all other rental income to the Committee and paying all operating expenses. Another group of citizens headed by Harry Helfman, a

## MASONIC TEMPLE

The Detroit Masonic Temple is the largest Masonic Temple in the world. It was designed by well-known Detroit architect George D. Mason in 1920 to house the expanding Masonic membership in the city, which had outgrown its former temple on Lafayette Boulevard. Construction began in 1920, and when the cornerstone was laid, on September 18, 1922, the trowel used in the ceremony was the same one that the nation's first Commander-in-Chief (and famed Mason) George Washington had used in laying the cornerstone of the nation's capital.

The building is massive, and includes three theaters, a Shrine, a chapel, two ballrooms, eight lodge rooms, a swimming pool, a bowling alley, and a 17,500-square-foot drill hall; while most of these rooms are no longer in use, at one time the 1,037-room structure required its own powerhouse to generate all the electricity needed to provide for the myriad activities that took place under its roof.

When the performance theater was opened on February 22, 1926, Gabrilowitsch led the orchestra in a celebration concert. After Orchestra Hall was foreclosed in 1937, the DSO could no longer afford to play in the old hall; they moved to Masonic Temple in 1939, where they played at the larger 4,600-seat performance hall until 1946, when Henry Reichhold moved them to the Music Hall.

The Masonic Temple remained a major performance venue for years in Detroit, hosting the performances of a wide variety of artists, from the Metropolitan Opera and the Royal Ballet to rock 'n' roll stars. In fact, one of those stars, Jack White of the White Stripes, saved Masonic in 2013, when it, too, was facing foreclosure. He paid the back taxes of $142,000 anonymously, though he was later identified as the donor; in gratitude, the management named the smaller performance theater in his honor.

Sources: Masonic Temple, http://themasonic.com; *Detroit Free Press*, June 5, 2013.

the Symphony Society. But although Murray Paterson worked tirelessly for months to work out a solution, both plans fell through.

By November 1938, the prospects for the DSO remaining in Orchestra Hall looked bleak. Paterson noted in the program that the Symphony Society's rent to remain in the Hall for the next season had been raised to $31,000. It was an unsustainable economic situation.[16]

## MOVING TO MASONIC TEMPLE

In January 1939, the Symphony Society met to decide where the DSO would play the following season. They had received an offer from Masonic Temple that represented a significant savings if the DSO was willing to move. It offered its two concert halls, one seating 4,600 and the other seating 1,600, which was a considerable increase over Orchestra Hall's total capacity of 2,200, and which offered the possibility of greater revenues through increased ticket sales. Masonic offered a rental arrangement of $550 per concert for the larger hall, $125 per concert for the smaller hall, $25 per rehearsal, and $200 per month for offices. Included in those costs were all fees for tickets, ushers, stage hands, light, and heat.

Based on those figures, Paterson estimated costs for the 1939–40 season at Masonic at $19,325, which covered the expenses of forty concerts, 120 rehearsals, and office space. He projected a budget

Detroit attorney, wanted to raise money to pay off the debt and give Orchestra Hall to for the season at $280,000, with half coming from higher ticket sales in the larger venue and half to be raised as part of the Maintenance Fund.[17]

When compared to the Bondholders' offer of at least $31,000 per year in rent and fees to remain at Orchestra Hall, the Symphony Society had an easy decision to make. The DSO would move to Masonic Temple.

In a letter published in the program of February 11, 1939, Mrs. John S. Newberry, President of the Symphony Society, announced the move, which she called "the most important decision in [the Society's] history." Noting that the move was motivated by "economy and expansion," she claimed that "POPULARIZATION OF THE DETROIT SYMPHONY ORCHESTRA is the KEYWORD of the new plan. The orchestra MUST BE FOR ALL OF DETROIT and at Masonic Temple where hundreds upon hundreds of seats can be sold at the lowest prices ever offered anywhere this can be accomplished" (capitalization for emphasis is hers).[18]

The last concert played in Orchestra Hall was given on March 18, 1939, an all-Tchaikovsky program played in memory of Gabrilowitsch, and conducted by Kolar. Edith Rhetts Tilton remembered that final evening:

The curtain, which the audience had never seen closed, started to lower slowly during Auld Lang Syne, and

at the end it was closed. It was a dramatic, moving, and final adieux.[19]

So the DSO moved from Orchestra Hall to Masonic Temple, hoping that those "hundreds upon hundreds" of seats would be filled with a new and more broadly based group of patrons.

The 1939–40 season opened at Masonic Temple, with "1,500 new persons," including new season ticket holders in the audience, according to Murray Paterson. He continued to publish his "Plain Statement of Facts" in the programs, giving all interested readers an insight into the continuing financial challenges facing the symphony. He especially stressed the importance of donating to the orchestra, noting that "in every city in the United States where there is a symphony orchestra, gifts are necessary to carry on the work." He continued in all subsequent programs to appeal for more revenue, more members of the Symphony Society, more season ticket buyers, and more contributors to the Maintenance Fund.[20]

## PROBLEMS IN THE DIRECTOR'S CHAIR

But the DSO was facing artistic as well as financial challenges. While Franco Ghione and Victor Kolar continued to share conductor's duties for the DSO, there were serious problems with Ghione's skills as a director. Perhaps most importantly, he spoke no English, which created myriad communication problems between him and the musicians. He also reportedly had a fiendish temper, as mentioned by Herman Wise in his contribution to Edith Tilton's history of the DSO:

> His hot Italian blood . . . frequently boiled over at rehearsal and in his attempts to make himself understood his frustrations often reached the explosive stage. In fairness, he was as much annoyed with himself as with his players. Several times he started to take lessons in English, but to no avail. He found it impossible to go beyond a single word or two.[21]

Unfortunately, Ghione's limitations were not only related to his language skills. He was primarily an operatic conductor, and both his knowledge and expertise in the symphonic repertoire were limited. The grumblings from the orchestra were soon joined by those of the newspaper critics and the audiences, who grew tired of the uninspired programming. Even though he had signed a three-year contract in 1937 that should have taken him through the 1940–41 season, Ghione asked to have his contract terminated at the end of the 1939–40 season; his request was accepted.[22]

## EARLY YEARS IN MASONIC TEMPLE

The Symphony Society's plan to increase revenue by increasing ticket sales in a larger venue was a success in its first years. "More people than ever bought tickets for the orchestra's 1939–40 season," according to Lynne Mattson.[23] And there were more tickets available at lower prices than had been possible at Orchestra Hall, too. For performances in the larger hall, there were 1,000 season tickets available at five dollars for the season, the lowest price ever offered by the DSO; individual concert tickets were priced as low as twenty-five cents each, all helping to realize, in part, Mrs. Newberry's ideal of an orchestra for "all the people of Detroit."

Yet the orchestra also continued to be plagued by money problems. The tireless Murray Paterson kept the audiences up to date on the DSO's precarious financial situation in interviews and program notes. When people told him that the growing audiences must mean growing income for the symphony, he responded in print, "Nothing could be further from the truth," and announced that the shortage for the current season amounted to $46,000.[24]

His announcement prompted a widespread campaign to raise money for the symphony, with newspapers and radio programs promoting the cause. Even Mayor Jeffries made an appeal to the people of his city: "I suggest to the people of Detroit that it does not seem in harmony with the times or the prestige of our city that for lack of proper sponsorship the symphony should fail. Pride alone should cause us to rally to the rescue of this institution with its fine music at popular prices. The people will not feel that as a city we can allow such a worthy organization to suffer from our neglect."[25]

Yet by early February 1940, the DSO was still in need of funds. As part of Paterson's continuing pleas for donations, there was a "Save the Symphony" campaign that was publicized throughout the area. It was a "long uphill climb," according to the manager, that also saw the birth of a new organization, the Friends of the Detroit Symphony Orchestra, headed by the poet laureate of Detroit, Edgar A. Guest, with membership "open to all, with the cost of $1 per year." With this final push, the organization was able to raise the total needed by the end of the season to cover the deficit.[26]

In the 1940–41 season, Victor Kolar took over again as sole director of the DSO, and assembled a group of outstanding guest conductors as well. They included Leopold Stokowski, Georges Enesco, Richard Strauss, Siegfried Wagner, Fritz Reiner, and Bruno Walter, among the finest directors of the international musical community. Among the soloists to appear with the DSO were violinist Jascha Heifetz, pianist Vladimir Horowitz, and cellist Gregor Piatigorsky.

There was a wide variety of programming, with audiences hearing the familiar nineteenth-century repertoire

Kolar with Henry Ford, who sponsored the Ford Radio Hour. (Courtesy DSO Archives)

of Beethoven, Brahms, and Schubert, but also more modern pieces, including Richard Strauss's tone poems, with the composer conducting. The Ballet Russe continued to perform in Detroit and was a very popular concert draw. Performances by the Fisk Jubilee Singers, with Leonard B. Smith as trumpet soloist, were another favorite for Detroit audiences, as was Percy Grainger, who performed his own compositions on the piano.[27]

While the combination of outstanding programming and solid advance ticket sales made the outlook for 1940–41 season bright, in one critical area revenue was falling. Income from the Ford Sunday Evening Hour broadcasts, which had brought in around $30,000 per year from 1934 to 1938, began to decline, falling to $19,750 in

1938–39 and to $16,500 in 1940–41. This was due largely to the steep decline in fees paid by Ford to the DSO per concert, which fell from $1,000 per week in 1934 to $500 per week in 1938.[28]

The total decline in revenue from all sources amounted to a deficit of around $32,000 at the end of 1941. Dr. Fred T. Murphy, the nephew of William H. Murphy and the President of the Symphony Society at the time, stated to the group's Board that he did not think that a public campaign was the way to erase the deficit. Rather, he encouraged members of the board to contribute $1,000 each to cover the deficit.[29]

This effort erased most of the shortfall, and improved the DSO's balance sheet. According to the condensed financial report of the 1940–41 season, total expense for the period was $277,000, total income was $271,303, leaving a loss of $5,696.[30]

Paterson estimated the budget for the 1941–42 season at $265,000, with projected revenue of $120,000, and a Maintenance Fund of $145,000, about $43,000 of which needed to be raised before the end of the season. Despite the continuing financial challenges, the Manager ended his report stating that "we can all enter this year with a great deal of optimism."[31]

The preliminary programming planned for the 1941–42 season also showed promise: Bruno Walter and Sir Thomas Beecham had agreed to be guest conductors, and outstanding soloists, including

pianist Sergei Rachmaninoff and soprano Kirsten Flagstad, were scheduled to appear. The season was to include fourteen Thursday night concerts, eight Friday night pops concerts, as well as performances on six Friday afternoons, six Saturday mornings, and six free school children's concerts.[32]

But labor problems soon arose between the musicians and the management of the DSO that threatened the entire season. The core of the problem had to do with the length of the season: at twenty weeks, the DSO's schedule was below the average twenty-six-week season of most American orchestras at the time. The American Federation of Musicians, the bargaining representatives for the Detroit branch of the musicians' union, wanted the number of concerts to be expanded so that the musicians could make an adequate living. Paterson countered that in light of the $43,000 that the Society needed to raise before the end of the season, and because hundreds of patrons had already bought season tickets for a twenty-week schedule, the only way that concerts could be added was through a special festival series at the end of the regular concert season.

The dispute continued into the opening of the season, in October 1941, and was finally resolved when a representative of the Masonic Temple Association named C. W. Van Lopik presented an offer to pay for an additional week of concerts, to be given at the end of the season.[33]

Then, just two months later, the orchestra, the city, and the country found themselves transformed by a devastating new reality.

## DETROIT AND WORLD WAR II: THE "ARSENAL OF DEMOCRACY"

On December 7, 1941, the Japanese attacked the United States at Pearl Harbor in Hawaii. The US declared war on Japan, Germany, and Italy, and Detroit geared up to play a crucial role in supplying the Allies, becoming the central force in the nation's "Arsenal of Democracy."

The changes in the city were immediate. The day after Pearl Harbor, army personnel began guarding the border crossings at the Windsor Tunnel and the Ambassador Bridge. The population mobilized for war, as more than 200,000 Detroiters joined the armed forces. More than 100,000 Detroiters also served at home, training as air raid wardens, medical volunteers, special police, and firefighters.

The factories that once produced the nation's automobiles were transformed into plants that manufactured the tanks, aircraft, munitions, and other materials needed to supply the troops, employing thousands of Detroiters. William S. Knudsen, former president of General Motors, became a lieutenant general in the army and the director of the Office of Production Management. The government built plants that were run by the auto companies, with Chrysler running the tank plant in Warren, Ford producing B-24 bombers at Willow Run, General Motors building tanks in Flint, and Hudson Motors running the Navy's gun production in Center Line.[34]

The DSO played its part for the war effort, too. With revenues falling and its season in jeopardy, the orchestra announced the Allied Music Festival, a series of three concerts, each celebrating the music of the Allied nations—Great Britain, Russia, and the United States—to boost the morale of Detroiters through music in time of war. The programs were given on February 24, 26, and 28, 1942, and featured famous conductors, including Andre Kostelanetz, Efrem Kurtz, and Victor Kolar, and soloists, including pianists Alec Templeton and Oscar Levant and soprano Dorothy Maynor, with revenue going to support the DSO, whose financial fortunes had fallen precipitously after the country went to war. Masonic Temple donated the performance space, the soloists donated their time, and the musicians gave up the week of pay they had been promised in the previous labor negotiation.

As "The Commentator," W. K. Kelsey, wrote in the *Detroit News*, "It's a united effort for the good of the Orchestra, for the good of Detroit, for the good of the nation, for the good of the United

Kolar in his later years as conductor. (Courtesy DSO Archives)

Powers against the forces of evil and degeneration."[35] The Festival was a success, and brought in much-needed revenue of just under $10,000. But the DSO was about to face another blow.

### THE END OF THE FORD RADIO BROADCASTS

In the spring of 1942, Ford announced that it would no longer fund the Ford Sunday Evening Hour radio broadcasts. The announcement, while startling, was in line with similar cancellations. At the same time that Ford canceled its broadcasts, Chrysler cut the popular Major Bowes's broadcasts to a half-hour, and Lipton Tea ceased production of Helen Hayes's radio show.[36] While it was certainly understandable considering Ford's focus on the war

effort, it represented an unexpected loss in revenue at a time when funds were scarce and getting scarcer. Trying to keep the orchestra alive, a group of concerned supporters approached another possible sponsor, Max Osnos, who was the president of Sam's Cut-Rate, a popular discount department store. Osnos agreed to fund a series of twenty-one radio broadcasts, and to promote it as part of an effort to raise money for the war effort through the sale of war bonds.[37]

At the same time, negotiations were under way between DSO management and the musicians' union regarding the 1942–43 season. Earlier in the year, the union and management had signed a contract that called for a twenty-one-week season. But after the audit of the 1941–42 financial records was completed in March, Fred T. Murphy, president of the Society, presented the Board with a bleak assessment of the finances of the DSO. There was still a deficit of almost $26,000, and, with the nation at war and donations and tickets sales down, there was simply not the money to pay for a concert series of twenty-one weeks.

In an effort to save the season, Murphy wrote a letter to the musicians dated July 28, 1942, in which he outlined the financial problems facing the DSO. He noted that projected revenue was down significantly, then addressed a potentially devastating development: gasoline rationing was on the horizon, "which will so interfere with transportation as to make attendance at any series of concerts impossible."[38]

In light of that dire assessment, Murphy outlined a new offer: a season of fourteen weeks instead of twenty-one, with cutbacks in salary and office expenses on the management side that would parallel those of the musicians. Murphy expressed his deep regret at the proposed reductions, and wrote that the directors "realize that the wage return to the individual is too small, but in these times it may be a question of half a loaf being better than none at all."

Murphy ended his letter with a stern prediction: "I believe it can be said, and said with justification that if the concerts are given up for this season they will not be revived in the lifetime of many of us."[39]

The musicians rejected the proposal. In response, the Board canceled the season. These notes are from the Symphony Society records:

On September 29, 1942, the Directors of the Detroit Symphony Society voted that the series of concerts proposed for the 1942–43 season be canceled and that the Symphony suspend its activities in maintaining the Orchestra and giving concerts for the duration of the war. This action was taken after lengthy consideration of the present extraordinary conditions, fiscal and otherwise, caused by the war, the proposed

rationing of gasoline and the effect this will have upon the attendance at concerts, the sale of tickets, the payment of pledges to the Maintenance Fund, and the unwillingness of the Federation of Musicians to accept a shortened season.[40]

Privately, Fred T. Murphy wrote to Mrs. Julius Haass of the Symphony Board:

I never took any action which was more distressing than the vote today when we determined to cancel the series of concerts proposed for the '42–43 season.[41]

So the Detroit Symphony Orchestra went out of business again, the only major orchestra in the country to do so during the war. The reaction in the media was immediate and harsh. The *Detroit Free Press*'s J. D. Callaghan wrote:

Detroit has suffered a blow to its musical prestige with the suspension of the Detroit Symphony Orchestra season, from which it may not recover within the experience of this generation.

And all because one of the richest cities in the world was so money-timid that it would not guarantee the funds for a complete season. Thus the long arm of Hitler and his pals has reached into the citadel of war industry and made its musical leaders knuckle under.

Callaghan noted that the country's governmental and cultural leaders had stated that "music must not be allowed to be eclipsed by the war," yet now twenty-eight years of music "goes out the window" due to a labor dispute that appears to be little more than a "struggle for power."

He claimed, too, that the most important contribution of the DSO to the city had not been the gala concerts featuring the wealthy and glamorous; rather, it was the appreciation of music instilled in "500,000 children" of the city, who had learned the joys of classical music through the free concerts, as well as the many who had heard great music for as little as twenty-five cents when the DSO moved to Masonic Temple. This, he felt, was the true loss to the city.[42]

In the *Detroit News*, "the Commentator," W. K. Kelsey, laid blame for the ending of the DSO on several factors: the death of Gabrilowitsch, whose musicianship and leadership were never replaced; the deaths of the orchestra's original patrons, "who would gladly write checks for $20,000" because of their belief in the importance of the organization; and the lack of vision in the current management: "there were too few who came in at the last hour to the places of those who had passed away." For Kelsey, the Depression and the war had proved too much for those in charge: "the

spirit had fled. The long years of stringency wiped out more than men's fortunes. It made them timid, uncertain, hesitant, to make great decisions."[43]

*Musical America* was even more harsh, shaming Detroit for its lack of courage, commitment to culture, and public spirit:

In a time that calls for grit, perseverance and clear thinking, Detroit has come into the headlines with a sorry example of civic and cultural backsliding. Not only because it represents the one important break in a courageous, solid front among the major orchestras of the country, but because it comes as a flagrant lapse of public spirit.

Detroit is this country's fourth largest city. It is a city of wealth, and, in other activities, of progressive public spirit. Perhaps more than any other of the first half dozen American cities, it is profiting from a great rush of war manufacturing. Money flows freely. Hundreds of thousands of its inhabitants have more to spend than ever in the past. . . . Among these must be many who are eager to take advantage of the city's cultural advantages. It has let them down.

Detroit is to be sternly rebuked. Music is too vital to the public morale, and therefore to the entire war effort, for any such major disaffec-

tion to be accepted without the cen-
sure it so emphatically deserves.[44]

Whether such hostile shaming was
deserved on the part of management,
the musicians, or civic leaders, the Detroit Symphony Orchestra had ceased to
be. The only concerts played during the
1942–43 season were the radio broadcasts
funded by Sam's Cut-Rate, with the DSO
musicians playing under the name "the
Detroit Orchestra," still under the direction of Victor Kolar.

The Detroit Symphony Orchestra,
while briefly extinguished, was soon to
rise again, this time under the control of
an autocratic industrialist whose tenure
was as brief as it was mercurial.

# The Reichhold Era, 1943–49: A One-Man Band

RESOLVED, that the Detroit Symphony Society approve the action of the President and the Directors in extending good wishes and every hope of success to the Detroit Orchestra, Inc., in their efforts to revive the symphonic concert.

Resolution passed by the Detroit Symphony Society,
September 24, 1943[1]

THE DETROIT SYMPHONY ORCHESTRA HAD FALLEN SILENT IN THE FALL of 1942, a victim of declining ticket sales and donations during the Second World War and an unresolved labor dispute between the orchestra and management. When the DSO disbanded in 1942, it was thought that it would remain out of business for the duration of the war. But other forces supporting the return of symphonic music in Detroit continued to fight on its behalf. The most influential was an industrialist named Henry Reichhold, who brought about the rebirth of the symphony and oversaw both its rapid expansion and tempestuous demise, all within six years.

## HENRY REICHHOLD

Henry Helmuth Reichhold was born in Berlin in 1901, the son of a chemist. He studied at the Universities of Berlin and Vienna, and after graduating joined his father's chemical company. In 1923, he moved to Detroit, where he began to work for the Ford Motor Company as a lab assistant in the paint department, at a salary of $6.80 per day. He was ambitious and hardworking, and was promoted to the head of the department within the year.

Reichhold's ambitions included starting his own company, and in 1927 he got his chance. His father's chemical company in Germany was producing phenolic resins, an important paint additive that cut the time it took paint to dry from days to hours. The process cut manufacturing time for any painted product—especially automobiles on the assembly line—significantly.

Reichhold first set up his business in a friend's garage, then, after being denied a forty cent raise by Ford, went off on his own. His new company, first called Beck, Koller, and Company and later Reichhold Chemical, was located in the Detroit suburb of Ferndale, and became a tremendous success, in large part because Ford became the chief buyer of his products.[2]

By 1942, Reichhold was a wealthy man; he was also an amateur violinist with a strong interest in the arts. After the DSO folded in September 1942, he sponsored a chamber music series at the Detroit Institute of Arts. Through his in-terest in music, he met Raymond Hall, a cellist who had played with the previous DSO and was part of a group of musicians trying to bring the symphony back. Through Hall, Reichhold met Karl Krueger, an American-born conductor, who had trained in Europe and led orchestras in Seattle and Kansas City.

Reichhold decided he had found the man to lead a new Detroit Symphony. He pledged $160,000 to sponsor a new season, to begin in 1943 under Krueger's direction. The new DSO was under the management of a new group, the Detroit Orchestra Inc., with Reichhold as president. Many of the musicians from the former DSO were still living in Detroit, and were hired to play in the new ensemble.[3]

## KARL KRUEGER

The first American-born conductor to lead the DSO, Karl Krueger was born in Atchison, Kansas, in 1894, the descendent of pioneers who had emigrated from Sweden and Germany. He learned to play the cello and the organ as a child, and went on to major in music at Midland College in Atchison, receiving his bachelor's degree in 1913. He continued to study at the New England Conservatory of Music, taking courses in composition and organ, and completed a master's degree in music at the University of Kansas in 1916.

After serving as a church organist in New York for four years, Krueger moved to Vienna, where he studied composi-

Karl Krueger, music director of the DSO from 1943 to 1949. (Courtesy DSO Archives)

that orchestra, too, to a widely apprecia-tive audience: during his first three years there, the ensemble had the largest sub-scription audience in the country.[4]

After ten years in his post in Kansas City, Krueger was ready for a change, and when the conductorship of the DSO was offered to him, he accepted. On the eve of his first appearance with the DSO, an article in the *Detroit News,* dated August 21, 1943, noted the situation in Kansas City when Krueger had taken over the or-chestra and anticipated the new maestro's success in his new city:

> There had been an interruption in the community's symphonic activities. The situation called for a musician capable virtually of building a new orchestra. But it also required a man of broad cul-tural background, magnetic per-sonality, and—above all—great enthusiasm, to catch the imag-ination of the public and make that orchestra a dynamic force in the life of the city. Mr. Kreuger proved brilliantly equipped for both these tasks.[5]

Detroit got its first glimpse of Krue-ger on October 21, 1943, when he con-ducted his first concert, a memorial tribute in honor of Gabrilowitsch. The audience and the critics responded en-thusiastically, finding him an "unusually

tion with Robert Fuchs, whose previous students had included Jean Sibelius and Fritz Kreisler. He also began studies in conducting under Arthur Nikisch, Felix Weingartner, and finally Franz Schalk, who was then the director of the Vienna Opera. Schalk made Krueger his assistant, and after working with him claimed, "I have no doubt that Krueger will play an important role among the leading con-ductors of his time."

Krueger returned to the United States in 1926 to conduct the Seattle Symphony Orchestra, a position he held for six years. When he left Seattle in 1932 for Kansas City, he was credited with raising the quality of musicianship of the symphony to the highest level in its history. As director of the Kansas City Philharmonic, he set about improving gifted man," who "on the stand is a figure of great polish, personal as well as artistic. He seems to have, as they say, what it takes."[6]

The schedule for the 1943–44 season contained eighteen subscription concerts, featuring various solo guest artists, ranging from pianist Artur Schnabel to harmonica virtuoso Larry Adler. Krueger, known as a champion of American composers, added many works by contemporary national musicians to the DSO's repertoire from his first years with the symphony.[7]

Detroiters responded to their new maestro and the reborn DSO by snapping up some eighty-four percent of all season tickets between the first and second concerts. And this occurred even though ticket prices had been raised significantly, ranging from eighty-five cents for balcony seats to $2.75 for main floor seating. It looked like the symphony was finally headed in a positive direction.[8]

Reichhold began an aggressive membership campaign, with enrollment forms in the programs, requesting contributions "from civic minded, public spirited lovers of music and the cultural arts" to the Maintenance Fund. The requested levels of giving were significantly higher than earlier seasons as well, with a "Sponsor" membership requiring a contribution of "$5,000 and over," a "Patron" giving "$1,000 to $4,999," "Sustaining" members giving "$500 to $999," and six more levels

of giving, ending with "Contributing Associates," giving "less than $5."

By the end of the season, there were fifteen "Program Sponsors," including some of the major businesses in Detroit: Bundy Tubing, Detroit Trust, Dow Chemical, Chrysler Corporation, Cranbrook Central Committee, Ford Motor Company, Grinnell Brothers, General Motors, Great Lakes Steel, Himelhoch's, J. L. Hudson, Manufacturers National Bank, and Reichhold Chemical. Reichhold made sure their names, as well as the names of all givers at all levels, were updated in each new program.[9]

The DSO program for November 4, 1943, included the return of another proud sponsor: Sam's Cut-Rate, the discount department store that had paid for the 1942–43 radio broadcasts, announced that it would also be sponsoring eighteen broadcasts in the 1943–44 season. It began its ad noting that: "The Detroit Orchestra has passed its dark days, and now emerges with more brilliance than ever." Now, the company that was "happy indeed in lending support to the orchestra at a time when its destiny hung in the balance" would once again carry the broadcasts "as a public service and aid to the War Bond effort."[10]

Also of note in the program was an informal letter from Karl Krueger to the audience, inviting patrons to share their reactions to each piece on the program, marking each with an "A" if they liked the composition, a "B" if they disliked it, or "C" if they were indifferent. He then wrote a few paragraphs about whether or not audience members should applaud after individual movements or wait until an entire piece was completed to clap. He told them it was "custom" to wait until a piece was over, but also encouraged them to applaud when they "feel like it," respecting each individual's reaction to the piece.[11]

This approach appeared to be part of Krueger's attitude toward non-professional music lovers, for whom he expressed great respect. In a book on the history of music directors published in 1958, Krueger made the following dedication: "This little book is for the musical amateur to whom we musicians owe so much." He encouraged amateur listeners to trust themselves: "The music lover has need of nothing but the music itself, he gets along better without any 'explanations' and the more he is alone in his listening, the better the quality of his listening will probably be."[12]

Krueger's approach to his new audience further endeared him to Detroiters, and they responded with the highest attendance figures in the symphony's history. According to statistics given in the DSO programs, more than 70,000 people attended concerts at Masonic Temple during his first season, and 65,000 also heard the DSO perform its new summer series of outdoor concerts at the University of Detroit's football stadium. Krueger also brought back the DSO's popular Sat-

urday morning concerts for school children, another positive move made by the new director.[13]

Yet despite the successes of the new DSO under Reichhold and Krueger, the orchestra still needed more money, and, as in previous seasons, the programs contained continuous pleas for more contributions to insure that there would be another season. These campaigns were successful by the end of the season, and in an endnote to the final program in 1944, Reichhold announced that "Detroit will have a series of symphony concerts throughout the 1944–45 season," and also that Krueger had signed a three-year contract to remain with DSO.[14]

## "THE WORLD'S LARGEST SYMPHONY" AND THE "SYMPHONY OF THE AMERICAS"

Reichhold had even greater ambitions for the 1944–45 season. He had said repeatedly that he wanted the DSO to eventually become a "self-sustaining" orchestra, and he made several changes to enhance the commercial success of the ensemble, including the size of the orchestra, the number of musical performances, and even the types of music performed.

In the fall of 1944, he increased the number of musicians in the orchestra from ninety-two to 110, promoting it nationwide as "the world's largest symphony." There were even listings in the programs to show that the DSO now had sixteen more musicians than the Boston Symphony Orchestra, nine more than Philadelphia, and four more than the New York Philharmonic. When long-time concertmaster Ilya Schkolnik left the DSO to become the concertmaster and assistant conductor of the Baltimore Symphony Orchestra, Reichhold hired the distinguished violinist Josef Gingold, then second concertmaster at the NBC Symphony, to take his place. That same season, Valter Poole became the assistant conductor of the symphony, moving from the viola section, where he had played for eighteen years.[15]

The season was expanded to include twenty Thursday evening subscription concerts, twenty Saturday concerts, as well as sixteen school children's concerts. And to provide more of a national audience for the DSO, Reichhold signed a contract with the Mutual Broadcasting System for the orchestra to appear on a regular Saturday evening radio broadcast. He also negotiated a contract with the prestigious Victor Red Seal label to produce a series of recordings of the DSO under Krueger.[16]

In December 1944, Reichhold made another move to enhance the prestige of the orchestra: he announced that he was sponsoring a composition contest, called the "Symphony of the Americas" prize, a competition for North and South American composers. He stipulated that the piece had to be a complete symphony, no more than thirty minutes long, and

offered a grand prize of $25,000 for first place, $5,000 for second, and $2,500 for third place. It was a huge amount of money, unlike any other offered at the time to a composer.[17] (For comparison, the 2014 Pulitzer Prize in music, awarded to John Luther Adams, included a cash award of $10,000.)

Each of the twenty-one countries of North and South America could submit one entry. The panel of judges included major figures in symphonic music, including Krueger, composers Howard Hanson and Roy Harris, and other distinguished musicians.

Reichhold even established a new radio series to promote the contest: the "Symphony of the Americas" broadcasts were directed by new assistant conductor Valter Poole, and featured a smaller ensemble playing lighter works for orchestra as well as music from Central and South America not usually represented in the American symphonic repertoire.[18]

As another part of his ventures to make the DSO a profitable, self-sustaining entity, Reichhold determined that the DSO could make money by dividing the orchestra into even more ensembles. These groups would play different kinds of music, to be performed for different radio broadcasts, thus appealing to a broader range of potential listeners and commercial sponsors. So in addition to the "Symphony of the Americas" broadcasts, he inaugurated programs featuring a dance orchestra conducted by the popular Jean Goldkette, a program of light classical music, and an ensemble playing popular music of a more sentimental nature.

According to an article in the *Detroit News* outlining his ambitious radio broadcast project, Reichhold forecast that the additional revenue for these series would reach $250,000 dollars, furthering his goals of a self-supporting ensemble.[19]

## BACK TO CARNEGIE HALL

While Reichhold was busy expanding the commercial possibilities of the DSO, the artistic ambitions for the ensemble continued under Krueger, who led the orchestra in a concert at Carnegie Hall on January 30, 1945. According to Olin Downes, the influential critic of the *New York Times*, the orchestra played well and was rapturously received by the audience, though the program was, for him, "rather poorly made." And although he was a bit put off by the promotion of the DSO as "one of the largest orchestras" in the country, Downes did find that the symphony's sound was "prevailing good and well balanced."[20]

He praised in particular the playing of Josef Gingold: "a violinist, a concertmaster with all the attributes of authority and leadership which this position requires." Downes also praised the string section, especially in their playing of Rachmaninoff's Symphony no. 2 in E

Minor. And though he quibbled with Krueger's choice of the piece and what he found as overly emotional playing in sections, it was, in the end, a "well-coordinated performance, effective and eloquent." Of special note for the critic was the orchestra's final piece, the final scene from Richard Strauss's *Salome*, with the soprano Marjorie Lawrence, in which he found "the orchestral virtuosity at its pitch."[21]

Back at home, local music critics were far more effulgent in their praise for their orchestra. According to the *Free Press*, the DSO had "skyrocketed" to "a place among the first few symphonies in the world." Giving in to hyperbole, the critic continues: "So eminent has its position become, especially in the treatment of tone color, and so outstanding have been its performances under the guiding hand of Karl Krueger, that it is difficult to list the best without overstepping the limits of newspaper space."[22]

The hyperbole wasn't limited to the newspapers. Reichhold announced that he had negotiated a contract with Krueger to remain at the helm of the orchestra for ten more years. "All great institutions are lengthened shadows of personalities," he said in praise of the conductor in an article in the *Detroit News*. "Krueger's achievement here has been the talk of the whole country and we feel confident he will make it the peer of any orchestra in the world."[23]

## CONCERTMASTER: JOSEF GINGOLD (1944–47)

Josef Gingold, concertmaster of the DSO from 1944 to 1947, was one of the finest violinists to play with the orchestra in its history. He was born in Brest-Litovsk, Russia, on October 28, 1909, and immigrated to the United States with his family in 1920. He studied violin with Vladimir Graffman in New York, then in Brussels with the legendary teacher Eugene Ysaye, who told his mother in accepting him as a student that he was "born to the instrument."

Returning to the United States in 1929, Gingold found full-time work playing in Broadway pit orchestras, while continuing to study with Adolfo Betti and Harold Morris. In 1937, he auditioned for Toscanini and the NBC Orchestra, and was accepted in the first violin section. He played there for seven years, moving up to assistant concertmaster and playing with the NBC String Quartet with Mischa Mischakoff, who was then the concertmaster of the NBC ensemble and would follow Gingold to Detroit.

Gingold accepted Karl Krueger's offer to become the DSO's concertmaster in 1944, and was widely praised for his playing, performing fourteen times as a soloist during his brief three-year tenure with the orchestra. While in Detroit, Gingold also became the teacher of a twelve-year-old gifted violinist, "Joey" Silverstein, who would go on to become an outstanding concertmaster himself with the Boston Symphony Orchestra.

Gingold's rich tone and flawless technique made him a legendary figure in the DSO's history, but he is also remembered for the tempestuous way in which he left the orchestra. Lured away by George Szell to play with the Cleveland Orchestra, his departure caused a firestorm in February 1947.

Gingold was concertmaster with Cleveland for thirteen years, leaving in 1960 to teach at Indiana University's School of Music, where he became one of its finest and most revered faculty members. When he turned seventy-five, his contributions to the field were celebrated at IU's music center, where dozens of his former students appeared and played to honor their teacher, many of them soloists and concertmasters in their own right, causing the dean of the music school to note, "There are more superb violinists per square inch in this hall tonight than in any other place in the world."

Gingold also helped establish the International Violin Competition in Indianapolis, gave master classes in Paris, Tokyo, Copenhagen, and Montreal, and held the Mischa Elman Chair at the Manhattan School of Music.

Sources: David Blum, "Profiles: A Gold Coin," *The New Yorker*, February 4, 1991; Andrew Adler, "Josef Gingold Gala," *High Fidelity*, March 1985; Anne Mischakoff Heiles, *America's Concertmasters* (Sterling Heights: Harmonie Park Press, 2007), 219–21.

## RETURNING TO A HOME OF THEIR OWN: MUSIC HALL

Just a few months later, in June 1945, the tireless Reichhold announced that he had bought the Wilson Theater as the new home of the Detroit Symphony. Renaming it "Music Hall," he claimed that Masonic Temple was too large a space for concert performances. This was, of course, in direct contradiction to the forces behind the orchestra's move from Orchestra Hall in 1939, when the number of seats in Masonic was deemed important to the DSO's plans of expanding their audience. Yet Reichhold also championed the move because he wanted to be able to house all the symphony's activities in one building, whether concerts, recordings, or broadcast performances.

In an indication of both his ambition and his independent stance toward all things dealing with the orchestra, Reichhold made the purchase with his own funds, and without the approval or knowledge of the board of Detroit Orchestra Inc. According to a glowing profile in the Detroit Athletic Club's *DAC News*, Reichhold faced little opposition from the board, who were referred to in the article as having "dummy director" roles, and ridiculed as "powerless to do anything but submit and go along quietly."[24]

Reichhold's precipitous move to Music Hall did cause some immediate logistical problems: the DSO's 1945–46 concert season had to be performed at Masonic Temple because, despite his protestations that Masonic was too large, the seating in the new hall could not accommodate the 3,000 season ticket holders who had already paid for their subscriptions. But the other ensembles now connected with the DSO, including the smaller broadcast orchestras and Gus Haenschen's All-String Orchestra, began using the new facility in the fall of 1945. Once again, Reichhold took a hands-on approach, helping the workmen move the equipment into the new building on Madison Avenue in downtown Detroit.[25]

Soon, there were many performers booked into the new Music Hall, providing a wide range of music: the Grand Opera Quartet, the Trapp Family, Yehudi Menuhin, Sigmund Romberg and Andre Kostelanetz and their orchestras all played in Music Hall in its inaugural season. Other groups, including the Boy Scouts, the Lutheran Missionary Rally, and J. L. Hudson's Bridal Fashion Show, rented the hall, bringing income to Reichhold and the DSO.[26]

Another new series of concerts began in the summer of 1945, when the first free concerts at the State Fairgrounds took place, under the baton of Valter Poole. These continued for decades and were one of the most popular and enduring efforts of the DSO. And there were more developments initiated by Reichhold: in September 1945, he announced that the DSO was going into the business of making and distributing records, which were to be pressed at a plant in Ferndale.[27]

With World War II over and thousands of GIs returning to Detroit, Reichhold expanded his musical empire even further, hoping to appeal to an even wider population of potential listeners. In 1946 he bought *Musical Digest* magazine, which was then a popular guide to orchestral and operatic performances, and he planned to put all profits from the magazine into the orchestra. Reichhold placed full-page ads in the DSO programs for the magazine and announced that it would become a monthly of "global proportions," focusing on the "dynamic importance of music in this electronic age."[28]

In the spring of 1946, Karl Krueger began a series of guest conductor performances in Europe, in a gesture of post-war outreach that enhanced his and the DSO's reputation. He appeared in ten cities, launching with a concert by the GI Symphony Orchestra in Frankfurt, Germany, broadcast over the NBC radio network. These concerts took him to Paris, Helsinki, Stockholm, Copenhagen, Oslo, Vienna, Prague, and Madrid, and were described in the DSO programs as winning warm praise from European critics, who called him "a grand seignor of the baton" and "a virtuoso of virtuosos," who brought "the brilliance and power of other days" to the capitols of Europe.[29]

During the 1946–47 season, the DSO performed all of its concerts at the Music Hall, and brought back the Friday evening concert series as well as the regular Thursday night subscription series, for a season of eighteen performances, and one special concert, featuring the famed contralto Marian Anderson. Guest artists that season included tenor Jussi Björling, pianist Artur Schnabel, and bass Alexander Kipnis. The school concerts continued as well, with Valter Poole conducting eighteen performances.

Krueger continued to offer concerts featuring a wide range of music, from baroque masters such as Handel and Bach, to classical stalwarts of the nineteenth century like Beethoven and Brahms, but also providing Detroit audiences with their first exposure to such modern composers as Vaughan Williams and Howard

Hanson, and, in what must have been a first in the city, an all-Hindemith program. He also continued to ask for audience input in both programming and recommendations for guest artists, and offered an all-request program at the end of the season.

In an effort to expand the usage of Music Hall, Reichhold added another new series to the venue's programming for 1946–47, a recital series featuring twenty-four concerts with many well-known musicians, including violinist Fritz Kreisler, mezzo-soprano Risë Stevens, bass Ezio Pinza, guitarist Andrés Segovia, and pianist Leon Fleisher.[30]

Reichhold's ambitions for the Music Hall also included a new recording studio, and in 1947 he announced that the DSO would record exclusively for Vox records, where he had just been named the chairman. Not only did Reichhold believe that the DSO would sell more records with Vox than with RCA Victor, he also believed the enterprise would be more profitable if it was housed with the rest of the DSO's ventures, and under his control.[31]

Yet another radio program became the next venture to be broadcast from Music Hall. The "Music for Michigan" series, with Valter Poole conducting, was heard every Tuesday at 7:30 p.m. over radio station WWJ. Sponsored by Detroit Edison, the concerts were promoted as a "Solid Half-Hour of America's Concert

Margaret Truman performs with the DSO, March 1947. (Courtesy DSO Archives)

Favorites," another of Reichhold's efforts to broaden the audience for the DSO.[32]

## MARGARET TRUMAN APPEARS WITH THE DSO

On March 16, 1947, the DSO hosted the debut of soprano soloist Margaret Truman, daughter of President Harry Truman. While her voice, described as "immature, unremarkable, and unobjectionable" in the *Free Press*, did seem to most critics unequal to the task of a solo performance, the concert was in many ways a coup for the orchestra, as the president's daughter brought in a radio audience numbering 15 million when it was broadcast from the Music Hall.[33]

## DECLINE AND FALL

Yet, despite all the concerts, broadcasts, recordings, and rather relentless self-promotion of the DSO under Reichhold, things began to go awry. In February 1947, Josef Gingold, the highly regarded concertmaster of the orchestra since 1944, left the symphony abruptly to join the Cleveland Orchestra. It turned out that he had been offered the concertmaster's post in Cleveland by their famed director, George Szell. Szell, who had appeared as a guest conductor in Detroit during the previous season, initially made the offer in November 1946 and was at first rebuffed by Gingold. Yet, according to music critic and Cleveland Orchestra historian Donald Rosenberg, when Szell told Gingold his plans were "to take the Cleveland Orchestra to the top," the violinist signed the contract, with both agreeing to "button their lips until the appropriate time."[34]

When the news hit Detroit on February 4, 1947, it caused an uproar. Krueger wrote a letter to Szell, accusing him of "piracy" in poaching his man. "Szell, rightly, sneered at claims made by the people of Detroit," according to Rosenberg. The Cleveland conductor told a reporter: "Any organization is entitled to approach any artist in perfectly good faith for a time for which he is not legally committed to another organization."[35]

But Krueger was livid. He wrote an open letter to Szell that appeared in papers all over the country, continuing the fight:

I cannot for a moment believe that the estimable members of the governing body of the Cleveland Orchestra could be guilty of collusion with you in your snide negotiations in this case. For Mr. Gingold I have only the warmest good wishes. But whether Mr. Gingold is active in Cleveland or Detroit is quite beside the point. The issue in this instance is your method. To me it appears reprehensible.[36]

The press had a field day with the dispute: "Sympho Slugfests Not for Fun! Longhair Scraps Put Even the Dorseys to Shame" claimed a headline in *Downbeat*. "Cleveland Orchestra Poo Poohs 'Piracy' Charges" wrote the *Dayton News*.[37]

In Detroit, the conflict exposed an undercurrent of unhappiness with both Krueger and Reichhold, among musicians and concert-goers. "Mr. Gingold's departure means a very real loss to Detroit. However, the quality of the Detroit Symphony is unworthy of Mr. Gingold, not due to the members of the symphony, but rather due to the poor conducting of Karl Krueger," read a letter to the *Free Press* from February 21, 1947.[38]

The ruckus eventually died down, and the DSO management focused on more positive news. In December 1947 the winner of the $25,000 prize in the "Symphony of the Americas" contest, which had been

## CONCERTMASTER: OTIS IGELMAN (1947–49)

Otis Igelman is one of the lesser-known concertmasters in DSO history. He was born in Indiana in 1905, and showed great promise as a young violinist. After winning the National Federation of Music Clubs competition in 1922, he joined the DSO as its youngest member, just eighteen years old. He left Detroit in 1945 and moved first to California, where played for radio performances and with the Los Angeles Philharmonic, then was hired by the Utah Symphony as assistant conductor and concertmaster.

In 1947, he was hired by Karl Krueger to replace Josef Gingold, telling the press, "I consider Mr. Igelman one of the most outstanding violinistic talents that America has produced." Igelman made his debut as concertmaster in October 1947, in the Glazunov Concerto. He and cellist Georges Miquelle shared the stage in 1949 to perform Brahms Double Concerto, but unfortunately, Igelman's tenure as concertmaster was short-lived: the orchestra went out of business later that year.

Source: Anne Mischakoff Herles, *America's Concertmasters* (Sterling Heights, MI: Harmonie Park Press, 2007), 222.

## THE TWILIGHT SUMMER CONCERT SERIES

One of Reichhold's innovations for the DSO was the Twilight Summer Concert Series, which took place at the University of Detroit stadium in the 1940s, representing one of the earliest attempts at a summer concert series outside of Belle Isle and the Fairgrounds during the war years. An undated article from the *Musical Leader*, a Chicago-based magazine published from 1900 to 1967, describes the concerts:

Under the guiding genius of Henry Reichhold, President of the Board of Directors, Detroit Symphony Orchestra Inc., Detroit has chalked up one more tremendous success with a series of Twilight concerts under the sponsorship of the Grinnell Foundation of Music.

Our hats are off to Henry Reichhold, Karl Krueger and everyone who planned and executed this "magic" . . . who are applying the American ideal to music . . . who are designing musical programs not only for the few but for the many. "Music to speak to the heart of Man, to inspire courage, to lift ideals, to brighten the horizon of daily living." Here in these Twilight Concerts, we have a fine example of the fruits of their efforts.

Source: "Detroit Twilight Concerts Attract Thousands," *Musical Leader*, undated article circa 1942, DSO Archives, Karl Krueger Collection.

renamed the Henry H. Reichhold Symphonic Awards, was announced. Leroy Robertson, a fifty-one-year-old music professor from Utah, won the contest, and his composition, Trilogy for Orchestra, was performed by the DSO and broadcast on the ABC radio network on December 14, 1947.[39]

At the end of the 1947–48 season, the symphony went on a tour of several US and Canadian cities, then returned to Detroit for what turned out to be the final season of the DSO under Krueger and Reichhold.

## ANOTHER FINAL SEASON

As the 1948–49 season began, there were mounting rumors of dissatisfaction among musicians and concertgoers. An article in the *Free Press* from February 1949, remarking on Reichhold's efforts to control all aspects of the orchestra, noted that:

> The Detroit Symphony is unique in the Nation in that it has a board of directors which is rarely called on to function. It is an imposing array of names. . . . The orchestra is, in all essentials, a one-man concern, and that man is Henry H. Reichhold.[40]

Why had it taken so long for these opinions to come out? What happened next indicates that it was because Reichhold had stifled dissent, inspiring fear rather than any open discussion of key issues, whether concerning satisfaction with Kreuger, the expansion of musical activities related to the symphony, or labor relations between the musicians and management. According to an article in *Time* magazine published in February 1949, the problems had been festering for some time:

> For the last three years, some Detroit Symphony musicians had been muttering an obbligato behind their music sheets about the musical methods and tastes of their conductor, Karl Krueger.[41]

*Time* then quoted Reichhold's reply to those who chose to criticize the director:

> Perhaps the American public hasn't learned to appreciate the German school of conducting of which Krueger is a disciple. I like this way of playing music, and it's the kind of music Detroit is going to get.[42]

Then Reichhold fired principal cellist Georges Miquelle in the middle of the 1948–49 season; it caused a firestorm. Miquelle, a distinguished musician who had begun his tenure with the orchestra in 1925 under Gabrilowitsch, stood accused by Reichhold of "apologizing" to guest violinist Erica Morini for a substandard performance of the DSO, which had accompanied her in the Tchaikovsky Violin Concerto in January 1949. Although both Miquelle and

Morini denied the accusation, Reichhold fired the cellist for what he claimed was "disloyalty" to Krueger.[43]

But it was the way that he fired Miquelle, who had already agreed to resign at the end of the season, that shocked, then riveted the attention of Detroit and the entire country. According to the article in *Time*, Reichhold stormed across the stage at Miquelle after a rehearsal, shouting, "Out! Out! Out! Right now! You're through! Get the hell out of here and don't come back!"[44]

The other musicians were threatened with dismissal, too: "I think a good shake-up and house cleaning is just what the Detroit Symphony needs," thundered the president of Detroit Orchestra Inc. "Troublemakers had better resign now before I fire them."[45]

Such expressions did little to help relations between the orchestra and Reichhold, which had become understandably strained. The American Federation of Musicians' Detroit chapter disbanded the negotiating committee that had been working on a contract with management. The next move was Reichhold's, who canceled the 1949 spring tour, though he claimed it was not related to the union's action.[46]

The press continued to follow the deteriorating situation and its effect on the DSO's performances. Shortly after Miquelle was fired, the critic for the *Detroit Times*, Harvey Taylor, wrote a review of a concert in which he complained that the orchestra's playing was "a morass of spotty mediocrity . . . the low point of the season."[47]

Reichhold's response to Taylor's review caused even more controversy. Following the next concert, he confronted the musicians backstage, telling them: "This is an ultimatum. Either the orchestra does something immediately about the press, or 90 men will be out of a job. Dr. Krueger and I have fought bad publicity long enough. Now it's up to you."[48]

He ordered the musicians to support the orchestra against any criticism, then ordered them to sign a paper demanding that the *Times* critic be banned from any further concerts. Several contacted Taylor, who delightedly printed the entire story on the front page of the paper. Under the headline, "Reichhold 'Lowers Boom' on Symphony: Asks Curb on Critic," Taylor began, "The Detroit Symphony Orchestra has a new problem today, and it's a beaut."[49]

Krueger and Reichhold met with the press and tried to control the damage, but Reichhold wasn't through expressing his will. He continued to threaten the musicians, claiming that if any more news of the internal problems of the organization leaked to the press, he would withdraw his funding.

But the end was near: even though Reichhold announced on February 8, 1949, that there would be a full season the following year, just two weeks later he fired all the musicians. He did this, he claimed, to clear the way for a new labor contract, one that offered them a season that was five weeks shorter than the previous year's, and paid $15 less in minimum pay.[50]

As the story continued to play out in the press, the *DAC News*, which had published a positive profile of Reichhold in 1946, now took one of the club's own members to task:

> The one-man band parading under the aegis of the Detroit Symphony Orchestra may have played its last notes. Finally, the dissension, uncertainty, and contradictions produced by the unconventional methods of operation which have characterized the Orchestra for the past several years have pyramided into a situation that can only mean the end.[51]

The article outlined both the positive and negative aspects of Reichhold's management style:

> Mr. Reichhold has made of his presidency of the organization a reign of contradictions. He has brought to it, in many cases, rare enthusiasm, genius, and sincerity of purpose; but in others, mere flamboyance and a tinselly glitter covering an inferior product.
>
> Largely, however, the fortune which could have been concen-

trated on building a really outstanding symphonic orchestra was channeled into a bewildering network of projects—a magazine, two recording outfits, a nationwide broadcast—all of which failed to accomplish what was supposed to be their prime purpose, that of making the Detroit Symphony both great and self-supporting.[52]

Krueger, too, came in for criticism, faulted for his lack of musicianship as a conductor:

> [The] anemic and uninspiring direction of Mr. Krueger could not, and cannot, bring out the best in his men. Critics knew that and so did all the symphonic fans in town.[53]

By June 1949, there was still no contract between Reichhold and the musicians. A new organization, the Detroit Philharmonic Society, was formed to provide financial support for the DSO if no agreement was signed. And the Detroit Federation of Musicians financed the five-week concert series at the Fairgrounds that summer, keeping some semblance of symphonic music alive while negotiations continued.[54]

In August, Reichhold claimed that there was little chance that the DSO would have another season:

> Let's face it and call a spade a spade. We're flat broke, there are

not even tangible promises of money, and—as far as I can see it now—the symphony is all washed up. Apparently, if I don't support the musicians single-handed, Detroiters don't care enough about their orchestra to make a move.[55]

Blind to any fault on his part, Reichhold continued, calling the situation a "shocking disgrace," of which all Detroiters "should be ashamed."[56]

In September, Karl Krueger resigned as conductor of the DSO, making his announcement in a New York newspaper. Claiming that he had "better uses for his time than combating tawdry intrigues of disappointed and obscure local musicians," he left Detroit for New York, where he became the director of a new ensemble, the American Arts Orchestra of New York. [57]

Reichhold, who found out about Krueger's plans in the newspaper, was blindsided by the resignation. He sought the help of the American Federation of Musicians to try to hammer out a contract with the musicians and continue the orchestra. But no agreement could be reached.

At last, Reichhold, too, gave up. He submitted his resignation as president of the Detroit Orchestra Inc., and once again the DSO went out of business, for the third time in its history.

In leaving, Reichhold took a final swipe at his and Krueger's detractors, claiming:

> Those Detroiters who reputedly refused to support the orchestra because of Krueger's presence as conductor haven't that argument any more. His resignation may save the situation. At least we'll know whether those potential supporters were sincerely opposed to Kreuger or bluffing.[58]

Georges Miquelle issued a statement in support of the resignations:

> I consider that all the troubles the orchestra has gone through are due to the incompetence of Karl Krueger.
>
> It is now possible to go ahead and build a new orchestra, under a first-class conductor. And it must be maintained by a board of sensible and responsible citizens who realize that nothing but a first-class orchestra and a number one conductor will obtain public support in Detroit.[59]

What Miquelle had predicted did eventually come true, but it would be two long and dreary years before the DSO would reemerge and know an era of greatness once again.

# Another Rebirth, 1952–63

## The "Detroit Plan," Paul Paray, and a New Golden Age

There has been an economic revolution in this country. The so-called wealthy people, who in the past have financed the deficits of symphony orchestras, grand operas, and were the large contributors of all civic enterprises, have been drastically curtailed by taxes. It was therefore imperative that we turn to the source of money, which is now, obviously, corporations, foundations, the community at large, and labor.

John B. Ford, "The Detroit Story"[1]

IN 1949, THE DETROIT SYMPHONY ORCHESTRA WENT OUT OF BUSI-ness for a third time, following the troubled tenure of Henry Reichhold, a millionaire industrialist who had, in the words of critic Bernard Asbell, "agreed to pay the fiddlers—and proceeded to call the tune."[2] The paradigm that he presented—a wealthy patron who was the single largest contributor, with the single greatest clout in making decisions about music and management—had proven to be untenable.

From 1949 to 1951 there was no symphony orchestra in the nation's fourth largest city. About thirty members of the old DSO continued to perform as the "Little Symphony," but they certainly could not replace, in size or scope, the offerings of a full orchestra.

Then, in April 1951, the stirrings of a new movement to bring back the DSO began. The Women's Association of the Detroit Symphony Orchestra had stayed together and stayed committed to raising money for the DSO's next incarnation. They met with Jerome Remick Jr., whose father had been one of the earliest and most important members of the Detroit Symphony Society, and who had served as its president and helped finance Orchestra Hall.

The Women's Association told Remick that they stood ready to start a drive to raise $250,000 to bring back the symphony, but first they wanted him to find someone who could lead the initiative. Remick chose John B. Ford Jr.[3]

## JOHN B. FORD JR.

John B. Ford Jr. was a member of what Detroiters still call the "Chemical" or "Salt" Fords, to distinguish them from the unrelated family of carmaker Henry Ford. He was a descendent of John Baptiste Ford, an industrialist who made his fortune in glass in the nineteenth century. He had come to Michigan in the late 1800s to build the Michigan Alkali Company, later Wyandotte Chemical, along the Detroit River, choosing the site to take advantage of its rich deposits of salt and soda ash, which were crucial to glassmaking.[4]

In 1951, John B. Ford Jr. was a major civic leader in Detroit: an executive at Wyandotte Chemical, a founder of the National Bank of Detroit, and a longtime supporter of the DSO. He had been a member of the Board of Directors of the Detroit Symphony Society, which had folded in 1943, when Reichhold took over the DSO. He could also remember "in the early days of Ossip Gabrilowitsch when the boxes were auctioned off and at the end of the season a small group of men and women would make up the deficit."[5] So, when Remick approached him, Ford had been mulling over the symphony and its recent fate, and knew the time had come to develop an entirely new approach to the financing and running of an orchestra.

## "THE DETROIT PLAN"

"I felt that a new method of financing symphony orchestras was imperative," Ford wrote in a document titled "The Detroit Story." Then, he made the iconic comment that begins this chapter: "There has been an economic revolution in this country." With income tax rates for the richest Americans topping out at eighty-seven percent in 1951, there were far fewer wealthy patrons who could freely fund a symphony orchestra. Instead, Ford recommended a new model: a coalition of "corporations, foundations, the community at large, and labor."

Ford based his financial model on the highly successful fundraising of the United

Foundation. It had been established in 1949 as an independent entity that raised money for a coalition of aid and human services organizations through a funding campaign known as the "Torch Drive."[6] Detroit was the first major city to organize a United Foundation drive, and its success left many in the area, including John B. Ford Jr., deeply impressed. He called it "the soundest plan for civic giving yet developed in this country."

Ford outlined what he called the "Detroit Plan" which was based on the United Foundation's model with one important exception: each of the organizations, called "sponsors," would contribute the same amount—$10,000—and each would be entitled to a seat on both the Board of Directors and the Policy and Finance Committee. Further, Ford stipulated that the votes be of equal value "so that there could be no criticism of any one organization dominating the policy of the orchestra."

The sponsors would also agree to fund the orchestra for three years, allowing for a stability of funding necessary to secure performance space, union contracts, and the hiring of a permanent conductor.[7]

As described in the plan, Ford made a truly inspired move: the first organization he approached was the Detroit Federation of Musicians, the symphony musicians' union, through their president, Eduard Werner. Werner and his membership agreed wholeheartedly to the new model,

and signed on as a sponsor. Then Ford approached the leaders of major corporations in the city, winning their support. That first roster of sponsors included most of the major companies in the city: Briggs Manufacturing, Bundy Tubing, Chrysler Corporation, Cunningham Drug Stores, Detroit Edison, the *Detroit News*, Ford Motor Company, the Ford Foundation, Fruehauf, General Motors, Great Lakes Steel, J. L. Hudson, S. S. Kresge, the Kresge Foundation, the McGregor Fund, Manufacturers National Bank, Michigan Consolidated Gas, National Bank of Detroit, Packard Motor, Parke Davis, Pfeiffer Brewing, Sam's, Stroh's, the Women's Association of the DSO, and Wyandotte Chemical. And in every case, it was the presidents of these organizations who became members of the Board of Directors.[8]

Next, Ford approached the leaders of the City of Detroit. He stated that since the orchestra "was to be Detroit's own orchestra, we felt that the City of Detroit alone should be asked to contribute more than any of the sponsors." The city readily agreed.

Over a span of just twelve days, Ford received pledges amounting to $250,000; it was a spectacular success, but there was even more good news to come. The Women's Association was asked to approach the citizens of Detroit to add another $100,000 to the fund. They began a drive to raise money from specific groups, including doctors, lawyers, and small businesses, as well as individuals. The Women's

Association also met with great success, raising $15,000 more than their goal.[9]

The money raised was put to use right away: the musicians signed a three-year contract and the DSO rented Masonic Temple for a three-year series of concerts. Ford, as president of Detroit Symphony Orchestra, Inc., hired Howard Harrington as the new manager. Harrington, who came to Detroit after several successful years as head of the Indianapolis Symphony, set to work.[10] Valter Poole was once again named associate conductor, and most of the old DSO members were hired back to play.

Among those hired back was Georges Miquelle, whose tempestuous firing by Reichhold had garnered national headlines. Now, he was back as principal cellist, as the rebuilding of the orchestra continued.[11] One major new hire was Mischa Mischakoff as concertmaster. Mischakoff was a Russian-born and conservatory-trained violinist, who was concertmaster of the NBC Symphony under Arturo Toscanini. Mischakoff, who began playing with the DSO full-time at the end of the season, saw to it that his standmate from NBC, Henri Nosco, also joined the orchestra, and Nosco became the orchestra's concertmaster until Mischakoff's contract with NBC was fulfilled.[12]

Next, the search was on to find a new conductor for the new DSO. A series of guest conductors were engaged, with three—Paul Paray, Jonel Perlea, and Victor de Sabata—competing for the job of permanent conductor. Paray perhaps had an edge in the competition because the DSO had hired him as the musical adviser to the orchestra, so he was already making decisions regarding repertoire and guest soloists in preparation for the new season.

As that contest played out, the orchestra reestablished itself as the premier musical force in Detroit, its return a triumph of the city's cultural and industrial progress, and a tribute to the coalition of business sponsors whose sense of civic pride and responsibility brought about its rebirth, all in time for the 250th birthday of the city, July 24, 1951.[13]

## A NEW PARADIGM OF SUPPORT

The programs for the new season contained information about each concert, each guest conductor and soloist, but also much more. Each one also contained an editorial from one of the corporate sponsors of the new DSO. The first, from the City of Detroit, praised the group efforts of those sponsors: "Their faith made reality the dream of returning a great musical instrument to the community. Their civic action is an example of community betterment envied throughout the country." The editorial claimed "our new symphony is a possession of the people of the city," a source of civic effort and civic pride, which, perhaps most importantly, is shared at every level of its citizens: "ev-

## CONCERTMASTER: MISCHA MISCHAKOFF (1952–68)

When Mischa Mischakoff joined the DSO in 1952, he was considered the leading concertmaster in the country, and was well known to many Americans as the concertmaster of Arturo Toscanini's NBC Symphony Orchestra and the Chautauqua Symphony through their weekly broadcasts.

Mischakoff had been born on April 3, 1895, in Poskurov, Russia, and studied at the St. Petersburg Conservatory, whose distinguished alumni included Ossip Gabrilowitsch and Neeme Järvi. He graduated in 1912 and made his debut in Berlin the same year. Immigrating to the United States in 1921, he began a distinguished career as concertmaster of several major American orchestras, including the New York Symphonic Orchestra from 1924 to 1927, the Philadelphia Orchestra from 1927 to 1929, the Chicago Symphony from 1930 to 1936, and the NBC Orchestra from 1937 to 1952. (As an interesting side note, he changed his last name from Fischberg to Mischakoff soon after his arrival in America because there were so many violinists named Fischberg at the time.)

In 1951, when he was first approached to become the concertmaster of the DSO, it was rumored that Toscanini might retire, and, according to Mischakoff's daughter Anne Mischakoff Heiles, he was torn between his loyalty to Toscanini and his desire for stable employment. He was offered a good salary to come to Detroit, but other orchestras, including Chicago and Philadelphia, wanted him, too.

Mischakoff ultimately decided on Detroit for a number of reasons: the uncertainty regarding Toscanini's future, the personal guarantee of John B. Ford of a five-year contract, the lighter concert schedule in Detroit compared with other orchestras, and the promise that he would have an important role in developing the string section and the orchestra into a world-class ensemble.

Mischakoff signed a contract to come to Detroit in 1951, but had to remain with the NBC Orchestra for one more year to fulfill his obligations there, so the concertmaster's job was filled during that time by Henri Nosco. When he did arrive in 1952, he inaugurated a "golden age" of his own, raising the level of string playing through rehearsing, training, and teaching, as well as what he felt was a major responsibility, to "produce qualified players for the future," as related by Anne Mischakoff Heiles.

In an interview with the *Detroit Times* in 1951, Mischakoff provided a fascinating glimpse into the process he used in auditioning string players for the DSO. He told the reporter:

> When I audition [players] for an orchestra, I don't look principally for stunning virtuosity. I look for flexibility, good taste in playing, and above all the ability to adjust to new instructions—which is what every symphony man must be able to do. I gauge a man's value to the orchestra more by his ability to play Bach, Mozart, and Brahms than by his ability to play a spectacular concerto brilliantly.

The string section he formed was the foundation for the outstanding ensemble under Paul Paray, which won accolades in concerts and on recordings for its rich, resonant, virtuosic playing. Mischakoff continued as concertmaster with the DSO under Sixten Ehrling as well, retiring in 1968, at the age of seventy-three.

Sources: Anne Mischakoff Heiles, *America's Concertmasters* (Sterling Heights: Harmonie Park Press, 2007), 222–25; *New York Times*, February 3, 1981; *Baker's Biographical Dictionary of Musicians.* (New York: Schirmer, 2001); *Detroit Times*, September 4, 1951.

eryone may share in the pleasure it affords and share in its support."

Gone are references to the wealthy elites who had formed the backbone of support for the DSO since its inception. Instead, each sponsor outlined the support given by their companies, from the ranks of the executives to the rank-and-file.

In their editorials published in the programs, the sponsors declared their support for the DSO as part of their responsibilities to those they employed and to the region.

Briggs Manufacturing Company's editorial stressed its commitment to the "welfare of its people and the fact that a company can and should be a good citizen of its community," outlining the support for civic affairs by all ranks of employees within the company. In an example of the idea that prosperity for companies "lifts all boats," the editorial further notes its shared goal of promoting "a higher standard of living for all."

Similarly, the profile of the Bundy Tubing Company noted its history, its production statistics, and the "obligations of a successful organization." It stressed that it provides "good pay and ideal working conditions" brought about by "thoughtful decisions of Management," as embodied in its president, Wendell W. Anderson, who, as was the case with all the sponsoring organizations, served on the Board of Directors of the DSO.

Chrysler's editorial noted with pride that some "380,000 men, women, and children in Detroit gain their livelihood directly or indirectly through the work of the company," and that "playing a part in Detroit's civic and cultural life has always been important to the company." Cunningham Drugs predicted in its profile that the return of the symphony "will make for better neighbors, better friends, better families, and a better Detroit."

Detroit Edison's profile outlined the long-time links between the utility and the orchestra, from it executive ranks on down, noting that Valter Poole conducted the Edison company symphony, its Glee Club performed with the DSO at Orchestra Hall in the 1930s, and that both the Detroit Symphony and Detroit Edison were developed "on the firm foundation of community service and community betterment."

The DSO's first sponsor under the "Detroit Plan," the Detroit Federation of Musicians, proudly described its long history in Detroit in its editorial. An equal partner in the "public-spirited and culture-conscious corporations" who have funded the symphony's reemergence, the union also described its benevolent efforts on behalf of war bonds, veterans, and other charitable organizations. And in the spirit of the other sponsors, it also proudly stands by its efforts to insure fair wages for its membership: "The Federation has always jealously guarded the living standards of its members," as well as providing free hospitalization and surgical benefits.

The Ford Motor Company stressed its important role as a leader of industry and economic progress, as well as a major force in philanthropy, funding culture and education. The profile noted Ford's efforts to create not just an automobile, but one that was "within reach of nearly everyone," bringing about a "world-wide industrial revolution" and economic benefit for the entire region. After noting its many philanthropic efforts, from Henry Ford Hospital to the DIA, the Ford editorial ended with another impressive example of its beneficence to the city and the symphony: its $2.5 million contribution to the city to build the new Henry and Edsel Ford Civic Auditorium.

Fruehauf Trailer proudly told its history, from horse-drawn wagon days to the world's largest manufacturer of trailers, whose success, a triumph of the "American free competitive enterprise system," goes hand in hand with its commitment to civic affairs.

General Motors traced the history of its growth in parallel with Detroit's, noting that in 1951 it had grown to include ten plants in the city, which employed 40,000 people. It placed its support for the DSO within the context of the "widespread interest in the happiness and welfare of its own employees, and in the interests of being a good neighbor," a proud civic duty.

Like its fellow sponsors, Great Lakes Steel Corporation celebrated its commitment to "Detroit's cultural, as well as industrial, progress," calling attention to the fact that: "Private industry, well operated, provides many more benefits than meet the eye in business transactions." Declaring its support for the DSO as part of its company's equal commitment to providing "well-paid, good jobs for 12,000," Great Lakes Steel also noted its contributions, through taxes, to the city of Ecorse, Wayne County, and the federal government, indicating how its own prosperity and

growth have benefited the region and the country at large.

Sounding a note that still resonates in the memory of many Detroiters, J. L. Hudson's traced its history as interwoven with the city's, from the first days of the Opera House in 1881 to 1951, recounting how its downtown store had played host to generations of Detroiters buying everything from first shoes and bicycles to wedding gowns and washing machines. The editorial proudly concluded that all its employees, from salespeople to elevator operators to bakers, are "happy to help support the Detroit Symphony Orchestra because this wonderful musical organization helps make their hometown a better place in which to live."[14]

## THE FIRST SEASON OF THE NEW DSO: 1951–52

As the first season began, a spirit of good will and optimism greeted the new symphony, now fully staffed save one important position: a permanent conductor. From October 1951 to February 1952, the "contenders," Paul Paray, Jonel Perlea, and Victor de Sabata, conducted the DSO in a series of concerts.

The first was Paray, who, on October 18, 1952, led the orchestra in its first concert in two years to a full house, and amid much fanfare. His performance on the podium was rapturously received by audiences and critics alike. Harvey Taylor of the *Detroit Times*, who had been the infamous target of Reichhold's rage, wrote, "The Detroit Symphony Orchestra reaffirmed that all it has ever needed is a great conductor."[15] The *Free Press* concurred, claiming that "The orchestra not only made a comeback—it bounded back into full form."[16]

And what about the members of the orchestra? According to the *Detroit Times*, as the audience rose to give Paray a standing ovation, "the musicians—although the 'bravos' must have been sweet to their ears—needed no more reward than the rich satisfaction they must have got from making those sounds and to be able to play under a man who could bring them about."

Paray's series of concerts ended in mid-November, and he was followed by Perlea, and in February by Sabata. Although Perlea and Sabata were appreciated for their contributions, Detroiters had a clear favorite: Paray. The French conductor and composer, who had an established reputation as an outstanding musician and humanitarian, signed a three-year contract in January 1952, as both permanent conductor and music director. This was an important distinction, and was not granted to all conductors. Paray's responsibilities and authority included overseeing a broad range of orchestral activities, artistic and business alike, from programming to the selection of new DSO members,

guest artists, tours, and outreach to the community of Detroit.[17]

As Detroiters eagerly awaited the DSO's new leader, Paray completed his guest conducting duties with the Pittsburgh Symphony and Los Angeles Orchestra, as well as in Paris and Uruguay. He arrived in Detroit to assume his new role in October 1953, warmly welcomed to the city that would be his home for the next ten years.

## PAUL PARAY

Paray was born in 1886 in Le Treport, a coastal town in Normandy. He began studying piano with his father, who was organist of the local Catholic Church, as a child. Through his father, he also studied the oratorios of such eighteenth- and nineteenth-century masters as Haydn, Mendelssohn, Berlioz, and Saint-Saëns.

Paray attended the Saint-Evode choir school in Rouen, where he studied cello, timpani, piano, and organ, and also received a full education in the history of vocal music, from the Renaissance to the present. This early training certainly influenced his later claim that "all music worthy of the name must be able to be sung."

The precocious musician composed a Magnificat for Christmas at the age of fourteen. That same year, he played many of the great organ works of J. S. Bach at the cathedral at Rouen. He also began the close study of the scores of recent classical composers including César Franck, Anton

Paul Paray, music director of the DSO, 1951 to 1962. (Courtesy DSO Archives)

Bruckner, and Gabriel Fauré, whose work was a particularly important influence.

In 1903, Paray left Rouen for Paris, where he was a student at the Paris Conservatory, studying composition with Xavier Leroux and Georges Caussade. An early work from the period, a Christmas Pastorale, garnered him the welcome sum of 100 francs. But he didn't limit himself to classical music alone, playing cello in Sarah Bernhardt's theater orchestra and composing popular songs under the pseudonym of "Paul Apria."

Paray's compositions began to garner attention, and in 1911 he won the Prix de Rome for his cantata *Yanitza*; the prize was awarded by a panel headed by Camille Saint-Saëns. Over the next three years, he continued to compose, and began an oratorio based on the life of Joan of Arc, a figure who also inspired one of his greatest compositions, his *Mass for the 500th Anniversary of the Death of Joan of Arc.*

Paray's musical life came to an abrupt halt in 1914, when World War I began, and he was sent to the front as a soldier in the French army. He was captured by the Germans two months later, and spent the next four years as a prisoner of war in a camp in Darmstadt. Denied both instruments and paper, he nonetheless continued to compose, completing a string quartet that he committed to memory, writing it down soon after the war ended in 1918.

He made his conducting debut shortly after the ending of the war, leading the orchestra of the Casino de Cauterets. He made his Paris debut in 1920, and became the assistant conductor of the Lamoureux Orchestra, then under the baton of the distinguished French conductor Camille Chevillard. In 1923, when Chevillard died, Paray became principal conductor.

During the 1920s, Paray earned a reputation as a conductor devoted to interpreting both the works of the classical repertoire as well as modern composers, in a style characterized by lyricism, elegance, and precision. He became so well respected for his interpretive abilities that the world premieres of works by Fauré, Ravel, Ibert, and Duruflé had their first performances, at the requests of the composers, under his baton. He also introduced French audiences to the playing of outstanding young soloists, including violinists Yehudi Menuhin and Jascha Heifetz.

Paray left the Lamoureux Orchestra in 1928, then conducted several other major French ensembles, including the orchestras of the Monte Carlo and Paris Operas, and the Colonne Orchestra of Paris. He held the position at the Colonne until 1940, when the Nazis occupied Paris during World War

II. They demanded that Paray change the name of the orchestra because Colonne had been a Jew, and asked him to name all the Jewish members of the symphony.

Paray refused, and resigned in protest. He joined the Resistance, and moved to Marseilles, where he conducted radio concerts. When the Germans moved into that part of France and once again banned all Jewish musicians from playing, Paray quit and moved to Lyon.

There, in 1942, Paray again defied the Nazis. On May 16, the Germans staged a propaganda concert by the Berlin Philharmonic, featuring German music. Paray and the Resistance organized a concert for the following day, performing the "Sorcerer's Apprentice," by the Jewish composer Paul Dukas. Then, in a scene right out of the film "Casablanca," Paray asked the audience to rise and sing "The Marseillaise." They did, as tears streamed down their faces.

Next, Paray moved to Monte Carlo, where he once again led the Monte Carlo Opera orchestra, hiring Jewish musicians unable to find work in France. Following the liberation of Paris in 1944, Paray returned to the Colonne Orchestra, and he remained its principal conductor until 1952.[18]

Paray had made his American debut in 1939, conducting the New York Philharmonic in a program of French music, to wide praise. After the war, he continued to act as a guest conductor, in Europe and the United States, directing in Boston, Cincinnati, Philadelphia, Pittsburgh,

## VALTER POOLE

Valter Poole joined the DSO in 1927, as a violist under Gabrilowitsch, and became assistant conductor in 1944 and associate conductor in 1952. When he retired in 1970, after more than forty years with the organization, he had conducted more than 1,500 performances; but Poole's contributions to music went beyond his duties with the DSO. He was also the director of the Michigan WPA orchestra, which was organized in 1936 and part of the Federal Music Project during the Depression, and conducted by Poole from 1937 until the project ended in 1944. In 1964, Poole was interviewed as part of the Archives of American Arts New Deal and Arts project, and offered insights about the influence of the WPA orchestra on music in Detroit from the mid-1930s to the mid-1940s.

When the WPA orchestras were formed, they provided employment and pay for out-of-work musicians, but Poole had other ambitions: "to have the project become important and to present music played well enough so that it would attract the regular music lover." To augment but not duplicate the efforts of the DSO, the Michigan WPA orchestra presented many modern works to audiences throughout the state, bringing some sixty new works to the people of Michigan. Poole recalled offering Detroiters their first hearings of works by Shostakovich, Prokofiev, Honegger, Barber, and Bartók, but also of African American composer William Grant Still, whose works would later be recorded by Neeme Järvi and the DSO.

"My aim was to provide music that could be attractive and interesting for the community," Poole stated, and many young people in the state heard their first concerts performed by the WPA orchestra under his direction. Reaching out to all areas and ethnic groups, Poole conducted concerts for and featuring music of the Polish and Mexican communities of Detroit, including one concert on Belle Isle attended by 20,000 members of Detroit's large Polish population.

Of his efforts, Poole told his interviewer, "It developed many music lovers and intelligent concertgoers," a modest statement indeed for someone who did so much to keep music alive in Michigan during the Depression and World War II, and after the DSO disbanded in 1942. In typical self-effacing fashion, he concluded the interview this way:

I will just say that I'm forever grateful for the experience that I had of self-development with the WPA. I probably would have been a conductor just as well but whether I would have been one of the conductors of the Detroit Symphony as I am now I am not so sure, but I had this real opportunity of introducing world famous composers to Detroit and I am forever grateful for that opportunity.

Source: Oral history interviews with Valter Poole, 1954, Archives of American Art, Smithsonian Institution.

and Chicago, until he accepted his position in Detroit.

In January 1952, DSO manager Howard Harrington called a press conference to announce Paray's appointment, hailed by the city's newspapers, with an editorial in the *Detroit News* noting that "Paray on his first appearance in Detroit as a guest revealed himself as one in whom is combined an understanding of musicians, as well as music, with the hypnotist's gift for bringing more out of a subject than he knew he had."[19]

When Paray took charge of the symphony in 1952 as permanent conductor, it marked the beginning of a new era, reminiscent for many of the Gabrilowitsch years. During his first year, he brought in guest artists of outstanding caliber, including pianists Rudolf Serkin and Artur Rubinstein and violinist Isaac Stern. As part of his negotiations to join the DSO, Paray had requested more string players, and he got them: the number of musicians increased from ninety-two to 105, with a season of twenty-two concerts, and prices still as low as sixty cents. Paray also had risers installed on the stage of the Masonic auditorium, to improve the acoustics.

That first year also brought about the return of many popular music series for the DSO, as well as innovative new programming. The Saturday morning Young People's Concerts returned, conducted by Valter Poole and featuring, as commentator, Laurentine Collins, bringing back the role of educator so memorably developed by Edith Rhetts Tilton during the Gabrilowitsch era, exploring and explicating symphonic music for a new generation of young Detroiters. Two radio shows reached thousands of listeners each week: the Sunday Symphony series on WJR, with Poole conducting, and the other featuring Karl Haas offering introductions to each week's symphony's concerts, on WWJ.

Paray's programming for his first season indicated his affinity for the French repertoire, which he had championed since his earliest conducting days in France and included the work of such nineteenth- and twentieth-century masters as Berlioz, Fauré, Bizet, and Debussy, as well as the works of the German masters, notably Mozart, Beethoven, Brahms, Schumann, and Strauss, and such European luminaries as Dvořák, Tchaikovsky, and Chopin.

But Paray also programmed a breadth of music not heard since the days of Gabrilowitsch, from Bach to world premieres of modern works and including contemporary composers, known and unknown, such as Isaac Albeniz, Jacob Avshalomov, Frederick Delius, Gian Carlo Menotti, and Howard Swanson, as well as composers of popular American music, ranging from Leroy Anderson to George Gershwin to Sigmund Romberg, in all covering the work of an astonishing 100 composers during the course of his first season.

In each program, Paray also printed both a listing of the personnel of the orchestra, as well as a diagram of where each musician sat, giving the interested audience member a sense of the organization of the flow of music from the stage to the auditorium, and an insight into the special tonal color of each section—strings, woodwinds, brass, and percussion—and the blend they produced.[20]

## THE MERCURY RECORDINGS

Perhaps most memorable for the history of the DSO, in 1952 the orchestra signed a three-year contract with Mercury Records for their Living Presence label to record the symphony under Paray's direction. These seventy recordings are

Paray conducting the DSO during a recording session at Orchestra Hall, then the Church of Our Prayer. Note the single microphone above Paray's head. (Courtesy DSO Archives)

considered some of the finest and most highly prized performances ever produced; many are also considered the definitive recordings of certain works and feature Paray's interpretations of classical pieces with a style so distinctive that it earned for the symphony the title of the "greatest French orchestra in the world." Rereleased in the 1990s on CD, these recordings continue to inspire new generations of listeners.

The recordings were made at two major locations, Orchestra Hall and the auditorium of Cass Technical High School, situated blocks from Masonic Temple. They employed Mercury's singu-

lar method: for the first recordings, done in Orchestra Hall (which was then the Church of Our Prayer), they used only one microphone; at the high school they used three; and all recordings were made with no equalization, filtering, compression, or limiting.[21]

The first of these recordings, made on February 20, 1953, includes Ravel's *Rapsodie Espagnole*, in a performance showcasing what became the orchestra's signature sound under Paray: speed, clarity, elegance, and precision. In December 1953, Paray and the DSO recorded Fauré's *Pavane*, at a characteristically faster tempo than many listeners were used to, with lyrical elegance and dynamic, sparkling clarity.

One of the most astonishing of these early recordings is of Beethoven's Symphony no. 6 in F, the "Pastorale," recorded in November 1954, which is played at such a rapid clip that it inspired the critic from *Gramophone* to write, "I couldn't believe my ears, and darted to the turntable to see if it was set by mistake to 45 [rpm]." Indeed, the pace is bracing: fast, yet every note is clear and clean. And, as the *Gramophone* critic noted, Paray was following, as few conductors before or since had, Beethoven's intended pace, as stated in his metronome timings in the score.[22] And while it is an interpretation very few conductors have chosen to adopt since, it does make one used to more established readings sit up and listen with new ears.

One of the most highly acclaimed of Paray's DSO recordings is of Chabrier's *España*, recorded in 1960 at Cass Technical High School. The critic for *Sensible Sound* wrote that "Paray's is the most joyous, infectiously exciting, and spontaneous *España* I think I have ever heard." Echoing other commentators on Paray's Mercury works, the critic notes that the recording reveals a "transparency and openness" that proved to be a hallmark of the Mercury catalog.[23] This evaluation was seconded by Peter Gutmann in his "Classical Notes" reviews: he remarks on Chabrier's "fresh and spontaneous exuberance," and concludes that "The splendor

Chabrier: España, Suite Pastorale. (Courtesy Universal Music Group for Mercury Living Presence. Reprinted with permission. All rights reserved.)

of this record perhaps derives its inspiration from the composer—meticulous rehearsal to achieve precision and grace in a context of impulsive joy that beautifully recreates and realizes Chabrier's essence."[24] That clarity and transparency also reveals the quality of the acoustics at Cass Technical High School, which also warrants a few comments. "Cass Tech," as it has been known for generations, was one of the finest public schools in the state, offering a top-level prep school education in all areas, with state-of-the-art laboratories for science students and outstanding facilities for those in the arts.

The seminal DSO recordings, rereleased on CD in the 1990s, contain liner notes describing the work of the Mercury staff and their choice of recording sites and techniques. Of the Chabrier recording, the notes state that: "In these days of extreme recording fidelity, Mercury has proudly admitted that Living Presence recordings reproduce not only the exact sound of the music but the acoustical 'presence' of the auditorium as well."

Here is the description of the acoustical "presence" of the auditorium at Cass Tech:

> At first glance it seemed to be perfect: the right site, well-aged surfaces, full-blown acoustical resonance, an adequate stage for the orchestra. Tests by engineers and classical staff revealed that all these qualities were indeed the assets they seemed, and in addition the sound seemed to have a kind of French quality to it. French music seemed at home in it. In climaxes it was taut, in pianissimo sections it was sensuous. It was so good, in fact, that Mercury moved its equipment then and there, and all the Detroit Symphony Orchestra's last Living Presence recordings were done at Cass.[25]

These qualities were evident in another Mercury recording of the DSO under Paray, the Symphony in B-flat by Chausson. Paray was considered the supreme interpreter of the piece, and in fact was so well known for his interpretation that

critic Steven Haller wrote that "it was Paul Paray who may be credited with returning the Symphony to its classic form, making of this oft-abused treasure a glowing rhapsody of seamless and heartfelt melody."[26]

Another "classic" recording of Paray and the DSO features the Symphony of César Franck. When it was rereleased in 1996, it received a glowing review in the *American Record Guide* from critic John P. McKelvey, who noted Paray's many virtues displayed in the performance, beginning with the brisk pace: "His tempos tended to be quick, and this is (at 33:58) one of the fastest performances of the Franck in living memory." He also catalogs Paray's signature style of interpretation: "Paray's management of phrasing and shaping of melodic lines and his flexibility of pace and sure handling of tempo relationships keep his reading brisk and concise and still not overdriven. Indeed, superb articulation, splendid handling of balances and dynamics, and excellent orchestral playing contribute to making this one of the best versions around, despite speeds that would be excessive in less skilled hands."[27]

For a conductor known for his exploration of the French repertoire, Paray made classic recordings of German masterpieces as well, notably Brahms's Symphony no. 4 in E Minor, which he recorded only once, with the DSO. The performance from March 1955 reveals the rich complexity of

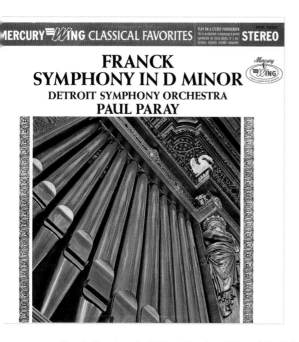 

Franck: Symphony in D Minor. (Courtesy Universal Music Group for Mercury Living Presence. Reprinted with permission. All rights reserved.); Chausson Symphony in B-flat. (Courtesy Universal Music Group for Mercury Living Presence. Reprinted with permission. All rights reserved.)

the string sound, the delicate, nuanced interplay between the strings and the winds, the clarity of attack and articulation in the brass, and the soaring lyricism of the melodic line.

Another of Paray's most warmly received recordings was of the complete Schumann symphonies and the Manfred Overture, reviewed in *American Record Guide* by critic Steven Haller. Haller compares Paray's interpretations to those of Leonard Bernstein, a noted conductor of Schumann, and finds Paray's work superior in many aspects. He contrasts the "effusive embrace of the young Bernstein," with the "far less flamboyant, yet by no means dispassionate treatment of Paray."

Bernstein he labels "downright indulgent" in certain sections, while finding in Paray "a cohesion, a pulling together of the widely disparate elements that make up these highly 'romantic' scores, that coming after the excesses of Bernstein's recordings makes these performances sound fresh and new, almost as if you were hearing the music for the first time."

Haller praises in particular Paray's tempo in the Symphony no. 1 in B-flat Major, the "Spring" Symphony, describing Bernstein's tendency to impose an "indulgent" pace that causes him to "fairly plod" through portions of the symphony. This he contrasts to Paray's "bracing" tempo, which "builds tension" in sections,

## MEMORIES OF PARAY

Oliver Green was the bass clarinetist of the DSO for over fifty years and was hired by Paul Paray. When he auditioned for Paray he was twenty-eight years old and had played in other orchestras but wanted to return to Detroit, his hometown. This is his memory of that audition:

> Paray had acquired two bass clarinet players he didn't like, then I went to play for him, and he liked it. He turned around and smiled at the personnel manager and I thought, "Shoot, I've got tenure!"

Source: Telephone interview, June 16, 2015.

Concertmaster Mischa Mischakoff recalled that in 1962 Paray paid him

> the biggest compliment since I have known him—how thrilled he was the night before when he started *Psyche* of Frank and heard me do certain accents at the beginning of the piece, which help clarify the rhythm, and how conscientiously and always with the same great effort I play all the concerts, etc., etc.—the best concertmaster he ever played with.

Source: Anne Mischakoff Heiles, *America's Concertmasters* (Sterling Heights: Harmonie Park Press, 2007), 225.

Violinist Jim Waring remembered Paray this way:

> In 1953, at age 67, Paul Paray was the Music Director and Conductor of our DSO. 1953 was also my first year as a member of the violin section. For the first rehearsal at the Masonic Temple I was in my assigned chair early and eager to begin playing when from the wings entered this man; little did I know then what a strong and lasting influence he was to be on my life personally and musically.
>
> His walk was filled with dignity, energy, joy, and command, some of the many powerful qualities he brought to the podium and, as I learned, most essential to the work of preparing and performing the symphony repertoire. Following his "Bonjour, ladies and gentlemen," he called for La Valse, a piece he truly owned, having studied it with Ravel himself. What followed was an unforgettable experience for me, one which I will treasure forever, that moment when notes on a page become magic.
>
> From Paul Paray I learned many things on a deeper level than I had previously known. First, last, and above all else is to love the music with the same intense love that motivated us as students and brought each of us to this level.

Source: Jim Waring, "Paul Paray Remembered," in Orchestra Report, 1993. Used by permission of the author.

and causes others to "sing from first note to the last." For him, one hears "more of the sheer joy of the music bounding forth with Paray." In his assessment of the two conductors' interpretations of the C Major symphony, Haller praises how Paray's consistent brisk tempo "brings everything together, flowing effortlessly in the opening pages and soaring straight ahead in the mercurial coda as if in one sustained breath."[28]

Perhaps the quintessential statement of just what made the DSO under Paray such a "French" orchestra can be found in Peter Gutmann's review of the Mercury recording of Ravel's *Le tombeau de Couperin*. He calls it "one of the world's greatest French conductors and one of the world's finest French orchestras playing the very essence of French music." For him, the fourth movement, the "Rigoudon," reveals both the genius of the ensemble and its leader:

> The conductor and 'his' orchestra transform Ravel's gracious and respectful tribute to his cultural forbear into an ecstatic shout of joy. Played deliriously fast yet with breathtaking precision, this is a pure celebration of the apex of French culture—graceful yet powerful; complex yet elegant, understated yet emotional, committed yet relaxed, respectful of tradition yet thoroughly modern, each instrument gleaming with individual pride yet perfectly nestled in the ensemble, utterly natural yet exquisitely polished, deeply cultured yet an invitation to all to enjoy and partake of its wonder.[29]

It was this outstanding ensemble that Paray took on tour in January 1954, performing a series of concerts that took them to major cities in the northeast, mid-Atlantic, and southern states, and included a performance at New York's Carnegie Hall. That concert, given on January 15, 1954, made a deep and positive impression on the New York critics, winning praise for both the new conductor and the ensemble under his direction. The concert included Weber's Overture to the Opera *Der Freischütz*, Beethoven's Symphony no. 7 in A Major, Wagner's Prelude and Love-death from *Tristan and Isolde*, Duruflé's *Deux Danses*, and Ravel's *Bolero*. Composer and critic Virgil Thomson, whose music had been played by the DSO over the years, wrote in the *Herald Tribune*:

> [Paray] never forced his orchestra's sound or strained its balances. He never sacrificed a work's grand line to momentary emotivity. Like a great actor, he "threw away" small

Ravel: *Le tombeau de Couperin*. (Courtesy Universal Music Group for Mercury Living Presence. Reprinted with permission. All rights reserved.)

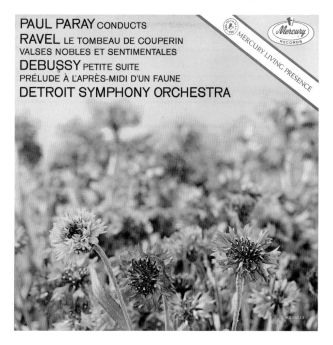

PAUL PARAY CONDUCTS
RAVEL LE TOMBEAU DE COUPERIN
VALSES NOBLES ET SENTIMENTALES
DEBUSSY PETITE SUITE
PRÉLUDE À L'APRÈS-MIDI D'UN FAUNE
DETROIT SYMPHONY ORCHESTRA

effects to make each piece monumental and shapely. . . . The orchestra itself gave off a lovely sound, a disciplined and unified sonority. It was Paul Paray that kept my mind on the evening's music. The Beethoven Seventh seemed to be its old, real self, with all the dirt washed off, its eloquence restored.[30]

Ronald Eyer, critic for *Musical America*, joined in praising the ensemble, claiming:

The new orchestra is a precision instrument of high quality. Its attacks and releases were impeccable; the intonation of the various choirs, singly and in combination, was never in question, and there were the vivacity, the *esprit de corps*, and the bright-eyed alertness of a young, enthusiastic organization determined to make the most of every moment and give the best it had all of the time.[31]

Olin Downes, the influential critic of the *New York Times*, who had reviewed the orchestra since the days of Gabrilowitsch, gave this assessment:

Paray succeeded notably in clearness and perfection of detail, exceptionally artistic phrasing, balance of tone and cohesion of the sections in ensemble interpretation, one of the most eloquent readings of the music that we had heard in many a day. The orchestra with which Mr. Paray has already accomplished so much is a symphony body to be reckoned with in its own city and in the nation.[32]

The musicians themselves remembered their years under Paray with reverence. An article in the DSO's *Performance* magazine relates the recollections of musicians who noted their maestro's fondness for "rhythm": he was known to occasionally visit the percussion section of the DSO "to demonstrate exactly what he wanted." A member of Paray's orchestra, violinist Felix Resnick, remembered his "unique ability to discover and communicate the rhythm particular to each composition." Cellist Mario DiFiore recalled it this way: "Rhythm and ensemble—under Paray we rediscovered our world-class roots."[33]

The year 1955 marked an important one in the history of Paul Paray and the DSO. The maestro signed a two-year contract to remain in Detroit, and the "Ford Plan," which had helped bring back the orchestra in 1951, was also renewed for another three years. That meant that the DSO was on firm footing, both musically and financially.

The conductor and musical director was pleased on all fronts: "In all my musical life, I have never had so fortunate and so friendly an association. Everything that I was promised when I came to Detroit three years ago has been fulfilled to the letter. It is this state of affairs that has enabled me to devote my entire efforts to building the orchestra. And under the same conditions, I can see a future of increasing excellence for the organization."[34]

Paray, who had received a thorough education in choral music and composed choral works since his youth, also reestablished a professional symphonic chorus in Detroit, the Rackham Symphony Choir. Under the direction of Maynard Klein, director of choirs at the University of Michigan, this distinguished ensemble made an important contribution to the expansion of the repertoire: for the first time since Gabrilowitsch, major symphonic works requiring a chorus could be performed by the DSO, including Bach's *St. Matthew Passion*, Berlioz's *L'Enfance du Christ*, the Fauré *Requiem*, and, for the first time in Detroit, Beethoven's Symphony no. 9 in D Minor in its entirety, including its dramatic final movement. It also readied the orchestra and chorus for the debut of their new home, the Henry and Edsel Ford Auditorium, and the performance of one of Paray's major compositions, his *Mass for the 500th Anniversary of the Death of Joan of Arc.*

## FORD AUDITORIUM

In 1955, the DSO once again had a performance space of its own: Ford Auditorium, built on the banks of the Detroit River at the cost of $5.7 million dollars, with funds coming from the city of Detroit and major donations from the Ford family, Ford Motor Company, and Lincoln and Mercury dealers around the country. Designed by the architectural firm of O'Dell, Hewlett, and Luckenbach, the building was set as a centerpiece of the redesigned Civic Center, with the front of the building facing Jefferson Avenue, the main east-west street that stretches from downtown Detroit to the eastern suburbs, along the Detroit River.

The design of Ford Auditorium was based in part on Eliel Saarinen's plan for a Civic Center developed by the architect in 1924 and reflected the precepts of modern functionalism: that "form follows function." The building was designed to look like what it was—an auditorium—and both the interior and exterior were simple and unadorned to the point of severity. In their book *AIA Detroit: The American Institute of Architects Guide to Detroit Architecture*, architect Eric J. Hill and journalist John Gallagher write: "Its visual impact depends on its elementary massing, its subtle interplay of material and texture, and color contrast."[35]

The exterior façade was made of dark granite, containing flecks of blue and set

Ford Auditorium, home of the DSO from 1956 to 1989. (Courtesy DSO Archives)

in a basket-weave pattern, with window-less sidewalls made of white marble. For many Detroiters of later generations this was a puzzling design choice: a riverfront auditorium without windows, and situated in such a way that it blocked the view of the water from Jefferson. As all aspects of the building's design, it was most likely a choice made to adhere rigorously to form following function. As architect Elmer Kiehler said, in noting its shape, "Even the tilt of the auditorium floor can be visualized by the slope of the marble on the exterior wall." Contrasting it to the design of such classic performance spaces of the earlier era as Orchestra Hall, Kiehler said, "Theater buildings used to be rectangular. Now we build them like a slice of pie, and every seat has a complete view of

the stage . . . and there are no chandeliers to distract you."[36]

The auditorium's interior was a tribute to modernism as well, as simple as its exterior: it included bold colors in décor and the sparest use of sculpture as accents. The auditorium itself sat 2,920 on the main floor and the balcony, and the seats were upholstered in turquoise fabric, which contrasted with the gold velvet curtain that ringed the stage. The foyer contained paneling made of wood, marble, and granite. There were also sculptures by Marshall Fredericks, whose "Spirit of Detroit" had been commissioned the same year. The three Fredericks sculptures, made of bronze, copper, and aluminum, depicted three distinct scenes: on the north wall was the "Ford Empire," 120 feet long; the east wall featured "Harlequin," "Ballerina," and "Orchestral Parade"; and the west wall showed "Harlequins: Juggler, Acrobat, and Lovesick Clown" and "Circus Parade."[37]

The building's modern majesty was heralded in the reports that accompanied the dedication of the auditorium on October 15, 1956. It was a national event, with reporting from the *New York Times*, and live television broadcasts of the *Ed Sullivan Show* coming from Ford Auditorium.[38]

Paray and the DSO gave the first concert in their new home three days after the dedication, on Thursday, October 18, 1956, in a program that opened with Beethoven's overture "The Consecration of the Hall." It was followed by Paray's *Mass for the 500th Anniversary of the Death of Joan of Arc.*

### MASS FOR THE 500TH ANNIVERSARY OF THE DEATH OF JOAN OF ARC

Paray first composed a piece based on the life of the French saint in his oratorio *Jeanne d'Arc* in 1913, a narrative of the story of the French military and religious heroine, whose statue graced a church in Le Treport, where he was born.

In 1931, he returned to Joan of Arc, writing a Mass to commemorate the 500th anniversary of her death, conducting its world premiere at Rouen Cathedral, near the place where she was martyred in 1431. It was this work that Paray chose to inaugurate the new auditorium in Detroit,

with full orchestra and the Rackham Symphony Choir.

The piece has four parts that follow the traditional mass: Kyrie, Gloria, Sanctus, and Agnus Dei. Praised since its first performance, it was called "one of the great works of choral literature" by Steven J. Haller in the *American Record Guide* when the DSO's recording of the work under Paray was rereleased on CD in 1997. Haller noted the "unique harmonic fingerprints of the composer" in the Kyrie, which contrasts to the "almost Oriental flavor" of the Gloria, with a "frenzied danse generale, striking in its jagged rhythms and sonic splendor." For Haller, the Sanctus creates a fervor of sound in which the orchestra and chorus seem to "explode, sending shards of sound in all directions," followed by a calming Benedictus, and concluding with an Agnus Dei whose "ineffable beauty and soaring, seamless melodic line" could "make the angels rejoice."[39]

Paray the composer received another important showcase in 1957, when the Women's Association of the DSO presented more of his compositions at a concert given at the DIA. The performance on March 23, 1957, featured three chamber works by Paray: the Sonata for Violin and Piano, the Sonata for Violincello and Piano, and his String Quartet. All of these works were the products of Paray's earliest endeavors, and were written between 1908 and 1919. J. Dorsey Callaghan of the *Free Press* praised the "intense vitality" of

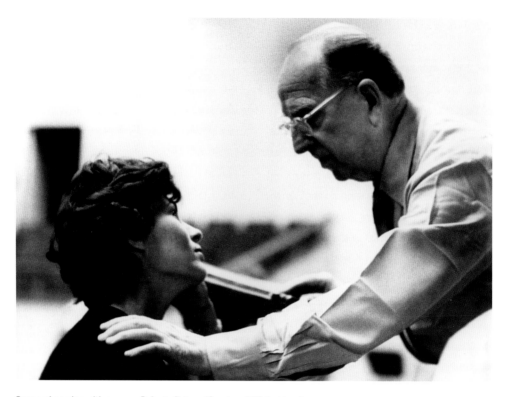

Paray rehearsing with soprano Roberta Peters. (Courtesy DSO Archives)

the music, and noted that, "Even in the questing spirit of the slow movement of the cello-piano sonata, the musical probing reflects an inquiring mind rather than one that despairs."[40]

That same year Paray signed another three-year contract to remain in Detroit, through the 1959–60 season.[41] He also received another award, this time from the nation of his birth. For his work in bringing French culture to the United States, and especially to Detroit, Paray was named a commander of the French Legion of Honor.[42]

In the fall of 1957, the celebrated organist Marcel Dupré, who had played

with the DSO under Gabrilowitsch in 1924 at the dedication of the Murphy Organ at Orchestra Hall, once again returned to Detroit, to inaugurate a new instrument in a new hall. On October 11, 1957, Dupré played at the dedication of the new Kanzler Memorial Organ at Ford Auditorium. The program included the Symphony no. 3 in C Minor by Saint-Saëns, the "Organ Symphony," and the Sinfonia from the 146th Cantata, for Organ and Strings, by Bach.[43]

## PROBLEMATIC ACOUSTICS

Despite its outstanding maestro and growing reputation as an orchestra of the first-tier, the DSO did have problems with the acoustics in its new home, Ford Auditorium, from the very first concert. The same modernist principles that evoked a new era in performance space proved to be woefully inadequate to one of the main principles of concert halls: minimalist architectural concepts, including bare, straight walls and the lack of adornments, lead to poor acoustics.

These problems were noted as early as the first performances. Harold C. Schonberg, music critic for the *New York Times*, called Ford Auditorium "an acoustical horror." "This writer was present at several of the inaugural concerts and departed shaking his head," he wrote. "There seemed to be no reverberation in the hall, bass notes could not be heard and there was no warmth to the sound." He noted the faults in the very design of the hall: the single balcony shaped "something like a town hall, only twice as large." This resulted in totally different patterns of sound projected to audiences in the balcony and those on the main floor.[44] Schonberg also attended the dedication of the Kanzler Memorial Organ, noting that "it was as if an acoustic blotter had been placed over the organ, and over the orchestra, too, for that matter."[45]

In 1957, Eleanor Ford contributed funds to correct the problems, which resulted in the installation of a plywood shell to act as a better reflector of sound. While many, including Schonberg, believed the acoustics were improved, they remained problematical for years; for musicians and listeners alike the problem was not resolved until the DSO departed the auditorium permanently when Orchestra Hall was restored in 1989. Ford Auditorium was demolished in 2011, as part of the redesign and rebuilding of the riverfront section of downtown Detroit.

## WORCESTER MUSIC FESTIVAL

As Paray's tenure with the orchestra continued, the reputation of the DSO steadily grew. In 1958, the organization received another important honor when it was chosen as the orchestra in residence at the famed Worcester Music Festival. From its origins as a choral festival in 1858, it was, at its 100th anniversary, the oldest musical event of its kind in the nation. It had become a showcase for the finest national and international soloists and ensembles, hosting such luminaries as the young pianist Ossip Gabrilowitsch in 1902.

The Philadelphia Orchestra, under the baton of both Leopold Stokowski and Eugene Ormandy, had been the resident orchestra from 1944 to 1958, but when its fees became too high, the festival management decided to look elsewhere. That they settled on Paray and the DSO said much for the ensemble's reputation. According to the *Detroit News*, the festival's president, Robert S. Heald, and board chairman, John Z. Buckley, decided on Detroit "because of its artistic growth and integrity and the magnificent artistry of its great conductor."[46]

The DSO and Paray received accolades from around the musical world for its performances at Worcester in October 1958. John F. Kyes wrote in *Musical America* that "Not only were the orchestral offerings very creditable, and the instances of co-operation with artists outstanding, but the orchestra played for T. Charles Lee, choral conductor, in a manner that enhanced the quality of the 250-voice chorus and helped it reach new heights."[47]

The *Musical Courier* concurred, claiming that "one applauds the choice of the Detroit Symphony under Paul Paray," citing its singular style and the "clarity, distinction, and fervor" of its playing:

Mr. Paray's directions, clean-cut and authoritative, produced fine readings. The orchestra and conductor also proved to be excellent as accompanists, a field important to the Festival structure. Above all, one sensed that this was not just a routine job, but that the orchestra was on its mettle and that this was a valued and meaningful experience for all concerned.[48]

The DSO remained the orchestra in residence at the Worcester Festival for many years, and is remembered with great fondness: "The one-week annual residency by the Detroit Symphony Orchestra in the fall was one of excitement musically and socially," said executive director Stasia B. Hovenesian, and included gala dinner parties in which residents feted the visiting musicians. The relationship ended in 1975, when a labor dispute between the musicians' union and management of the DSO brought an end to the arrangement.[49]

## CONCERT AT THE UNITED NATIONS

In 1959, the DSO and Paray received another honor: United Nations Secretary General Dag Hammarskjöld invited the orchestra to play a concert for the General Assembly to commemorate the anniversary of the Proclamation of the Universal Declaration of Human Rights. The historic document was written in part by former First Lady Eleanor Roosevelt, and outlined the UN's commitment to preserving the rights of all people of all nations.

The concert was given on December 6, 1959, and was broadcast to every member nation throughout the world. The DSO performed Rimsky-Korsakov's *Le coq d'or* suite, Schumann's Symphony no. 4 in D Minor, and Duruflé's *Deux Danses.* The soloist that evening was famed violinist Jascha Heifitz, who came out of retirement after a car accident to perform the Beethoven Concerto in D Major for Violin and Orchestra. When Heifitz was asked if the Human Rights celebration had motivated him to play, he replied that it was, but also "partly it was my great admiration for Paul Paray as a musician."[50]

## PARAY AND THE MUSICIANS: LABOR RELATIONS

Under Paul Paray, the DSO enjoyed an era of peaceful labor relations. During his tenure, the musicians' union and management successfully negotiated four consecutive three-year contracts, a record that has never been matched in the orchestra's history. While the reasons behind this relatively cordial relationship are many, they begin with the establishment of the Detroit Federation of Musicians as an equal partner in supporting the rebirth of the symphony under the Detroit Plan in 1951, as well as its continued role in the management of the orchestra from the level of the board of directors. The union was given a voice in shaping policies, both musical and managerial, and was considered an important ally in developing the orchestra into the fine ensemble it became under Paray.

## PARAY AND DETROIT: HIS RELATIONSHIP WITH THE CITY AND ITS PEOPLE

The DSO's success under Paray inspired lavish praise from critics and the concert-going public, but their musical achievements affected the lives of Detroiters in other ways as well. An article in the *Reporter* magazine examined the DSO six years into Paray's tenure. It quotes Kurtz

Meyers, head of the music and drama department at the Detroit Public Library, saying, "A good orchestra seems to give the Detroiter a feeling of prestige in relation to people he visits in other places. The Detroiter is conscious that he's from the city of belt-line production and dirty fingernails—the city of the [1943] race riots but not of the arts. He feels culturally insecure and wants to be assured that Detroit is not in the backwoods."[51]

This sentiment was echoed in the statements of a wide variety of Detroiters. Charles Brownell, the treasurer of the DSO and a Detroit banker, noted that, even though he didn't attend many concerts, the orchestra was "like a good automobile, I guess," providing "pride of ownership." Another opinion was voiced by an attorney who had raised money to support the symphony, who said, "I have my children to think about. Frankly, my work for the symphony helps build a solid position for them in the community."[52]

The article also included comments from the owner of a machine shop, who had given $100 to support the DSO: "All my life I have worked with my hands and made a little success of it. Now the Detroit Symphony Orchestra comes to me to have my name on their program," sharing space with the likes of General Motors and the Ford Motor Company. This was perhaps one of the most remarkable results of the Detroit Plan, described by Cecil Smith, music critic for the *Chicago*

*Tribune* this way: "Detroit's insistence on full representation for diverse social, religious, and racial groups reveals a realization of the fact that an orchestra today must be a democratic institution rather than the quasi-private possession of a privileged group."[53]

For his part, Paray professed a deep appreciation for the music-loving public of Detroit. He felt it was expressed in the quality of the community orchestras in the region: "Consider that a city the size of Mount Clemens or Plymouth can support an orchestra, drawn mainly from the pool of instrumental ability within themselves . . . *c'est formidable.* For ten years I have watched the steady growth of musical appreciation among Detroit audiences. Despite the reputation of the city as an industrial and manufacturing center, it has become an intensely interesting center of musical life." He was also impressed by the variety of music enjoyed by Detroiters: "I have found that in Detroit, discussion of music culture need not be confined to the symphony. A desire to know all the facets of music seems to be characteristic of people here."[54]

## GUEST CONDUCTING

Paray continued to be a highly sought-after guest conductor, and had several lengthy guest turns with such outstanding orchestras as the New York Philharmonic. When Guido Cantelli died suddenly in 1956, Paray agreed to conduct a portion of the remaining concerts of the season. He was enthusiastically received by New York audiences, praise which he deflected with characteristic humility: "I like to believe that this kindness, this applause, is a tribute less for me personally than for our achievements in music in Detroit."[55]

The New York Philharmonic called on Paray again in 1960, following the death of Dmitri Mitropoulos, who had been scheduled to conduct a series of concerts in January of that year. Paray again conducted in New York, and again won praise for his work.

## THE CHANGING ECONOMICS IN DETROIT

Despite the dazzling accomplishments of the DSO under Paray, there were economic changes happening in Detroit that affected the symphony's finances, as well as those of its traditional supporters under the "Detroit Plan." The most significant changes were occurring in the auto industry, the backbone of Detroit's economy. Between 1954 and 1960, several major plants shut down, including those owned by two of the original sponsors of the Detroit Plan, Briggs and Packard. In all, some 70,000 jobs were lost on the east side of Detroit during the 1950s.[56]

The era brought about a wave of consolidation in the auto industry, which resulted in the tremendous growth of the "Big Three," Ford, GM, and Chrysler,

Paray in concert with soprano Elisabeth Schwartzkopf. (Courtesy DSO Archives)

which all remained major contributors to the DSO. But it also marked the change in status or disappearance of many others. In comparing the list of sponsors from the programs of 1951 and 1962, the following names are missing entirely: Briggs, Fruehauf, the Kresge Foundation, Packard, Pfeiffer Brewing, and discount clothing retailer Sam's. Several sponsors had changed their status, moving to a lower level of donation, including Cunningham Drugs, Great Lakes Steel, J. L. Hudson, and S. S. Kresge.[57]

Examining the statements of the DSO's Financial Policy Committee is also revealing: in the 1952–53 season, the orchestra received $285,886 in income from sponsors; by 1958–59, that number was down to $210,461, with a total deficit of $22,259.[58]

These figures help place in context the plea from DSO President Allen G. Barry that appeared as a "Special Report" in the front of the first program for the 1959–60 season. He begins with a statement that will certainly sound familiar from similar appeals dating to the orchestra's earliest years: "All the foremost orchestras encounter a deficit which must be made up by private giving. If

## THE DECLINE OF ORCHESTRA HALL

To understand the dramatic transformation of Orchestra Hall before its rescue in 1970 and renovation in the 1980s, it is important to comprehend just how far the formerly great hall had fallen. Here is a description of what it looked like in the 1960s, from *Stages*, published in 1994 to commemorate the seventy-fifth anniversary of the opening of Orchestra Hall:

An acoustical legend, it was now on its last legs. Abandoned and ignored, decaying from the inside out. The very place that had attracted lovers of classical, then jazz, then devotional music, was now possessed by pigeons, whose nests and feathers littered even the best seats in the house. Its maple and pine wood stage, which had once supported the world's most famous performing artists, was now a runway for rats.

All around, it was a vision of hopelessness—peeling paint, cracked and crumbling plaster, streaked wood paneling, rotting carpeting and drapes. Its singular touches—the *trompe l'oeil* paintings, carved moldings, leafy scrolls, winged cupids, ornamental grillwork, and convex balcony fronts—were all but unrecognizable in their decomposing state.

Vandals and street people had found their way inside, and their trash was strewn throughout. Water damage from the leaking roof was severe. The stench of mold and garbage hung heavily in the air.

This was Orchestra Hall during the decade of the 1960s, slowly but surely dying. A building whose past was its only hope for the future.

Source: *Stages*, 61.

every concert were sold out these deficits would decline but would not be wiped out my any means."

Then Barry makes a very revealing statement regarding the economic constraints facing the lower-level contributors to the DSO:

We now have 2,600 donors as compared to last season's 3,985— a decrease of 1,385 contributors to whom we now make a very special appeal. The number represents a loss of nearly $15,000 in the face of increasing costs of operation.

This was followed by a financial report noting operating revenue of $410,150 and expenses of $801,600, which, minus contributions of $363,000, left an estimated deficit for the year at $28,450. These numbers indicate that the downturn in the economic fortunes of Detroit, which left thousands unemployed and major names gone from the rosters of the wealthiest in the region, also hit the ranks of the smaller donors to the DSO. Pleas for more and larger donations continued in the programs throughout the 1950s and 1960s, indicating that the Detroit Plan, though revolutionary in its breadth and the continuity of the funding it provided, was not the ultimate solution to all the orchestra's financial needs.[59]

## PARAY ANNOUNCES HIS RETIREMENT

In 1961, Paray, at the age of seventy-five, was ready for a new phase of his career: he announced that he planned to step down from his full-time directing duties to pursue guest conducting, and that the 1961–62 season would be his last.

His decision was met with an outcry from the people of Detroit. According to Lynne Mattson, "hundreds of petitions calling upon the orchestra management to ask Paray to remain were circulated."[60] Soon, the newspapers took up the cause as well:

> The utterly spontaneous petitions to Paul Paray to put off, at least for another year, his retirement as commander of the Detroit Symphony Orchestra are proof of this community's appreciation of what that gentleman, scholar, and generally great man has done not only for the Detroit community, but in a far wider field.
>
> The combination in one individual of such knowledge of the literature of music, such toleration of its many schools, such ability to gain and keep the enthusiastic cooperation not only of those playing under him, but also of the board of directors (an entirely different matter, frequently not achieved) is so rare that it is small wonder that the prospective loss of Paray shakes the musical public like the thought of a disaster of nature.
>
> Will he not grant us a reprieve? At least one more season after this?[61]

Paray was deeply moved by the outpouring of support from Detroiters, but he remained firm in his decision, with a few adjustments: he agreed to conduct through the 1961–62 season, as well as the first nine weeks of the 1962–63 season. He shared that final season with a roster of co-conductors that included Thomas Schippers, Josef Krips, Werner Torkanowsky, and Sixten Erhling; Ehrling would go on to become the next conductor of the DSO.[62]

Paray's gifts as a conductor remained undiminished as his time in Detroit drew to a close, and he continued to add to the lengthy and distinguished discography of recordings with the DSO. In 1961, two recordings by Paray and the DSO received the prestigious Grand Prix du Disque, awarded for outstanding musical performance, one for the recording of the Symphony no. 3 in C Minor by Saint-Saëns, the "Organ Symphony," with organist Marcel Dupré, and the second for the recording of *La Tragédie de Salomé* by Florent Schmitt.[63]

Further proof of Paray's enduring musical achievements with the DSO is evidenced by the rapturous reviews his later

Mercury recordings with the DSO received in the modern era. Of the reissue of a 1962 recording of works by Ibert and Ravel, made in Paray's final year with the DSO, music critic and editor of *Stereo Review* Richard Freed wrote:

> Paul Paray conducted the premiere of Jacques Ibert's "Escales" in 1924, and a sense of self-renewing affection for the piece may be felt in the performance he recorded in Detroit in 1962. It comes with the even more magical ones of "La Valse" and four other Ravel works——an especially striking example of Mercury's success in balancing warmth and shimmer, a "round" sound with startling sharpness of detail.[64]

As Paray began his last season with the DSO, he also received the title of conductor emeritus, with the understanding that he would return to Detroit each year to conduct four weeks of concerts. The title was offered by the DSO board of directors in a unanimous decision, and Paray accepted.[65]

Paray's final concert as conductor of the DSO took place on March 30, 1962, featuring an all-Beethoven program: the Overture to *Fidelio*, the Symphony no. 1 in C Major, and the Symphony no. 9 in D Minor, with the Rackham Symphony Choir.

Detroit bid a fond and tearful adieu to the maestro, greeting him with a standing ovation, and sending him off with the same. As Josef Mossman wrote in the *Detroit News*:

> A king of music departed, and was given a royal farewell.
>
> At the close of the concert, the audience arose to applaud and shout for a full five minutes, until the house lights were turned up and concertmaster Mischa Mischakoff signaled the orchestra to play "Auld Lang Syne."
>
> It was an emotional outpouring of affection and gratitude from a public that cherishes Paray for giving Detroit one of the world's great symphony orchestras.[66]

As Detroiters said goodbye to Paray, they looked forward to his regular return visits, first in the opening concerts of the 1962–63 season, then as guest conductor for many subsequent seasons. The cordial relationship between Paray and "his" orchestra continued for several years, then ended abruptly in 1968, during the tenure of his successor, Sixten Ehrling.

On March 14, 1968, during his scheduled four-week guest conducting term, Paray mounted the podium and made an announcement that astonished the audience. According to Morris Hochberg, Professor of Music at Wayne State University:

Paray handed his baton to a member of the Detroit Symphony Orchestra, turned to the audience and, in a solemn voice that was vibrant with emotion but, nonetheless carried to every corner of the auditorium, announced that this appearance was to be his last and that this was not of his own choosing but that of the management and certain members of the board of directors of the Detroit Symphony.[67]

The audience and the musicians were stunned. Because the incident occurred during a newspaper strike in Detroit, it wasn't until several months later that the local press weighed in on the incident. *Free Press* music critic Collins George wrote that despite the outpouring of anger and demands for an explanation from Paray's many supporters, "The management still offered no word of general ex-planation (although it was pointed out that 'for life' was mentioned nowhere in contracts.) . . . Attempts to get true facts from each side are met with either emotion or polite evasions."[68]

Surely, this was no way to treat the man who had, through the quality and integrity of his musical vision and artistry, brought back the DSO from the edge of extinction, and raised it to the highest level of performance it had known since Gabrilowitsch. Indeed, as Collins George wrote, "the management seems to have been singularly inept and undiplomatic" in its handling of the case.[69] It cast a cloud over both the DSO's management and of Sixten Ehrling. And while Ehrling would become known as a conductor who introduced a broader range of repertoire to Detroit, he never reached the people of the city in the same way as the man whose memory still invokes the second "Golden Age" of the DSO, and the phrase, "the genius of Paul Paray."

CHAPTER SEVEN

# Changing Times, 1963–76:
## Sixten Ehrling and the Changing Fortunes
## of a City and Its Orchestra

My objective is to preserve the greatness of the Detroit Symphony as
it now is, and also to have a part in its natural growth in the years to
come. . . . Certainly I have been placed in charge of an orchestra that
is so great that it would be ridiculous for me to speak of changes.

Sixten Ehrling[1]

WHEN SIXTEN EHRLING TOOK OVER THE POST OF CONDUCTOR AND
music director from Paul Paray in 1963, both the orchestra and the city of Detroit were full of optimism for the future: the DSO had become an outstanding
ensemble with a national reputation under Paray, and the city had a strong
industrial economic base and pride in its cultural institutions. Over the course
of the next thirteen years, from 1963 to 1976, much of that would change. The
orchestra would continue to gain distinction for its musical achievements and
its new summer music festival, yet would also endure labor disputes and work
stoppages, wild fluctuations in its finances, and the loss of all funding from the
city that had been its home for almost a century.

During the same period, Detroit began a decline from which it has yet to
recover. It suffered one of the worst race riots in the nation's history, precip-

itating profound demographic changes, including a substantial loss of population and businesses, as well as a major recession, leading to the loss of one third of the city's jobs.

Yet the seeds of these profound changes seemed almost unimaginable when Ehrling took the helm of the DSO. Praised for his youth, vigor, and dedication to modern works, he was only forty-five when he began his decade in Detroit.

## SIXTEN EHRLING

Ehrling had devoted his life to music from childhood. He was born on April 3, 1918, in Malmo, Sweden, the son of a banker, who wanted his son to follow him into a job in finance. But Ehrling showed such remarkable musical gifts, especially as a pianist, that his father relented and sent him to the Royal Academy of Music in Stockholm, where he studied piano, violin, organ, composition, and conducting.

While still a student, Ehrling worked as a rehearsal pianist at the Swedish Royal Opera in Stockholm, and made his professional debut as a conductor there in 1940. The next year, 1941, he moved to Europe, where he studied conducting with Karl Boehm at the Dresden State Opera; Ehrling was able to travel to Nazi Germany during World War II because Sweden remained neutral during the conflict.[2]

Returning to Sweden, Ehrling was named the conductor of the Gothenburg Orchestra in 1942, and in 1943, rejoined

Sixten Ehrling, music director of the DSO from 1963 to 1972. (Courtesy DSO Archives)

the Swedish Royal Opera as an assistant conductor. At the Royal Opera, Ehrling became a champion of modern music, conducting a concert performance of Igor Stravinsky's *The Rite of Spring* in 1950 that, according to Martin Anderson of the *Independent* in London, "put Ehrling on the map; it was to become one of his visiting cards."[3] The work, today considered a regular part of the orchestra repertoire, was at that point still considered with "caution" by orchestras and audiences alike, according to Anderson.

Ehrling continued to promote modern works when he was named musical director of the opera company in 1953, introducing audiences to such works as Alban Berg's *Wozzeck* and Karl-Birger Blomdahl's *Aniara*, an opera about space travel, which Ehrling performed in Sweden and also at the Edinburgh Festival in 1959. King Gustav VI gave him the title of Premiere Royal Court Conductor of Sweden, and, as his reputation grew, he became one of the best-known conductors in Europe.[4]

Ehrling also developed a reputation as an exacting and rigorous conductor, and one who prized "subtlety and efficiency over showiness," according to Allan Kozinn of the *New York Times*[5]; his seven years as music director of the Swedish Royal Opera are considered by many critics to be the company's "golden age." In addition to new work, he presented performances of such favorites as Bizet's *Carmen* and Verdi's *Un ballo en maschera*, and also achieved fame for his interpretations of Wagner's operas, and for performances that were noted for both their lyrical beauty and precision. One anecdote from the British critic Martin Anderson sums up the astonishing perfectionism of his approach:

> Wagner's *Die Meistersinger von Nürnburg* was among the works that [Ehrling] conducted a large number of times. Among the stage-manager's tasks was the exact timing—minutes and seconds— of every single performance of every opera. Once I was shown the book with these entries, a kind of logbook. I could see that the difference in total playing time be-

tween Ehrling's fastest and slowest performance of this opera was less than one minute.

*Die Meistersiger* is four hours long.[6]

Ehrling's uncompromising artistic vision was also expressed in his reputation for brusque treatment of musicians under his baton, which led to his departure from Sweden in 1960, when he resigned rather than apologize for the tongue-lashing he gave to the orchestra's musicians for what he considered subpar playing on their part.

In leaving Sweden, Ehrling claimed that he had been unjustly criticized for demanding more of the players: "At the Stockholm opera, they wanted me to apologize for the way I led the orchestra, which I refused," he said. "I moved to America instead."[7]

Detroit was actually the first place Ehrling visited in the United States. He came to the city for the first time in November 1961 to lead the DSO as a guest conductor, and was introduced in the program as a "noted pianist often in demand as a soloist" and as the master of a repertoire that "includes more than 500 symphonic works encompassing music from the early classics to the present day."[8]

After his debut in Detroit, Ehrling continued to conduct in the United States and Europe, returning to the city in December of 1962 as a guest conductor once again. In January 1963, when he was named the DSO's permanent conductor, he praised the maestro he was replacing:

> Before I speak of my own plans in Detroit, I wish to pay tribute to Maestro Paray first of all. As a student I heard him conduct the Colonne Orchestra in Paris. He played works by Schumann and Ravel, and it was an exciting and thrilling occasion that I have always remembered.[9]

## CONFLICT BETWEEN MUSICIANS AND MANAGEMENT

But before Ehrling officially took over the orchestra in the fall of 1963, a labor dispute erupted in the spring that threatened his first season. After twelve years of relative peace between the musicians and management, the orchestra members' union, the Detroit Federation of Musicians, requested a pay raise, which the DSO's executive board promptly refused.

At that point, Robert Semple had taken over for John B. Ford as president of the orchestra. Semple was an executive and colleague of Ford at Wyandotte Chemical, and he shared his love of music and the DSO; he was, in fact, a good amateur clarinetist. As the chairman of the Executive Board at the time, Semple first claimed that there was no money available at all for raises. Then, he offered a total of $25,000 for all musicians, to be paid over three years, which would have added to the musicians' weekly salary of $140 an increase of about three dollars per week per musician. The union countered with a request for "the same income percentage-wise as the ratio of orchestra salaries to city workers" in the cities of Boston, New York, and Philadelphia.[10]

In July 1963, Semple went to the press to present management's side of the dispute, and claimed that management did not have the money, that the three large city orchestras cited in the union's request had "fantastic box office response, playing to full houses four or five times a week," and that, "In Detroit, we are lucky to fill the house twice a week." He then went on to note that "those orchestras also have lucrative recording contracts," and that Detroit "has not established itself firmly in the recording field."[11] It is hard to understand the reasoning behind that statement, given the seventy highly praised—and popular—Mercury recordings done during the ten years of Paul Paray's conductorship, which were still producing royalties.

By July 9, the two sides had still not reached an agreement, and the Michigan Labor Mediation Board stepped in to help resolve the dispute. When that effort failed, and as the entire season hung in the balance, Detroit Mayor Jerome Cavanaugh presented a plan that saved the season. His proposal offered to increase the city's contribution to the DSO to include payment for the school concert series and the summer concerts on Belle Isle, which they had not paid for before. The musicians

Ehrling onstage with the DSO. (Courtesy DSO Archives)

and management agreed to the proposal, which meant that, in the new contract, the musicians' base pay would increase from $140 per week, for a season of twenty-eight weeks, to $175 per week, for a season of thirty weeks.[12]

### THE DSO UNDER EHRLING

With the labor problems resolved, DSO audiences eagerly awaited the arrival of their new conductor. As Ehrling officially took the helm in December 1963, he made clear that he would be introducing his new city to new music:

> As far as the public is concerned, [my goal] is to get them to know music not played here. You can't frighten them, but I'm not going to give them the safe stuff. I look

forward to a first Detroit performance every week.[13]

Ehrling was as good as his word. In his ten years with the DSO, he conducted a total of 722 works of music, including twenty-four world premieres, a record never matched in the orchestra's history. And in just his first months with the symphony, he led them in the American premiere of Carl Nielsen's Symphony no. 3, the "Sinfonia Espansiva," as well as first performances in Detroit of works by Jakov Gotovac, Bozidar Kunc, Guillaume Landré, and Francis Poulenc. He also increased the number of players, from ninety to 101, augmenting the string section in particular.[14]

Detroiters were mightily impressed with Ehrling, and were somewhat in awe of their charismatic new conductor. In a segment from Edith Rhetts Tilton's "History of the Detroit Symphony Orchestra" published in 1965, DSO marketing executive Cliff Drozda describes the impression he made:

From the moment Sixten Ehrling strides out crisply from the wings to take command of his Orchestra, there is something distinctly Scandinavian about his bearing, demeanor, and conducting. But the music he makes is international.

Ehrling's tremendous physical vitality is immediately apparent. The more subtle qualities of the man's genius show themselves as he works. He has been called persuasive, precise, authoritative, dramatic, and inspired. A New York critic recently said of him, "Ehrling has a strong, ordered musical intuition which, backed by all of his other assets, makes him remarkably apt at his job."[15]

Other critics around the country concurred. Writing in the *Minneapolis Star* shortly after Ehrling's appointment in Detroit, music critic John K. Sherman wrote, "The Detroit Symphony has accomplished the musical coup of the year in signing Sixten Ehrling," and called him "a magical interpreter, a master of orchestral expression, and particularly

skillful in creating the myriad shadings and hues by which the big instrument tells its story."[16]

Reviews of Ehrling's first season with the DSO noted the breadth of the repertoire presented, and a firm conviction that his presence in Detroit was further confirmation that the symphony had reached that coveted status as "one of the country's major orchestras," as *New York Times* music critic Harold Schonberg claimed in February 1964.[17]

One of the highlights of the 1964 season was the DSO's performance of the Fifth Symphony of Dmitri Shostakovitch, a modern masterpiece then relatively new to Detroit audiences. Collins George of the *Free Press* wrote:

The Shostakovitch Fifth . . . is a large musical canvas of the sort Ehrling likes to conduct. It has one of the most astonishing slow movements in musical literature, one from which Ehrling extracted every drop of meaning. It was, under his hands, a thing of great sensual beauty.[18]

Boris Nelson of the *Toledo Blade* also witnessed the performance and claimed:

In the last movement [of the Shostakovitch], we heard a great orchestra. The greatness is inherent and we look forward to watching Sixten

Ehrling haul it to the surface and nail it there for future use.[19]

As Ehrling's first season came to an end, another new chapter in the DSO's history unfolded: the inauguration of a summer music festival, to rival Boston's Tanglewood and Chicago's Ravinia.

## MEADOW BROOK MUSIC FESTIVAL

The Meadow Brook Festival debuted on July 22, 1964, at the new Baldwin Memorial Pavilion on the campus of the new Oakland University. The idea for the festival had been brewing since earlier in the year, when a group of music lovers, led by automobile executive Semon "Bunkie" Knudsen, proposed a new concept for the DSO: a summer concert series "which would provide an opportunity for everyone in the community to enjoy great music of great artistic value at low cost in a beautiful setting."[20] Oakland University had recently been founded, thanks to the generosity of Matilda Dodge Wilson, who, with her husband, Alfred, had donated 1,300 acres of their 1,500-acre estate, called Meadow Brook, as well as two million dollars to build the college.

Wilson and the Kresge Foundation also funded the amphitheater that was built as the performing space for the DSO. It was designed by the architectural firm of O'Dell, Hewlett, and Luckenbach, the same firm that had designed Ford Au-

ditorium. Mrs. Wilson served as the Festival Committee Honorary Chairman, and the pavilion was built near the bottom of a wooded ravine on the property, at her suggestion.

Designed by engineer Christopher Jaffe as a natural amphitheater, the Baldwin Pavilion was completed in just five months, and included a covered stage area, pavilion seating, and a specially designed acoustical shell that could be adjusted to the requirements of a variety of musical performances. At the time, it was considered "the finest quality acoustical setup of any outdoor system in the country," and was clearly superior to the acoustics available at Ford Auditorium.[21]

In its first year, the Meadow Brook Festival hosted four weeks of concerts; within two years, it had been expanded to eight. There was also a music school, which was headed by celebrated conductor Robert Shaw and featured some of the finest musicians in the world, who gathered to study, teach, and perform at Meadow Brook. Members of the faculty included many DSO members, as well as such famous orchestral and choral conductors as James Levine and Roger Wagner. Students from high school and college could earn credit in applied music, ensemble, theory, and music history.[22]

The famed trio of Eugene Istomin, Isaac Stern, and Leonard Rose held a chamber music residence program at Meadow Brook for several years as well.

Istomin, Stern, and Rose also appeared as part of an outstanding group of international soloists who performed in the festival's early years, including pianists Claudio Arrau, Alfred Brendel, Vladimir Ashkenazy, and Van Cliburn; violinists Henryk Szeryng, Itzhak Perlman, and Gidon Kremer; cellists Mstislav Rostopovich and Lynn Harrell; and singers Elisabeth Schwarzkopf, Maureen Forrester, and Jessye Norman.[23]

The festival also produced several new chamber ensembles, including the Meadow Brook Wind Quintet, the Meadow Brook Chamber Orchestra, and the Meadow Brook String Quartet. These were all composed of DSO musicians, who played chamber music during the fall and winter at Oakland University.[24]

Sixten Ehrling changed his summer schedule so that he could conduct all of the concerts in the first season, and in 1966 conducted the world premiere performances of three works commissioned specifically for the DSO and Meadow Brook. The composers had been paid in part by a $20,000 grant from the Rockefeller Foundation, signaling a source of money for the DSO and other US orchestras that would become ever more significant in the years to come.

The 1964–65 season was celebrated as the fiftieth anniversary of the DSO (most published sources at the time dated the orchestra's birth to 1914, rather than 1887), and the future looked bright

## MOTOWN AND THE DSO

In the mid-1960s, amidst all the serious classical music-making in Detroit, several members of the orchestra, notably a group of string players led by assistant concertmaster Gordon Staples, were also moonlighting with a very special, very Detroit group of musicians: the Funk Brothers, the legendary Motown house band who created the inimitable "Motown Sound."

Founded in 1959 by Berry Gordy Jr., Motown was the most successful independent record label of the twentieth century. Its musical roots were urban rhythm and blues, but Gordy wanted his music to appeal to all young people, and it became one of the most successful efforts in "crossover" music in history. With the slogan "the Sound of Young America," Gordy launched the wildly successful careers of such stars as Marvin Gaye, Smokey Robinson and the Miracles, the Temptations, Diana Ross and the Supremes, Stevie Wonder, the Four Tops, and many more.

One of the foundations of Motown's success was the songwriting trio of Brian Holland, Lamont Dozier, and Eddie Holland, who, along with Smokey Robinson, wrote most of the Motown hits. Then, in the small studio at their headquarters on Grand Boulevard in Detroit, Hitsville USA, the composers, the Funk Brothers, and the Motown singers would work on new recordings, often accompanied by a group of DSO musicians, far into the night.

On tracks like the Temptations's hit "Don't Look Back," one can hear the string section complementing the work of the Funk Brothers, creating a sound that is clear, soulful, and swinging. The DSO musicians who played for Motown included violinists Staples, Alvin Score, Beatriz Budinzky, Felix Resnick, James Waring, Lillian Downs, Linda Snedden Smith, Richard Margitza, Virginia Halfmann, and Zinovi Bistritzky; violists Anne Mischakoff, David Ireland, Edouard Kesner, Meyer Shapiro, and Nathan Gordon; cellists Italo Babini, Edward Korkigian, Marcy Schweickhardt, and Thaddeus Markiewicz; and harpists Carole Crosby and Pat Terry. The group also made a record, "Strung Out," for Motown, as Gordon Staples and the String Thing, in 1970.

Sources:http://www.discogs.com/Gordon-Staples-And-The-String-Thing-Strung-Out/release/561823; https://www.motownmuseum.org/story/motown/.

under Ehrling: the orchestra numbered 101 musicians, and they visited Carnegie Hall with their new director in a concert that drew wide praise from the New York critics, including Harold Schonberg of the *New York Times*, who offered one of the earliest evaluations of the orchestra under their new director:

Only last season, the Detroit Symphony Orchestra was, in a way, one of the poorer relatives in the United States symphonic family. A fine orchestra, it nevertheless was somewhat short on strings. But its new conductor, Sixten Ehrling, must be a persuasive man. The Detroit Symphony Orchestra now has a full complement of players. And it has achieved maturity in more ways than one, as indicated Thursday night in Carnegie Hall. . . .

There could be nothing but praise for the way he and the orchestra handled the music. Indeed, the entire program testified to the work of an orchestra of considerable technique, solid musical ideas, and complete integrity. The Detroit Symphony by now is one of the country's superior symphonic organizations, ready to compete in any company. It is well-drilled with responsive ensemble and excellent solo playing all around. In short, it is as good an orchestra as one is likely to hear.[25]

Ehrling scored another triumph in the final concert of the 1964–65 season, where he presented, for the first time in Detroit, Benjamin Britten's *War Requiem*, a massive piece that had premiered in 1962 and that expressed the composer's condemnation of war. The work requires multiple choirs and two orchestral ensembles, and Ehrling conducted some 350 musicians on the stage of Ford Auditorium for the event. Boris Nelson of the *Toledo Blade* praised the work, which he termed "a passionate denunciation of war by an adamant pacifist and conscientious objector," as well as Ehrling's direction, which he called a "cooperative venture of many forces" that "came off well" save for the poor acoustics of Ford Auditorium, which muffled the choirs' sound.[26]

## MORE NEW MUSIC

Ehrling continued to champion new music, at home and on tour. In November 1966, he led the DSO in a concert at Carnegie Hall in New York, in a program that featured Witold Lutosławski's Concerto for Orchestra. Writing in the *New York Times*, Harold Schonberg continued his praise of Ehrling, and also gave an insight into the quality of the sound of the orchestra under their conductor, as well as its strengths and weaknesses:

Mr. Ehrling is bringing the Detroit Symphony smartly along. Indeed, he is making a virtuoso ensemble of it. . . . [They play] with a great deal of finesse, sharp and clear attacks, strong solo work.

Tonally the Detroit Symphony is still somewhat on the hard side. Part of that is due to the caliber of the musicians. The strings, especially, do not have the polish of the very top international ensembles.

And part is due to the conductor. Mr. Ehrling is a very sound man with a precise beat and a good deal of spirit. But he has the kind of musical mentality more interested in movement than in color or nuance. He likes to keep things in motion, to build to climaxes, to maintain clarity. Never is there the least hint of sensuality or romanticism in his conducting.[27]

Ehrling programmed more modern music for the DSO at home as well, with seven world premieres in 1966–67, including works by Roger Sessions, Carlos Surinach, Natanael Broman, Donald Erb, Norman Kay, Harold Laudenslager, and Paul Creston. Creston's work, "Chthonic Ode," was commissioned by the DSO and was dedicated to Erhling and the orchestra.

For the more "traditional" music lover, the DSO also offered a series of pop con-
certs in April, with guest conductors like Arthur Fielder, which featured popular music from Broadway as well as lighter classical fare, such as opera overtures and arias. The concerts were performed at the Light Guard Armory, with seating designed to look more like a nightclub than a concert hall, featuring cocktail tables for four.

At Meadow Brook in the summer of 1966, there were world premieres of works by Kay and Surinach, classical favorites with guest artists such as Van Cliburn and Henryk Szeryng, and large choral masterworks, including the *Mass in B Minor* by J. S. Bach and the *War Requiem* by Britten.[28]

## "VIOLENCE IN THE MODEL CITY"

The following summer brought a very different spirit to Detroit. It was the summer of "Violence in the Model City," as the title of Sydney T. Fine's lauded study on the Detroit riot of 1967 defined it, when a city that prided itself on racial harmony descended into racial hostility, hatred, and violence that left a mark on the city and its surrounding suburbs still felt today.

The Detroit riot began on July 23, 1967, when police raided an illegal after-hours bar on Twelfth Street near Clairmont. A crowd of several hundred African Americans gathered as the men arrested in the raid were taken into custody, and began to jeer at the police. Soon, the crowd was out of control, and looting and fighting began. The police who arrived at the scene did nothing to stop what had become an unruly mob.[29]

The riot spread throughout the city, and Governor George Romney called in state police and the National Guard; when they could not control the fighting, looting, and arson, members of the Army's airborne division arrived to bring order. Over the span of six days, 400 state police, 7,300 national guardsmen, and 4,700 army troops battled thousands of rioters, black and white, who had armed themselves and fought not just each other, but, according to author Arthur Woodford, pitched "a battle against authority, whatever its skin color." At the end of the riot, there were forty-four dead and 7,331 arrested in one of the largest civil disturbances in the country's history.[30]

The people of Detroit, the state, and the nation were stunned by what had happened. What followed was an effort to rebuild Detroit and its institutions through a coalition of political, social, and business leaders, many of whom served on the board of the DSO. Led by Governor Romney and Mayor Cavanaugh, they met and established the "New Detroit Committee," with the goal of developing programs to address an array of problems that affected the people of the city, especially its poor African American citizens. As Woodford

explains, the focus of this first "urban coalition" in the United States was:

> education, employment and economic action, housing and neighborhood stabilization, health, drug abuse, community self-determination, Minority economic development, public safety and justice, anti-racism, and the arts.[31]

Reviewing the programs and press releases of the DSO in the aftermath of the riot, one finds no immediate and official response to a piece of history that had rocked the city to its core. However, a personal account was offered by Beatriz Budinszky Staples, wife of concertmaster Gordon Staples, who recalled that her husband, who lived near the center of the uprising in 1967, was scheduled to perform the Berg violin concerto at Meadow Brook the day the riot began. She remembered that he "almost could not get out of the area as streets were cordoned off and buildings were set on fire. Finally, he arrived at Meadow Brook, quite shaken, a nerve-racking experience for him and a difficult time for all that will never be forgotten."[32]

However, the DSO did take part in an art festival sponsored by New Detroit, held a year after the riot, as part of an outreach effort to the African American community of Detroit. The orchestra moved its first five Belle Isle concerts to the steps of the Rackham Building, across the street from the Detroit Institute of Arts in downtown Detroit. There, in what a summary by New Detroit Inc. called the DSO's "sincere and earnest [efforts] in trying to reach more city residents," they performed concerts that included four African American soloists who had been auditioned specifically for the five-night concert series. The performances were well received by the community, and Collins George of the *Free Press* wrote that the DSO had "inadvertently hit upon a formula to use native talent as soloists."[33]

On November 7, 1968, the DSO presented an important first, for itself and for the African American community. Conductor James Frazier, a native Detroiter, graduate of Wayne State, and a graduate student at the University of Michigan, became the first African American to lead the orchestra in a full-length program. His story was captured in a television documentary, "Milestone in D Minor," which aired on local station WXYZ. Frazier, who won a conducting prize at the International Competition in Liverpool, England, also conducted at Interlochen and at the University Michigan. He went on to lead the Leningrad Philharmonic and guest conduct several other major orchestras.[34]

In the late 1960s, the DSO's regular schedule grew to include an annual concert at Carnegie Hall, where Ehrling con-

tinued to burnish the reputation of the DSO under his baton. Music critic Theodore Strongin wrote of the "well-oiled precision," of one such performance, commenting on the coolness and clarity of the ensemble under Ehrling, and noting the conductor's precise, almost chilly reserve. He begins by describing the DSO as

a very clean, well-kept orchestral machine. Its edges are sharp, its surfaces are shiny and it functions with the accuracy of a computer. Mr. Ehrling himself gives the impression that no complexity would be too much for him. He would get everything sorted out and shipshape in no time at all.

This kind of conducting lays bare the craftsmanship of composers so that it can be recognized and admired. But last night Mr. Ehrling did not go much deeper than that. One could appreciate the neatness. . . . But it was not easy to be moved.[35]

The year 1970 marked the retirement of one of the hardest-working, longest-serving members of the DSO. Valter Poole retired from the organization, after conducting over 1,500 performances, including most of the school concerts, as well as the public concerts at the Fairgrounds and on Belle Isle. He was praised by gen-

The DSO's Paul Ganson, with Duke Ellington and Paul Freeman at an educator's conference in Detroit, 1970. (Courtesy DSO Archives)

## THE DETROIT SYMPHONY YOUTH ORCHESTRA

The year 1970 brought an important new initiative to the orchestra. That year, the Detroit Symphony Youth Orchestra was founded, sponsored by the DSO and under the guidance of DSO bassoonist Paul Ganson, to provide musical instruction to talented young musicians from the Detroit area, and also a training ground for the orchestra itself. As the first auditions got under way, some 350 young instrumentalists played for members of the DSO and local music educators; the 112 hardworking and accomplished musicians who won a place in the ensemble gathered to rehearse on Saturdays, under the baton of Sixten Ehrling, the Music Advisor to the organization, as well as other outstanding conductors.

It also marked the debut of Paul Freeman, who joined the DSO as conductor-in-residence and the first conductor of the Symphony Youth Orchestra. Freeman, who had received his bachelor's, master's, and doctoral degrees from the Eastman School of Music, came to Detroit after conducting with Robert Shaw in Atlanta and serving as associate conductor of the Dallas Symphony. In Detroit, he championed African American music and, during his nine years with the orchestra, was the conductor on a series of recordings with the DSO, which were featured on Columbia Record's Black Composer Series.

Source: Paul Ganson, *Civic Circle*, Spring 1997.

erations of musicians and audiences for his contributions to the musical life of Detroit.

Ehrling continued to challenge DSO audiences with new music, and to take the orchestra on annual trips to New York, where they took part in the International Festival of Visiting Orchestras at Carnegie Hall. In 1970, he led the DSO in a performance of Mahler's Symphony no. 4 in G Major, which was praised by critic Raymond Ericson, who wrote that the orchestra was a "first-rate ensemble, clean and balanced in tone," and its director "an honest musician who does not overdramatize the works he is dealing with." He praised Ehrling's "care in delineating the many complex instrumental textures of the score," and the "fine use of rubato and those brief hesitations that set off a succeeding chord of unusual sweetness or an abrupt change in harmony." Finally, he concluded that "The performance lacked the ultimate seamlessness and tensile strength, which might have made it sublime, but it had its moments of calm radiance."[36]

It is certainly a loss to contemporary listeners that Ehrling made no studio recordings with the DSO during his tenure. The sole recording available is a collection from 1974 that includes Ehrling conduct-

The exterior of Orchestra Hall, 1970. (Courtesy Library of Congress); The interior of Orchestra Hall, indicating the degree of deterioration, 1970. (Courtesy Library of Congress)

### SAVING ORCHESTRA HALL

While the musical future of the DSO was being developed in the new Detroit Symphony Youth Orchestra, a splendid artifact of the orchestra's past was about to face the wrecking ball. On September 17, 1970, a guard at a bank across the street from Orchestra Hall, which had been boarded up after years of neglect, noticed two men working on the hall. He contacted his building's leasing manager, Dick Magon, who discovered that the men were from the water board, and that the acoustical marvel that had served as the DSO's first home had been sold that day and was scheduled to be demolished in two weeks.

Magon in turn contacted Paul Ganson of the DSO, and the campaign to rescue Orchestra Hall began. The group acted quickly, first securing the help of Mel Ravitz, who was then president of the Detroit Common Council, to stay the demolition order. Next, they formed the Committee to Save Orchestra Hall (SOH), made up of musicians, music lovers, architects, historical preservationists, and other concerned members of the community. The group's first order of business was gaining time to apply for historical landmark status for the building. Orchestra Hall had just turned fifty years of age, and was therefore eligible for protection under federal law governing buildings of historic significance.

While that effort was in progress, the group contacted Gino's Inc., the fast-food chain owned by former football great Gino Marchetti, that had bought the hall. Then, just as the Save Orchestra Hall initiative got going, Gino's made a surprising decision. They offered to sell the hall back to SOH and also gave them time to raise the funds to do so, and only for the price they had paid, in addition to the costs associated with the sale. It granted the great old Hall a reprieve, and fundraising efforts began immediately.

Source: *Stages*, 61, 71, 75–76.

ing a piece from a live concert, made at Ford Auditorium, and is one of several excerpts also featuring Gabrilowitsch, Kolar, Krueger, and Paray. Recording was clearly not a priority for Ehrling, as it was for such conductors as Paray; in fact, he made only thirteen recordings during his long career as a conductor. As such, it leaves interested listeners without a way to compare how the symphony sounded under Ehrling with his predecessors and successors; we must, at best, try to glean from the critics just what it was that made his interpretations distinctive.

## EHRLING DEPARTS, AND ALDO CECCATO JOINS THE DSO

In 1972, Ehrling announced that he planned to leave the DSO. He wanted to return to guest conducting and had also been hired as the head of the conducting programs at the Juilliard School in New York. Notes from the meeting of the Executive Committee of the Board of Directors of the symphony in April 1972 include comments from classical music host Karl Haas, who approached the Board and asked that Ehrling be encouraged to stay; that suggestion, however, was not followed. There was instead a motion to engage "a principal guest conductor for two years before a final determination is made." That motion was approved.[37]

However, just one month later, that decision was reversed, and it was announced that thirty-eight-year-old Italian conductor Aldo Ceccato had been signed to a two-year contract as principal conductor of the DSO, beginning with the 1973–74 season. This was an unusual action by the Board because Ceccato had never been a guest conductor with the orchestra, nor had he ever appeared in Detroit.

A "President's Report" in the concert program from the 1972–73 season notes that "A number of our Board members heard Mr. Ceccato appear as a guest conductor with several major orchestras and were deeply impressed," claiming that he was "uniquely qualified to enhance our Orchestra's prestige among the world's major symphonies."[38]

However, unlike his predecessors, Ceccato was not given the designation of music director. When queried about that, Robert Semple, president of the Executive Board, replied that giving Ceccato the title of principal conductor would "give everyone concerned an opportunity to evaluate what is best for the orchestra's future."[39]

## ALDO CECCATO

As the 1973–74 season got under way, DSO audiences met their new conductor. Born in Milan on February 18, 1934, Ceccato had studied at the Verdi Conservatory in Milan from 1948 to 1955, then with Albert Wolff and Willem van Otterloo in the Netherlands, and finally at the Hochschule für Musik in Berlin. He served as the assistant to Sergiu Celibidache at

Aldo Ceccato, conductor of the DSO from 1973 to 1976. (Courtesy DSO Archives)

the Academy of Music in Siena in 1960, whom he claimed as a major influence on his career, as was conductor Victor de Sabata, who had once been considered for the conductorship of the DSO. Ceccato was actually Sabata's son-in-law, having married Eliana de Sabata in 1968.[40]

Ceccato made his debut in the United States in 1969, when he led the Chicago Lyric Opera. He was a popular guest conductor in the 1970s, leading the orchestras in Chicago, Philadelphia, and Cleveland, as well as the New York Philharmonic over several seasons, where he garnered praise as a "graceful, forceful" conductor by music critic Harold Schonberg, who also noted that he lacked a strong rhythmic sense, letting things "get a little out of control," with performances becoming "rhythmically limp."[41]

Just before he took over his post in Detroit, Ceccato acknowledged that the particular way in which he was hired had created a certain distance between him and the orchestra, noting that while he was flattered to be chosen as conductor, "it made things a little more difficult" with the musicians, who had never worked with him. "I spoke out to the orchestra and said I could understand their thoughts, being unknown to them," said Ceccato, "but now I feel we understand each other marvelously."[42]

Ceccato outlined his plans for the DSO: he wanted to "install a Detroit

## CONCERTMASTER: GORDON STAPLES (1968–88)

Gordon Staples became concertmaster of the DSO in 1968, replacing Mischa Mischakoff. A gifted musician, he was born in Los Angeles in 1929, and started playing the violin at the age of five. At fourteen, he began playing for the CBC Orchestra, and when the family moved to Vancouver, he studied with Gregori Garbovitsky. Staples attended the Philadelphia Academy of Music, and after he graduated, became concertmaster of the US Navy Symphony in Washington, DC.

From Washington, Staples moved on to the New Orleans Symphony, where he was associate concertmaster, and from there to Detroit, where he was assistant to Mischakoff. He is remembered as a warm and unpretentious man, able to relate to fellow musicians and conductors alike. His wife, DSO violinist Beatriz Budinszky Staples, recalls, "Not everybody in that chair has the people skills he had."

Staples often performed as a soloist with the orchestra and was known for bringing distinctive styles to the wide variety of music he played. "He got to the essence of the music," said Budinskzy. "Style, rather than technical perfection, marked his playing."

But it was the stylings that Staples and members of the DSO string section brought to their work for Motown that brought them to the attention of an international audience. He called the sessions, "a little thing I do on the side," but he also praised the complexity of the arrangements: "They write very involved string parts for some of these things," he claimed. "It's not all gutbucket rock 'n' roll." His work for Motown was important in other ways, too: it augmented his income by thousands of dollars per year, allowing him to buy a Stradivarius, the "Halir" Stradivari, made in 1694.

Staples performed his duties as concertmaster until 1988, when he decided to step aside from the position, but to remain part of the orchestra's first violin section. He felt that the constant demands of the position had taken their toll on him—"It's like being a 24-hour shrink," he told Nancy Malitz of the *Detroit News*. He wanted to have the "pleasure of making music without the full measure of responsibility that rests on the concertmaster's shoulders."

Sadly, his respite from the demands of the role were short-lived: he was diagnosed with cancer within months and died in 1990. But the Staples name remains a part of the DSO: Gordon's wife Beatriz played with the orchestra until her retirement in 2014, and their son Gregory joined the violin section in 1999.

Sources: Anne Mischakoff Heiles, *America's Concertmasters* (Sterling Heights: Harmonie Park Press, 2007), 227–31; *Detroit News*, October 29, 1986; *Detroit Free Press*, October 29, 1986.

Chamber Orchestra." He also wanted to "enlarge the repertoire," focusing especially on Dvořák, Bartók, Bruckner, and Brahms, a curious goal after the broad sweep of music presented during Erhling's years.

Detroiters got their first glimpse of Ceccato in September 1973. He was announced to concertgoers with much fanfare, with much attention paid to his background and also to dashing good looks. Ceccato impressed both audiences and the Board of Directors, who approved the renewal of his contract in May 1974, adding the title of Music Director, and securing his appointment through the 1976–77 season.[43]

Ceccato took the DSO to Carnegie Hall in 1975, where critic John Rockwell found the orchestra "an efficient ensemble capable of highly musical performances," though "not of the very top rank of American orchestras," lacking "precision" and "sonorous tone." He faulted Ceccato for his conducting, claiming that he was most concerned with "easygoing plasticity of phrasing." And, in a criticism raised by several commentators, Rockwell faulted Ceccato's inability to set and keep a consistent tempo, producing music in need of "sharper rhythmic definition."[44]

Back in Detroit, the Executive Board of Directors had become disenchanted with their relatively new maestro. The notes from the Executive Committee of October 1, 1975, state that "Ceccato will not renew his contract," although this was not made known publicly. He resigned in 1976, and the process began to find his successor.[45]

## THE FINANCIAL PICTURE

Ceccato directed the DSO at a turbulent time in the organization's financial history. In fact, both he and Ehrling conducted the DSO during an era when the finances of the organization fluctuated widely, with ever-increasing budgets; ongoing, sometimes ruinous deficits; occasional surpluses; and dynamic changes in sources of revenue, es-

pecially those generated from foundations and the federal government.

When Ehrling joined the orchestra in 1963, the DSO's budget included total costs of $970,995, income from all sources of $948,500, and a deficit of $22,500. The organization had been carrying a deficit of around $22,000 for several years at that point, but then the funding paradigm changed significantly.[46]

In 1964, the Ford Foundation gave the DSO two million dollars to establish a permanent endowment, half as a gift and half as a matching grant, to be paid out over five years. It was a first for the symphony and tested the powers of the DSO to fundraise in response to what is now commonly known as a "challenge grant." The first contributors to the matching grant were well-known supporters of the symphony: Eleanor Ford gave $750,000 and John B. Ford gave $250,000. The endowment was projected to produce $200,000 per year for the orchestra, once the fundraising goal had been met.[47]

Still, the DSO continued to seek financial assistance from its established base of donors: in the programs for 1965, full-page ads noted that "Every Minute of Music Costs $90" and that "Your ticket dollar pays for only 30 seconds out of every minute," with the other half paid for by "generous contributors." So, even with John B. Ford's original sponsorship program still in place and endowment funds on the horizon, the organization still continued to ask patrons for financial help.[48]

Yet the goal of financial stability continued to elude the organization. Throughout the mid-1960s, the total budget for the orchestra grew at an ever faster pace. From a total of $970,000 in 1963–64, expenses for the DSO grew to $1.464 million in 1965–66, to $1.890 in 1966–67, to $2 million in 1967–68, and to $3 million by the early 1970s.[49]

While there were years when there was a surplus, there were also years of catastrophic losses. The president's report of 1971–72 reports that "expenses exceeded all income by a significant margin," leaving an operating deficit of over $1.5 million and a total loss of $210,000 for the year. In order to pay for the season, the organization had to spend all of its cash reserves, take out bank loans, and borrow against future earnings from the endowment fund to get through the end of the fiscal year.[50]

These were dire financial straits indeed. The report lists several reasons for the losses, including inflation, which was running at about 3.4 percent in 1972, and would get much worse by the end of the decade. The organization had also lost a grant from the Ford Foundation of about $100,000 per year. While the notes from the Executive Committee indicate that the organization's president, Robert Semple, was then approaching the Big Three auto companies for $75,000 each, as well as

appealing to the McGregor, Kresge, and Wilson Foundations for donations, the Board continued to seek out long-time donors to increase their contributions, with a goal of $1.5 million per year for three years.[51]

## AN OIL EMBARGO, AND A RECESSION

But even grimmer economic news was to come. In October 1973, there was an embargo on oil coming out of the Middle East. Gas and oil prices escalated immediately, with gas jumping from an average of forty-two cents per gallon to $1.30, and oil prices rising by an incredible 350 percent. There were gas shortages around the country, and prices of everything, from food to manufactured goods to raw materials, escalated dramatically, as the country confronted an economic recession fueled by a worldwide energy crisis.

In Detroit, the damage was particularly dire. In response to the gas shortages, Americans wanted small, fuel-efficient cars, and the Big Three simply couldn't make the changes to their fleets quickly enough. Car sales plummeted to levels not seen since the late 1940s. It was also the time of the first emergence of Japanese compact cars, and the market share of companies from Japan grew to ten percent by 1978.

The recession took hold in Detroit with a vengeance. Over the span of just ten years, Detroit lost one-third of its total jobs, 208,000 in all. The population dropped as well, to 1.3 million, down twenty-eight percent from its peak in 1950.[52]

All these changes in the fortunes of Detroit had a significant impact on the financial health of the symphony. Summaries in the financial records for the 1973–74 season state that in income and attendance, the DSO was in "last place among [orchestras] with budgets in excess of $3 million, and only one-third of the average of the top three in dollar sales." Ticket sales had lagged, with Detroit ranking twelfth among the major orchestras. Some long-term commitments were cut, including the DSO's residency at the Worcester Festival, because management determined in 1974 that the fee the orchestra was paid was "not keeping up with inflation," in the words of Robert Semple; the DSO ended their participation in the festival in 1976. Yet there were no new ideas put forward by the Board. The answer to the money woes was the same they had offered for many years:

Contributions and grants must make up any shortfall. Detroit has traditionally been the leader in support from business and industry and ranked second in total contributions in the last year (1973) for which complete data is available. Our foundations and many individuals have been most generous. *But* only about 2,500 individuals (1974) have been interested enough to lend their personal support. Seven other orchestras have 2 to 3½ times as many contributors—several in cities with much smaller population.[53]

## MORE LABOR PROBLEMS

On September 30, 1975, the musicians were unable to reach an accord with management over a new three-year contract and began a two-month strike. Their issues were wages and also a greater role in artistic decisions regarding the orchestra. An agreement was reached in early December that ended the work stoppage. It provided for an increase in base pay to $400 per week in the third year of the contract and a fifty-one-week season, but more importantly for many of the musicians, it provided for the creation of a six-member artistic advisory committee and a fifteen-member nonrenewal committee of orchestra musicians, which would vote on nonrenewals requested by the orchestra's music director.[54]

The DSO's labor woes forecasted a new era in orchestra and management relations, not just in Detroit, but around the country. According to a front-page story in the *New York Times*, the DSO was one of seven orchestras that had gone on strike during the 1974–75 and 1975–76 seasons. In addition to Detroit, there were work stoppages in Dallas, Denver, New Jersey, Omaha, Pittsburgh, and Kansas City, representing orchestras from among those with the highest budgets, including Detroit and Pittsburgh, and those with far more modest budgets, such as Omaha.

The article noted that the "accumulated deficits of major symphony orchestras had increased 150 percent" from 1970 to 1975, a figure that dwarfed private contributions, which had risen by roughly thirty-three percent, from $24 million to $32 million, in the same time frame. And how would that gap in funding be filled? The article's author, C. Gerald Fraser, notes that while musicians and management disagreed on many issues, they shared the belief that "Federal support is the only real salvation for fiscal stability."

They also agreed that musicians would continue to demand more control over all aspects of their orchestras. The final quote in the article comes from Sixten Ehrling, the DSO's own former maestro, who noted that it wasn't only the source of funding that was changing: "the power of the conductor seems to be diminishing. All the great orchestras were built under dictators," he said. "Whether they can be maintained with a more democratic system is difficult to say."[55]

In April 1976, Detroit Mayor Coleman A. Young, in a move to shore up the city's finances, cut all funding to the DSO,

which represented a loss of income to the organization of $175,000. The Executive Board tried to reinstate the funds through a direct appeal to the City Council, but failed, which resulted in an estimated deficit for the 1976–77 season of $140,000.[56]

The decline in funding from the city of Detroit occurred at a time when the economics of the symphony orchestra, in Detroit and elsewhere, was shifting dramatically. A study done by the American Symphony Orchestra League comparing the levels of tax-supported grants, income from concerts, maintenance funds, and other sources covering the seasons 1971–72 to 1975–76 is particularly illuminating on this point. It provides figures for American orchestras large and small, from Boston to Honolulu, comparing the data in several categories. For the DSO, it shows income from tax supplemented grants totaling $578,000 for 1975–76, with the city averaging around $165,000 for the five-year period, with money from the state rising from zero to $211,000, and federal grants growing from $130,000 to $208,000.

The findings in the study indicate that the future of funding for symphony orchestras lay in appeals to the public sector, buttressed by ever-increasing amounts from foundations, which proved to be the new paradigm for the DSO. For 1977, grants to the orchestra included $760,000 from the Michigan

## THE WOMEN'S ASSOCIATION FOR THE DETROIT SYMPHONY ORCHESTRA

Since 1918, there has been a women's group associated with the DSO devoted to supporting the orchestra through fundraising, furthering the reach and appreciation of the symphony, and, in one crucial case, providing funding that brought the DSO back to life.

In her history of the DSO, Edith Rhetts Tilton wrote:

> The Women's Association for the Detroit Symphony Orchestra is dedicated to furthering the interest of our Orchestra in daily contacts, in financial support, and increasing the appreciation of it as a force in civic life.

The involvement of women in the organization of the symphony harkens back to Miss Frances Sibley and her group of women willing to pledge $100 each to form a group in 1914. In 1918, Gabrilowitsch oversaw the creation of a women's DSO Auxiliary to be an "integral part of symphony structure," to raise money, especially to buy tickets to DSO concerts for students.

In 1928, the formal Women's Association of the DSO was formed, and it was responsible for selling 1,000 tickets to DSO concerts each year. During the Depression, the Association raised $25,000 to continue the free student concerts and young people's concert series.

The means of fundraising seem a bit old-fashioned by today's standards—fashion shows, parties, teas, and dress balls—but the Association was made up of hardworking, committed women who got things done. After the DSO folded in 1942, the group stayed together, devoting themselves to raising money for the war effort. Their success was phenomenal: they sold $2,270,740 worth of war bonds, and received a citation from Treasury Secretary Henry Morgenthau Jr. for their efforts.

The Association then set up an endowment fund and incorporated, so that they were ready, when the war was over, to commit themselves to the "reflowering of musical interest and activity." They even stood up to Henry Reichhold: when the Detroit Symphony Society folded in 1948, its assets, including instruments and music, were given to the Women's Association and held as part of their endowment. Then, in April 1949, Reichhold publicly accused them of pulling their support from the orchestra. It was untrue, and they defended themselves and the truth vigorously.

In 1951, they helped John B. Ford bring back the DSO through fundraising, and were one of the organizations that contributed $10,000 per year under the Detroit Plan, with representation on the Board and the Finance Committee as well. In 1952, they gave back the assets of the Symphony Society they had held in their endowment—"the music library, instruments, and all orchestral equipment"—to the DSO "so long as it remains a major symphony orchestra."

Founded in 1939, the Junior Women's Association's fundraising initiatives over the years have included a series of popular cookbooks, in addition to galas, parties, and fashion shows. The organization continued to be a major source of revenue for the DSO into the 1980s: in 1983–84 alone, the Association contributed $571,751 to the orchestra, in total revenue from benefits, donations, and ticket and subscription renewals. The endowment, valued at $100,000 in the 1950s, had grown to more than $450,000 by 1986.

In 1989, the Women's Association of the DSO ended as an independent entity, supplanted by the Volunteer Council, whose mission is also to support the DSO through fundraising and a variety of educational and volunteer services.

Sources: *The First Thirty Years of the Women's Association for the Detroit Symphony Orchestra: with Preface* (Detroit, 1958?). Unpaged. Written and published by the Women's Association for the Detroit Symphony Orchestra; Edith Rhetts Tilton, "The History of the Detroit Symphony Orchestra," from Programs for the 1964–65 Season; The Detroit Symphony Orchestra Hall Inc. Collection, Box 7, Folder 2, Walter P. Reuther Library, Archives of Labor and Urban Affairs, Wayne State University.

Council for the Arts, one million from the National Endowment for the Arts, one million from the Kresge Foundation, and $250,000 from the Mellon Foundation, representing altogether more than $3 million in grants alone.[57]

This, then, was the financial picture of the orchestra as the era of Sixten Ehrling and Aldo Ceccato drew to a close, with many issues, including consistent funding, labor relations, and artistic direction, still unsettled. In an effort to grasp, in the words of Robert Semple, "our one chance to go world class within a span of almost a generation," the Board reached an agreement with a new conductor, Antal Dorati, whose tenure began in 1977.[58]

Here was someone who promised a new direction: a musician of international stature, who announced a new tradition of festivals devoted to classical music giants, a return to the recording studio, and, for the first time, a European tour for the DSO. Perhaps this would be the combination of talent, ambition, and appeal that would at last resolve the problems of the orchestra and lead to yet another golden age.

# An Orchestra and a City in Flux, 1977–90: Antal Dorati, Günther Herbig, and a City in Decline

It was after much deliberation that I decided to join you, and I did so with definite purpose and aims. I am proud to serve this vast community and happy to put at its disposal my talent, energy, and the experience of a lifetime.

Antal Dorati, DSO Program, November 2, 1977[1]

WHEN ANTAL DORATI TOOK THE REINS OF THE DETROIT SYMPHONY in 1977, he came to the city with "talent, energy, and the experience of a lifetime" that belied his seventy years. Within months of his arrival, he had inaugurated the first of a series of music festivals that continue to this day. He negotiated the return of the DSO to the recording studio, and added to his own distinguished discography that would eventually number over 600 recordings. And he began laying plans for a first for the orchestra: a European tour, designed to burnish the reputation of the DSO and reestablish its bona fides as a major orchestra of international stature.

## ANTAL DORATI

Dorati was born on April 9, 1906, in Budapest, Hungary, into a musical family: his mother was a piano teacher and his father was a violinist with the Budapest Philharmonic Orchestra. He began piano lessons with his mother at the age of

Antal Dorati, music director of the DSO from 1977 to 1981. (Courtesy DSO Archives)

five, and he added cello studies a few years later. An excellent student, he was admitted to the Franz Liszt Academy of Music in Budapest at fourteen, the youngest student to attend the school in its history.

At the Academy, Dorati studied with two major figures of twentieth-century music, Béla Bartók and Zoltan Kodály, who became great influences on his life as a conductor and composer. When he graduated in 1924, he became the youngest person to complete a degree at the Academy in its history, and also made his conducting debut at the Budapest Royal Opera, where he directed for four years.

Dorati's ascent as a gifted young conductor was swift: in 1928, he became the assistant of Fritz Busch at the Dresden Opera, and in 1929 was named the music director of the Munster Opera. He next moved into the realm of ballet, serving as a conductor with the Ballet Russe de Monte Carlo from 1933 to 1941. During his years with the Ballet Russe, Dorati actually conducted the DSO during the 1936–37 season, when the orchestra accompanied the acclaimed dance company during a tour of the United States. He also began to accept an ever-growing number of guest conducting offers and made his US debut directing the National Symphony in Washington, DC, in 1937.

Dorati stayed in the ballet world after leaving the Ballet Russe, moving to New York, where he conducted the orchestra for the American Ballet Theater from 1941 to 1945. He next returned to the orchestral world, accepting the position as conductor of the Dallas Symphony Orchestra, which he is credited with building, literally from the ground up, into a fine ensemble. In his memoir *Notes on Seven Decades*, Dorati recalled meeting a group of businessmen and one journalist, the local music critic, who was the only one who actually knew what a symphony orchestra was.

He was interviewed for the position in an airport bar, where the businessmen asked him just how much a "good" symphony orchestra would cost. He'd written down an amount on a piece of paper and shared it with them. "And can you guarantee us that it will be a good orchestra?" they asked. Dorati said yes. And what would he do if it was not? "I hang myself," Dorati replied. He was hired.[2]

Dorati spent four years in Dallas, from 1945 to 1949, then accepted the post of conductor and music director of the Minneapolis Symphony (later the Min-

---

## PAUL FREEMAN

Paul Freeman, conductor-in-residence with the DSO from 1970 to 1979 and founder and music director of the Chicago Sinfonietta, is a champion of African American music and has devoted his career to bringing the musical legacy of black composers to audiences in the United States and throughout the world.

Freeman was born on January 2, 1936, in Richmond, Virginia, then part of the segregated South. He once noted the challenges of that background: "Growing up in segregation in Richmond . . . to have fulfilled my personal dreams and to have helped to found an entity that brings dreams to others, even I sometimes can't believe what we've done."

He showed an early talent for music, studying piano at five, then adding the clarinet and cello. He went on to receive his bachelor's, master's, and doctoral degrees from the renowned Eastman School of Music, also winning a Fulbright fellowship to study conducting in Berlin with Ewald Lindemann.

Freeman's conducting career took off after he won the Dmitri Mitropoulos competition in 1967: he filled in that same year at the San Francisco Symphony for conductor Andre Cluytens, then was named assistant to Atlanta Symphony music director Robert Shaw for a series of concerts held at Spelman College that featured the music of black composers from the eighteenth to the twentieth centuries.

Freeman called the experience "a revelation" because it was the first time he had heard the works of the African American composers he would later champion throughout his career. In 1968, he was named the associate conductor of the Dallas Symphony Orchestra, and in 1970 came to Detroit as conductor-in-residence.

Freeman's years in Detroit were distinguished by his work with the Detroit Youth Symphony and his continued quest to bring to light the music of unknown and overlooked black composers. Addressing what Steve Smith of *Billboard* called "a gaping hole in the classical recording lexicon," he conducted the nine albums of the "CBS Black Composers Series," leading the DSO and other ensembles in the works of William Grant Still, Olly Wilson, George Walker, and other African American composers, many for the first time on record. The series was reissued on the DSO's own label in 2002.

Freeman left Detroit in 1979 to become music director of the Victoria Symphony Orchestra in Victoria, British Columbia. While continuing in that role, he founded the Chicago Sinfonietta in 1987, established to give classical musicians from Minority groups more opportunities, and served as its music director until 2011.

Sources: *Billboard*, April 13, 2002; *Contemporary Black Biography* (Farmington Hills: Gale, 2003); http://www.chicagosinfonietta.org/about/paul-freeman/.

nesota Orchestra). In his eleven years with the organization, Dorati made what some consider his major contribution to American classical music. His years in Minnesota parallel Paul Paray's in Detroit, and both of them developed reputations as outstanding conductors and interpreters of the classical repertoire through their recordings on the Mercury label's Living Presence series.

In all, Dorati made more than 100 recordings with Minneapolis, and many became benchmark recordings of individual works. According to music critic Rob Cowan, these recordings "inspire a sense of wonderment to this day," especially his interpretation of Igor Stravinsky's *Rite of Spring* that "raised the roof," as well as seminal recordings of symphonies by composers as different as Copland, Beethoven, and Tchaikovsky.[3]

Dorati became known in Minnesota for his close, sensitive readings of a variety of composers, as well as world premieres, including the Viola Concerto of his former teacher, Béla Bartók. He was a very popular figure with the concert-going public and gave lectures on music at a local college and conducted the children's concerts of the orchestra himself.

Dorati was also notorious for his sometimes fiendish temper, which he acknowledged in his memoir, calling it his "cross to carry." He was an exacting, conductor, who took seriously the "guardianship of the level and the integrity of our music making." When this led to an out-burst of anger at a particular musician, the results became the stuff of legend.

Minneapolis trumpeter Ron Hasselman recalled that when he made a mistake during a performance of Debussy's *La Mer*, "it was like [Dorati's] teeth grew six inches, and his hair just flew. He glared at me and conducted the rest of the piece with his fist."[4] Such anger would quickly dissipate, however, and Dorati was known to take the chastised musician out to dinner to make amends.

While Dorati was making a name for himself as the director of American orchestras, he remained close to his musical colleagues in Europe. In 1956, while he was in Minneapolis, the Soviet Union invaded Hungary, and many musicians fled to Vienna. There, they founded what became the Philharmonica Hungarica. Dorati chose this ensemble to help him realize a dream: he wanted to record the complete symphonies of Haydn. At the time, it was an astonishing idea: Haydn was not the staple of the orchestral repertoire he became later in the century, and Dorati's label, Decca, was very resistant. But Dorati and the Philharmonica Hungarica triumphed in the end: the recordings of all 104 symphonies, which began to appear in the 1970s, were rapturously received, and have sold more than half a million copies to date.

After eleven years in Minneapolis, Dorati moved to Europe, where he became a successful guest conductor of a variety of ensembles, and also served as music director of the BBC Symphony Orchestra from 1963 to 1966, the Stockholm Philharmonic from 1966 to 1970, and the Royal Philharmonic of London from 1974 until his final years.

While he maintained those conductorships in Europe, Dorati also accepted the post of music director with the National Symphony Orchestra in Washington, DC, in 1970. He spent seven years with the symphony and is credited with once again performing the task of "orchestra builder" with the ensemble, expanding its repertoire to include works that were then played by other orchestras, but were little known in Washington, such as Bartók's *Miraculous Mandarin* and *Bluebeard's Castle*. He also conducted the inaugural performance at the orchestra's home, the concert hall of the John F. Kennedy Center for the Performing Arts.[5] Dorati had great ambitions for the National Symphony, including a recording of Olivier Messien's *La Transfiguration de Notre Seigneur Jesus Christ*, which unfortunately sold only eighty-eight copies in its first months. Such artistic aspirations, as well as the financial commitment required to achieve them, found Dorati ever more in conflict with the orchestra's board of directors; it eventually proved to be too much for the relationship between music director and the management, and they parted ways in 1977.[6]

## ARRIVING IN DETROIT

Dorati had begun negotiations to take on the job as music director in Detroit in 1976, and was very clear about what it would take to raise the profile and the playing of the orchestra, to bring it to the "world-class" status the Board had established as their goal. So when he arrived in Detroit in 1977, he had already outlined his ambitious plans: annual music festivals, a return to the recording studio, and a European tour.

A man of grand gestures, Dorati introduced himself to his new city in a note that prefaced the first program of the 1977–78 season. Addressed to the "Large and Growing Musical Family of Detroit," he starts with the words that begin this chapter. He continues in an intimate tone, talking about the nearly mystical relationship that exists between audiences and musicians:

> Music is a demanding art—perhaps the most demanding of all. It could be partly for this reason also that its rewards are so uniquely cherishable. It asks for the complete dedication and one might say superhuman concentration of musicians; it demands utmost efforts from everyone who undertakes to help make the production of great music possible; it also exacts a very definite investment from the listener, an investment of readiness, receptiveness, attention, and surrender of a 'fixed amount' of that most precious treasure, time—minutes,

DETROIT SYMPHONY ORCHESTRA/ANTAL DORATI·MUSIC DIRECTOR

# Beethoven Festival

Program from the Beethoven Festival, 1977. (Courtesy DSO Archives)

hours, never recurring particles of our lives, which we must relinquish to the musical experience.

Looking forward to sharing the celebration of such affectionate sacrifice with all of you, I send my warmest greetings, as heralds, to all friends and colleagues, on the stage, behind the stage, and in front of it.[7]

## BEETHOVEN FESTIVAL

Detroiters received their formal introduction to Dorati on November 2, 1977, when he led the DSO as music director for the first time, conducting Beethoven's Symphonies 1, 4, and 5, to begin the Beethoven Festival. Held over two weeks, the series featured performances of all the symphonies, as well as chamber music performed by outstanding ensembles, including the Juilliard String Quartet, the Istomin-Stern-Rose Trio, and works featuring soloists from the DSO. Another prominent soloist was pianist Ilse von Alpenheim, a distinguished musician who had appeared with major orchestras all over the world, and was also the wife of Dorati.

In addition to musical performances, the festival included a "Beethoven Congress," a series of lectures and presentations devoted to the composer, which were given by more than twenty leading Beethoven scholars, critics, and other experts, and which took place on the campus of Wayne State University. It was a rich cultural offering, unlike anything that had ever been sponsored by the DSO.

Dorati truly took the city by storm: for the first time in Detroit, scalpers hawked tickets in front of Ford Auditorium. His face looked down from billboards on the freeways. Television and newspapers from around the country covered the opening of the festival, which was universally hailed as a triumph. "A renaissance man for our city," claimed the *Free Press*.[8] "From now on, the history of the Detroit Symphony will be written AD—after Dorati arrived," claimed the *Windsor Star*.[9] Speaking of the NBA franchise that played down the street, the *New York Times* noted that, "Last night the Detroit Pistons had to play in the shadow of the Detroit Symphony."[10]

The DSO gained a nationwide following from the event as well. Its performances of the Beethoven symphonies were videotaped for broadcast on the PBS network, with Dorati discussing the composer and his works with actor E. G. Marshall. The television program was paid for by a grant of $325,000 from the Ford Motor Company. The orchestra expanded its radio audiences, too, thanks to a $100,000 grant from the Ford Foundation, which funded a broadcast series that aired over public radio stations, which were produced through Wayne State's radio station, WDET-FM.

During his first season with the DSO, Dorati programmed an astonishing variety of music, including fifteen different series, from the regular classical concerts on Thursday, Friday, and Saturday evenings, to coffee concerts, family concerts, pops concerts, chamber orchestra performances, a Christmas Festival that included an annual performance of the *Nutcracker Ballet* and a sing-along *Messiah*, young people's concerts, the continuing concerts at the Light Guard Armory, and the summer series at Meadow Brook. These programs together represented nearly 300 works of music that first season, including some thirty-seven pieces heard in Detroit for the first time, ranging from the works of such baroque

masters as Bach and Buxtehude to modern composers like Charles Ives and William Boyce. Dorati also took the orchestra on tour, performing in the Upper Peninsula of Michigan and several cities outside of the Detroit metropolitan area, including Bay View, Grand Rapids, East Lansing, Ann Arbor, Flint, and Interlochen.[11]

His first year also featured outstanding guest artists, including cellists Mstislav Rostropovich and Janos Starker, soprano Jessye Norman, violinists Itzhak Perlman and Pinchas Zukerman, pianist Alicia de Larrocha, and, making his appearance with the DSO for the first time, flutist Jean-Pierre Rampal.

Dorati accomplished all of these things despite the fact that he himself was only in Detroit approximately eleven weeks of every year. In his memoir, *Notes of Seven Decades*, he wrote about the life of the symphony orchestra director in the modern era, lamenting that by the 1970s, most music directors had the responsibility for several major ensembles at once, as he did, due, he thought, to the modern audience's appetite for an ever wider variety of music.

In his memoir, Dorati also provided an interesting insight into the effects of the 1967 riot, in what was perhaps the first public assessment by anyone in the orchestra's higher echelons, claiming that "perhaps no other large American city suffered so much damage, so great a setback from that kind of unrest as the Motor City." He had been a visitor in the 1930s, so could speak from experience how the city's "once flourishing, attractive downtown district has been all but abandoned completely," yet also of the hope promised in the "renaissance" of Detroit.[12] Dorati arrived in Detroit just as the Renaissance Center, a riverfront development project spearheaded by Henry Ford II, opened; its gleaming towers on the river offered the promise of rebirth and of better times to come in the city, and many shared the same hope for the DSO.

Dorati claimed that when he arrived, the DSO "had become a competent performing body, without special distinction, respected but hardly cherished, accepted rather than admired." His mandate when he was hired was "to upgrade it into what is called, for want of a better name, a 'world-class' orchestra."[13] He claimed that the management of the orchestra did not realize that "the upgrading of an orchestra means budgetary expansion commensurate with the orchestra's rise in quality and scope." As it had in Washington, such opinions gave rise to what became a constant battle between Dorati and the Board regarding the financial commitment it would take to improve and sustain the orchestra's artistic ascendance.

Dorati also offered intriguing insights into the quality of musicianship of the DSO in 1977:

It turned out that the orchestra had far greater reserves in talent than I, even optimistically, had anticipated. Therefore, there was nothing else to do than to make the performers feel, individually and collectively, that they were artist-musicians rather than musician-workers. Once they truly recognized their real status, their playing shone in new, splendid colors, overnight, as it were.[14]

## RECORDINGS

Dorati achieved another goal with the newly energized orchestra, signing a major recording contract with the London label in 1977. The first three albums were recorded in 1978, at the United Artists Theater in downtown Detroit. They included an all-Tchaikovsky recording, featuring the ever-popular *1812 Overture*; a collection of rhapsodies, including works by Dvořák, Ravel, Liszt, and Enesco; and an album of two works by Bartók.

These recordings won broad praise for the orchestra, with Abram Chipman of *High Fidelity* claiming that in the recording of the Bartók Suite no. 1 "Dorati really sets the five movements of the suite on fire with the authority and razzle-dazzle temperament of his best days."[15] The all-Tchaikovsky album became a bestseller within weeks of its release, and was soon the best-selling classical record in the country. These were the first of what would total sixteen recordings of the DSO under Dorati, works that include a diversity of composers and reveal an orchestra of wide range and ability.

In 1981 and 1982, the orchestra re–corded three famous works of Stravinsky: *Petrushka*, *The Firebird*, and *The Rite of Spring*. Critics were lavish in their praise, with David Hall of *Stereo Review* noting the "clarity and sonic impact" of *The Firebird*, as well as Dorati's ability to bring to bear on the music "all the dramatic flair at his command, which is considerable," and "the Detroit players with him all the way."[16]

Edward Greenfield of *Gramophone* concurred in a review of *The Firebird* recording that gives an insight into what the orchestra sounded like in the early 1980s. He writes that "one marvels that textures can be made so clear yet well-coordinated, too. The clarity and definition of dark, hushed passages is amazing, for example, with the contra bassoon finely focused, never sounding wooly or obscure, and with string tremolos down to the merest whisper uncannily precise."[17] The DSO's recording of the *The Rite of Spring* went on to win the first Grand Prix du Disque for a compact disc recording.

Under Dorati, the orchestra also distinguished itself in a recording of the works of a giant of American classical music, Aaron Copland. A 1982 album containing *El Salón México*, *Appalachian Spring*, Four Episodes from *Rodeo*, *Dance Symphony*, and *Fanfare for the Common*

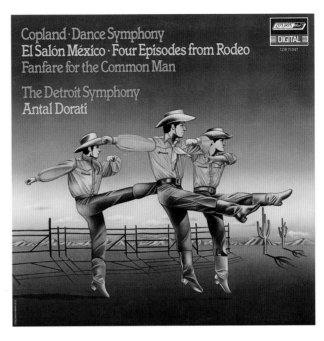

Copland: *Dance Symphony*, *El Salón México*, Four Episodes from *Rodeo*, *Fanfare for the Common Man*. (Courtesy Universal Music Group for London/Decca. Reprinted with permission. All rights reserved.)

*Man* received praise for its clarity and rhythmic drive, as Gerald S. Fox claimed in a review in *American Record Guide*, calling Dorati's interpretation of the Four Dance Episodes "as good as they come."[18]

Dorati had gotten his start as a director of opera, and that experience informed his direction of the DSO on another highly praised collection of the works of Richard Strauss, including *Der Rosenkavalier Suite*, an arrangement written by Dorati himself, as well the symphonic fantasy Strauss wrote to his *Die Frau ohne Schatten*. Writing in *Stereo Review*, Richard Freed claimed that "Dorati's achievement in Detroit is documented by the recordings," calling the works "stunning show-

Bartok: *The Miraculous Mandarin*, Music for Strings, Percussion and Celesta. (Courtesy Universal Music Group for London/Decca. Reprinted with permission. All rights reserved.)

chords," the driving tempos, sharp attacks, and the solo clarinet that weaves "seductive" and "highly decorated arabesques." He also noted the musical portrait of the Mandarin himself, "painted in sound with a pentatonic theme harmonized in tritons and played by muted trombones with shrill outbursts on wind and strings."[20]

## FUNDING SOURCES

As Dorati's second season began in the fall of 1978, praise for the orchestra continued to roll in, as did funding from a variety of sources, including grants, contributions from individuals, and, from a very welcome source, the city of Detroit, which restored funding to the DSO in the form of a $105,000 grant, as well as the proceeds from its city-wide garage sale of $90,000.

But Board president Robert Semple continued to sound the plea for more money from all sources, public and private, from businesses, individuals, and foundations. He announced in his 1978 report that the total expenses for the previous season had grown to $5.5 million, with an increase of more than $1 million spent on salaries, benefits, and travel. This led to an operating deficit of $2.3 million for the year, and resulted in a total loss for the season of $55,000.[21]

Charged with continuing to increase the orchestra's profile, while the Board focused on increasing sources of funding, Dorati entered his second season. It included a second music festival, this one

pieces for an orchestra brilliant enough to handle them, and in Dorati's hands the Detroit Symphony tosses them off with the flair one associates with the very top rank of world-class ensembles. Whether or not the orchestra actually sounds like this week in and week out in its subscription concerts, what we hear in this recording is sheer glory."[19]

Freed was also full of praise for the DSO's recording of Bartók's *Miraculous Mandarin*, calling it "spectacular" and "stunning." Originally a ballet score, it was a work that Dorati, with his background in dance, was well familiar with. The recording is vibrant, alive, and full of atmospheric tension as it paints its portrait of lust and murder. Timothy Day noted the "scurrying strings and hammered-out woodwind devoted to the music of Schubert and the Viennese school, featuring compositions by nineteenth- and twentieth-century classical masters—Brahms, Schumann, and Strauss, as well as Schoenberg, Webern, and Berg.

## SCHUBERT/VIENNA FESTIVAL

The Schubert Festival took place in November 1978, with a program that featured four of Schubert's symphonies and also several concerts devoted to his chamber music, including piano trios, string quartets, and quintets. There was also an entire concert of lieder, both Schubert's and those of other Viennese masters, including Brahms, Schumann, Wolf, and Strauss. More of Schubert's range was on display at an evening devoted to his famed song-cycle *Die Winterreise* and the US premiere of one of his operas, *Alfonso and Estrella*.

Once again, musicologists from around the world came to Detroit to attend the Schubert Congress and present papers and demonstrations of his music. Claiming that "the heart of a festival is celebration," the programs encouraged non-musicians to attend both the concerts and the lectures, to engage with the scholars on all aspects of the music, and to enjoy concurrent exhibits at the Detroit Public Library, the Rackham Auditorium, and Ford Auditorium, which displayed a collection of photographs relating to Schubert from the Austrian Embassy.[22]

The Schubert Festival was less financially successful than the Beethoven offering was, but it did nothing to deter Dorati from continuing to prepare the next festival, devoted to Brahms, which took place in 1979. Nor did it deter him from claiming:

> Artistically and morally . . . the festivals were unquestionably great successes. . . . Many other local musical organizations were involved and manifold musical interests were served. . . . Also for the first time they made the name "Detroit" internationally known for its cultural assets rather than for its industry.[23]

In the spring of 1979, Dorati continued his efforts to expand the musical horizons of Detroit. He presented concert performances of two operas by Richard Strauss: *Elektra*, and one of the most iconoclastic operas of the twentieth century, *Die äegypitsch Helena*. With Metropolitan Opera stars Gwyneth Jones and Willard White, as well as Glenda Kirkland, the *Helena* concert especially was quite a sensation, with John Guinn of the *Free Press* claiming that the "performance was inspired, from the opening arpeggio to the final D-major chord."[24]

Dorati took the performance of *Helena* on tour, conducting the opera at Carnegie Hall in New York, where Harold Schonberg of the *New York Times*

Dorati giving a talk on Richard Strauss in Detroit, March 1979. (Courtesy DSO Archives)

claimed that he and the DSO "acquitted themselves honorably."[25] In Washington, they presented the work at the Kennedy Center, Dorati's former home, where Paul Hume of the *Washington Post* praised the conductor's "superb awareness."[26] The DSO also made a recording of the opera—the first to include the entire piece—so lengthy that it required three discs.

In October 1979, Dorati led the DSO in a concert that took place in Orchestra Hall, to commemorate the sixtieth anniversary of the first concert, conducted by Gabrilowitsch in 1919. The performance was sold out, and it gave Detroiters a chance to revel in the acoustics of the hall, which were undiminished despite years of neglect, and to see the renovations then going on that would one day bring it back to its former greatness.[27]

## EUROPEAN TOUR

With his next initiative, the DSO's first European tour, Dorati set out to prove that the orchestra deserved to be known as a cultural asset of international renown; by nearly all accounts, he achieved that goal admirably.

The European tour took place in November 1979, and included twenty-four sold-out concerts in twenty-three cities, with the orchestra visiting Belgium, France, Germany, Great Britain, Norway, Spain, Sweden, and Switzerland. The response from the European audiences was overwhelmingly positive: more than 60,000 people hailed the DSO and Dorati, and they received lavish praise in print and standing ovations wherever they performed.

Horst Koegler of the *Stuttgarter Zeitung* wrote that, "In contrast with their colleagues from New York, Chicago, and Cleveland, Detroit seems to exhibit more warmth, fluidity, softness, and tonal opulence." Hans Schurmann of the *General-Anzeiger* claimed that "the concert in Bonn indeed proved that the Detroit Symphony has by now made the leap to the first rank of the great American orchestras."[28]

For Dorati, it was a vindication of the achievement of the musicians themselves: he called "the emergence of the orchestra itself from routine satisfactoriness to overall excellence the most gratifying single feature" of his tenure with the ensemble. On their triumphant return to Detroit, Dorati wrote a program note to the DSO audiences, outlining his feelings of "deep satisfaction and pride." "Your orchestra— for never forget that it is yours—had been 'discovered' in Europe and recognized as one of the top orchestras in the world."[29]

In his memoir, Dorati claimed that the DSO "had never before played as beautifully as it did throughout that tour

**INTERNATIONAL BRAHMS FESTIVAL**

**Detroit Symphony Orchestra·Antal Dorati** music director

Program for the Brahms Festival, April 1980. (Courtesy DSO Archives)

of Europe," and further that the orchestra "so far has been accepted and acclaimed at its full value only in Europe."[30]

The European tour was enormously successful artistically, but it was also enormously expensive, and the cost overruns led to a huge deficit and a battle of the wills between Dorati and the Board. Despite corporate sponsorship, including substantial gifts from the Knight Foundation, BASF Wyandotte, Burroughs, Ford, GM, American Motors, Touche Ross, Manufacturers National Bank, and the National Bank of Detroit, the losses amounted to an operating deficit of $1.9 million, $732,000 of which was attributed directly to the tour.[31]

In this atmosphere of ever-growing concern about finances, the 1979–80 season drew to a close, with Dorati overseeing the third music festival, this one devoted to the music of Brahms, held in April 1980. Once again, outstanding artists and scholars from around the world came to Detroit to celebrate and share in the music of Brahms, in what was the most comprehensive series devoted to the composer in North America to that point. The festival comprised a series of nineteen performances, from Brahms's *Ein Deutsches Requiem* with Dietrich Fischer-Dieskau, and the Alto Rhapsody with Maureen Forrester, to chamber music performed by the Amadeus Quartet and concertos featuring soloists such as pianist Vladimir Ashkenazy.[32]

The festival proved to be an artistic and financial success, but did little to stanch the red ink that had accumulated on the DSO's books. The Board approached Dorati to try to reduce future costs; notes from meetings include "questioning the need for all Dorati innovations to achieve world class," and that future "orchestra programs be made as cost-effective as possible without sacrificing artistic integrity."[33]

## FINANCIAL WOES FOR THE ORCHESTRA AND THE CITY

Yet these efforts proved ineffective, and by the middle of 1980, both the orchestra and the city were in dire economic straits. Detroit was in the throes of another recession, which affected the auto industry especially. As had happened in previous downturns, Detroit was especially hard hit: Chrysler nearly went out of business, saved from bankruptcy by $1.5 billion in federal loan guarantees. Interest rates and inflation rates rose to eighteen percent. Michigan's unemployment rate was the highest in the country; in Detroit it reached 18.5 percent. Wayne County, home of Detroit, was facing a deficit of $20 million.[34]

The orchestra had suffered right along with the city: Detroit withdrew is annual commitment of $105,000 to the DSO, the grants from the Michigan Council for the Arts were cut by nine percent, the amount of the state appropriation was no longer guaranteed, and donations dwindled. In response, the Board created the Five-Year Plan in July 1980. It included estimates of growth in income rising from $6.35 million in 1979–80 to $9.3 million in 1983–84, a smaller rate of growth in expenditures, from $8.4 million in 1979–80 to $9.8 million in 1983–84, and relied on a "Bridge Fund," made up of yields from its endowment, which the plan projected would amount to more than $3.5 million over the five years, bringing the budget of the orchestra into balance by 1983–84.

The plan also included cutbacks: tours to New York, Washington, and other Eastern US cities were canceled and all funding to the Detroit Civic Orchestra and to WDET were withdrawn, which led to the cancellation of the radio broadcasts of the orchestra.[35]

While the Board worked on the Five-Year Plan, they also met with Dorati to negotiate his contract to remain in Detroit; in the end, they could not come to an agreement. In September 1980, after years of battles over the need for the financial resources he thought necessary to secure the orchestra's artistic future, Dorati decided to go public with his concerns. He wrote an open letter to Board president Robert Semple, published in the *Free Press*, in which he threatened to resign if the city and the people of Detroit did not come up with enough money to continue funding the orchestra.

The conflict became the talk of Detroit, and received national attention, too. Dorati made it clear that he understood the precarious financial position the city was facing at the time. Yet he believed the money could be raised, especially from the wealthy people of the region, and that the operation of a "world-class" ensemble "while expensive, is not of that size that Detroit could not afford it, if it wished."[36]

But the Board had neither the resources nor the will to mend the rift. Unable to reach an agreement, Dorati resigned as music director, though he agreed to stay on to conduct the orchestra through the end of the 1980–81 season, then assume the role of Conductor Laureate.

It was a bruising battle and was seen by many observers as a major mistake on the part of management. *Detroit News* music critic Nancy Malitz described it as the "darkest hours" of the DSO's recent history; she claimed it revealed the Board's lack of leadership and business sense, showing that they were "maddeningly naïve about money," made "promises they couldn't keep," and "reneged on just about everything trustees can renege on."[37]

Malitz also faulted the orchestra's management for not realizing the importance of the positive response to the DSO in Europe: "In a major publicity blunder, they ignored the orchestra's success and created big, bitter headlines of their own about the tour breaking the organization's back, the doomed dollar in Europe, and Dorati's wild demands."[38] After Dorati's departure, there were changes in the boardroom: in 1981, Robert Semple moved to the position of "honorary chairman," and was replaced by Walter McCarthy. McCarthy, an executive with Detroit Edison and a philanthropist, was serving as CEO of the utility when he took over for Semple.

Dorati's last season as music director began with birthday celebrations of three major American composers—Aaron Copland, Samuel Barber, and William Schuman—with the composers visiting Detroit and attending a concert series in their

Aaron Copland with Dorati in Detroit, during the DSO's celebration of Copland, October 1980. (Courtesy DSO Archives)

honor. Schuman gave the Detroit premier of his "baseball cantata," *Casey at the Bat*, based on the famous poem by Ernest L. Thayer. The performance featured famed bass-baritone Donald Gramm in the lead role, and he was accompanied by three local vocal ensembles, the Brazeal Dennard Chorale, the Kenneth Jewell Chorale, and the Cantata Singers. There is a photo to commemorate the event, with Tiger greats Al Kaline and Charlie Gehringer, and Schuman and Dorati in Tiger uniforms.[39]

For the final music festival under his direction, Dorati chose the work of Belá Bartók, his teacher and mentor, in a program that brought musicians and

musicologists from all over the world in a celebration of the 100th anniversary of Bartók's birth. Yehudi Menuhin performed Bartók's Concerto no. 2 for Violin and Orchestra on a program that also included the composer's fiery *Miraculous Mandarin* and his *Concerto for Orchestra*.

In May 1981, the DSO bade farewell to Dorati, in a concert celebrating his seventy-fifth birthday. The Board had previously announced that the position of music director would not be filled immediately. Instead, conductor Gary Bertini was hired to serve as music advisor to the DSO following Dorati's departure; he would remain in the position for two years.[40]

## GARY BERTINI

Gary Bertini was born in the city of Brichevo, in what was then the Soviet Union, on May 1, 1927. His family moved to Palestine when he was young, and it was there that he began his musical studies, starting with the violin. He attended the Milan Conservatory and graduated in 1948, then continued his studies first at the Tel Aviv College of Music, then in Paris, where he was a composition student with Arthur Honegger, Olivier Messiaen, and Nadia Boulanger.

Bertini's professional career began in Israel, where he directed several of his country's major musical ensembles, including the Rinat choir, the Israel chamber Ensemble Orchestra, and the Jerusalem Symphony Orchestra. Bertini also served as principal guest conductor of the Scottish National Orchestra from 1971 to 1981, and began a distinguished career as a guest conductor with such outstanding ensembles as the Berlin Philharmonic, the BBC Symphony, the National Orchestra of France, and the Washington National Symphony. He first conducted the DSO in January 1978.[41]

Bertini began his new position in Detroit in the fall of 1981, and, while working in an advisory capacity to program music and hire guest artists, he also conducted the orchestra for eight weeks during the season.

Gary Bertini, musical advisor of the DSO from 1981 to 1983. (Courtesy DSO Archives)

## MORE LABOR WOES

In 1982, during Bertini's second year as advisor, the musicians and management went to battle over a critical concession linked to the cost-saving goals of the Five-Year Plan of 1980. In their contract negotiations that year, the musicians had accepted a minimal wage increase in exchange for greater artistic control in management decisions, specifically a clause in the contract that gave them the right to approve Dorati's successor as music director and principal conductor. Although some European ensembles did allow musicians the right to approve a new conductor at that time, the clause was a first for an American orchestra.

When negotiations for a new contract began in 1982, the management attempted to eliminate the provision, claiming that the musicians' right to veto power over the appointment of a new director had been granted for one year only. The musicians refused to give up the right, and voted to strike.[42]

## A STRIKE

The musician's strike began on December 9, 1982. Once again, the conflict played out in the press, locally and nationally.

DSO clarinetist and spokesman Douglas Cornelsen told the *New York Times* that the musicians insisted on maintaining their veto because they believed that the Board, dominated by businessmen, would select a conductor based on his willingness to accept a limited budget and to bow to management's wishes, not because of artistic qualifications:

The record, with the exception of Dorati, is not good. The board is afraid of the financial commitment needed to hire a conductor with a world name and they want someone who is manageable. Dorati was not manageable and he's not in the picture anymore.[43]

In the city and throughout the region, the battle lines were drawn in the dispute, with the Board, backed by many of its corporate sponsors, outlining their stance in terms reminiscent of the hostile negotiations between the United Auto Workers and the Big Three automotive companies. Oleg Lobanov, managing director of the orchestra, stated management's position:

If the authority is not with the board, then who is it with?[44]

His opinion was echoed by the new Board chairman, Walter J. McCarthy Jr., who sent a letter to the musicians claiming, "The authority is necessary both because the orchestra's donors rightly expect it and because the individual in question is, in fact, an employee of the board and your supervisor."[45]

The conflict played out in the press, with both major newspapers, the *Detroit News* and the *Detroit Free Press*, siding with management. The *Free Press* mocked the musicians' stance on artistic control, calling it akin to "patients selecting the head of the mental institution in which they are being treated."[46]

With the lucrative Christmas concerts on the line, the strike was finally settled on December 21, when the musicians ratified a new contract that granted them limited artistic control in the selection of a new conductor. Aided in part by a compromise suggested by Michigan Governor William Milliken, the contract stipulated that there would be a "pre-selection" committee made up of three musicians and three members of management who would determine a list of conductors. In the case of a tie, a vote of the entire board would determine the outcome.

The orchestra went back to work immediately. Douglas Cornelsen, speaking on behalf of the musicians, stated, "We feel it is still the best conductor-selection clause in the business." Management was satisfied with the compromise as well: Oleg Lobanov claimed that the contract language "keeps the authority sitting squarely with the board of directors, where it belongs."[47]

As Gary Bertini completed his two-year commitment as musical advisor, the search began for a new music director. Both management and the musicians were interested in one man in particular, Günther Herbig, who had first conducted the DSO in August 1982; he had also rehearsed with the orchestra and was preparing to conduct a concert when the musicians walked out on strike in December 1982. Although he later recalled that he had determined after that incident he would "never come back to Detroit again in my life," he reconsidered, and accepted the position of music director in November 1983.[48]

## GÜNTHER HERBIG

Herbig was born on November 30, 1931, in Usti-nad-Labem, Czechoslovakia, of Aus-

trian parents. His mother was a pianist and his father was an architect. Herbig began musical studies at the age of nine, playing the flute and the cello. Yet even at that young age, he was interested in conducting, in what he recalls as his fascination with the "totality of a musical work." When World War II arrived in 1939, his musical studies came to a halt; he began them again after the war, studying at the Franz Liszt Academy and the Hochschule für Musik in Weimar, then went on to train with several major conductors, including Herbert von Karajan. Herbig's first appointment was at the German National Theater in Weimar,

Günther Herbig, music director of the DSO from 1983 to 1990. (Courtesy DSO Archives)

where he was a conductor from 1957 to 1962. In 1962, he was named music director of the Hans Otto Theater in Potsdam, a position he held for four years, before moving on to the (East) Berlin Symphony Orchestra, where he served as a conductor from 1966 to 1972.

While in East Berlin, Herbig also took on music director responsibilities with the Dresden Philharmonic, and he became their chief conductor in 1972. After five years in that role, he returned to the Berlin Symphony, as chief conductor, a position he held from 1977 to 1983.[49]

Herbig's first appointment with an American orchestra came about in 1979, when he was named principal guest conductor of the Dallas Symphony. In 1983, he was approached by Oleg Lobanov, who told him that the DSO musicians had been so impressed with him when he led them in 1982 that they wanted him to return in a permanent capacity. His appointment, announced in 1983, took effect on September 1, 1984.

Herbig came to Detroit from East Berlin, which at that time was part of communist East Germany, and joined the DSO during the final years of the Cold War. It is a fascinating insight into the politics of those times to see the stories announcing his appointment. A report in the *New York Times* begins with the headline, "East German to Run Detroit Symphony," and includes quotes from a news conference in Detroit in which

Herbig was asked to confirm reports that his appointment had been held up by the East German government. He assured the reporters that he was free to travel and choose his posts, and this was seconded by Board chairman Walter McCarthy, who insisted the organization was "not worried about politics" concerning Herbig's new position.[50] Still, his past held an enduring interest for observers; during his years in Detroit, he was frequently quoted as saying he had never been a member of the Communist Party in East Germany and that he was a devout Catholic.[51]

Herbig's selection also prompted surprise in some parts of the musical world, where, as Nancy Malitz noted in a profile, the response was often "Günther who?" She claimed that what had happened to Dorati played a major part in Herbig's selection: Dorati's resignation and his problems with the Board had been a national news story, and affected the search for a new conductor when "thoroughly second-rate [candidates] swore they'd never come to Detroit because the Board didn't keep its promises."[52]

Yet Malitz saw signs of hope in Herbig's selection: by 1983, several members of the previous Board had left, replaced with people who realized that he had the qualities they needed to rebuild the orchestra and restore its place in the American and international orchestral world. Malitz called Herbig a "fully formed, thoroughly competent conductor," who was "far better than any American the DSO, in its crisis, could have seduced."[53]

Herbig knew the challenges he faced: "If an orchestra has three or four years in which a music director is not present, as was the case here, it always slips a little bit," he told the *New York Times*. So from his first rehearsals with the orchestra, which began during the Meadow Brook summer season in 1984, he worked on all areas: "ensemble, musicianship, intonation and balance, everything."[54]

Herbig also spoke about his plans for the orchestra in an article in *High Fidelity* magazine, written by John Guinn, music critic for the *Detroit Free Press.* He told Guinn that his efforts with the orchestra were "basically always directed towards creating a balance of emotion, logic, and perfection. I don't believe in being just technically oriented, and I don't believe a masterpiece is a playing ground for the ego of the performing artist. You have to put all you are as a human being into a work, but you have to be very cautious not to hurt the work itself."[55]

Herbig described what happened when all these elements aligned: "suddenly, after half an hour sometimes, if you are concentrated enough and lead in the right direction, you feel how a hundred musicians are suddenly breathing in a different way and feeling all in the same way."[56]

Herbig had a reputation as a fine interpreter of the music of the German Ro-

mantic movement, especially the work of Anton Bruckner, who was well-represented in the programming that inaugurated his first season as music director, 1984–85. He began with plans to expand the musical horizons of the orchestra as well, including return engagements at Carnegie Hall, and also wanted to bring back international tours. And while the orchestra still had commitments to the London label for its recordings with Dorati, Herbig hoped to sign a contract with another major label to record the DSO under his baton.

Detroiters embraced Herbig from his earliest appearance with the orchestra. In his first concert, he conducted the DSO in two symphonies by Beethoven—no. 3 in E-flat Major, the "Eroica," and no. 8 in F Major—both roundly applauded by the audience and critics. Within months, subscriptions were up thirty-five percent, and the list of donors increased by thirty percent. National radio broadcasts were reinstated, with sponsorship coming from General Motors, and the Detroit Civic Orchestra once again received funding.[57]

Still, Herbig was a bit perplexed by the lack of interest in the DSO among the people of Detroit in general. As a native of East Germany, he had come from a country where orchestras are state-supported and subscriptions to orchestra series are so popular that they are passed down through generations of families. "We have to struggle to get people to the concerts of one orchestra," he said of his new home, as

Herbig conducting the DSO. (Courtesy DSO Archives)

opposed to East and West Berlin, which, with a population the size of Detroit, had eight orchestras, almost all of which were sold out each season.[58]

In April 1985, Herbig and the DSO returned to Carnegie Hall in a concert that was deemed "a triumph for all concerned" by *New York Times* music critic John Rockwell. The program featured Mahler's Symphony no. 6 in A Minor, and Rockwell was glowing in his praise, claiming that Herbig "gave a deeply felt, thoughtfully conceived, impeccably musical interpretation, and he got his musicians to play up to and beyond their considerable capacities." Noting the "fine playing of the Detroit Symphony itself," Rockwell commented that "the music-making, both individually and especially corporately, sounded genuinely committed and responsive—responsive both to the score and to the ensemble as a whole."[59]

In the summer of 1985, Herbig took the DSO to new territory: they performed as part of the Casals Festival in San Juan, Puerto Rico. They also continued the tradition of playing a series of concerts in Northern Michigan and the Upper Peninsula. And in another first, they played a concert in Washington in commemoration of the Statue of Liberty's 99th birthday. They performed the world premiere of "The Lady Remembers," composer Richard Adler's symphonic suite dedicated to the iconic statue.[60]

In the fall of 1985, the DSO was back at Carnegie Hall, where they presented a program highlighted by a performance of Shostakovich's Symphony no. 7, a dramatic work depicting the siege of Leningrad during World War II. Will Crutchfield of the *New York Times* noted that Herbig did not take a "programmatic/patriotic" approach, offering instead a performance in which the "shrillness of the scoring was softened; the marching stride of the first movement was not insisted upon; the angularity of the themes was answered with moderating, not italicizing execution."

While he faulted details, such as a "tempo a bit staid, the string sound not wiry enough" in certain sections, Crutchfield praised "lyrical solos, "imaginative colors," and "the considerable abilities of a considerable orchestra," with "the care over balances, the purposeful shaping of phrases, the elegant string playing in the second movement and the generally fine wind playing throughout."[61]

In February 1986, Herbig introduced his own music festival, "Images," which took place over nine days and included concerts and discussions focused on music inspired by poetry, literature, and painting. Several months later, in June 1986, Herbig led the DSO in a work jointly commissioned by the orchestra, Carne-

gie Hall, and the American Symphony League, a piano concerto by Pulitzer-Prize winning composer Ellen Taaffe Zwilich.[62]

## ORCHESTRA HALL RECLAIMED

In February 1987, the DSO announced that it was returning to its first home in Detroit, Orchestra Hall. It was a triumph for the Save Orchestra Hall movement, and for many lovers of music and architecture in the region. Hailed as "an acoustical marvel, a gem among the world's concert halls," by Pablo Casals, the hall had been spared the wrecking ball in 1970, and in 1971, after its historic landmark status had been secured, fundraising and renovations began.

A brave group of musicians played in the hall as early as 1971, while pigeons flew among the rafters, for a group of potential investors. By the late 1970s, the space had been renovated to the point that the hall could once again host concerts, including several chamber music performances associated with Dorati's music festivals.

But it wasn't until 1987 that the DSO formally announced it would leave Ford Auditorium and return to Orchestra Hall to once again reclaim its first permanent home. Herbig was delighted, praising the hall's acoustics: "it responds and breathes like a human being."[63]

The musicians were every bit as delighted to return to Orchestra Hall, and to abandon Ford Auditorium. Plagued with problems since it opened in 1956, and de-

DSO bassoonist Paul Ganson playing on the rooftop of Orchestra Hall as renovations take place. (Courtesy DSO Archives)

spite costly renovations, it had remained "an acoustical nightmare," according to contrabassoonist Lyell Lindsey.[64]

## ANOTHER LABOR DISPUTE, ANOTHER STRIKE

But while the plans were underway for the DSO's return to Orchestra Hall, another labor dispute between the musicians and management put the 1987–88 season in jeopardy. Negotiations on a new contract had begun early in 1987, but by September, when the contract expired, no agreement had been reached. The musicians offered to work under their old contract at their previous wage while negotiations continued, but management refused. A federal mediator was called in, and several concerts had to be canceled.

The negotiations took a negative turn when, in mid-September, management told the musicians they could return to work, but only if they took an eleven percent cut in pay. The Board claimed that they had an operating deficit of $1 million, and that a pay cut was the only way to balance the budget. The musicians refused to take the pay cut, and, claiming they had been locked out, stopped working. Management, who claimed that the musicians were on strike, began to cancel more concerts, including a scheduled trip to Carnegie Hall in October.[65]

In mid-November, Mayor Young met with the head of the musicians' union, Carl Austin, and Board chairman Walter McCarthy to try to break the impasse. The meeting was productive: management dropped the demand for a pay cut, the musicians' union withdrew its complaint of unfair labor practices against management, and both sides returned to the bargaining table.

Yet the dispute dragged on, as the two sides traded accusations. In mid-November, the musicians rejected an offer that would have increased their base pay from $47,320 to $49,660 per year by the third year of the contract because the work stoppage had already resulted in a fifteen percent cut in their income for the year. Further, they believed that the current offer indicated that management "remains unwilling to commit to keeping a major symphony orchestra in Detroit."[66]

Management's reply was offered by McCarthy, who acknowledged that the work stoppage had achieved the savings that management sought, but now said he feared that the situation threatened the future of the DSO as an organization.[67]

The dispute continued into December, threatening the important Christmas season, when the orchestra made approximately ten percent of its annual income. Finally, on December 14, 1987, the musi-cians voted 85 to 8 to ratify a new contract, ending the longest strike in the DSO's history to that point. The new contract raised the base pay to $53,560 in the third year, which brought the musicians in line with similar pay at such major American orchestras as Los Angeles and Cleveland. The Christmas season was saved, and concerts were rescheduled, including the DSO's return to Carnegie Hall.[68]

## HERBIG ANNOUNCES HIS PLANS TO LEAVE

While the labor dispute simmered in November 1987, Herbig announced that he would become the artistic advisor of the Toronto Symphony, to begin in 1988. He had been a guest conductor with Toronto, and was completing a two-week stint with the orchestra when the announcement was made.[69]

Herbig claimed that he had no intentions of leaving Detroit, but just seven months later, in May 1988, he announced that he would leave at the end of the 1989–90 season. Claiming that the orchestra's management was financially unable to meet his requirements, Herbig said, "There's no reason to go on when you get told that the goals are not obtainable." Specifically, he stated that the DSO management had told him that three of his major goals for the orchestra could not be realized, due to economic constraints: the orchestra would not return to recording, he could not increase the roster from

## CONCERTMASTER: EMMANUELLE BOISVERT (1988–2011)

When Emmanuelle Boisvert won the concertmaster position with the DSO in 1988, she became the first woman to hold the position in a major orchestra in the United States. She was born in Quebec in 1963, and showed talent at a young age, beginning violin lessons at age three. She began attending the Conservatoire de Musique de Québec at the age of six, and graduated at seventeen, then continued her studies at the Meadowmount School of Music in New York, founded by revered violinist Ivan Galamian, with whom she studied for three summers.

Boisvert also studied with David Cerone, at both Meadowmount and the Curtis Institute in Philadelphia, where she also played with the Concerto Soloists Chamber Orchestra and at the Marlboro Festival. In 1986, at the age of twenty-three, she joined the Cleveland Orchestra, and in 1988, auditioned for, and won, the concertmaster position with the DSO, then under the direction of Günther Herbig.

Boisvert's commanding technique and strong leadership skills made her a highly regarded member of the orchestra, noted for helping to develop and maintain the signature sound of the string section—lush, fulsome, and with clarity in tone, tempo, and rhythm—as well as her solo performances, which revealed her consummate ability and fine tone. She told Anne Mischakoff Heiles, "Every second I make a decision about what a conductor is doing, interpreting that motion and leading the rest of the section." She also said she relied "on what the principals have to say. We constantly check with each other through eye contact during a performance."

Boisvert also became a beloved member of the music community in Detroit, noted for her outstanding musicality as well as her glamorous, charismatic stage presence. Praised by the *Detroit News* music critic as "brilliant, endlessly imaginative, daring," she also played on a distinguished instrument, a 1718 Stradivari, known as the "Marquis de Rivière," which she said was "like playing a Rembrandt." She recalled that the "sound is so rich and dark and pure but powerful."

When Boisvert announced her resignation in May 2011, in the wake of a long and bitter strike, it was a shock to music lovers in Detroit and around the country; it was also perhaps the most significant resignation from the DSO during a time of uncertainty and discord. And although Boisvert left at a time of upheaval and unrest, she is still remembered for her consummate musicianship and leadership over twenty-three seasons. She is now the associate concertmaster of the Dallas Symphony Orchestra.

Sources: Anne Mischakoff Heiles, *America's Concertmasters* (Sterling Heights: Harmonie Park Press, 2007), 232–42; *New York Times*, May 26, 2011; *Crain's Detroit Business*, May 25, 2011; https://www.mydso.com/about-us/people/bios/emmanuelle-boisvert,-associate-concertmaster-the-robert-e-jean-ann-titus-family-chair.aspx.

ninety-seven to 103 musicians, and the planned 1990 tour of the Far East had been canceled.[70]

### A EUROPEAN TOUR

Yet one goal Herbig was able to achieve was a second European tour for the DSO. The trip began on January 23, 1989, and included performances in fourteen cities in Switzerland, Germany, Austria, Spain, France, and Great Britain. Once again, they played to sold-out houses and standing ovations, with the music critic of the *Süddeutsche Zeitung* of Munich writing, "perfection, brilliance, and discipline are indeed discernible immediately as the DSO begins playing. . . . Herbig can hold the musical fabric in a transparent, chamber-like fashion because these musicians from Detroit are all first-class."[71]

Richard Morrison of the *Times* of London also praised the DSO, noting how Herbig "has nurtured a particularly fine string sound—beefy in timbre, incisive in attack, yet sensitive in dynamic shading." While he found some sections lacking, he noted that "Herbig's interpretations had considerable merits." "The quick movements [of Beethoven's Symphony no. 7] were emphatically accented without ever becoming bloated, and Herbig counterpointed the power with an occasional welcome touch of gentleness."[72]

## A CASH CRISIS

But while the orchestra was receiving rave reviews in Europe, a huge gap in short-term cash required to keep the orchestra running precipitated another financial crisis. General Motors, which had given $600,000 to the orchestra to sponsor the tour, had to give an immediate grant of $500,000 to meet the organization's short-term cash needs; Ford and Chrysler were called upon for similar commitments, and each of them donated $300,000, for a total of $1.1 million in emergency funds to end the crisis.

The cash woes of the organization prompted stern statements from the leaders of the Big Three. GM Chairman Roger Smith said that his company would suspend further donations until the management could develop a sound business

### THE RESTORATION OF ORCHESTRA HALL: OSCAR GRAVES

When Orchestra Hall reopened in the fall of 1989, it was a true triumph of vision, will, and artistry. Among the hundreds of artisans, artists, and craftsman who helped restore the crumbling hall to its former magnificence was sculptor Oscar Graves.

Graves had been born in Detroit in 1921 and had studied art at the Cranbrook Academy and Wayne State University. He worked for many years as an assistant to Marshall Fredericks, whose *Spirit of Detroit,* as well as the interior sculptures in Ford Auditorium, made Fredericks, and later Graves, a well-known artist in the city.

By the 1980s, Graves had established his own reputation as a sculptor with works on display in Detroit that included a bronze portrait of Martin Luther King Jr. at the corner of West Grand Boulevard and Rosa Parks Boulevard, and a bronze tablet with bronze relief of Bishop Richard Allen, the founder and first bishop of the African Methodist Episcopal Church, which is in Richard Allen Park, facing the Ebenezer AME Church in Detroit.

Graves's contributions to the restoration of Orchestra Hall are delineated in *Stages,* which was published to commemorate the rebirth of Orchestra Hall:

Graves examined nearly obliterated plaster decorations to reproduce designs virtually from scratch. The work required the reproduction of hundreds of delicate designs in many sizes, some of which, while appearing the same in all respects, were actually configured differently for the left and right sides of the Hall. Graves built new molds, cast new ornaments, and worked with a crew of three to four plasters for up to 20 hours a day, all to help preserve the interior's original eccentricities, and thus its mystical acoustic properties.

Source: *Stages: 75 Years with the Detroit Symphony Orchestra and Orchestra Hall* (Detroit: Detroit Symphony Orchestra Hall, 1994), 77.

plan, and also seek out new donors. "It is essential that [the DSO] achieve broad and continuing support from the entire community to assure its financial stability," Smith said.[73]

Stanley Seneker, executive vice president and chief financial officer of Ford, who was also a member of the Board of the DSO, concurred, stating that "we need to see a comprehensive business plan that takes into account all the ongoing financial requirements of the Symphony, as well as related capital and other expenses such as those required in the move to Orchestra Hall." He also noted the need for the organization to get funding "from all sections of the community it serves. . . . It is unacceptable for the Symphony to continue to go from financial crisis to financial crisis and expect foundations, corporations, and individuals to support it indefinitely."[74]

## AFFIRMATIVE ACTION AND THE DSO

Yet the problems of the DSO extended beyond financial crises. While the musicians were still on tour in Europe, they were confronted with yet another crisis, this one of a social and political nature.

In February 1989, state legislators decided to withhold nearly $1.3 million in state subsidies to the DSO unless more black players were hired. Once again, a story about the DSO received national exposure, with the *New Republic* quoting

the state senator who sponsored the move. "Music is music," claimed David Holmes. "Do-re-mi-fa-so-la-ti-do. I learned that in school." Other Michigan legislators joined the protest, and threated to boycott and picket the orchestra.[75]

The source of the legislators' concern was that only one member of the DSO was African American, which they claimed was a glaring example of discrimination in a city that was then sixty percent black. The DSO's response was to add one more African American musician to the orchestra immediately, a move that was actually in violation of their own labor agreement.

By this point, the DSO had established a tradition of "blind" auditions, where all candidates play behind a screen, so that neither discrimination nor favoritism could influence the selection of a new orchestra member. In a meeting held overseas while they were on tour, the musicians voted to allow a one-time exemption to that practice, and to offer a permanent position to bassist Richard Robinson, who had been playing as a substitute with the orchestra for the past year.

Deborah Borda, who had been appointed as the first executive director of the DSO in January, issued a press release, which read in part:

The musicians, their union, and the management of the Detroit

Symphony Orchestra have stepped forward to take this action. This signals our clear and strong commitment to affect an aggressive affirmative action program.[76]

As might be expected, the story was commented on by many in the press, including Isabel Wilkerson of the *New York Times* and Clarence Page of the *Chicago Tribune*. For Wilkerson, the incident raised the issue of artistic integrity and independence for the modern symphony orchestra, as well as its reliance on public funding and the political motives that might affect it. By 1989, the DSO was reliant on state aid of $2.5 million, which represented twenty percent of its annual budget; in contrast, the New York Philharmonic's contribution from the state of New York was $475,000, or about two percent, of its budget. "It is this heavy reliance that has made the Detroit Symphony especially vulnerable to attack," she wrote.[77]

Wilkerson also reported that the response among black musicians was overwhelmingly negative, describing that they "fear that abrogating standard procedures diminishes their legitimate and hard-won achievements." Michael Morgan, assistant conductor of the Chicago Symphony and an African American, agreed, saying that, "Now even when a black player is hired on the merits of his playing, he will always have the stigma that it was to appease some state legislator."[78]

Richard Robinson himself questioned the way the decision to hire him was made. "I would have rather auditioned like everybody else," he said. "Somehow this devalues the audition and worth of every other player."[79]

In 1989, only one percent of the 4,000 musicians in major orchestras in the United States were black. Both Wilkerson and Page believed that the small percentage of African American musicians in symphony orchestras was the result of the very small number of black classical musicians, not discrimination. Page wrote that "Few black youngsters have the desire, the money, the exposure, the time, or the educational resources to encourage aspirations toward a career in classical music."[80]

Wilkerson placed her position in a similar context: "Few blacks seek careers in classical music. Many inner-city schools provide little, if any, exposure to it, and poor black families are unable to afford the years of classical training required to be a symphony musician."[81]

Violinist Joseph Striplin, who up to Robinson's hiring had been the only black member of the DSO, claimed that he had seen no evidence of racial discrimination in the orchestra's hiring practices. And he suggested that the Michigan legislators, in making claims against the DSO, were taking attention away from true instances of discrimination. "This is like hockey," he said. "If the New York Rangers had to have 10 or 12 black players, they might have a lot of trouble finding them."[82]

For the DSO's new executive director Deborah Borda, however, it was an issue that needed airing. "It's healthy to think about this," she claimed. "This is not an institution of the 18th century. The symphony world is changing."[83]

And Borda, in her new role, was part of that change. She had replaced Oleg Lobanov and was part of a new management team for the DSO that also included a new chairman, Robert S. Miller Jr., vice president of Chrysler, who had led that company's financial turnaround, and who replaced Walter McCarthy. They began their new duties in early 1989 and oversaw the rocky financial crisis of February 1989 and another that summer, when the DSO's management had to ask the state of Michigan for emergency funding to meet payroll.

The state gave the orchestra $1 million in emergency aid, and Borda went to work on the budget. She set up meetings with the musicians' union to discuss their contract, and in just a few weeks, they were able to reach an agreement. By a vote of 82 to 8, the musicians agreed to take a pay cut of close to ten percent over four years, in order to help management reduce a debt that had grown to a startling $11.7 million dollars.[84]

These were dire times again for the DSO, but as Herbig's final season with the orchestra began, there was a light of hope. The DSO returned to Orchestra Hall to play their first concert of the season, and Borda was able to secure an outstanding successor to Herbig, Estonian conductor Neeme Järvi, who would win the hearts of musicians and audiences alike, and lead the DSO to another era of musical greatness.

CHAPTER NINE

# The Orchestra and the City Rebound, 1990–2005: Neeme Järvi and Another Golden Age

The orchestra has had its share of ups and downs. But it is perceived as being one of the big winners in this community. It's on the threshold of something special. We've got the right conductor and the right kinds of programs. But the jury is out on whether we'll make it happen.

Mark Volpe, Executive Director of the DSO, November 1991[1]

A few days before the gala opening of the Max M. Fisher Music Center in October 2003, the musicians of the Detroit Symphony Orchestra assembled onstage at Orchestra Hall for their first rehearsal in their new $60 million digs. As music director Neeme Järvi made his way to the podium, the musicians welcomed him back, as they always do when he's been away for a while, with warm applause.

When the ruckus died down Järvi gestured broadly to the spruced-up surroundings of Orchestra Hall and the adjacent palatial glories of the Max. "We did this," he said to the players. Then he said it again with even more force: "We did this."[2]

Mark Stryker, *Detroit Free Press*, May 22, 2005

WHEN NEEME JÄRVI TOOK OVER AS MUSIC DIRECTOR OF THE DSO IN 1990, the prospects for the future of the ensemble were bleak indeed. The previous year had been disastrous, from a financial, business, and political perspective. The deficit had reached $11.7 million, management had to seek two million dollars in emergency funds from the Big Three automakers and the state of Michigan just to make payroll, and, in an attempt to right the orchestra's disastrous financial situation, the musicians took a pay cut of almost ten percent. There were major changes in the top management ranks, too, with the appointment of a new board chairman, Robert S. Miller, and executive director, Deborah Borda. And just as they began their new roles and adding to the atmosphere of upheaval, there were accusations of racial bias in hiring that threatened state funding and put the orchestra in a negative national spotlight once again.

But if Järvi had any qualms about taking on an orchestra in such a troubled state, he showed no signs of it. When he greeted DSO audiences as their new music director for the first time in 1990, he radiated consummate artistry and leadership, as well as charm and optimism, delivered with the wit of "an artist who has learned how to play an audience and market himself American-style."[3] It was a combination that endeared him to Detroit and would make him one of the most popular and successful directors in the orchestra's history.

## NEEME JÄRVI

Neeme Järvi, whose surname is also spelled "Jarvi," had shown his enthusiasm for music from an early age. He was born in Tallinn, Estonia, then a part of the Soviet Union, on June 7, 1937, and first studied percussion and choral conducting at the Tallinn Music School. He claims to have made his first public performance even earlier: "I made my public debut when I was four, playing two simple pieces on a xylophone," he told the *New York Times*. "And in my teens I once played a violin concerto on a xylophone."[4]

After graduating from the Tallinn School, Järvi attended the prestigious Leningrad Conservatory, formerly the St. Petersburg Imperial Conservatory, where Ossip Gabrilowitsch had graduated with highest honors. Järvi spent five years at the school, from 1955 to 1960, studying conducting with Yevgeny Mravinsky and Nikolai Rabinovich; in later years, Järvi called Rabinovich his "musical father."

At the conservatory, Järvi heard some of the greatest orchestras of the era, including the major American orchestras and their famed conductors: the Boston Symphony Orchestra under Charles Munch, the Philadelphia Orchestra under Eugene Ormandy, the Cleveland Orchestra under Georg Szell, and the New York Philharmonic under Leonard Bernstein. "It was a great time to be there," he recalled. "I learned a lot from them and, of course, from the Leningrad Philharmonic and its conductors."[5]

After graduating in 1960 with a double degree in percussion and conducting, Järvi returned to Estonia, where he served as the music director of the Estonian State Symphony Orchestra from 1960 to 1980 and the Estonian Opera Theater from 1964 to 1977. The energetic, curious conductor even formed a chamber orchestra "because I love the music of Bach, Corelli, Haydn, and Mozart," he said. And even though Estonia was under Soviet control and works of Christian art were frowned upon and often banned, Järvi conducted masterpieces of sacred music, including Bach's *B Minor Mass* and his *St. Matthew Passion* and *St. John Passion*, as well as Handel's *Messiah* and Haydn's *The Seasons*.

Järvi brought modern opera to Tallinn, too. "I did *Porgy and Bess*, which I think was the first Soviet production of it," he recalled. "I'm very fond of Richard Strauss, and I did *Salome* and *Der Rosenkavalier*. I believe the production of the latter in Tallinn was one of the few it has ever had in the Soviet Union." Soon, he was conducting other major operatic works in Tallinn: "Rossini's *Turk in Italy*, Verdi, Puccini, *Carmen*, and, of course, many Estonian operas."[6]

Even then, Järvi was a champion of the music of his homeland, and he celebrated it on the podium and later in the recording studio. He was fiercely proud of his musical heritage, and took part in Estonia's tradition of song festivals for am-

Neeme Järvi, music director of the DSO from 1990 to 2005. (Courtesy DSO Archives)

ateur choruses from childhood. Known as Laulupidu, the music festival, held every five years, includes thousands of choristers performing in front of hundreds of thousands of listeners; it is estimated that in this country of 1.3 million people, nearly half have participated in the Laulupidu festivals.

While continuing his directorial duties in Estonia, Järvi also continued to study conducting. He attended the Accademia di Santa Cecilia in Rome, where he won first prize in a conducting competition in 1971. The award brought him greater attention

## LESLIE B. DUNNER

Leslie B. Dunner was the resident conductor of the DSO from 1987 to 1999, and played many important roles with the orchestra, as assistant and associate conductor of the orchestra as well as music director of the Detroit Civic Orchestra and Dearborn Symphony. In his eleven seasons with the DSO, he gained the reputation as a versatile interpreter of a wide variety of music, from pops to the classical repertoire.

Dunner was born on January 5, 1956, in New York, New York. He began to study clarinet in school, and also developed a lifelong love of dance. He went on to the prestigious Eastman School of Music, where he received his bachelor's degree in 1978; he continued his musical education at Queens College in New York, earning his master's degree in 1979. Moving on to Cincinnati, he received his PhD from the University of Cincinnati College-Conservatory of Music in 1982.

Dunner taught music at Carleton College in Minnesota from 1982 to 1986, then accepted a position as music director of the Dance Theatre of Harlem, a position he continued while serving as resident conductor in Detroit.

In addition to his director's duties, Dunner also conducted the DSO on an acclaimed recording, *Ellington and the Modern Masters: Music of African-American Composers*, which was taken from taped performances in Orchestra Hall between 1994 and 1998, and featured former winners of the Unisys composers competition.

When Dunner left the DSO, he was honored at a Classical Roots concert, "with speeches, gifts and an especially warm audience reception," according to Mark Stryker of the *Free Press*. He went on to lead the Annapolis Symphony Orchestra, where he was music director from 1999 to 2003. Since then, he has led the Joffrey Ballet as music director, as well as continuing guest conducting stints with the New York Philharmonic, and the Atlanta, Baltimore, Chicago, Dallas, St. Louis, San Francisco, and Seattle Orchestras, as well as many other orchestras around the nation and the world.

Sources: *Contemporary Black Biography* (Farmington Hills: Gale, 2004); *Detroit Free Press*, February 15, 1999.

from the world of classical music outside Estonia, and in April 1979, he was chosen, by a Soviet artists' agency, to replace Yuri Simonov at the Metropolitan Opera, where he made his American debut conducting Tchaikovsky's *Eugene Onegin*, in a performance described as "very impressive" by the *New York Times*.[7]

In 1980, Järvi immigrated to the United States with his wife and three children. From that point, he began to accept several offers to guest conduct, and made his debut with the New York Philharmonic in February 1980 in an all-Sibelius program. That performance prompted praise from the critics, including the *New York Times*, which noted, "Mr. Järvi is a musician with his own ideas, and a first-rate baton technique to carry out those ideas."[8]

Järvi expanded his guest conducting to include long-term stints with several ensembles, including the Birmingham Symphony Orchestra, where he conducted from 1981 to 1984, the Scottish National Orchestra, which he directed from 1984 to 1988, and the Swedish National Orchestra of Gothenburg, once led by another DSO conductor, Sixten Ehrling, with which Järvi began a long and fruitful alliance in 1983 that lasted until 2004.[9]

Järvi took the Gothenburg Orchestra on an eighteen-city tour in 1983, conducting its American debut at Carnegie Hall, where he led them in a program that featured the Scandinavian works he championed, including Sibelius's Symphony no. 2 in D Major and Hugo Alfvén's Swedish Rhapsody no. 1. While the *New York Times*'s Donal Henahan found fault with some aspects of the performance, he found much to praise: "The prevailing sound was full and hearty, occasionally overbalanced in favor of an excellent brass section."[10]

With the Scottish and Gothenburg Orchestras, Järvi also began a series of ambitious recording projects, mainly for the Chandos and Bis labels, which brought his name, and the ensembles he led, to an international audience. These, too, were predominantly works of Scandinavian and Slavic composers, and included the works of nineteenth- and early twentieth-century Russian masters.

The Scandinavian works Järvi recorded with the two orchestras included the complete works of Sibelius as well as compositions by Franz Berwald, Wilhelm Stenhammar, Niels Gade, and, in a first for many listeners, the music of Järvi's fellow Estonian, Eduard Tubin, whose work lay especially close to his heart. Among the Slavic composers he recorded were

Dvořák, as well as the well-known Russian composers Rimsky-Korsakov, Prokofiev, and Shostakovich, and the lesser-known Mily Balakirev and Anatoly Liadov.

The recordings won much praise for both Järvi and his orchestras, with John Rockwell of the *New York Times* calling him a "serious, self-effacing leader who places the music before the projection of flashy personal image." Rockwell called Järvi's recordings "exemplary," noting that "he has further assured himself a valued niche in record collectors' libraries by concentrating on the Scandinavian and Slavic music he clearly finds congenial." Of the specific performances, he noted their "ample idiomatic flavor, yet they retain an inherent Classicism, even in Romantically supercharged music. He manages the tricky task of seeming the servant of the composer, yet not supine."[11]

Järvi first led the DSO as a guest conductor in 1983 during the summer season at Meadow Brook, returning again in 1984 and 1989. By 1990, he had established a reputation as an outstanding interpreter of a wide range of repertoire, had a discography that numbered 160 recordings, and had conducted all the major American orchestras, including New York, Boston, Los Angeles, and Chicago, as well as the leading orchestras of Europe and Japan.

Järvi's appointment as the DSO's eleventh music director was announced in January 1990. Detroit and the music world in general gave a sigh of relief. "Things may be looking up for the troubled Detroit Symphony Orchestra," wrote Susan Heller Anderson in the *New York Times*.[12]

According to Detroit music critic Lawrence B. Johnson, Järvi was a man "with a mission": "His driving purpose is to explore, to discover, to shed light—in particular, to champion less familiar Romantic and Neoromantic symphonists."[13]

Järvi told Johnson, "I believe it's every conductor's duty to help composers become known, to find the very great qualities that have not been noticed. I'm always happy to pick out a composer who has not been at all known."[14]

### DETROIT DEBUT

When Järvi took the stage on October 25, 1990, to conduct the DSO for the first time as its music director, it was the fulfillment of another mission: he had wanted an American orchestra of his own, and at the age of fifty-three, he finally had one. The program he chose for that first concert announced both his range and his plans for the DSO. It featured works by Carl Maria von Weber, Paul Hindeminth, Howard Hanson, and Carl Nielsen, indicating a wide view of the symphonic repertoire: the nineteenth-century German classical tradition, German modernism, American modernism, and a Danish modernist, for good measure.[15]

The rapport between music director, musicians, and audience was immediate,

and electric. Ticket sales grew by twenty-two percent in Järvi's first year, reaching more than a quarter-million individual tickets by the end of the season, and the number of sold-out concerts doubled.[16]

Within months of becoming music director, Järvi signed a two-year, five-record contract with Chandos to make recordings with the DSO, featuring what became a best-selling and critically acclaimed collection, the American Series. In typical Järvi fashion, these recordings contained the compositions of well-known American composers, including Aaron Copland, Samuel Barber, and Charles Ives, as well as less-known and often neglected musicians like Amy Beach and George Chadwick; another volume in the series featured the compositions of the little-known African American composer William Grant Still, paired with a work of a giant of American music, Duke Ellington.

The recordings were made in Orchestra Hall and were funded by grants from the National Endowment for the Arts and a special organization, the Friends of Detroit Symphony Orchestra Hall. The first CD to appear in the American Series contained Barber's Symphony no. 1 and the overture to *The School for Scandal* as well as Beach's Symphony in E Minor, the Gaelic symphony. Joseph Horowitz of the *New York Times* deemed the recording of the Beach symphony "important" and "impressive," noting that the work had been

Järvi with the DSO on stage at Orchestra Hall. (Courtesy DSO Archives)

unjustly neglected and praising Järvi's efforts to bring it back to the classical mainstream: "No European country would so ignore a native symphony as tuneful, skilled, and picturesque; its American neglect betrays insecurities of a borrowed high culture fixated on pedigreed 'greatness.'"[17]

## ANOTHER FINANCIAL CRISIS

Just as Järvi's second year as music director began, the DSO was confronted with another financial crisis. In 1991, the state of Michigan faced a $1 billion budget deficit, and Governor John Engler announced cuts to the state's arts organizations, including $1.9 million in support that had been budgeted for the DSO.[18]

It was a grim time for the state, and for Detroit as well. The Big Three automakers had experienced a sharp decline in sales, with the US share of the market falling from eighty percent in 1980 to 63.8 percent in 1990.[19] Over the decade, Detroit had lost thirty percent of its jobs, resulting in an unemployment rate of twenty percent, a poverty rate of more than thirty percent, and a continuing erosion of its population to the suburbs.[20]

The orchestra's annual budget of $17 million needed to be trimmed immediately to make up for the loss in state funding. That job fell to Mark Volpe,

Charles Ives: Symphony no. 1, Samuel Barber: *Three Essays for Orchestra*. (Courtesy Chandos Records Ltd.)

who was the new executive director; he had taken over for Deborah Borda, who left the DSO after only eighteen months to run the Minnesota Orchestra. He told the press, "We analyzed our options, and we determined that to maintain our viability both with our creditors and with the community, we had to take $1 million out of the budget while maintaining our core programs."[21]

Everyone on the orchestra's staff, including Volpe, took an immediate pay cut of 4.5 percent. The musicians had already taken a ten percent reduction in pay in their recent contract negotiations, so were not faced with further cutbacks. But the recital series had to be canceled, as were tours within the state, and mem-

bers of the symphony choir, who up to that point had been paid, were asked to donate their services.

Volpe worked on a plan with the orchestra's management to reduce the deficit and, once again, to fund an endowment. The plan, called the Extraordinary Operating Initiative, was begun in 1991 and among its goals was to utilize contributions from the state and business donors to pay down the deficit, and to begin an endowment campaign to raise $18 million over five years.[22]

## TRIUMPHANT RETURN TO CARNEGIE HALL

One month later, in November 1991, the DSO returned to Carnegie Hall under their new maestro, in an acclaimed concert that featured works by Järvi's fellow Estonian, Arvo Pärt, as well as Sibelius and Ives. Allan Kozinn of the *New York Times* wrote about the concert in the context of the orchestra's financial woes, noting that the ensemble's struggles to survive showed its determination, as well as its "grace and grit." Perhaps most important, he also noted that:

> [The] musicians showed that what is at stake is a first-class ensemble with a sound that is impressively polished and warm. Its lower strings, in particular, provided a rich, glowing foundation in Arvo Pärt's ruminative "Cantus

in Memory of Benjamin Britten." And the transparency of the wind and brass playing gave the last two movements of the Ives First Symphony an alluringly springy, Romantic sound.[23]

Kozinn also praised Järvi as "not a flashy conductor, but his gestures are clear and expressive, and sweeping when they need to be." He was especially impressed with the Ives symphony, in which Järvi "went a long way toward shaping it into a likable, cohesive piece," with the orchestra responding to his efforts "admirably" and playing the symphony "as if it were a top-drawer masterwork."[24]

Järvi had wanted to take the DSO on another European tour, but the financial situation in the early 1990s precluded that. So, the ever-resourceful director chose another medium—radio—to convey the quality of his new ensemble. On October 12, 1992, the orchestra performed as part of a live broadcast that marked the 500th anniversary of the first voyage of Columbus to the New World. The DSO was the only major American orchestra to take part in the performance, which featured a number of smaller ensembles from all over the United States and was broadcast to twenty-two European nations.

The orchestra also continued the radio broadcasts of its concerts, which had been sponsored by GM since 1984. It is estimated that these concerts, broadcast over 300 stations in the United States and Canada, were heard by up to one million listeners each week, hosted by television talk show personality Dick Cavett.[25]

By 1992, two years into his time in Detroit, the relationship between music director, musicians, audiences, and management was still warm and collegial. That year, Järvi's contract was extended by two years, and included an "evergreen" clause, which allowed for the agreement to be renewed indefinitely, as long as management and the music director could agree on terms. Järvi's contract was negotiated, in part, by Alfred R. Glancy III, who had taken over as chairman of the Board from Robert S. Miller in 1992. He had served on the DSO's board since 1975, and, as CEO of Michigan Consolidated Gas, brought the business knowledge of running a large utility to the position.

Järvi shared his thoughts on his first two years with the orchestra with *Free Press* critic John Guinn, commenting on his relationship with the musicians and his sympathy and understanding of their abilities and their sacrifice. He noted that he enjoyed conducting the DSO "much more than some of the highly touted national and international groups" he had led. The reason? "The Detroit musicians have suffered," said Järvi. "So they make better music. They play from their hearts."[26]

Järvi and the DSO continued their ambitious recording schedule for Chandos, which by 1992 included two best-selling CDs on the classical charts, the Barber and Beach recording, which was the first volume in the American Series, and one featuring Ives and Barber, the second volume of the series. Containing Ives's Symphony no. 1 and Barber's *Three Essays for Orchestra*, it was Järvi's 100th release on Chandos, and the disc was pressed with a gold finish. Released with much fanfare, the recording received great reviews, and maestro and musicians graced the covers of several international music magazines, including *Gramophone*, *CD Review*, *Fanfare*, *Luister*, and *Diapason*.

The orchestra also released a recording of works by the French composers Roussel and Ravel, which was praised by critic Richard Freed in *Stereo Review*, who claimed that Järvi

> seems to relish the unique rhythms and colors of [Roussel's Symphony no. 3 in G Minor and *Bacchus et Ariane*]; he catches their spirit splendidly, and—by no means incidentally—he has the Detroit Symphony playing like a true virtuoso ensemble. The textures are marvelously achieved: just dry enough in the symphony's remarkable scherzo, ablaze without passing into neon in the starry climax of Bacchus.[27]

The orchestra released another disc of French music in 1992, once again featuring Roussel, this time his Symphony no. 4 and *Sinfonietta*, which received a review from Thomas Godell, who, while faulting some of Järvi's interpretations, had nothing but praise for the sound he elicited from the orchestra: "Järvi obtains a glorious sound from the Detroit Symphony—by far the best since the halcyon days of Paul Paray. The strings are rich and solid, the woodwinds colorful and the brass crisp."[28]

The third volume in the American Series of recordings featured the works of two African American composers, William Grant Still and Duke Ellington. Still was the first African American composer to produce a symphony and was virtually unknown to the world of classical music; on the CD he was represented with his Symphony no. 1, called the Afro-American. Ellington, a master of American jazz, was represented with his *Suite from "The River."* The recording was reviewed by Carl Bauman, who claimed that Järvi did "a remarkably fine job with [Still's] score," and that the DSO "responds more effectively to Still's idioms" than any other recording of the piece.[29]

Bauman wrote that while he would have preferred a heftier work to balance the Still symphony, he did find things to praise in the Ellington selection: "Obviously, jazz is ever-present and the results here are really very fine. Järvi has his Detroiters swinging, though not to the degree that Ellington himself might have."[30]

Further broadening his and the orchestra's reach, Järvi and the DSO next recorded the work of the little-known American composer George Frederick Bristow, his Symphony in F-sharp Major, paired with Barber's Symphony no. 2 and Adagio for Strings, which appeared as the fourth volume in the American Series. Writing in the *American Record Guide*, Steven J. Haller claims that Järvi's interpretation is a revelation:

> Neeme Järvi has this music in his blood; in his able hands Bristow's noble score fairly bursts at the seams with motor energy and the sheer infectious joy of music-making. Moreover, this splendid ensemble proves itself no less the master of Bristow's passionate lyricism than of Barber's jagged rhythms and sonorous brass writing.[31]

Haller also reviewed the sixth volume in the American Series, which included George Whitefield Chadwick's Symphony no. 3 in F Major, paired with several shorter works by Barber. Well known at the turn of the nineteenth century, Chadwick had once been called the dean of American composers, but was little remembered and performed in the late twentieth century.

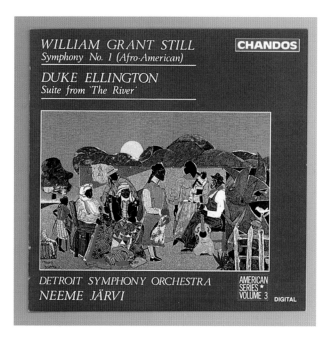

William Grant Still: Symphony no. 1 (The Afro-American), Duke Ellington: *Suite from "The River."* (Courtesy Chandos Records Ltd.)

Haller described Chadwick's Symphony, which he had submitted to a competition chaired by Antonín Dvořák in 1894, as "skillfully developed," and noted how the recording of the work's final movement "makes the most lasting impression: bursting forth at once in the horns in the robust manner of Brahms's First Serenade, there soon commences a syncopated fanfare motif in the trumpets that spurs on the orchestra to a breathless conclusion, producing a rich skein of sound."[32]

"That last movement stirs the blood in wondrous fashion under the knowing hand of Neeme Järvi," wrote Haller. "Gifted with a superb orchestra . . . and ensconced in the warm, all-embracing

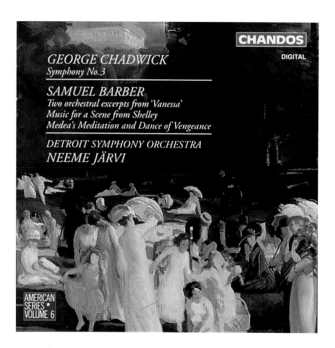

George Chadwick: Symphony no. 3, Samuel Barber: Two Orchestral Excerpts from "Vanessa," etc. (Courtesy Chandos Records Ltd.)

the symphony received to serve as the orchestra-in-residence at the Lucerne International Music Festival in the spring of 1994. Although it was only a week-long residency, it showcased the quality of the orchestra under Järvi, and planted the seeds for the viability of a more lengthy European tour in the future.

## CONDUCTING STYLE

Much has been written about Järvi's ability to draw the very best performances out of the ensembles he conducted, before and during his time in Detroit. In a review of the DSO's Carnegie Hall concert in April 1994, Bernard Holland described it this way:

> Conducting technique has no standards, but few have that unexplainable gift for conveying musical wishes by bodily attitude. Mr. Järvi is one of them.
>
> Saturday night at Carnegie Hall presented Mr. Järvi as orchestra builder and music director. Judging from the performance by the Detroit Symphony Orchestra of Rachmaninoff's First Symphony, he is as good at distinguishing his players as he is himself. There is a heft and resonance from this substantial if frequently troubled orchestra that I cannot remember from the past. When string players play well, they have a way of

acoustics of Detroit's venerable Orchestra Hall, Järvi plays the music for all it's worth; indeed, he makes one wonder how such a fine piece of work could have been hidden from us for so long?"[33]

Haller also praised the Barber works on the recording, noting Järvi's "prodigious mastery" of the pieces, especially "the Mahler-like schattenhaft writing of the 'Scene from Shelley' and the motor-driven closing pages of 'Medea's Dance of Vengeance.'" He concluded: "If you have any sympathy for turn-of-the-century American music—indeed any interest in romantic music at all—you owe it to yourself to buy this record."[34]

A tribute to the rising reputation of the DSO under Järvi was the invitation activating the floor beneath them, and on Saturday Carnegie Hall's stage parquet became an added instrument.

The richness of the string sound together with the clarity of Rachmaninoff's music told us that size and weight move lightly indeed when there is inner agreement between orchestra sections, when crescendo and decrescendo are understood to the farthest back desks of the violin section and when players tune their playing to the intonation of colleagues.[35]

Järvi's conducting style reflected his belief in spontaneity, in rehearsal and performance. Often, he would rehearse a piece one way, then change his interpretation during a concert. According to music critic Lawrence B. Johnson, this taught the musicians to be "quick and adaptable":

> At any given performance, the musician who does not pay attention to the man up front may well find himself out of sync if he simply assumes the music flying by will go just the way Järvi did it in rehearsal or even in the previous performance.[36]

According to veteran cellist Haden McKay, "There's always the element of the unexpected with Neeme, which is wonderful in a concert. Of course, that kind of risk-taking can also be scary, knowing we have to follow on the spot in front of an audience. But that's Neeme. He can bring out something we didn't even know was there. It's not intellectualized. It's just a force of character that comes out in the music."[37]

Associate concertmaster Kimberly Kaloyanides Kennedy concurred. "He always keeps us on our toes because we don't know what he'll do next. He can make something so original out of any piece. That spontaneity is what keeps everything fun and lighthearted—which is what we feed off. There is nobody like him."[38]

For Järvi, the interpretation of a piece was an ever-evolving concept. The idea that a conductor would repeat programs, or interpretations of individual pieces, over and over was horrifying. "I cannot be like this!" he told Scottish music critic Stephen Johnson.

> A human being can't be a machine, doing always the same thing. You must never copy. You find conductors who do the same 12 or 15 pieces over and over again—in the same way, again and again. That's a very boring life—for everybody. You must feel what you do—and that means always doing it as though for the first time.[39]

Yet for all his reliance on spontaneity, Järvi also insisted on providing what he firmly believed every symphony orchestra needed: a clear, consistent artistic vision.

The music director brings that by making the same demands every day, over and over. We have become accustomed to each other. Now, I can make just a little demonstration of a string bowing and they've got it. We don't even have to stop. They just make the adjustment, and we keep going.

That sort of daily training is important, even for the Berlin Philharmonic. It's not an easy thing for an orchestra to be completely confident, to keep good intonation, to stay on its toes. A guest conductor can never achieve that. The chief conductor is the person who says we're good but we need to be better. . . . It isn't a matter of philosophy but of detailed work.[40]

Järvi's conducting style was part of an ebullient musical persona, through which he forged a special relationship with musicians and audiences alike. For harpist Patty Masri-Fletcher, he had "a unique ability to bridge the gap between audience and musicians through personal rapport, programming, and even his conducting style. He brings so much

joy to it. His whole body gets involved—even his tummy."[41]

A former clarinet intern with the DSO, Stephen Millen, who moved into a management position with the symphony after his internship and knew Järvi from both sides of the stage, insisted that the joyous, warm persona on the podium was the real thing. "He puts aside all the cares of the world and focuses on making the art of music joyful," he claimed.[42]

Audience members agreed, too. Sterling C. Jones, a symphony subscriber from Detroit, was quoted in the *Detroit Free Press* about the maestro: "It's not just charisma," he said. "It's the ability to make people in the audience feel that the music is being made just for them."[43]

That was Järvi's stated purpose throughout his career in Detroit: "I play for the audience. I'm not doing it for myself. I love what I'm doing but I need to feel it goes to the audience. We do it for people who enjoy our music-making."[44]

Another of Järvi's performance staples was the playing of encores, which he chose from a broad range of orchestral repertoire, and which were a favorite with audiences. In fact, the DSO made two recordings of them. The first, *Encore!*, released in 1993 by Chandos and featuring brief pieces by composers as diverse as Chabrier, Sibelius, Ellington, Debussy, Gershwin, and John Philip Sousa, became an instant best-seller and remained a favorite with listeners.

Järvi conducting the DSO, Orchestra Hall. (Courtesy DSO Archives)

## DIVERSITY INITIATIVES

Järvi was also concerned with developing the audience for classical music among Detroit's largely African American population—by 1990, the city was seventy-five percent black—and continued to include the work of both little-known and well-known black composers in concerts.[45] He was also involved in the annual Unisys African-American Composers Forum and

Symposium, which attracted black audiences and became a showcase for the work of young black composers.

The Unisys African-American Forum was begun in the late 1980s, after accusations of discrimination in hiring by the DSO were raised by state legislators. Through financial support from the Unisys Corporation and run under the auspices of the DSO, it was one of the most important initiatives to come out of the discussions surrounding increasing diversity in the orchestra and the audiences for performances by the symphony.[46]

The Forum included an annual music competition, one of the few places where young African American composers could present their work. They were judged by a panel of musicians, and the winning pieces were given their premiere performances by the DSO. It was often an important first step for young composers, as in the example of Anthony Kelley, whose work won the competition in 1993, and was performed by both the DSO and the North Carolina Symphony. "My exposure in the Unisys competition made others aware of me," he told *American Visions* magazine, and, for Kelley, it paved the way for further competitions as well, as he was chosen to present new works at the New Choral Music Program for Emerging Composers at Macalester College in Minnesota the following year.[47]

Järvi was also instrumental in bringing the work of these young composers

to an even larger audience. In 1999, the DSO released a CD of the world premieres of pieces presented at the Unisys competition, recorded in Orchestra Hall between 1994 and 1998, and made available on the orchestra's own label. Included are works by Jonathan Holland from Flint, Michigan, who has gone on to a distinguished career as a composer and was in his twenties when the orchestra performed his works, *Martha's Waltz* and *Fanfares and Flourishes*. The recording also features Olly Wilson's *Shango Memory*, Anthony Davis's *Notes from the Underground*, and Alvin Singleton's *BluesKonzert*. A review of the CD notes that, "Neeme Järvi leads committed performances throughout, particularly noteworthy for their rhythmic elan. This is an important release that deserves an audience."[48]

One of the most important initiatives in developing greater diversity in the ranks of classical musicians, in Detroit and around the country, began in 1998 with the founding of the Sphinx Organization. This national association was created by Dr. Aaron P. Dworkin, who had begun his own violin studies as a child, and noticed the lack of people of color both onstage and in the audience at the concerts he attended.[49]

While an undergraduate at the University of Michigan, Dworkin began the Sphinx Competition for Black and Latino string players. Hosted every year by the DSO and held in Orchestra Hall, it represents an unprecedented opportunity for young musicians to learn and compete under the direction of outstanding musicians from around the world, including members of the DSO. Part of the organization's mission is to reach out to underserved communities in Detroit and nationwide, and it offers free violins and lessons for elementary students, and a summer chamber music academy for students in middle and high school.[50]

In addition to its support for the Sphinx Organization, the DSO under Järvi also brought back an important recording of music by composers of African descent, which had been made under the direction of former resident conductor Paul Freeman in the 1970s. Originally recorded as part of the CBS Black Composers Series, the set had gone out of print but was reissued under the DSO label in 2002.

Emil Kang, executive director of the symphony in 2002, said that the idea originated in the Classical Roots Committee of the orchestra, a group that seeks to build greater diversity in programming and audience development. "What's at the crux of this is our belief that the Detroit Symphony Orchestra has to be reflective of Detroit," he told Steve Smith of *Billboard* magazine. "It goes beyond race in that sense. It's really about how we represent our community."[51]

## MORE RECORDINGS

The indefatigable Järvi also continued to record with the DSO on the Chandos label, making recordings that included some rather unusual pieces and performers. In 1995, they released a CD with the Turtle Island Quartet that contained nontraditional works, such as the *Spider Dream Suite* by David Balakrishnan, a member of the Quartet, a work described in a review by Paul Cook as "a Stephane Grappelli–like romp that has distinct elements of Armenian music, all propelled by the force of rock and roll-jazz tempos, off-beat key signatures notwithstanding." These, along with a diverse group of other pieces by Miles Davis, Dizzy Gillespie, Bach, and Tower of Power, round out the recording. Cook called the music "alluring" and gave credit to the recording's success to Järvi: "He has to be one of the most adroit conductors on the planet. His affinity for so many different kinds of music is astonishing."[52]

Chandos ended its recording agreement with Järvi and the DSO in 1996, due to declining sales and increasing costs, but many more CDs appeared, more than twenty in all, during Järvi's tenure. These included a recording in the American Series that featured the Symphony no. 2 by Paul Creston and the Second Symphony of Ives. It was lavishly praised by Justin R. Herman, who wrote: "What a fine CD! Sonically superior, repertoire badly in need of top-notch advocacy, and, most important, Järvi and his orchestra so sympathetic to the idioms and composers." He concluded by calling the recording "A valuable release; the jewel of the Chandos American Series."[53]

Järvi and the DSO also released a recording of Richard Strauss's *Schlagobers*, or "Whipped Cream," a piece described as an "overstuffed Viennese cream puff, one of those delectable desserts that you dig into greedily but can't finish," by Anthony Tommasini of the *New York Times*, when the DSO performed the piece in New York. While acknowledging that the work was rather high in schmaltz and low in musical depth, Tommasini also noted that, in performance, "It certainly provided Mr. Järvi with a chance to show off his orchestra's precision, power, and color."[54]

### ORCHESTRA PLACE

In March 1996, the DSO announced an unprecedented plan for growth and expansion in Detroit: Orchestra Place, an $80 million project that would redevelop the area around Orchestra Hall and include a new complex of buildings for the DSO and other ensembles, a high school of the performing arts, and offices for the Detroit Medical Center.[55]

The project was envisioned to complement other ongoing urban renewal projects in a city where things were finally looking up economically. Michigan's economy had recovered, largely on strong results from the Big Three auto-makers, and an era of low inflation and unemployment helped the entire state to prosper. In 1997, unemployment in Michigan had fallen to just 3.9 percent, and building and renovation were beginning in downtown Detroit.[56]

Theaters like the Gem and the Fox, which were built during the flush days of the 1920s and had fallen into disrepair, were renovated and drew new crowds to a growing entertainment district downtown, as did the spectacular new Detroit Opera House, which opened to much acclaim in 1996. In addition, there were plans for three new casinos to be built in the downtown area, and two new sports stadiums, for the Detroit Tigers and the Detroit Lions, were also in the early stages of development.[57]

Orchestra Hall, situated almost a mile north of downtown, was in an area sorely in need of updating. The concept for Orchestra Place came in large part from real estate developer Peter D. Cummings, with suggestions from his famous father-in-law, Max Fisher. Fisher had made a fortune in gasoline and real estate, and by the 1990s was a nationally known philanthropist and community leader. Cummings had moved to Detroit with his family in 1989 and had joined the board of the DSO, whose members encouraged him to try to elicit a donation to the orchestra from Fisher.

Although Fisher wasn't particularly drawn to the idea of supporting the orchestra—Cummings said that Fisher didn't especially like music—he encouraged his son-in-law to "think bigger" when Cummings first described modest improvements to the Orchestra Hall area. With Fisher's suggestion as a catalyst, Cummings spearheaded an ambitious plan to expand Orchestra Hall into a new educational and entertainment area: the performing arts high school would be part of the Detroit Public Schools, the expanded performance area would present a broader range of musical entertainment, and new commercial buildings would house offices for the Detroit Medical Center, all integrated into the community and part of Detroit's renewal.

Since moving back to Orchestra Hall in 1989, the organization that ran the symphony, renamed Detroit Symphony Orchestra Hall, or DSOH, had acquired eight acres of property surrounding the Hall. This would be the land for the Orchestra Place expansion, to be completed in phases over several years, and designed to reach out to the nearby Medical Center and the surrounding community, and to integrate the new development into the neighborhood.

"We have been looking for an opportunity to become involved in a project in the city to help in its revitalization," said Peter Cummings's redevelopment partner, Robert Sosnick. "Orchestra Place, with its strategic location on Woodward and its historic alliance among the symphony, the Detroit Public Schools, and the Detroit Medical Center, is clearly a major step forward in that revitalization."[58]

Phase One of the plan included a 175,000-square-foot office building on Woodward, just south of Orchestra Hall. It would become the corporate headquarters of the Detroit Medical Center, which then operated seven hospitals in the area, as well as administrative offices for the orchestra, retail businesses, and a restaurant. The plans also included a 500-car parking deck to provide parking for the businesses during the day and music patrons at night.

The size and scope of the development demanded an ambitious fundraising plan as well, and it got off to a spectacular start: on September 30, 1997, DSOH announced contributions of $22.1 million for the project, the largest amount ever given to the organization, and among the largest in the history of Detroit's cultural institutions. The Fisher family gave a total of $6 million, with $5 million coming from Max Fisher and his wife, Marjorie, and $1 million from Peter and Julie Fisher Cummings. Another $6 million was donated by real estate developer and DSO patron Samuel Frankel and his wife, Jean; the Kresge Foundation gave a challenge grant of $6.5 million, with matching funds coming from philanthropist Shirley Shlager and businessman David Handleman and his wife, Marion.[59]

The Kresge Foundation's John Marshall praised the partnership that gave rise to the building of Orchestra Place, and noted the foundation's hope for its success and its meaning for Detroit:

We wish to endorse the development of Orchestra Place and the unique partnerships it represents; to applaud the exemplary artistic accomplishments of the Orchestra; to recognize the economic impact the project will have on the future stability of the Orchestra and the revitalization of its Woodward neighborhood; and to celebrate the Orchestra's ability to attract the largest gifts to a Detroit cultural institution in recent memory.[60]

Järvi also acknowledged the donations and their importance to the DSO:

These very generous gifts will help the Orchestra to fulfill a great destiny. They will help us to become even more a part of the fabric of our city and state. The Orchestra Place neighborhood will take on a new life with the advent of the high school and the hall expansion, which will make us an even more desirable destination for audiences. We will strive for our music-making to reflect the overwhelming and magnificent spirit of these gifts.[61]

## A EUROPEAN TOUR

In the midst of the renovations of Orchestra Place, the DSO embarked on its first European tour in nine years. It took place in the spring of 1998, and included performances in seventeen cities in nine countries over three weeks. The tour was paid for by Michigan-based Guardian Industries, one of the world's largest makers of automotive glass.[62]

Guardian's president and CEO, William Davidson, had developed a close friendship with Neeme Järvi, and saw the tour as an opportunity that would benefit the DSO, improve the reputation of Detroit, and also serve as a thank you to his company's European employees:

During the last 16 years, Guardian has made significant investments throughout Europe, with facilities in Luxembourg, Spain, Hungary, and Germany. During that time, we have learned a great deal about our European friends and their culture, including their deep appreciation for classical music. By working together with the DSO, we're not only showcasing Detroit's world-class Orchestra in Europe, but giving something back to the European communities where we conduct business every day.[63]

The tour was hailed by the DSOH board as further evidence of the musical and cultural stature of the orchestra, as well as the importance of Järvi and his effect on the fortunes of the organization. "This is an important indicator of the Orchestra's fine artistic reputation," said Board chairman Alfred Glancy, "and demonstrates how it serves as our region's cultural ambassador to the world. Also, the live experience of this Orchestra and its music director is unique, and now we have an opportunity to share this magic with an international audience."[64]

Järvi himself was deeply moved by the gesture: "I am so pleased that I will be able to show our Orchestra in these major European music capitals," he said. "In Europe, audiences are already familiar with our many recordings and radio broadcasts, and now they will have the opportunity to hear this American orchestra for themselves, in performances featuring American repertoire. We are very grateful to Guardian for making this exciting tour possible."[65]

Over the course of twenty-one days, the orchestra performed in Manchester, Birmingham, Brighton, and London in the United Kingdom; in Madrid and Barcelona, Spain; in Hamburg, Frankfurt, Berlin, Cologne, and Stuttgart in Germany; in Luxembourg; in Vienna, Austria; in Prague, Czech Republic; in Budapest, Hungary; and in Järvi's hometown of Tallinn, Estonia.

Järvi's choice of repertoire played on the tour reflected the many American works he championed at home and recorded on the Chandos American Series, including Barber's overture to *The School for Scandal*, Copland's *Billy the Kid*, and Still's Symphony no. 1 (the Afro-American Symphony). Traveling with the DSO as soloists were American violinist Pamela Frank and Norwegian pianist Leif Ove Andsnes.

As the tour began, Järvi spoke of his relationship with Detroit in an interview with the *Birmingham Post*. "I have been here eight years and it's wonderful," he said. "The honeymoon goes on and on." Of the American repertoire showcased on the tour, he reinforced his goal to "always do some American music which is not well known."[66]

> What do we know from American music: Copland, Bernstein and Gershwin. There's a lot of good music with a jazz influence, and from the Boston school—Chadwick and Mrs. Beach. We also do a lot of Barber's music which is not played very much.[67]

Järvi spoke of the DSO with pride: "It's a hugely professional orchestra which can swing very well in American music and play jazz very well. Detroit is a strong jazz city and the influence goes on and on. It helps to keep an American orchestra's image when you can swing a little."[68]

The orchestra received outstanding reviews throughout their tour. Their first concert, in Manchester, was praised by Gerald Larner of the *Times* of London, who noted that they played "with refreshing vitality and great skill in a programme so varied that it might almost have been designed to catch them out." Järvi was singled out for particular praise for his ambitious programming, as well as his well-known conducting principles:

His belief in spontaneity is such that he is less likely to drill his instrumentalists into a routine than take them by surprise—as he does when he mounts the rostrum, briefly acknowledges the audience and then turns to the orchestra with the down-beat already in motion.[69]

In Birmingham, the DSO's performances were similarly greeted with warm praise. Aprella Fitch of the *Birmingham Post* noted the orchestra's distinctive sound in *The School for Scandal* this way: "Whispering, chattering, and at times fulsome strings, attractively punctuating brass and percussion, together with eloquent winds." She also lauded the playing of pianist Leif Ove Andsnes in the Piano Concerto no. 3 by Prokofiev as "wonderfully mature and musical." Of the Symphony no. 10 by Shostakovich, she wrote that the orchestra's performance displayed "virtuosic individual and ensemble strength."[70]

Perhaps the highest praise came from the *Guardian*, whose critic, Edward Greenfield, began his review of their London concert by noting that Detroit, while not among the "top five" orchestras—New York, Boston, Philadelphia, Cleveland, and Chicago—was a virtuosic ensemble nonetheless, capable of dazzling an audience.

On this showing it would be hard to exaggerate the achievement of the Detroit Symphony Orchestra, whose tour of Britain culminated in a Barbican concert not just of dazzling brilliance—we expect that of American players—but of stirring warmth, too. The programme could hardly have been more taxing, a sequence of orchestral showpieces, American repertory in the first half, Prokofiev and Ravel in the second. If dazzle was what we expected and got, it was the inspired conducting of Neeme Järvi that set the performances on a higher plane. He did not just bring out pinpoint ensemble, but persuaded the players to perform with a flexible expressiveness akin to what one expects of a solo player, not a whole orchestra geared to precision.[71]

After their triumphal tour of Europe, the DSO ended their trip in their music director's hometown of Tallinn, Estonia. "That was the highlight for the orchestra," claimed Järvi. "It's like a postcard."[72]

## A TOUR OF JAPAN

Just months after their successful European trip, the DSO announced another tour, this time to Japan, for their first visit to Asia. Sponsored by Northwest Airlines and taking place in November 1998, the Detroit Symphony Orchestra/Northwest Airlines Friendship Tour was a ten-day, eight-concert visit to two Japanese cities with significance for Detroit. The first stop was Toyota City, the Sister-City of Detroit, and the second was Otsu City in the Shiga Prefecture, the Sister-State of Michigan.

The tour featured eight concerts and inaugurated two new performance spaces in Japan, the Toyota City Concert Hall and Otsu's Biwako Hall. In announcing the tour, Järvi said, "We are very honored by this invitation, to be the first American orchestra to perform in these spectacular new halls. These historic concerts will celebrate the special relationship our city and state [have] with our friends in Japan. In Japan, they love classical music and are very familiar with our recordings, but they have never heard the Detroit Symphony Orchestra live in concert."[73]

Three of the concerts featured Järvi conducting the orchestra in established pieces of Western classical music, with symphonies by Mozart and Mahler, as well as Dvořák's Symphony no. 9, ("From the New World"). Five of the eight concerts were explicitly educational in nature, and specifically for junior high school students, and were presented as a graduation gift from the mayor of Toyota City. These concerts were conducted by resident conductor Leslie B. Dunner, and featured a wide selection of American composers, including Barber, Copland, Ellington, and Gershwin.

During the tour, Orchestra Hall and the Toyota City Concert Hall established an agreement between their two cities, to enhance the exchange of culture between them. The Harmonius Concert Hall Agreement was signed by Detroit Mayor Dennis Archer and Toyota City Mayor Masaichi Kato in a ceremony held on November 12, 1998.[74]

## ORCHESTRA PLACE, PHASE TWO

By the end of 1998, Phase One of the Orchestra Place renovation, the 175,000-square-foot office building and parking deck, was nearing completion, and work began on Phase Two. This included the performing arts high school, to be built on 2.5 acres of land behind Orchestra Hall that the DSOH had donated to the city, and a 50,000-square-foot expansion of the existing building that housed Orchestra Hall, including a renovation of the hall and a new recital hall that would host other musical performances, to enhance and complement the offerings of the DSO.

By 2000, the scope of Phase Two, and the money required to realize it, had grown. Peter Cummings, now Board chairman, had demonstrated great success in generating millions in gifts to build Phase One of Orchestra Place, and that success had inspired other donors interested in helping to fund the project. According to Joseph Serwach of *Crain's Detroit Business*, "It proved to be an idea the DSO could sell to a bigger audience that would never have bothered to see a symphony orchestra concert."[75]

With new donations on the horizon, Cummings reenvisioned Orchestra Place. The scope of the project grew to include an even larger expansion of Orchestra Hall, from 50,000 to 135,000 square feet, to be called The Max M. Fisher Music Center. It included a 450-seat performance hall named the Music Box, a music education center, additional performance and administrative space, and rental space.

This new vision required new funding, so the original fundraising goal of $80 million was raised to $125 million. While that original amount had once seemed "an impossible dream," in the words of former chairman Alfred Glancy, for Cummings, it was an inevitable outgrowth of the Orchestra Place concept that brought in donors from outside the symphony's regular contributors.

"We raised this in a different way," said Cummings. "We didn't just go to the Big Three. We went to individuals. We reached out to other partners." The amounts were stunning: by early May 2000, they had raised $91 million of their $125 million goal. It included $37 million from members of the DSO board of directors, $20.1 million from other individuals, $12.9 million from foundations, $10.7 million from the state of Michigan, and $10.2 million from corporations. Of particular note was Max Fisher's own contribution, which he doubled from $5 million to $10 million, and the donation of Bernard and Marilyn Pincus, who gave $6 million to create the Jacob Bernard Pincus Music Education Center.[76]

Much of the credit for the increased interest in giving to the Orchestra Place project was attributed to the influence of Fisher, whose involvement, according to *Crain's* reporter Sewach, "helped turn heads beyond the world of traditional arts supporters." That included Michigan Governor John Engler, like Fisher, a Republican, who, after years of funding cuts to the DSO, had supported the large state commitment to the campaign; although Fisher claimed he had done no political arm-twisting to receive state support, it did indicate the breadth of his influence into sources of backing for the project.[77]

Cummings was grateful for the support of another politician, this time a

The Max M. Fisher Music Center. (Benjamin Beytekin/picture-alliance/dpa/AP Images)

Democrat: he praised the efforts of Detroit Mayor Dennis Archer, who, he claimed, "created an environment in which people want to invest in the city."[78]

The fundraising progress had an overall positive affect on the finances of the DSOH as well. By the time the second phase of the Orchestra Place project was outlined, the organization announced that it had paid off its accumulated deficit for the first time in twenty years, and was also able to add to its endowment.

## A NEW GUEST CONDUCTOR

The beginning of the new millennium was a positive time from a music-making point of view, too. In January 2000,

the DSO announced that famed violinist Itzhak Perlman would become principal guest conductor in 2001. Järvi was delighted with the appointment: "He can make wonderful things happen," he said.[79]

Perlman had guest conducted the DSO the previous fall, and there appeared to be a mutual spark between the orchestra and the man on the podium. "By the first break in rehearsal, I felt we had something going," Perlman told the *Free Press*. "When I asked for a certain sound, the orchestra was able to dig in and come up with something just so gorgeous, and I was really quite affected by that."[80]

Järvi and the musicians weren't the only ones pleased with the possibilities of

## PETER D. CUMMINGS, CHAIRMAN OF THE BOARD OF THE DSO, 1999–2003: ON THE DSO TOUR OF EUROPE, OCTOBER 9, 2001

Last week, the Detroit Symphony Orchestra departed for Europe, 155 strong. Musicians, stagehands, staff, and spouses are traveling abroad for nearly three weeks, starting in Dublin and finishing in Barcelona. The decision to go in these troubled times was a difficult one. I want to share with the community both why we went and how the decision was made.

We went because we were scheduled to go and extensive plans were already in place in communities across the European continent. In addition to the twelve concerts, we had arranged ten pre- and post-concert gatherings. Government officials, diplomats, business people, and musicians were to meet and exchange ideas. DaimlerChrysler, our lead sponsor, and Guardian Industries, which has established a Touring Fund to support these trips and to enable planning, were at the heart of the arrangements and had invested significant time and resources in helping to organize them.

In short, our sponsors and the DSO itself had made commitments that we were loath to back away from, for any reason.

Even after September 11.

September 11 left us all feeling devastated and vulnerable. Unfortunately, this feeling, and the reality behind it, will not soon recede. So the management of the orchestra, led by President Emil Kang, worked tirelessly to respond to the valid concerns of the musicians regarding safety and security. Certain travel arrangements were altered. A security firm was hired. Every reasonable step was taken to reassure the group.

And yet, doubts persisted. Much as we wanted to honor commitments to the host communities in Europe, and to our sponsors, we were fearful about traveling at this time and leaving the comfort of family and home.

Then, during the week before our departure, a strong consensus developed within the orchestra itself that we must turn to the business at hand and do what we do best: perform concerts at the highest level of musical excellence.

The fear began to dissolve, replaced by a collective will to go. A handful of musicians elected not to go, citing personal reasons. Of course, these individual decisions were respected.

We have a right to be proud of our orchestra, all ninety-eight players. The oldest is eighty-three and the youngest twenty-two. There are seventy-one men and twenty-seven women. They hail from more than twenty different countries and represent many different cultures. They are a fabric of diversity, and yet somehow they managed to make a collective decision to proceed while still respecting the rights of the few who needed to stay at home.

What better ambassadors to send abroad at a time like this? They are a gifted and courageous group that will do Detroit, Michigan, and all of America proud.

Their journey to Europe stands as the Detroit Symphony's tribute to the victims, families and rescue workers of September 11, whose stories of courage and compassion continue to unfold, day by day.

Powering this tribute—from Ireland and England, to Germany, Austria, and Spain, and finally home again—will be the music, healing and uplifting, which has a lure beyond language.

Source: *Detroit Free Press*, October 9, 2001.

Perlman joining the organization. Denise Davis-Cotton, principal of the Detroit High School for the Fine and Performing Arts, then under construction, was delighted with the prospect of Perlman conducting master classes and coaching students. "I simply cannot write a lesson plan that will have the magnitude of impact Perlman will provide," she said. "This will provide students with a breadth of knowledge they wouldn't otherwise be exposed to."[81]

## A PERMANENT TOURING FUND

Another positive development in 2000 was the announcement of a permanent touring fund for the DSO, provided by William Davidson and Guardian Industries. Davidson established the fund with an initial $2 million, to pay for both domestic and international touring.

In announcing the gift, Davidson said, "It is critical that we support the efforts of key Detroit and Michigan institutions to promote the unique attributes of our community. We are home to world class cultural institutions, such as the DSO, and it's time the rest of the country and the entire world were better aware of that."[82]

Järvi praised the initiative: "I am grateful to my good friend Bill Davidson. We were honored to have him support our 1998 European Tour and join us for some of the concerts there. Bill knows how important this is for the Orchestra and for

our community. In the United States, people know the Detroit Symphony from our radio broadcasts, but have not had the chance to hear us perform live."[83]

The DSO made use of the funds right away: they began planning a European tour for the fall of 2001, and traveled to Florida in January 2001 for the "Guardian Sunshine Tour." The opening concert of the tour, played in Palm Beach's Kravis Center, was warmly reviewed by Sharon McDaniel of the *Palm Beach Post*. She praised the strong programming and the virtuoso playing of violin soloist Joshua Bell, calling the entire evening "rich enough to overdose on."[84]

## A SUDDEN MEDICAL CRISIS

In the midst of all the positive news for the DSO, a sudden medical crisis threatened the future of the ensemble and its leader. On July 9, 2001, Järvi suffered a stroke while visiting Pärnu, Estonia. After several anxious days, the family revealed that his condition had stabilized, but that he would require surgery to repair a broken artery. His doctors predicted that he would make a full recovery, though it would take several months. The DSO, relieved at the news, now faced a new challenge: to find a new conductor to lead them on their upcoming European tour.[85]

In August, the DSO announced that Finnish conductor Leif Segerstam would take Järvi's place on the tour, which was scheduled for October and included performances in twelve cities over seventeen days. Segerstam, principal conductor of the Helsinki Philharmonic and the Royal Opera of Stockholm and well regarded throughout Europe, had conducted the DSO in three concerts in April 2001 and was pleased to be selected. "The concerts that I performed with the DSO last spring gave me much creative musical stimulus and inspiration," he said. "I am eagerly looking forward to making music with them again, and creating the rich musical interpretations that they so generously and spontaneously let me enjoy."[86]

## EUROPEAN TOUR

As the orchestra prepared for its European tour, the terrorist attacks of September 11, 2001, brought the nation, and the world, to a halt. After a series of meetings to determine how, or if, they wished to proceed, the musicians decided that the tour would go ahead as planned. They were determined to prove themselves musically under the baton of a new maestro, while, at the same time acknowledging the fear and anxiety of those difficult times. "I think we're all feeling the stress," said concertmaster Emmanuelle Boisvert. "We're looking forward to the tour, but there are concerns, too."[87] As they prepared to leave, extra security measures were put in place to guard the musicians' safety through-

out the tour, and, in early October, they became the first US orchestra to travel after the terrorist attacks.

Because of Segerstam's previous commitments, the orchestra was unable to rehearse with their new conductor until they reached Dublin, Ireland, just ten hours before their first concert. Yet, despite the problems and constraints they faced, the musicians displayed unmatched artistry and flexibility in Dublin and everywhere on the tour, performing at the highest level and receiving praise from the European press.

In Dublin, they played to a sold-out crowd of 1,200, where the audience demanded, and received, four curtain calls. They next played at London's Royal Festival Hall, in a performance attended by British critic Stephen Pettitt, who noted the DSO's signature sound:

a solidity of tone in the body of strings, a pleasingly robust woodwind section and impressively incisive percussion playing. . . . It also has a brass section that sings rather than shrieks, unlike the brass in certain more self-consciously showy American orchestras. It is a sound I like very much, and it was put to excellent use Saturday evening. There was a cogent performance of Rachmaninoff's Symphonic Dances—a complex but uniquely rewarding work, frequently spare of texture and abstract in approach.[88]

The orchestra traveled on to Wales, Germany, Austria, and Spain, where they were again met with sold-out audiences, standing ovations, and critical praise. Critics in each of the cities praised the DSO's solid musicianship and rich sound, as well as the programming that showcased that sound. The one work critics couldn't agree on was DSO resident composer Michael Daugherty's *Rosa Parks Boulevard*, which drew mixed reviews, but the overall positive light in which the orchestra was received burnished their reputation at home and abroad.[89]

## A BELOVED MAESTRO RETURNS

The DSO returned to Detroit at the end of October, and in November welcomed their maestro home. Järvi returned to the city and the orchestra he loved on November 25, 2001, with his health, vigor, and special blend of musicianship and showmanship intact. As Lawrence B. Johnson wrote in the *Detroit News*:

The instant Järvi appeared from the right stage entrance for the first time Friday night, the audience of 2,200 rose and cheered "Bravo, maestro!" and "Bravo, Neeme!" After barely a minute, he turned to the orchestra and lifted his baton. By the time this con-

cert was over, any lingering doubt of Järvi's recovery was gone, exorcised by the pounding, intricate rhythms of *The Rite of Spring* in an edge-of-the-seat thriller of a performance.

After numerous standing ovations, and with a huge bouquet of flowers tucked under his arm, Järvi conducted a signature encore, "with his free hand, mugging all the while," according to Johnson. He was back, to the delight of audiences and musicians alike.[90]

## JÄRVI ANNOUNCES HIS RETIREMENT

Just six months later, in April 2002, Järvi announced that he would leave the DSO in 2005. While he radiated good health and energy, he knew it was time to slow down from the fevered pace which he had kept up for many years. The announcement came as something of a shock to many music lovers in Detroit, though Järvi, in his fifteen years as music director, was second only to Gabrilowitsch in the length of his tenure. He believed it was a decision whose time had come:

I am at the age now where I want to cut back on my schedule and spend more time with my family. The demands of a music directorship are great, and during my tenure with the Detroit Symphony

Orchestra we have accomplished much. [But] in 2005, it will be time for me to slow down.[91]

Speculation began immediately about who would be chosen as his successor, as Järvi continued to direct the DSO in preparation for the opening of "The Max," the Max M. Fisher Music Center.

## THE OPENING OF THE MAX

On October 11, 2003, the Max M. Fisher Music Center opened, with a gala celebration to inaugurate the 135,000-square-foot addition, as well as the completion of new facilities for the musicians in Orchestra Hall. A sold-out crowd attended the opening, where patrons marveled at the four-story glass atrium, the new "Music Box" recital hall, and the Jacob Bernard Pincus Education Center, the new home of the four youth ensembles sponsored by the DSO.

As education director and music director Charles Burke told Lawrence B. Johnson of the *Detroit News*, the new center provided rehearsal and performance spaces for the Civic Symphony for students aged seventeen to twenty, the Sinfonia for those twelve to sixteen, the Sinfonia Chamber Players for musicians fifteen to sixteen, and the Civic Jazz Orchestra for players ages fourteen to twenty.

At the opening, Peter Cummings praised the contributors who had raised the funds to make "The Max" a reality, but especially Järvi, for "elevating the image of the DSO as an orchestra of national importance." Järvi replied by praising the musicians, who throughout the renovation had been making do with trailers in the lots around the Hall. "The musicians deserve this. They are hard workers, and I appreciate what they have achieved under very bad conditions. They are heroes."[92]

The gala concert that inaugurated the new complex was a marvelous mixture of old and new. Järvi chose a world premiere called *Motor City Dance Mix*, written by Jonathan Holland, who had been a winner of the Unisys African-American Forum in the 1990s; Beethoven's Violin Concerto in D Major with guest Itzhak Perlman; and Copland's Third Symphony, which Järvi had recorded with the DSO years before, and which features a reworking of Copland's *Fanfare for the Common Man*, an apt selection harkening back to the industrial roots of the city.

## THE PROMISE AND THE PROBLEMS

Whether or not the promise of the new space would be realized remained to be seen, and it was on Peter Cummings's mind at the gala opening. "We've built the Max, but we haven't operated it yet," he told the *Detroit News*. "Now we face the challenge of showing that we can actually

The Orchestra Hall/Max M. Fisher Music Center renovation, completed October 2003. (Benjamin Beytekin/picture-alliance/dpa/AP Images)

make this space come alive and fulfill the dreams of many people."[93]

And financial problems did arise: in late 2003, shortly after the opening of the Max, an unexpected deficit of $1.8 million dollars, as well as an equally unexpected cut in state funding of fifty percent, led to dramatic financial cutbacks in salaries for musicians and staff, and the resignation of Emil Kang as executive director. The reductions amounted to $4 million, and, after nearly a decade of successful contract negotiations between management and the musicians' union, the musicians' contract had to be renegotiated and salaries cut across the board.[94]

By that point, Järvi had announced that he had accepted the post of music director at the New Jersey Symphony Orchestra, to begin with the 2005–06 season. The commitment was considerably lighter than his duties with the DSO, comprising a ten-week concert season, and he had already promised to return to Detroit on a regular basis, as music director emeritus.

As Järvi's final year in Detroit approached, there were plans for a concert series to commemorate his fifteen years with the DSO, including a "Järvi Fest" to celebrate his contributions to music in Detroit, and featuring his three children, all professional musicians in their own right.

The atrium of the new Max M. Fisher Music Center, October 11, 2003. (Paul Warner/AP Images)

CHAPTER NINE

Järvi himself contemplated his achievements in terms of his relationship with the orchestra. "Step by step, we have grown together for 15 years," he told Lawrence B. Johnson of the *Detroit News*. "We're really a good team," which Johnson called an "understatement."[95]

The Estonian-born conductor and this mid-American orchestra have evolved into a championship team. They have changed together, flowered together, triumphed together. Especially over the last half-dozen seasons, they have turned what once were highlights into a lofty new standard of excellence at Orchestra Hall.[96]

Asked to recall the highlights of his years with DSO, Järvi said:

For me, the highlights are in the quality of the relationship, the mutual understanding. What have we achieved? Look at the spaces around the Max. It was the ugliest place when I came here—empty. But now we have the Max and the music school and many other new buildings going up. The DSO achieved this. The vision was right.[97]

The musicians expressed their feelings for their departing director, with harpist Patty Masri-Fletcher noting his enduring support for the musicians: "He urged the community to value the orchestra," she said. "He's always been on the side of very good music played by world-class musicians."[98]

Järvi's final concert, given on June 19, 2005, was reviewed by Mary Ellyn Hutton in the *American Record Guide*. Originally scheduled to be conducted by his son Paavo, who had to cancel due to a hand injury, the ever-ready Järvi stepped in and conducted a program described by Hutton:

Järvi opened with an energized Overture to Mozart's Clemenza di Tito and closed with the Schumann Rhenish Symphony. Son Paavo would have led a more ardent slow movement, but you could feel the waves of the Rhine in the Scherzo, and the outer movements brimmed with elan. The concert's most poignant moment was the encore, Sibelius's Romance in C, performed by DSO concertmaster Emmanuelle Boisvert, whose tender, brushed tone spoke volumes about the players' affection for their retiring leader.[99]

Järvi returned the compliment in his departing words to Lawrence Johnson:

Detroit is a great musical city, and Orchestra Hall is one of the very best places in the world to create music. It is always such a pleasure to hear that sound open up. I really don't want to go to the so-called Big Five as a guest conductor because I can't get that result. I would rather come back here. This is a truly great orchestra.[100]

The popular and charismatic Järvi departed in 2005, leaving a legacy of artistic excellence as well as financial stability, based in part on his appeal to audiences as well as donors. But there were problems on the horizon. After he left, no successor was named for three years, and without a permanent music director and well-defined artistic vision, the orchestra's future and direction were far from clear.

And while the Järvi era had also been a time of highly successful fundraising and important expansion for the symphony, the approach to financing Orchestra Place represented a significant departure from earlier models, especially the Ford Plan.

Järvi bows to the audience at the opening of the Max, October 11, 2003. (Paul Warner/AP Images)

As Peter Cummings had said, "We raised this in a different way. We didn't just go to the Big Three. We went to individuals. We reached out to other partners."

Unlike the Ford Plan, which was predicated on a large number of corporate sponsors contributing equal amounts and sharing the responsibilities of serving on the Board, the majority of the $91 million raised to fund Phase Two of Orchestra Place in 2000 came from a small group of rich donors: $37 million from board members alone, and another $20 million from other individuals. And as would become evident in the next few years, the debt to fund the building of the Max utilized a high-risk financing model that, during the financial crisis of 2008, led to crippling financial losses.

These problems would precipitate a bitter conflict between the orchestra and the organization that managed it, playing out in a city facing the largest municipal bankruptcy in the nation's history and threatening the viability of the DSO and all the major cultural organizations in the city.

# Musical Artistry in an Era of Uncertainty, 2005–Present: Leonard Slatkin and the Future of the Modern Symphony Orchestra

As the musicians took the stage, applause and cheering erupted. "We love you guys!" a concertgoer yelled. A violinist mouthed, "Wow," another tapped her music stand with her bow in appreciation, and the awe-struck players stood facing a packed-to-the rafters audience for five minutes while the love flowed over them.

The Detroit Symphony Orchestra was back.

The men and women in black and white appeared in Orchestra Hall on Saturday night for the first time after a corrosive six-month strike.[1]

WHEN NEEME JÄRVI LEFT DETROIT IN 2005, HE LEFT AN ORCHESTRA whose artistry was celebrated around the world; at home, the DSO was playing in a refurbished Orchestra Hall that was part of a spectacular new addition, the Max M. Fisher Music Center. Järvi's final year had been noteworthy for economic reasons, too: his farewell season had prompted a spike in revenue, as attendance and ticket sales rose and donations to the endowment grew.[2]

Yet there was trouble on the horizon for the DSO, and for the city it called home, as internal and external forces threatened not only its artistic and economic foundations, but its very existence. It was a world in flux, where both a 120-year-old symphony orchestra and a 305-year-old city struggled for relevance and viability, and for the leadership and vision to sustain them.

As the 2005–06 season got underway, there was still no music director. The season was programmed in large part by DSO vice president Stephen Millen, who scheduled a number of concerts that featured concerto or solo roles for the musicians of the orchestra, displaying the musical virtuosity of its members. There were also a number of guest conductors, including Roger Norrington, Charles Dutoit, and Rafael Frühbeck de Burgos, and orchestra watchers scrutinized them in hopes of discovering among them Järvi's replacement.

An active member in the search was the DSO's new president and executive director, Anne Parsons, who joined the orchestra in 2004 after the departure of Emil Kang, who had left in the wake of heavy financial losses after the opening of the Max. Parsons came to Detroit from New York, where she had been the general manager of the New York City Ballet for six years. During her tenure with City Ballet, Parsons had been responsible for the negotiations of union contracts. In that role, she, along with ballet master-in-chief Peter Martins, made the decision to continue performances of *The Nutcracker* during a strike by the organization's musicians in 1999, the first time in the ensemble's forty-five-year history in which

the performance took place with recorded music. Prior to her years in New York, Parsons had been the general manager of the Hollywood Bowl, and also served in management positions with the National Symphony in Washington, DC, and the Boston Symphony Orchestra.

In June 2006, the DSO announced a new principal guest conductor and artistic adviser, Peter Oundjian, who provided musical guidance over the next two years, selecting repertoire and guest conductors as the search went on. Relations between the musicians and management remained positive, and in the fall of 2006, the musicians' union announced that they had agreed to extend their existing contract for one year with no changes in salary or benefits.

A list of guest conductors for the next season included one that intrigued many Detroiters. Leonard Slatkin, a prominent American conductor credited with reviving the musical profile of the St. Louis Symphony and about to complete his twelve-year tenure with the National Symphony Orchestra in Washington, DC, was scheduled to conduct the orchestra in June of 2007.

Slatkin's appearance in Detroit was widely praised, with Mark Stryker of the *Free Press* calling the performance, especially the rapport between the musicians and the conductor, "sizzling."[3] Just months later, in October 2007, the DSO announced that Slatkin had been selected as the orchestra's twelfth music director, and he would begin his duties in the 2008–09 season.[4]

## LEONARD SLATKIN

Slatkin began his tenure in Detroit as one of the most prominent American-born conductors in the country, noted for his championing of American music, especially of modern composers. After the announcement, Drew McManus, an influential arts consultant whose special field is the business of symphony orchestras, wrote: "Leonard will be a really good fit in Detroit. He has a reputation as a real orchestra builder in terms of helping a group develop a unique, original sound, building reputation through recording, outreach, and pulling in new donors."[5]

Leonard Slatkin was born in Los Angeles on September 1, 1944, into a musical family. His father, Felix Slatkin, was a violinist and conductor, and his mother, Eleanor Aller, was a cellist; both worked as musicians in the film industry and were also founding members of the Hollywood String Quartet. Leonard began to study the violin at the age of three, and later added viola, piano, and composition.

Slatkin studied at Indiana University and Los Angeles City College and completed his bachelor's degree at the Juilliard School of Music in 1968, training under Walter Susskind. He became the assistant conductor of the St. Louis Symphony Orchestra that same year, and, advancing through the conductorship ranks from assistant to associate over the years, was named music director in 1979.

During his years in St. Louis, Slatkin is credited with developing the orchestra to a high level of musicianship and also founding the youth orchestra for the symphony. He took the St. Louis Symphony on a European tour in 1985, further enhancing its reputation.

While conducting in St. Louis, Slatkin also took on several major roles with other orchestras, notably as the music director of the summer programs for the Pittsburgh Symphony Orchestra's Great Woods Performing Arts series in 1990 and the Cleveland Orchestra's Blossom Festival in 1991. Also in 1991, he made his debut at the Metropolitan Opera, conducting Puccini's *La Fanciulla del West.*

In 1996, Slatkin left St. Louis to become the music director of the National Symphony Orchestra in Washington, DC, a position once held by former DSO maestro Antal Dorati. In Washington, Slatkin once again became known as a champion of American music, including the music of such major contemporary composers as John Corigliano and Elliott Carter. He also conducted the inaugural performances at the orchestra's renovated concert hall at the Kennedy Center.

While his musical directorship continued in Washington, Slatkin took on the roles of principal guest conductor with the Philharmonia Orchestra in Lon-

Leonard Slatkin, music director of the DSO beginning in 2008. (Associated Press)

don and the chief conductor of the BBC Symphony Orchestra. He also became an outspoken advocate for music education in the Washington, DC, area, campaigning to raise money for the DC Youth Orchestra, and, in 2000, becoming director of the National Conducting Institute, which trains young conductors.

Slatkin also made a series of recordings with a number of ensembles, including St. Louis and the National Symphony Orchestra, many of them featuring American composers. These included a 2004 recording of William Bolcom's *Songs of Innocence and Experience* with the University of Michigan Symphony and Chamber Choir, which won three Grammy awards. An-

other distinctively American work, *Made in America* by Joan Tower, was recorded by Slatkin and the Nashville Symphony Orchestra in 2007; that recording, too, went on to win three Grammys.[6]

## ECONOMIC PROBLEMS

Soon after Slatkin's appointment was announced, the DSO had to grapple with bad economic news. After three years of balanced budgets, there was a deficit of $190,000 at the end of 2007, a figure that would have been $2 million had several donors not stepped in to make contributions that allowed about $1 million that had been restricted as gifts to the endowment to be transferred to the fund for operations

## PETER OUNDJIAN

Peter Oundjian (pronounced "Un-jinn") played a crucial role as principal guest conductor of the DSO from 2006 to 2010 and as musical advisor to the DSO after Neeme Järvi left Detroit and before the appointment of Leonard Slatkin. Oundjian helped guide the DSO with artistry and outstanding musical leadership from 2006 to 2010, helping out in all areas, from programming to auditions to fund-raising and education initiatives.

Oundjian was born in Toronto on December 21, 1955, and was raised in London, England, where he began studying the violin at age seven. He went on to the Charterhouse School, and next to the Royal College of Music, then left the United Kingdom to continue his studies at Juilliard, where his teachers included Ivan Gallamian and Dorothy DeLay. Taking a Minor in conducting, he once had to direct a work sight-unseen for the formidable Herbert von Karajan, who praised his efforts.

Oundjian joined the Tokyo String Quartet in 1981 as first violinist, but his career as a player was cut short by a neurological disorder in his left hand that made playing the violin more and more difficult. So, at the age of forty, Oundjian switched careers, becoming a conductor, a role in which he has excelled for more than two decades.

Oundjian first conducted in Detroit in 1997 at the Great Lakes Chamber Music Festival, and he soon became a valued guest conductor for the DSO and many other ensembles worldwide. In 2004, he was named music director of his hometown orchestra, the Toronto Symphony, but was also able to take on the roles of artistic advisor and principal guest conductor for the DSO in 2006, while the search for a new music director in Detroit continued.

"I'm going to be an artistic anchor," said Oundjian of his new role in 2006. "There are times when an organization doesn't have a music director and it's difficult to feel stable. I'll be happy to provide some stability and creative direction that will allow the orchestra to forge ahead."

He accomplished that and more, directing the orchestra with a style praised for its spirit of collaboration, deep musical knowledge, and experience. In addition to making programming decisions, hiring guest musicians, and taking part in auditions, Oundjian also brought new music festivals to Detroit, including "8 Days in June," which featured a wide variety of music and performance genres, from orchestral concerts and chamber music to jazz, hip-hop, lectures, and spoken word pieces. Jazz giant Wynton Marsalis performed during the festival, as did actor F. Murray Abraham, who appeared in a performance of Stravinsky's *A Soldier's Tale*.

Some Detroiters thought that Oundjian was a top candidate for the music director's position, but he had already committed to Toronto, and in 2011 he added the Royal Scotland National Orchestra to his musical director duties. He still appears as a guest conductor with the DSO, as well as a number of orchestras around the globe.

Sources: *Detroit Free Press*, June 20, 2006; April 9, 2007; http://www.tso.ca/en-ca/About-the-TSO/peter-oundjian.aspx; http://www.rsno.org.uk/live/artistic-team/peter-oundjian/.

expenses. This occurred as the musicians and management signed a new three-year contract, in negotiations that at times grew contentious, but was settled without a strike, with the musicians agreeing to a giveback of $10,000 each over two years.

But there was another financial move involving the endowment at the end of 2007 that proved to be both risky and ill-advised. Management approved a withdrawal of $800,000 from the endowment to pay for expenses in 2007, which was, according to Anne Parsons, warranted due to weakness in Michigan's economy that had led to lower than expected revenue and a shortage of cash.

While, according to Parsons, it was a "temporary decision" and that management had decided to "borrow from our own bank account" with "a plan to pay it back," that would not prove to be the case. And while it would be months before the financial crisis and the worldwide recession took hold, by the end of 2007 there were already signs of weakness in the Michigan economy that was reflected in declining revenue. In addition to a drop in ticket sales, the DSO had expected $652,000 in funding from the state and instead received only half of that amount, and the Max M. Fisher Music Center, which had been expected to provide growing rental and retail income, brought in $250,000 less than the previous year.[7]

The following year brought even worse economic news. An analysis of the orchestra's finances at the end of its fiscal year in August 2008 showed a deficit of $512,000, which would have been far greater had not donors stepped in once again with $2 million in donations to shore up the orchestra's bottom line. The value of the endowment fell as well, from $95 million in 2007 to $85 million as of August 31, 2008, as the stock market lost value in the months prior to the financial crisis.[8]

## THE FINANCIAL CRISIS AND ITS IMPACT ON DETROIT

When the financial crisis did hit in September 2008, it left the city, the state, and the nation reeling in what would become the worst economic downturn since the Great Depression. To provide stability in the economy and prevent the collapse of the financial system, the government and the Federal Reserve began a plan to provide over $700 billion in funding to prevent the largest financial institutions from failing. In the weeks that followed, some banks and brokerage houses did fail or were forced to merge, while, despite the government's efforts, the stock market nearly collapsed.

According to the Dow Jones Industrial Average, a benchmark of the value of major stock holdings in the United States, the value of investments fell nearly forty percent in eight months, with the Dow declining from its historical high of 13,930 in July 2008 to 7,063 in February 2009.[9] Individual consumers and businesses saw the value of their investments plummet, and, over the next two years, an estimated $12.8 trillion in investment and market capital were wiped out.[10]

As had happened in previous recessions, Detroit and Michigan were particularly hard hit. Annual vehicle sales plummeted from just over sixteen million units in 2007 to ten million in 2009, and unemployment in Detroit rose to 27.8 percent and in the state to

15.3 percent, the highest in the nation. Two of the Big Three, GM and Chrysler, were near collapse and had to be bailed out by the federal government under the TARP (Troubled Asset Relief Program); both went through government-audited bankruptcies in early 2009, from which they exited quickly, then set strategies for recovery.[11]

While these programs are credited with saving the US automobile industry and more than one million jobs, the economic crisis wreaked havoc on the budgets of businesses and nonprofits throughout the country, and exacerbated the financial woes facing the DSO. By December of 2008, the endowment had fallen to $56.8 million, having lost more than $38 million in just over one year.[12] The crisis affected Detroit's other major cultural organizations as well, with the Detroit Institute of Arts losing $17 million in 2008, and the Michigan Opera Theater posting a loss of $800,000.[13]

### SLATKIN'S DEBUT

This was the atmosphere in Detroit in December 2008, when Slatkin made his debut as music director "at the epicenter of America's economic crisis, in the hometown of an embattled domestic auto industry," in the words of music critic Lawrence B. Johnson. The city put out the red carpet, literally, as his debut "commenced with search-lights sweeping the sky, a red carpet rolled out for patrons, and a

packed, anticipatory house." At the end of the night, Slatkin was greeted with "a wild ovation for a performance of Carl Orff's riotous cantata *Carmina Burana* that was equal parts superb music-making and delightful theatrics."[14]

Slatkin had, from that first appearance, given "every indication that he would be both the imaginative musical guru and the tireless fund-raiser that the financially challenged DSO hoped he would be," according to Johnson. Even before his arrival, he had been reaching out to potential donors, "working the streets, the phones, and the homes of donors who had seen their portfolios shrink as the stock market sank," and successfully, too: "the result has been palpable excitement at the development office and in Orchestra Hall," claimed Johnson.[15]

Over the span of the five weeks he spent in Detroit that season, Slatkin delighted DSO audiences with concerts that featured well-known works, like Rachmaninoff's *Rhapsody on a Theme of Paganini*, featuring the dynamic piano playing of Olga Kern, as well as world premieres, including African American composer James Lee III's *A Different Soldier's Tale* and Belarus composer Alla Borzova's *Songs for Lada*, which featured the Michigan State University Children's Choir.

"The orchestra's rapport with its new music director has been clear and gratifying," wrote Lawrence Johnson. "Despite the three-year interval since the departure of Neeme Järvi, the orchestra has preserved its technical discipline, and Slatkin has quickly raised that precision leavened by rhythmic fluency."[16]

Slatkin also began to record with the DSO, releasing a CD of new music, with new musical collaborators, *The Melody of Rhythm: Triple Concerto & Music for Trio*. It was a true departure for the DSO, featuring a trio that included Bela Fleck on banjo, Ustad Zakir Hussain on tabla, and Edgar Meyer on double bass. The recording received a Grammy nomination, and was praised in the journal *India Currents* for "its ability to surprise you with its wide and varied sound-scapes, regional influences, musical genres, and original refrains."[17]

## A MEDICAL EMERGENCY

In the fall of 2009, just months into Slatkin's first full season as the DSO's music director, the orchestra's new maestro faced a serious and sudden medical emergency. While conducting the Rotterdam Philharmonic in the Netherlands on November 1, Slatkin suffered a heart attack. He had emergency surgery to unblock an artery, and returned to the United States to recuperate.[18] He took two months off, and returned to the podium in February 2010, where he led the DSO in a six-concert tour in Florida.

## MORE FINANCIAL WOES

But while Slatkin returned to the podium with his health restored, the financial situation of the DSO continued to deteriorate. When the figures for the 2009 season became available, they revealed a desperate financial state: the deficit had grown to $3.8 million, and despite cost-cutting measures that trimmed $1.6 million from the budget and included layoffs and pay cuts on the part of the management staff, there was one glaring problem: the endowment had fallen below the $54 million mark, the amount that had been sold in bonds to build the Max Fisher Music Center in 2001. That put the DSO in violation of the loan covenant, which required that the endowment exceed the principal of the loan; with the endowment falling to $22 million in 2010, they defaulted on the loan, and the debt on the Max became the responsibility of a consortium of banks, which pushed for payment.

This startling state of affairs brought to light the debt arrangement developed under former Board chairman Peter Cummings in 2001 to pay for the building of the Max: it had utilized an arbitrage plan that was predicated on a high rate of investment return to pay off the bonds, which became unsustainable after the market collapse.

In 2001, the DSOH raised $54 million in pledges to build the expansion. As the money was received, the organization issued low-interest and tax-exempt bonds to the bondholders, and placed the pledge funds into the endowment, also paying the building costs from proceeds from the bond sale. The balloon payment on the $54 million owed to the bondholders was due in thirty years.

As Cummings explained to *Crain's Detroit Business*, the Board decided that the organization would pay only the interest due on the bond, and any income from the investment beyond the interest would fund operations and the endowment:

> The theory was that you would be able to get 5 to 8 percent on your money, and over a 30-year time frame, that arbitrage between paying 2.5 or 3 percent on the bonds to build the building and getting 6, 7, 8 percent on the growing endowment would have paid off the bonds.[19]

Of course, no one could have predicted the 2008 crisis, but the decisions made regarding the structure of the debt led to an even greater economic burden: by 2010 the organization didn't just owe the $54 million in real estate debt to the bank consortium; after the default, the interest payment on the debt rose to $2.4 million per year, adding to an already precarious financial situation.[20]

In February 2010, Slatkin announced that he had agreed to donate four weeks of concerts in the following season as a way to help out the organization's finances, stating that he would perform for sixteen weeks and reduce his salary, although the amount of the reduction was never disclosed.

## CONTRACT NEGOTIATIONS

Similarly, talks began between the musicians and management to renegotiate their contract, which was set to expire at the end of August 2010, in an effort to find a way to further reduce costs through concessions on pay. But talks between the two sides broke down in March, without an agreement.

The most important issue for the musicians was parity in pay with other US orchestras considered in the top tier, which they claimed was crucial in both hiring and retaining the best players. Although they were willing to share in the cost-cutting necessary to keep the orchestra viable, the musicians also wanted the new contract to contain guarantees that would bring their compensation back to previous levels once the finances of the organization had improved.

The orchestra management was most concerned with cutting costs, especially in light of the $54 million owed to the bank consortium, and the need to reach financial stability so that donors would once again contribute.[21]

In an essay that looked at the precarious position of the major arts institutions in Detroit—the DSO, the Detroit Institute of Arts, and the Michigan Opera Theater—Mark Stryker of the *Free Press* wrote about their shared purpose and their shared anxieties:

As Detroit's largest and most distinguished fine arts institutions, the DSO, MOT, and DIA play a leading role in defining the region's cultural identity. They entertain, inspire, and enlighten, offering the kind of top-drawer artistic experiences demanded of any city with high aspirations. With the disappearance of music and art in the schools, they've also become key sources of art education. And by investing more than $300 million into downtown real estate since the 1990s, they've been on the frontlines of revitalizing the city center.[22]

He then noted how those building expansions, including the Max M. Fisher Music Center, rather than securing the future of these institutions, had become sources of crippling debt. Adding to this, the continuing weak economy meant formerly generous contributors like GM and Chrysler had gone from giving millions each year to cutting nearly all donations to the arts organizations; similarly "consumers, many coping with job losses or pay cuts, stay home," and wealthy donors, "whose portfolios have shrunk," could no longer give at previous levels.[23]

An article in *Time* magazine from July 2010 put the situation of the DSO in the context of other orchestras facing difficult times in wake of the financial crisis. For example, in Baltimore, the musicians'

salaries had been reduced from $81,000 per year to $67,000; in Nashville the musicians had agreed on a wage freeze; and in Charleston a portion of the season had to be canceled because of financial losses. Perhaps most significant was the situation at the Philadelphia Orchestra, one of the elite "Big Five" orchestras, where the economic picture was so bleak that the organization filed for bankruptcy in 2011.

The article praised Slatkin for innovative programming, including playing concerts at Orchestra Hall that featured the film score to Alfred Hitchcock's *Psycho* and taking the orchestra to new venues, "from high school auditoriums in blue collar suburbs to a Salvation Army rehab center on the city's southwest side," in search of new audiences.[24]

Negotiations between the musicians and management were halted during this period, and by August they had still not reached an agreement, and remained far apart on several issues, most notably pay. The musicians offered to take a twenty-two percent cut in compensation, to $82,000 in base pay, rising to $96,000 during the three years of the contract. Management countered with two offers. The first, called Proposal A, called for a cut in base salary of about twenty-eight percent in the first year, to $74,880, with small increases for the second and third years of the contract, along with changes in work rules. The second offer, Proposal B, called for a two-tier approach to musicians' pay, with a cut of thirty-three percent in the first year to $70,200 for current players and a new base salary of $63,000 for new members.[25]

The musicians rejected the agreement on August 29, with Haden McKay, DSO cellist and member of the negotiating committee, noting that, "If there's one thing that really scares us, it's that $63,000," which was "about half of what players start at in top orchestras."[26] It was a major point of the musicians' stance throughout the negotiations that they needed to maintain levels of compensation that would attract and keep top-level players.

This point was seconded by orchestra consultant Drew McManus, who devoted many articles on his website, adaptistration.com, to the DSO's ongoing negotiations. He told Mark Stryker of the *Free Press*, "I consider Detroit a destination orchestra, and if the salaries fall to $75,000 to $80,000 and stay there for more than three years, it will become a stepping-stone orchestra for at least the next decade."[27]

This position was countered by management in a statement published by the *Free Press* from Anne Parsons, stating that "excellence is a by-product of more than salaries and includes factors such as artistic programs, community relevance, Slatkin's vision, and the talent and spirit of the players." Her stance throughout the negotiations was: "Without viability there can be no excellence."[28]

The two major papers in the city, the *Detroit News* and the *Free Press*, weighed in on the matter, with the *News* claiming that "the reality may be that this region can no longer support a world-class orchestra" and that Detroiters should get ready for the DSO to fade into second-class status or go out of business.[29]

The *Free Press*'s Brian Dickerson disagreed, and stressed the cultural legacy that was at stake:

> What's incredible, and ineffably sad, is the complacency with which Detroiters are shrugging off the disintegration of a cultural infrastructure our predecessors spent the entire twentieth century putting in place. And even that legacy is not as threadbare as our dwindling sense of obligation to the next generation, which stands to inherit a city whose music flows mainly from slot machines.[30]

## A LONG AND BRUISING STRIKE

When the two sides could not reach an agreement by the deadline of September 24, 2010, management imposed the terms of its final contract offer, based, in part, on their "B" proposal which, in addition to cutting base pay for current musicians by thirty-three percent, included a forty-two percent reduction in pay for new members, cutbacks in pension and health benefits, and a reduc-

DSO member Karl Pituch plays his French horn on the picket line after the musicians called a strike, October 4, 2010. (Associated Press)

tion in the total number of musicians in the orchestra.

On October 4, 2010, the musicians rejected the offer and announced that they would strike, as the first concerts of the season were canceled. Thus began the longest and most contentious strike in the orchestra's history, which played out in the press and in social media, with a tone that grew increasingly harsh and vituperative over six long months.[31]

The musicians and management remained $6 million apart in compensation, and also could not agree on changes to work rules. Management wanted to add mandatory teaching, chamber music per-

formances, and outreach responsibilities to the musicians' duties, without additional pay, a provision the musicians rejected.

These and other actions on the part of management were described as "punitive," by DSO cellist and negotiator Haden McKay; they included canceling the musicians' insurance and the insurance on their instruments, which they had agreed to pay on their own during the duration of the strike. Anne Parsons presented management's terse reply, saying, "We are following the letter of the law completely. If you walk off the job, you walk off the job," reflecting a tone that grew more rancorous on both sides over the months.[32]

The tone, and its possible consequences, was noted by Mark Stryker in the *Free Press*:

The parties remain deeply divided over pay cuts and work rules. But the biggest threat to the DSO may be the breakdown in communication and trust that could make it difficult, perhaps impossible, to rebuild in the wake of a settlement.

Players feel betrayed and frozen out of decision making; management says the players aren't listening and aren't acting responsibly.

Stryker quoted Robert Mnoonkin from Harvard Law School, on the stakes involved:

A serious strike could jeopardize the future of the orchestra. You see, in essence, a game of chicken where if there's a crack-up, it's plain there will be no winner.[33]

### THE PUBLIC REACTION

The conflict between musicians and management continued to play out in the press, with people coming down on both sides of the disagreement. Some sided with management, as revealed in an editorial in the *Detroit News*, which stated that, in light of the economic downturn and its devastating effect on Michigan residents, the musicians should be willing to make sacrifices similar to those made by the state's other workers: "Union-protected jobs with six-figure salaries are scarce in today's Michigan. The musicians should hang on to theirs with both hands, and pray along with the rest of us for a future that returns our state to prosperity."[34]

Yet in the court of public opinion evidenced in letters to the editor, management's position was faulted. One letter to the *Free Press*, from a negotiator who had argued on the side of management throughout his career, raised issues on the minds of many in the region:

I have to wonder what management is thinking and why they have gotten to a point of no return. I have never heard of a labor organization that would agree to a 20 percent-plus pay cut then still be told that it has to be 30 percent. . . .

I have not seen any serious questioning of the management of the Detroit Symphony. . . . How could they let the organization fall into financial problems if they were paying attention to what was and is happening in Detroit and the country?

Maybe management just wants to break up the orchestra and start over with a bunch of younger and much lower paid players with little or no experience. That would be but another blow to any chance Detroit might have to become a world-class city again.[35]

Many letter writers also stressed the importance of a viable DSO to the recovery of Detroit. A letter from a group of supporters that included Gloria Heppner, a member of the Board, noted that "the current labor dispute has the potential to undercut efforts to turn around the economy of Detroit and perhaps the entire southeastern Michigan economy."[36]

These opinions were shared by the majority of respondents who wrote to the *Free Press* during the course of the strike, and indicated broad support for the musicians' position and far less backing for management's stance.

As the strike entered its second month, management's response to the musicians' position was characterized by Drew McManus as "regrettable indifference" that was also "lurching toward a new level of antagonism." He cited as evidence an article on the dispute written by Ed Pilkington of the *Guardian* of London. Pilkington stated the musicians' stance this way:

The players believe that management wants to replace the traditional classical orchestra with a second-rank version. They say lower salaries and flexible working would dissuade the top play-

ers from coming to Detroit, and the orchestra's world-class status would be quickly squandered.[37]

Management's position, based on an interview Pilkington did with Anne Parsons, was described this way:

Management's reply can be paraphrased as: leave if you like. There are plenty of other good players in lesser-paid orchestras or straight out of college who would love to join the DSO, even with the 40% pay cut. Asked if Detroit can support a first class orchestra, Anne Parsons said, "Isn't it up to every [player] to answer that question: will they stay or will they go."[38]

The negative tone grew as the strike continued, and week by week, management canceled concerts. The two sides did not meet again until November 6, 2010, but talks broke off without a deal being reached; another meeting, held with a federal mediator on November 25, was also unsuccessful. The strike continued into December, as management canceled more concerts and the musicians held their own performances.

The strike also continued to garner national attention, as orchestras and other artistic organizations across the country, also stressed by the economic downturn, watched to see what would happen in

Detroit. A segment on NPR's "All Things Considered" outlined the issues, and the intractability, of the conflict. It quoted music historian Mark Clague, who noted that "Part of the reason why both sides are so inflexible is that each sees their response as being symbolic and having a domino effect all the way across the industry." The segment also suggested that only an "angel donor," such as the one who had saved the Cincinnati Symphony Orchestra with a gift of $85 million, could save the DSO at this point.[39]

On December 17, 2010, Michigan Governor Jennifer Granholm and US Senator Carl Levin tried to broker a deal to end the stalemate, but while some progress was made, no agreement was reached.

Throughout the dispute, the musicians posted articles by their own members and other sources supporting their positions on their own website, which they made clear was in no way linked to the formal DSO. Two essays in particular, by oboist Shelley Heron and clarinetist Doug Cornelsen, outlined the musicians' contention that management lacked the ability to handle two pressing issues: fundraising and the management of the debt incurred in building the Max M. Fisher Music Center. The site also became a forum for the opinions of those in favor of the musicians' position, and included letters to the editors of local newspapers as well as letters of support that revealed the escalating tone of rancor between the two sides as the strike dragged on.[40]

It is notable that, throughout the negotiations, Leonard Slatkin remained silent. Unlike Neeme Järvi, who had been an outspoken proponent of the musicians throughout his tenure and had conducted a benefit concert for the musicians of the Philadelphia Orchestra in 1996 during a labor dispute in that city, Slatkin did not come out in support of either side in the strike.[41] The significance of his stance was brought to light by the musicians of the Chicago Symphony Orchestra in January 2011, when, in demonstration of their solidarity with the DSO musicians, they distributed leaflets outlining their support for their colleagues prior to a concert. Noting that several DSO musicians were playing as substitutes in the concert, which was conducted by Slatkin himself, the CSO musicians urged him to "persuade the Board of the DSO to negotiate in a spirit of compromise and respect."[42] Slatkin maintained his silence.

The strike continued throughout January, with management continuing to cancel concerts. In February 2011, after contract talks mediated by Senator Carl Levin and Detroit entrepreneur and Quicken Loans owner Dan Gilbert failed to break the stalemate, management canceled the remainder of the season.[43]

The future of the DSO hung in the balance, as the *Free Press* noted on February 22, 2011:

Seldom has the axiom that no one wins in a protracted strike been more emphatically vindicated than in Detroit this past weekend, when the collapse of talks between the Detroit Symphony Orchestra management and players triggered an oft-threatened suspension of the orchestra's 2010–11 season.

Now an organization that has been bleeding its endowment to stay afloat will have to dig even deeper into its seed corn to satisfy subscribers demanding refunds, and a corps of talented musicians who balked at a 23% salary cut will earn no salary at all. If either side has struck a blow for some transcendent principle of economic justice here, we fail to discern it.

At stake now is the DSO's very existence. In the best-case scenario, the uncertainty surrounding performer and subscriber commitments for the 2011–12 season and beyond will exact short-term costs on the orchestra's quality; in the worst case, an organization nurtured by generations of performers, volunteers and arts-loving philanthropists will simply cease to exist.[44]

But there was more bad news to come. As both musicians and the public feared, DSO players began to leave the orchestra. On March 1, 2011, the three remaining percussionists announced their plans to leave; the fourth member of the section had left in 2009 and had not been replaced, so, with their departure, there were no permanent members left.

The musicians who left, including Brian Jones, Ian Ding, and Jacob Nissly, cited the continuing problems between musicians and management as a factor in their decisions.

Brian Jones, who left for a position with the Dallas Symphony, wrote:

Imagine my sadness and shock, then, as the downward direction toward which my organization is heading now, is forcing me back to where I never thought I'd have to go: the audition circuit. I feel close enough to some of my DSO friends to think of them as family, but I also have to work in an orchestra that earns me a secure living within which I can fulfill my responsibilities.[45]

Management's response to the loss of the percussionists was terse: "We send our best wishes with every colleague and wish them well on their journey," a further indication of the gap between the two sides.

As the strike entered its fifth month, the response from the public, as evidenced in letters to the editor of the *Free Press* and other sources, remained firmly in support of the musicians' position in the strike. One letter sent "To Supporters of the Detroit Symphony Orchestra" (with a copy sent to Drew McManus) was of particular interest. Dated March 17, 2011, it was from Sandra Reitelman, who had served as Director of Corporate Fundraising at the DSO from 2004 to 2006. Her candid and forthright letter claims that "the DSO management has not held up its end of the bargain in supporting the orchestra in its fulfillment of the organization's artistic vision and mission."

Reitelman made clear that she was not speaking of "mismanagement of finances, or of board negligence"; she did however voice her opinion that "internal flaws within the institution" reflect "an incomplete ability to draw audiences and financial support to enable this fine ensemble to maintain its legacy."[46]

## A RETURN TO WORK

Finally, on April 4, 2011, the DSO musicians and management reached a tentative agreement, ratified on April 8, which ended the bitter and bruising six-month strike. Under the terms of the agreement, the minimum salary dropped twenty-three percent, to $79,000, rising to $82,900 in the third year of the contract, with no two-tiered wage scale for current and new musicians. The total number of permanent players was reduced from ninety-six to eighty-one and the number of work weeks from fifty-two to forty. The

proposed work rule changes that would have required the musicians to perform outreach and teaching roles without compensation were changed to become optional, and paid.[47]

The orchestra announced free concerts for the public to take place on April 10 and 11. The settlement was cause for celebration in Detroit and was covered by the national press, including an illustrated story in the *New York Times*, which described the DSO's many supporters who were just as eager as the musicians to welcome back their orchestra:

Detroiters snapped up free tickets for the hastily arranged reunion. People stood in the back of the hall and a screen was set up for the overflow. Dozens were turned away. Many seemed to be newcomers to the hall, and dress was a mix of ties, bandannas, pearls and T-shirts. Couples clutched hands and some in the audience teared up. Shouts of "Yeah!" and whoops and whistles sounded amid the clapping.

The moment was about something more than the end of a bitter labor dispute. The sounds of music at the hall (along with the Tigers' victory in their home opener on Friday) were like the chirpings of a bird in the bleak days of late winter. It finally meant some good

Members of the DSO get a standing ovation as they walk on stage at Orchestra Hall after the settlement of the strike, April 10, 2011. (Associated Press)

news in a town so often described as hollowed out, shriveled up and abandoned.

Members of the audience concurred:

"This is a blue-collar factory town," said David Lewin, 56, a native of the city and a 10-year subscriber to the orchestra who works in advertising for the two Detroit newspapers. "Our image is the Rust Belt. Just down-and-out Detroit, and a lot of that is true," he said.

"But we have gems—the Detroit Symphony and this hall. What classical music represents, human expression at the highest level, juxtaposed with this hell hole we call

our city," he said, stopping to fight back tears. "It's remarkable."[48]

Despite the joy and relief of the public at the return of the DSO, there were concerns as well. Many people were struck by how similar the final contract specifics were to what the musicians had offered in August, and they wondered if the long and contentious strike had been necessary and how it would affect the relationship between management and the DSO in the future.

As an editorial in the *Detroit Free Press* noted:

The settlement that ended the players' epic six-month strike seems like one that could have been struck in half the time, with far less damage to the players, the management team and the concert-going public.

The total cost of the three-year contract is only marginally less than what the musicians had been willing to accept in January, and the compromise on work rules the two sides agreed to will allow management to institute an optional community outreach program that will reward participating players with higher salaries.[49]

To add to the concern, the problems of the DSO were far from over. The deficit for the year was projected at $3 million and the $54 million debt on the Max still loomed. There was also lingering bitterness and a sense of distrust among the musicians over the strike. Joseph Striplin, who had played violin in the orchestra for thirty-nine years, blamed management and board members, calling them, "a mix of politically reactionary right-wing figures who never saw a union they didn't hate" and a leadership with a "distorted vision of what a symphony orchestra should be."[50]

Sadly, the continuing atmosphere of distrust and animosity was on display just a month later, when the DSO's celebrated concertmaster, Emmanuelle Boisvert, announced that she was leaving Detroit for the associate concertmaster position with the Dallas Symphony. The announcement was made by members of the orchestra and included the following comments from Boisvert:

It has been a privilege for me to work with my colleagues and to make spectacular music both live and recorded with Maestro Neeme Järvi in our magnificent home— Orchestra Hall. I have been the fortunate recipient, through veteran musicians in the orchestra, of the wisdom of such DSO Music Directors as Paul Paray and Antal Dorati. I have also enjoyed sharing the duties of selecting new, amazingly talented musicians for the orchestra with the goal of ensuring the highest quality in classical music performances for Detroit and Michigan for many years to come.

This winter I performed with the Dallas Symphony on several occasions and marveled at their organization's commitment to classical music, the intrinsic respect offered to musicians by the administration and esteemed Music Director, Jaap van Zweden, and the emphasis they place on communication and teamwork at all levels. I had planned to stay in Detroit for my entire career, but Dallas presented me with an opportunity I simply couldn't refuse. Making the decision to leave Detroit has been heart wrenching.[51]

The story of Boisvert's departure galvanized the classical music community, and the story was picked up by more than 100 news outlets around the country. Her comments were parsed for what she said as well as what she didn't say, including any mention of current director Leonard Slatkin, as well as her praise for the management in Dallas.

As for the management of the DSO, Board chairman Stanley Frankel issued a statement described by Drew McManus as "profoundly indifferent":

> We thank Emmanuelle Boisvert for her many years of dedicated service and artistic excellence and wish her much happiness and success in her future endeavors with the Dallas Symphony Orchestra.
>
> Retaining and attracting top talent remains a priority for the DSO at every level and under the leadership of our Music Director Leonard Slatkin, the DSO will continue to achieve tremendous artistic success while building a sustainable and viable business model going forward.

In McManus's interpretation, Frankel's message was clear: "So long as Leonard sticks around we don't care who leaves and the more high-price salaries we can get rid of, the better."[52]

Then, more news from the management ranks reached the orchestra: during the strike, the Board had extended the contract of Anne Parsons, who had attracted criticism for her administrative style of management during the conflict. The news shocked both players and orchestra watchers who shared their concerns, and continued the atmosphere of rancor and mistrust long past the end of the contract dispute.

As the new season got underway in the fall of 2011, the financial problems of the DSO were once again in the news. Management now had to deal with the $54 million in real estate debt on which it had defaulted, and try to rebuild an endowment that had fallen to its lowest level in decades, just $19 million. The two goals were in many ways at cross purposes: potential donors didn't want all their gifts to the endowment to wind up with the banks, and the banks saw the donations as collateral for the debt they were owed.[53]

The negotiations between the DSO and the bank consortium that owned the debt went on for months and were finally resolved in June 2012. Although the terms were not released, the agreement settled the debt on the Max M. Fisher Music Center. Other real estate debts, dating from the building of Orchestra Place and

246

amounting to $16.2 million, were to be paid for by the revenue stream from the building's tenants.[54]

The DSO forged ahead in 2012 with innovative programming, inaugurating its new Neighborhood Series in January, in which they gave concerts in several key suburban communities, including Dearborn, West Bloomfield, Bloomfield Hills, and Grosse Pointe Farms.[55] In May, a rather unusual pairing appeared on the stage of the Fox Theater in Detroit: Kid Rock, a native Detroiter, and the DSO, under Slatkin, performed arrangements of Kid Rock's material, in a fundraiser to help rebuild the finances of the orchestra.

At the end of 2012, the management unveiled a new financial plan that reorganized the structure of the Board. Titled "Blueprint 2023," it called for "boosting the DSO subscriber base, increasing the annual fund, slowing the growth rate of expenses, and raising a permanent endowment fund," creating three "leadership spheres" to accomplish these goals. Among other changes, Phillip Fisher was elected chairman of the Board, replacing Stanley Frankel. Fisher, the son of Max Fisher, was, like his famous father, a businessman and philanthropist who had served on the Board for many years.[56]

The 2012–13 season offered what the *Free Press*'s Mark Stryker called "relentlessly moderate" fare, which he described as "designed to help rebuild and reassure a post-strike subscriber base by minimizing risk." The offerings included a Beethoven Festival and the works of such well-known composers as Rachmaninoff, Tchaikovsky, and Dvořák. He quoted Slatkin on making those programming decisions:

> We're still in a recovery mode and we are trying to make sure that we recapture not only our regular audience but attract a whole new subscriber base. If we threw right now an exotic set of programs at people, even with the low price,

## CONCERTMASTER: YOONSHIN SONG

In May 2012, Yoonshin Song, then thirty years old, was hired as the concertmaster of the DSO. She was born in Seoul, South Korea, where she began playing the violin at an early age. She went on to further studies in the United States, attending the New England Conservatory and Manhattan School of Music, and was a student of Donald Weilerstein, Robert Mann, and Glenn Dicterow.

Active as a soloist, recitalist, and chamber musician, Song was also the recipient of several international prizes, winning the Stradivarius International Competition in 2007. She joined the St. Paul Chamber Orchestra in 2010 and played with them for two years. After Emmanuelle Boisvert left the DSO in 2011, Kimberly Kaloyanides Kennedy became acting concertmaster, and the auditions for the permanent position began in 2012.

During the auditions, Song emerged as a finalist, and she played in a trial week with the DSO in April 2012. She established a strong rapport with the musicians and the director: "I had a really exciting week," she told the *Free Press*'s Mark Stryker. "In rehearsal, I felt so comfortable and got such positive feelings from people. I think Mr. Slatkin, we really interacted well. We had great fun, and I could feel the strong support behind me. They were willing to follow me."

Song's appointment to the position was announced from the stage of Orchestra Hall by Leonard Slatkin on May 6, 2012, and she started in her new position in the fall of that year. She plays a 1707 Vincenzo Rugeri violin, which is on loan to her through an anonymous patron who lives in Michigan.

Sources: *Detroit Free Press*, April 29, 2012; May 7, 2012; *American Record Guide*, July–August 2012, 23.

it wouldn't work so well, because we've got to regain trust.[57]

### A RETURN TO CARNEGIE HALL

The 2013 season saw the DSO return to Carnegie Hall, where they performed as part of "Spring for Music," an annual festival of orchestras from all over North America. The DSO also took on some of the music that was to have been performed by the Oregon Symphony, who had to cancel its appearance.

According to James Oestreich of the *New York Times*, the orchestra's "audacious" presentation of all four symphonies of Charles Ives, in chronological order, "made for an extraordinary journey." Be-

fore the performance, Slatkin told the *Times* that he wanted to show "how far the orchestra has come in a very short time," since the strike, and in Oestreich's opinion, they achieved that goal.[58]

He wrote that the DSO "performed nobly through the long haul of the Ives," as well as on the following night, when they played Rachmaninoff's *Isle of the Dead*, which Oestreich called "among the great sea pieces," stating that "Slatkin's atmospheric reading was especially evocative of surging waves." He claimed that the DSO "shone throughout" the evening, but in their performance of Kurt Weill and Bertolt Brecht's *Seven Deadly Sins* they were sensational, accompanying the soprano Storm Large in a show-stopper.[59]

## AND TO THE RECORDING STUDIO

The DSO and Slatkin also returned to the recording studio, continuing to explore the works of Rachmaninoff, whose Symphony no. 2 they had recorded in 2009, and which was noted by critic Geoffrey Norris as "a reminder of Leonard Slatkin's sympathy for Rachmaninoff's music and its emotional ebb and flow."

Of his interpretation of the Third Symphony and the Symphonic Dances, Norris noted how "Slatkin captures [the composer's] sense of sadness and world-weariness but, crucially, also recog-nizes the new piquancy of harmony, clarity of texture and rhythmic incisiveness that mark the works of Rachmaninoff's later years. The Detroit players have a sure instinct for the poignancy and sighs of the music, for its intricate but lucidly woven fabric and also for its passion and drive. Details of the scoring, so critical in any Rachmaninoff interpretation, are tellingly etched in here in the context of a perceptively chosen spectrum of dynamics."[60]

Yet there were other music commentators who faulted the sound of what they considered a diminished DSO. A review of their recording of Rachmaninoff's Symphony no. 1 and *Isle of the Dead* was faulted for "lacking in depth," in

## DETROIT SCHOOL OF ARTS

The Detroit School of Arts, part of the Detroit Public Schools, offers a college preparatory curriculum in academics and the arts for students in grades nine to twelve. Opened in 2005, the school was part of the vision of Max Fisher and was a key element of the renovation and new building that became the Max M. Fisher Music Center.

The DSO donated the land on which the school was built, and it is located on the same block as the Max. It is a 285,000-square-foot building and was constructed at a cost of around $125 million, making it one of the most expensive high schools in the nation. The Detroit School of Arts (DSA) replaced the former Detroit School for the Fine and Performing Arts, which was founded in 1992; many of the faculty members and the principal moved to the DSA when it opened in 2005.

The DSA offers a number of concentrations in the arts, including dance, theater, speech, radio and television production, and the visual arts. In the area of music, the school offers curriculum in vocal music, instrumental music, and music technology. The instrumental music curriculum includes concentrations in woodwinds, brass, percussion, strings, and keyboard, as well as composition for instrument and voice. In addition, public radio station WRCJ, which has its broadcast facilities within the school, provides internships to DSA students.

In 2014, there were 548 students in the DSA, drawn from the Detroit metro area. The students have access to master classes with DSO musicians, as well as outstanding visiting musicians such as opera star Denyce Graves. In 2013, 100 students from the DSA performed at Carnegie Hall, after a rigorous series of competitions. And in 2014, two films created by DSA students were shown at Detroit's Cinetopia film festival.

Sources: *Detroit Free Press*, March 1, 2005; June 19, 2010; http://dsa.schools.detroitk12.org/.

a review in *American Record Guide*. The critic claimed that the "Detroit strings seem thin," and that "Slatkin seems less involved, seems just to float through it."[61]

At the end of 2013, the DSO announced that its finances had finally turned around and that it had balanced its budget for the first time since 2007. Contributions to the symphony were up forty-three percent, to $18.9 million, coming from more than 10,000 donors. Of special note was the success of the orchestra's new online webcasts, called "Live from Orchestra Hall," which they claimed reached 300,000 viewers in 2013.[62]

The positive news continued in January 2014, when the musicians and management announced that they had reached an agreement on a new contract, eight months before the expiration of the old one. The agreement stipulated an orchestra with eighty-five musicians, plus two librarians, a thirty-six-week season, and an increase of 5.3 percent in wages over three years.

The contract continued the musician's neighborhood residencies in the suburban communities of Beverly Hills, Bloomfield Hills, Canton Township, Dearborn, Grosse Pointe, Southfield, and West Bloomfield. It also continued a provision from the previous contract that was of growing importance in the current era: an "integrated media agreement" that allowed for the live broadcasts of DSO performances, presented online free of charge.[63] The move to the streaming of the DSO concerts showed the orchestra in the vanguard of the practice. As the *New York Times* noted:

> [Perhaps] unexpectedly, given the dire state of Detroit's fortunes, the cutting edge for the phenomenon in this country lies here, where the Detroit Symphony Orchestra has the most ambitious free web-streaming program of any major American orchestra, as it looks online to help secure its future after surviving a bitter strike, the struggles of the auto industry, and the bankruptcy of its city.[64]

The orchestra also continued to broaden its efforts to reach out to a wider range of communities in the Detroit area with a variety of musical programming. In 2014, the Davidson Neighborhood Series sponsored concerts throughout the region: the DSO On-the-Go series offered ten free performances to neighborhoods in smaller communities in southeast Michigan, and the Concert of Colors, founded in 1992, continued to present a series of free concerts celebrating diversity in music to audiences in the city.[65]

In more efforts of outreach harkening back to the 1970s, the DSO continued to provide a forum for African American composers through its Classical Roots series. And, as part of its

New Music Readings for African-American Composers initiative, the orchestra performed the work of Jonathan Bailey Holland in 2014. Holland, who had won the Unisys composer's competition twenty years earlier, and was now a professor at the Berklee College of Music, was represented by his composition "Shards of Serenity."[66]

Continuing another initiative developed under Neeme Järvi, the DSO has sponsored a wide variety of jazz programming, which has featured the artistic direction of such jazz giants as Marcus Belgrave, Herbie Hancock, Chick Corea, Branford Marsalis, Wynton Marsalis, Michel Camilo, and Terence Blanchard since 2002.[67]

The DSO also continued its outreach into the community through a combination of its web-streaming and educational initiatives, launching a classroom edition of "Live from Orchestra Hall" in November 2014 to 30,000 students in Detroit and more than 50,000 across the country. The effort was praised by Detroit educator Jonathan Walker, who called it "ingenious": "It broadens [the students'] horizons, and it exposes them to something that they're typically not exposed to. I hope it sparks something and maybe one day they'll want to join [the orchestra], or maybe it will spark an interest in music."[68]

Another major educational initiative was announced in 2014 that further expanded the reach of the DSO into the community. The Wu Family Academy supports programs designed to develop young musicians throughout the region. The academy hopes to "change lives" by offering musical training to students from the elementary grades through high school. Their statement of purpose outlines the breadth and depth of the initiative:

> The vision of the Wu Family Academy for Learning and Engagement is to change lives by expanding the understanding of the arts, empowering everyone to have confidence in their creative decisions, and sparking a passion for music that will last a lifetime. We aim to change lives—whether as a hobby or a career—through life-long music making.[69]

At the end of 2014, the DSO announced that it was once again in the black, with a surplus of $60,000; Leonard Slatkin and Anne Parsons also had their contracts renewed. But consistent funding remained an issue. According to *Crain's*, in 2014 the DSO's revenue was down $280,000 from the previous year, the draw from the endowment was up $450,000, and contributions to the operating budget were down nearly 7 percent.[70]

In the summer of 2015, a name change for the Max was announced: the complex

Students from Detroit's Yes Academy watch the first webcast by the DSO. (Associated Press)

is now officially known as the Max M. and Marjorie S. Fisher Music Center, to acknowledge the many contributions of Marjorie Fisher to the DSO over the years. And in December 2015, Leonard Slatkin announced that he would step down from his position as music director of the DSO after the 2017–18 season, signaling the end of one chapter in the DSO's history and the beginning of a new one.

## THE RESOLUTION OF DETROIT'S BANKRUPTCY

As 2014 came to a close, so too did the bankruptcy proceedings involving the city of Detroit. The final resolution of the bankruptcy, with a swiftness Judge Steven Rhodes, who oversaw the case, termed "miraculous," centered on finding a way to fund the pensions of Detroit retirees that would not involve selling off the art collection of the DIA, which was owned by the city and represented the last and largest source of public funds remaining in the impoverished city, whose outstanding debt had grown to $18 billion when it entered bankruptcy in 2013.

In what was termed "the grand bargain," a consortium of foundations, businesses, the state of Michigan, and the DIA itself pledged $816 million dollars to fund the pensions. In return, the art in the DIA became the property of the museum, giving that venerable cultural institution control of its collection for the first time in over 100 years, and the city a fresh start.[71] So the city of Detroit, like the DSO, emerged from a series of economic crises that threatened its very existence to face a world in which the concept of the American orchestra, and the American city, had changed forever.

What had changed since the early days of the DSO, especially its first "golden age" during the Gabrilowitsch era? An article by James Oestreich in the *New York Times* about the state of America's top orchestras, and the viability of the concept of the "Big Five"—Boston, Chicago, Cleveland, New York, and Philadelphia—offers some insights:

A century or so ago, when classical music thrived in a nation of immigrants, orchestras were a powerful force, flagship institutions that helped to put American cities on the cultural map. And the Big Five, when it coalesced, helped, with its cumulative weight, to put American orchestras firmly on the international map. No other country could boast of such a constellation.

But this landscape has changed greatly over the last half-century, much as the country's economic, demographic, and cultural landscape has, and in many of the same ways. The economic fortunes of the flagship ensembles have changed with the fortunes of their cities.[72]

There are few cities who have endured such profound changes to its "economic, demographic, and cultural landscape" as Detroit. It has been through the Great Depression, several recessions, and bankruptcy; it has lost more than half its population, most of its industry, and seen its cultural institutions transformed by those changes.

The oldest of those cultural institutions, the Detroit Symphony Orchestra, has gone out of business three times since its founding in 1887, its finances rising and falling along with those of the city. It has, however, managed to come back from all these challenges, with its loyal audiences and supporters confirming its continued importance, a symbol of musical artistry in a city that cherishes its hard-won successes in the face of adversity.

The future of the DSO, and of the city it calls home, will be shaped by how they face the continued challenges of the ever-changing economic and social landscape of the modern era. Guided, as they have been since the days of Father Gabriel Richard, by an inextinguishable spirit, and a grittiness native to the city, they are both determined to survive: to adapt, to change, to hope, to "rise from the ashes" and be renewed.

According to the Russian legend of the Firebird, which inspired Stravinsky's great modernist work and celebrates the ever-renewing spirit of art, the feathers of the legendary Phoenix provide beauty and protection as it rises to live again; so, too, are the orchestra and the city entwined in a cycle of hope and renewal, and the will to survive, and to thrive, together.

# Notes

## CHAPTER ONE

1. Arthur M. Woodford, *This Is Detroit* (Detroit: Wayne State University Press, 2001), 39.
2. Ibid., 6, 10–12.
3. Ibid., 15.
4. Ibid., 32.
5. Mary Evelyn Durden Teal, "Musical Activities in Detroit from 1701 through 1870." (PhD diss., University of Michigan, 1964), 26.
6. "Judge Solomon Sibley and Sarah Whipple Sproat Sibley," *Sibley House Renewal*, published November 2012, http://sibleyhousedetroit.com/solomon-and-sarah-sibley/#sarahsibley.
7. Woodford, *This Is Detroit,* 47–49.
8. Teal, 26.
9. Woodford, *This Is Detroit,* 86.
10. J. Bunting, "The Old Germania Orchestra." *Scribner's Monthly,* November 1875, 98–107.
11. Teal, 374–75.
12. Ibid., 71.
13. Ibid., 205.
14. Eva Kolinsky and Wilfried van der Will, eds., *Cambridge Companion to Modern German Culture* (Cambridge: Cambridge University Press, 1998), 3.
15. John Spitzer, "Orchestras: American and European," in *American Orchestras in the Nineteenth Century,* ed. John Spitzer (Chicago: University of Chicago Press, 2012), 313.
16. Ibid.
17. See the image of the sheet music cover for "Bell Polka" in the Library of Congress, American Memory Collection, http://memory.loc.gov/music/sm2/sm1855/281000/281530/001.jpg.
18. Teal, 310.

19. Ibid., 223.

20. Ibid., 224.

21. Andrew Craig Morrison, *Opera House, Nickel Show and Palace: An Illustrated Inventory of Theater Buildings in the Detroit Area* (Dearborn: Greenfield Village and Henry Ford Museum, 1974.

22. Louis C. Elson, *The History of American Music* (New York: Macmillan), 1904.

23. Spitzer, 233.

24. *Detroit Free Press,* March 19, 1904.

25. *Detroit Free Press,* October 10, 1874.

26. *Detroit Free Press,* December 30, 1874.

27. *Detroit Free Press,* October 31, 1875.

28. *Detroit Free Press,* January 23, 1876.

29. *Detroit Free Press,* February 26, 1876.

30. *Detroit Free Press,* May 31, 1876.

31. *Detroit Free Press,* May 26, 1880.

32. *Detroit Free Press,* October 18, 1882.

33. Program, "First Symphony Concert, Monday, January 8, 1883."

34. *Detroit Free Press,* May 12, 1883.

35. Clarence M. Burton, When Detroit Was Young, from "Statistically Speaking," *Detroit History*, http://historydetroit.com/statistics.

36. *Detroit Free Press,* March 11, 1884.

37. "Detroit Philharmonic Club," unpublished brochure from 1885.

38. John Andrew Russell, *The Germanic Influence in the Making of Michigan* (Detroit: University of Detroit, 1927), 224–28.

39. *Detroit Free Press,* July 18, 1875.

40. *Detroit Free Press,* March 28, 1880; May 16, 1880; June 19, 1880; June 23, 1880.

41. *Detroit Free Press,* December 28, 1884.

42. *Detroit Free Press,* March 15, 1885.

43. *Detroit Free Press,* May 15, 1885.

## CHAPTER TWO

1. *Detroit Free Press,* December 18, 1887.

2. Woodford, *This Is Detroit*, 77, 82; Clarence Monroe Burton and Agnes Burton, eds. History of Wayne County and the City of Detroit, Michigan (Chicago: S. J. Clarke, 1930), 1048, 1141, 1436.

3. John Spitzer, "The Ubiquity and Diversity of Nineteenth-Century American Orchestras," in *American Orchestras in the Nineteenth Century,* 22.

4. *Detroit Evening News,* December 20, 1887.

5. *Detroit Free Press,* January 26, 1888.

6. *Detroit Free Press,* March 16, 1888; May 9, 1888.

7. *Detroit Free Press,* May 6, 1888.

8. *Detroit Free Press,* December 18, 1888.

9. *Detroit Tribune,* May 16, 1889.

10. *Detroit Free Press,* May 16, 1889.

11. *Detroit Free Press,* October 20, 1889.

12. *Detroit Free Press,* February 10, 1891.

13. *Detroit Free Press,* March 2, 1891.

14. *Detroit Free Press,* March 23, 1891.

15. *Detroit Tribune,* March 24, 1891.

16. *Detroit Free Press,* April 25, 1891.

17. John Spitzer, "American Orchestras and Their Unions," in *American Orchestras in the Nineteenth Century,* 80.

18. Fritz Kalsow, ledgers for the Detroit Symphony Orchestra, unprocessed collection of documents, Burton Historical Collection, Detroit Public Library, Detroit, Michigan.

19. Ibid.

20. Program, Detroit Symphony Orchestra, 1892–93; Detroit Public Library, Music, Art, and Literature Department, Detroit, Michigan; call number: R789 D48.

21. Kalsow, ledgers.

22. *Detroit Free Press,* April 18, 1893.

23. *Detroit Free Press,* May 22, 1893.

24. Kalsow, ledgers.

25. *Detroit Free Press,* April 29, 1894.

26. *Detroit Free Press,* July 15, 1894.

27. Kalsow, ledgers.

28. *Detroit Free Press,* January 20, 1895.

29. *Detroit Free Press,* March 28, 1895.

30. Program, Detroit Symphony Orchestra, 1894–95; Detroit Public Library, Music, Art, and Literature Department, Detroit, Michigan; call number: R789 D48.

31. Kalsow, ledgers.

32. *Detroit Free Press,* May 5, 1895.

33. Donald Rosenberg, *The Cleveland Orchestra Story: "Second to None"* (Cleveland: Gray and Company, 2000), 24–25.

34. Program, Detroit Symphony Orchestra, 1895–96, Detroit Public Library, Music, Art, and Literature Department, Detroit, Michigan; call number: R789 D48.

35. Ibid.

36. Kalsow, ledgers.

37. Program, Detroit Symphony Orchestra, 1896–97, Detroit Public Library, Music, Art, and Literature Department, Detroit, Michigan; call number: R789 D48.

38. Ibid.

39. Kalsow, ledgers

40. *Detroit Free Press,* December 16, 1897.

41. Kalsow, ledgers.

42. Ibid.

43. *Detroit Free Press,* March 15, 1899.

44. John Spitzer, "Orchestras: Local vs. National," in *American Orchestras in the Nineteenth Century,* 107.

45. Ibid., 108.

46. Mark Clague, "Building the American Symphony Orchestra: The Nineteenth-Century

Roots of a Twenty-First Century Musical Institution," in *American Orchestras in the Nineteenth Century,* 25–52.

47. Ibid.

48. *Detroit Free Press,* December 13, 1899.

49. Kalsow, ledgers.

50. *Detroit Free Press,* November 25, 1900.

51. *Detroit Free Press,* December 16, 1900.

52. *Detroit Free Press,* January 26, 1901.

53. *Detroit Free Press,* March 15, 1901.

54. *Detroit Free Press,* January 13, 1901.

55. *Detroit Free Press,* December 11, 1901.

56. *Detroit Free Press,* December 14, 1904.

57. *Detroit Free Press,* May 7, 1905.

58. *Detroit Free Press,* September 30, 1906.

59. *Detroit Free Press,* March 7, 1907.

60. *Detroit Free Press,* December 13, 1907.

61. *Detroit Free Press,* April 26, 1908.

62. *Detroit Free Press,* July 3, 1908.

63. *Detroit Free Press,* October 4, 1908.

64. *Detroit Free Press,* December 8, 1908.

65. *Detroit Free Press,* December 15, 1909; February 4, 1910.

66. George W. Stark, *City of Destiny: The Story of Detroit* (Detroit: Arnold-Powers, Inc., 1943), 478.

## CHAPTER THREE

1. Edith Rhetts Tilton, "The History of the Detroit Symphony Orchestra," from Programs for the 1964–65 Season, 18–19.

2. Ibid., 18.

3. *Detroit Tribune,* November 29, 1914.

4. Tilton, 19.

5. *Detroit Free Press,* May 8, 1910.

6. *Detroit Free Press,* March 3, 1914.

7. Tilton, 19.

8. Ibid.

9. Ibid.

10. Ibid., 52.

11. David Lee Poremba, ed., *Detroit in Its World Setting* (Detroit: Wayne State University Press, 2001); AMA, *Automobiles of America* (Detroit: Wayne State University Press, 1968).

12. Clarence Burton, *History of Wayne County and the City of Detroit,* vol. 3 (Chicago: S. J. Clarke), 59–60.

13. Ibid., 122, 125.

14. Clarence M. Burton, ed., *The City of Detroit, Michigan, 1701–1922,* vol. 4 (Chicago: S. J. Clarke, 1922), 308–13.

15. Tilton, 53.

16. *Detroit Free Press,* June 7, 1914.

17. *Detroit Free Press,* October 10, 1915.

18. Programs, Detroit Symphony Orchestra, 1915–16; Detroit Public Library, Music, Art, and Literature Department, Detroit, Michigan; call number: R789 D48.

19. *Detroit Free Press,* January 3, 1915.

20. Lynne Marie Mattson, "A History of the Detroit Symphony Orchestra" (master's thesis, University of Michigan School of Music, 1968), 7.

21. Ibid.

22. *Detroit Free Press,* January 3, 1915.

23. *Detroit Free Press,* February 25, 1917.

24. Programs, Detroit Symphony Orchestra, 1916–17; Detroit Public Library, Music, Art, and Literature Department, Detroit, Michigan; call number: R789 D48.

25. Woodford, *This Is Detroit*, 102.

26. Programs, Detroit Symphony Orchestra, 1916–17; Detroit Public Library, Music, Art, and Literature Department, Detroit, Michigan; call number: R789 D48.

27. Tilton, 53.

28. *Detroit Free Press,* December 15, 1917.

29. Clara Clemens, *My Husband, Gabrilowitsch* (New York: Harper and Brothers, 1938), 33.

30. Ibid., 1–5.

31. *New Grove Dictionary of Music and Musicians,* vol. 7 (London: Macmillan, 1980), 68.

32. *American Record Guide,* July–August 1993: 214.

33. Clemens, 45.

34. Ibid., 65–83.

35. Ibid., 127–28.

36. *Detroit Free Press,* December 28, 1917.

37. *Detroit Free Press,* December 29, 1917.

38. *Detroit Free Press,* March 2, 1918.

39. Ibid.

40. Jean Maddern Pitrone and Joan Potter Elwart, *The Dodges: The Auto Family Fortune and Misfortune* (South Bend, IN: Icarus, 1981).

41. Clemens, 104.

42. Ibid., 98–99.

43. Ibid., 104–05.

44. Ibid., 104.

45. Ibid.,105.

46. *Detroit Free Press,* June 27, 1918.

47. Clemens, 110.

48. Ibid., 111.

49. Ibid.

50. Program, Detroit Symphony Orchestra, 1917–18; Detroit Public Library, Music, Art, and Literature Department, Detroit, Michigan; call number: R789 D48.

51. Clemens, 121.

52. *Stages: 75 Years with the Detroit Symphony Orchestra and Orchestra Hall* (Detroit: Detroit Symphony Orchestra Hall, 1994), 5.

53. Robert Sharoff and William Zbaren, *American City: Detroit Architecture, 1845–2005* (Detroit: Wayne State University Press, 2005), 50.

54. Eric J. Hill and John Gallagher, *AIA Detroit: The American Institute of Architects Guide to Detroit Architecture* (Detroit: Wayne State University Press, 2003), 345.

55. Tilton, 176.

56. Ibid.

57. *Stages,* 5.

58. Sharoff, 33, 50.

59. "Concert Hall Acoustics, with Dr. Cyril Harris," http://www.aes-media.org/sections/pnw/pnwrecaps/1999/bhmc/.

60. *Stages,* 82.

61. *New York Times,* March 2, 1987.

62. Library of Congress, blueprints and drawings of Orchestra Hall, http://www.loc.gov/item/mi0023/.

63. Tilton, 176.

64. Clemens, 122.

65. *Detroit News,* October 24, 1919.

66. Ibid.

67. *Stages,* 17.

68. Detroit Symphony Society records, 1919–45, Box 3, Burton Historical Collection, Detroit Public Library.

69. Programs, Detroit Symphony Orchestra, 1992–93, Detroit Public Library, Music, Art, and Literature Department, Detroit, Michigan; call number: R789 D48.

70. Programs, Detroit Symphony Orchestra, 1922–23; Detroit Public Library, Music, Art, and Literature Department, Detroit, Michigan; call number: R789 D48.

71. Ibid.

72. Tilton, 117.

73. Ibid., 176.

74. Ibid., 208.

75. Ibid.

76. Ibid., 209.

77. *Stages,* 27, 31.

78. Programs, Detroit Symphony Orchestra, 1927–28; Detroit Public Library, Music, Art, and Literature Department, Detroit, Michigan; call number: R789 D48.

79. *Detroit Times,* January 9, 1925.

80. DSO program, October 16, 1927.

81. Clemens, 221.

82. Ibid., 336.

83. Ibid., 222.

84. Ibid., 339.

85. John Eliot Gardner, *Bach: Music in the Castle of Heaven* (New York: Knopf, 2013), 407.

86. Clemens, 337.

87. Ibid., 225.

88. Ibid., 319.

89. Ibid., 242–43.

90. Ibid., 123.

91. Ossip Gabrilowitsch papers, 1920–37 Collection, Box 1 Burton Historical Collection, Detroit Public Library.

92. Ossip Gabrilowitsch papers, 1920–37 Collection, Box 1, Burton Historical Collection, Detroit Public Library; Ossip Gabrilowitsch to Mignon Alger, March 24, 1930, Burton.

93. Ossip Gabrilowitsch papers, 1920–37 Collection, Box 1, Burton Historical Collection, Detroit Public Library; Ossip Gabrilowitsch to Joseph Weber, October 13, 1933, Burton.

94. Clemens, 147.

95. Ossip Gabrilowitsch papers, 1920–37 Collection, Box 6, Burton Historical Collection, Detroit Public Library; Ossip Gabrilowitsch to Walter Damrosch, November 15, 1922, Burton.

96. Woodford, *This Is Detroit*, 120–21.

97. Detroit Symphony Society records, 1919–45, Box 3, Burton Historical Collection, Detroit Public Library.

98. Clemens, 259–60.

99. Programs, Detroit Symphony Orchestra, 1932–33; Detroit Public Library, Music, Art, and Literature Department, Detroit, Michigan; call number: R789 D48.

100. Clemens, 261.

101. Tilton, 271.

102. Ibid., 272.

103. Clemens, 125.

104. Tilton, 270.

105. Clemens, 279.

106. Ibid., 281.

107. Ibid., 282–83.

108. Ibid., 283, 307.

109. Tilton, 240.

110. Clemens, 321.

## CHAPTER FOUR

1. Detroit Symphony Society Records, 1919–45, Box 3, Burton Historical Collection, Detroit Public Library.

2. Programs, Detroit Symphony Orchestra, 1936–37; Detroit Public Library, Music, Art, and Literature Department, Detroit, Michigan; call number: R789 D48.

3. Ibid.

4. Detroit Symphony Society Records, 1919–45, Box 3, Burton Historical Collection, Detroit Public Library.

5. Programs, Detroit Symphony Orchestra, 1936–37; Detroit Public Library, Music, Art, and Literature Department, Detroit, Michigan; call number: R789 D48.

6. Detroit Symphony Society Records, 1919–45, Box 3, Burton Historical Collection, Detroit Public Library.

7. Tilton, 328–29.

8. *New York Times,* May 16, 1936.

9. Detroit Symphony Society Records, 1919–45, Box 3, Burton Historical Collection, Detroit Public Library.

10. Programs, Detroit Symphony Orchestra, 1938–39; Detroit Public Library, Music, Art, and Literature Department, Detroit, Michigan; call number: R789 D48.

11. Ibid.

12. Ibid.

13. Ibid.

14. Detroit Symphony Society Records, 1919–45, Box 3, Burton Historical Collection, Detroit Public Library.

15. Programs, Detroit Symphony Orchestra, 1938–39; Detroit Public Library, Music, Art, and Literature Department, Detroit, Michigan; call number: R789 D48.

16. Ibid.

17. Detroit Symphony Society Records, 1919–45, Box 3, Burton Historical Collection, Detroit Public Library.

18. Programs, Detroit Symphony Orchestra, 1938–39; Detroit Public Library, Music, Art, and Literature Department, Detroit, Michigan; call number: R789 D48.

19. Tilton, 241.

20. Programs, Detroit Symphony Orchestra, 1939–40; Detroit Public Library, Music, Art, and Literature Department, Detroit, Michigan; call number: R789 D48.

21. Tilton, 329.

22. Ibid.

23. Lynne Marie Mattson, "A History of the Detroit Symphony Orchestra" (master's thesis, University of Michigan School of Music, 1968), 23.

24. *Detroit Free Press,* January 16, 1940.

25. *Detroit Free Press,* January 17, 1940

26. *Detroit News,* February 21, 1940.

27. Programs, Detroit Symphony Orchestra, 1940–41; Detroit Public Library, Music, Art, and Literature Department, Detroit, Michigan; call number: R789 D48.

28. Detroit Symphony Society records, 1919–45, Box 3, Burton Historical Collection, Detroit Public Library.

29. Ibid.

30. Ibid.

31. Ibid.

32. Programs, Detroit Symphony Orchestra, 1941–42; Detroit Public Library, Music, Art, and Literature Department, Detroit, Michigan; call number: R789 D48.

33. Mattson, 25.

34. Woodford, *This Is Detroit*, 152–55.

35. *Detroit News,* February 5, 1942.

36. *Time* magazine, February 2, 1942.

37. Mattson, 26.

38. Detroit Symphony Society records, 1919–45, Box 3, Burton Historical Collection, Detroit Public Library.

39. Ibid.

40. Ibid.

41. Ibid.

42. *Detroit Free Press,* October 4, 1942.

43. *Detroit News,* October 1, 1942.

44. *Musical America*, October 1942.

**CHAPTER FIVE**

1. Detroit Symphony Society records, 1919–45, Box 3, Burton Historical Collection, Detroit Public Library.

2. Mattson, 29–30.

3. *Detroit News,* August 29, 1943; Tilton, 360.

4. Mattson, 30–31; Programs, Detroit Symphony Orchestra, 1943–44; Detroit Public Library, Music, Art, and Literature Department, Detroit, Michigan; call number: R789 D48; "Krueger, Karl (Adalbert)," *Baker's Biographical Dictionary of Musicians,* vol. 3, ed. Nicolas Slonimsky and Laura Kuhn (New York: Schirmer, 2001).

5. *Detroit News,* August 21, 1943.

6. *Detroit News,* November 22, 1943.

7. Programs, Detroit Symphony Orchestra, 1943–44; Detroit Public Library, Music, Art, and Literature Department, Detroit, Michigan; call number: R789 D48.

8. *Detroit Free Press,* February 20, 1944.

9. Programs, Detroit Symphony Orchestra, 1943–44; Detroit Public Library, Music, Art, and Literature Department, Detroit, Michigan; call number: R789 D48.

10. Ibid.

11. Ibid.

12. Karl Krueger, *The Way of the Conductor* (New York: Scribner's, 1958).

13. Programs, Detroit Symphony Orchestra, 1943–44; Detroit Public Library, Music, Art, and Literature Department, Detroit, Michigan; call number: R789 D48.

14. Ibid.

15. *Detroit News,* June 12, 1944; June 18, 1944; August 13, 1944.

16. *Detroit Free Press,* September 17, 1944.

17. *Detroit News,* December 2, 1944.

18. *Detroit Free Press,* March 29, 1945.

19. *Detroit News,* April 14, 1945.

20. *New York Times,* January 31, 1945.

21. Ibid.

22. *Detroit Free Press,* April 1, 1945.

23. *Detroit News,* April 1, 1945.

24. *DAC News,* October 1946.

25. *DAC News,* November 1946.

26. Programs, 1945–46 season.

27. *Detroit News,* June 17, 1945.

28. *Detroit News,* December 19, 1946.

29. Programs, March 14, 1946, and October 24, 1946.

30. Programs, Detroit Symphony Orchestra, 1946–47; Detroit Public Library, Music, Art, and Literature Department, Detroit, Michigan; call number: R789 D48.

31. Ibid.

32. *Detroit News,* February 9, 1947.

33. http://www.biography.com/people/margaret-truman-266346#synopsis.

34. Donald Rosenberg, *The Cleveland Orchestra Story: "Second to None"* (Cleveland: Gray and Company, 2000), 247.

35. Ibid., 249.

36. Ibid., 249.

37. Ibid., 249.

38. *Detroit Free Press,* February 21, 1947.

39. *New York Times,* December 14, 1947.

40. *Detroit Free Press,* Feburary 13, 1949.

41. *Time,* February 14, 1949.

42. Ibid.

43. Ibid.

44. Ibid.

45. Ibid.

46. Ibid.

47. Ibid.

48. *Detroit Times,* February 5, 1949.

49. Ibid.

50. *Time,* March 14, 1949.

51. *DAC News,* April 1949.

52. Ibid.

53. Ibid.

54. *Detroit Free Press,* June 11, 1949.

55. *Detroit Times,* August 25, 1949.

56. Ibid.

57. *Detroit News,* Sept. 26, 1949.

58. *Detroit News,* September 26, 1949.

59. Ibid.

**CHAPTER SIX**

1. John B. Ford, "The Detroit Story," Board Members Collection, Box 1, Folder: Ford, John B., Detroit Symphony Orchestra Archives, Detroit, Michigan.

2. *The Reporter,* February 7, 1957.

3. Ford, "The Detroit Story."

4. http://www.michmarkers.com/startup.asp?startpage=L1790.htm.

5. Ford, "The Detroit Story."

6. http://www.liveunitedsem.org/history.

7. Ford, "The Detroit Story."

8. Ibid.

9. Ibid.

10. *New York Times,* May 26, 1951.

11. *Detroit Times,* April 10, 1954.

12. *New York Times,* September 16, 1951.

13. Tilton, 393.

14. Programs, Detroit Symphony Orchestra, 1951–52; Detroit Public Library, Music, Art, and Literature Department, Detroit, Michigan; call number: R789 D48

15. *Detroit Times,* October 18, 1951.

16. *Detroit Free Press,* October 15, 1951.

17. *New York Times,* January 26, 1952.

18. Paray biographical resources: *New York Times*, October 13, 1979; Tilton, 422–23; *Baker's Biographical Dictionary of Musicians* (New York: Schirmer, 2001), 2712–13; www.paul-paray.com.

19. *Detroit News,* January 29, 1952.

20. Programs, Detroit Symphony Orchestra, 1951–52; Detroit Public Library, Music, Art, and Literature Department, Detroit, Michigan; call number: R789 D48; Tilton, 423.

21. Liner notes to Mercury Living Presence/Chabrier, Roussel, Paul Paray/Detroit Symphony, CD transfer recording, 1991.

22. *Gramophone,* January 1957.

23. *Sensible Sound,* July–August 2005.

24. Peter Gutman, "Paul Paray: A Frenchman in Detroit," http://www.classicalnotes.net/columns/paray.html.

25. Liner Notes to Mercury Living Presence/Chabrier, Rouseel, Paul Paray/Detroit Symphony, CD transfer recording, 1991.

26. *American Record Guide,* November–December 1994.

27. *American Record Guide,* November–December 1996.

28. *American Record Guide,* July–August 1999.

29. Peter Gutman, "Paul Paray: A Frenchman in Detroit," http://www.classicalnotes.net/columns/paray.html.

30. *New York Herald Tribune,* January 16, 1954.

31. *Musical America,* February 1, 1954.

32. *New York Times,* January 16, 1954.

33. *Performance,* vol. 10, no. 4.

34. *Detroit Free Press,* Janaury 23, 1955.

35. Eric J. Hill and John Gallagher, *AIA Detroit: The American Institute of Architects Guide to Detroit Architecture* (Detroit: Wayne State University Press, 2003), 14.

36. http://www.historicdetroit.org/building/ford-auditorium/.

37. *Hour Detroit,* April 2012.

38. *New York Times,* October 15, 1956.

39. *American Record Guide,* November–December 1997.

40. *Detroit Free Press,* March 25, 1957.

41. *Detroit News,* February 7, 1957.

42. *Detroit News,* March 18, 1957.

43. Programs, Detroit Symphony Orchestra, 1957–58; Detroit Public Library, Music, Art, and Literature Department, Detroit, Michigan; call number: R789 D48.

44. *New York Times,* February 15, 1954.

45. *New York Times,* October 12, 1957.

46. *Detroit News,* January 5, 1958.

47. *Musical America,* November 15, 1958.

48. *Musical Courier,* January 1959.

49. http://www.telegram.com/article/20091004/NEWS/910040565/1011.

50. *Detroit Free Press,* December 10, 1959.

51. *The Reporter,* February 7, 1957.

52. Ibid.

53. Ibid.

54. *Detroit Free Press,* March 4, 1960.

55. *Detroit News,* November 18, 1956.

56. Woodford, *This Is Detroit,* 162.

57. Programs, Detroit Symphony Orchestra, 1951–52 and 1961–62; Detroit Public Library, Music, Art, and Literature Department, Detroit, Michigan; call number: R789 D48.

58. The Detroit Symphony Orchestra Collection, Box 14, Folder 48, Walter P. Reuther Library, Archives of Labor and Urban Affairs, Wayne State University.

59. Programs, Detroit Symphony Orchestra, 1959–60; Detroit Public Library, Music, Art, and Literature Department, Detroit, Michigan; call number: R789 D48.

60. Mattson, 60.

61. *Detroit News,* September 4, 1961.

62. Mattson, 61.

63. *Detroit News,* March 29, 1961.

64. *New York Times,* September 30, 1990.

65. *Detroit News,* January 12, 1962.

66. *Detroit News,* March 30, 1962.

67. *Impressario* magazine, July 1968.

68. *Detroit Free Press,* August 11, 1968.

69. Ibid.

## CHAPTER SEVEN

1. *Detroit News,* January 6, 1963.

2. *New York Times,* February 16, 2005; *Daily Telegraph* (London), February 21, 2005.

3. *Independent,* February 17, 2005.

4. *New York Times,* February 16, 2005.

5. Ibid.

6. *Independent,* February 17, 2005.

7. *The Guardian,* April 21, 2005

8. Programs, Detroit Symphony Orchestra, 1961–62; Detroit Public Library, Music, Art, and Literature Department, Detroit, Michigan; call number: R789 D48.

9. *Detroit News,* January 6, 1963.

10. The Detroit Symphony Orchestra Hall Inc. Collection, Box 14, Folder 48, Walter P. Reuther Library, Archives of Labor and Urban Affairs, Wayne State University.

11. *Detroit News,* July 1, 1963.

12. *Detroit News,* July 26, 1963.

13. *Detroit News,* December 27, 1963.

14. Programs, Detroit Symphony Orchestra, 1963–64; Detroit Public Library, Music, Art, and Literature Department, Detroit, Michigan; call number: R789 D48.

15. Tilton, 676.

16. *Minneapolis Star,* January 19, 1963.

17. *New York Times,* February 16, 1964.

18. *Detroit Free Press,* February 7, 1964.

19. *Toledo Blade,* February 7, 1964.

20. Tilton, 606.

21. http://library.oakland.edu/archives/buildings/building.php?building=361.

22. Mattson, 67–68.

23. http://www.detroitsymphonymusicians.org/archives-2010-11/what-we-think/meadow-brook-remembered/.

24. Programs, Detroit Symphony Orchestra, 1964–65; Detroit Public Library, Music, Art, and Literature Department, Detroit, Michigan; call number: R789 D48.

25. *New York Times,* November 17, 1964.

26. *Toledo Blade,* April 6, 1965.

27. *New York Times,* November 2, 1966.

28. Programs, Detroit Symphony Orchestra, 1966–67; Detroit Public Library, Music, Art, and Literature Department, Detroit, Michigan; call number: R789 D48.

29. Woodford, 180–81.

30. Ibid.

31. Ibid., 183.

32. http://www.detroitsymphonymusicians.org/archives-2010-11/what-we-think/meadow-brook-remembered/.

33. The Detroit Symphony Orchestra Hall Inc. Collection, Box 18, Folder 12, Walter P. Reuther Library, Archives of Labor and Urban Affairs, Wayne State University.

34. http://www.worldcat.org/title/milestone-in-d-Minor/oclc/43371877.

35. *New York Times,* November 3, 1967.

36. *New York Times,* November 7, 1970.

37. The Detroit Symphony Orchestra Hall Inc. Collection, Box 6, Folder 22, Walter P. Reuther Library, Archives of Labor and Urban Affairs, Wayne State University.

38. Programs, Detroit Symphony Orchestra, 1972–73; Detroit Public Library, Music, Art, and Literature Department, Detroit, Michigan; call number: R789 D48.

39. *New York Times,* May 17, 1972.

40. *Baker's Biographical Dictionary of Musicians* (New York: Schirmer, 2001).

41. *New York Times,* November 11, 1970; April 7, 1973.

42. *New York Times,* August 12, 1973.

43. The Detroit Symphony Orchestra Hall Inc. Collection, Box 6, Folder 22, Walter P. Reuther Library, Archives of Labor and Urban Affairs, Wayne State University.

44. *New York Times,* January 31, 1975.

45. The Detroit Symphony Orchestra Hall Inc. Collection, Box 6, Folder 22, Walter P. Reuther Library, Archives of Labor and Urban Affairs, Wayne State University.

46. Program of January 27, 1963, from Programs, Detroit Symphony Orchestra, 1962–63; Detroit Public Library, Music, Art, and Literature Department, Detroit, Michigan; call

number: R789 D48.

47. Mattson, 66.

48. Programs, Detroit Symphony Orchestra, 1965–66; Detroit Public Library, Music, Art, and Literature Department, Detroit, Michigan; call number: R789 D48.

49. The Detroit Symphony Orchestra Hall Inc. Collection, Box 4, Folder 26, Walter P. Reuther Library, Archives of Labor and Urban Affairs, Wayne State University.

50. Programs, Detroit Symphony Orchestra, 1972–73; Detroit Public Library, Music, Art, and Literature Department, Detroit, Michigan; Call number: R789 D48.

51. The Detroit Symphony Orchestra Hall Inc. Collection, Box 6, Folder 22, Walter P. Reuther Library, Archives of Labor and Urban Affairs, Wayne State University.

52. Woodford, 222–24.

53. The Detroit Symphony Orchestra Hall Inc. Collection, Box 6, Folder 22, Walter P. Reuther Library, Archives of Labor and Urban Affairs, Wayne State University.

54. *New York Times,* December 21, 1975.

55. Ibid.

56. The Detroit Symphony Orchestra Hall Inc. Collection, Box 6, Folder 23, Walter P. Reuther Library, Archives of Labor and Urban Affairs, Wayne State University.

57. Ibid.

58. The Detroit Symphony Orchestra Hall Inc. Collection, Box 6, Folder 2, Walter P. Reuther Library, Archives of Labor and Urban Affairs, Wayne State University.

**CHAPTER EIGHT**

1. Programs, Detroit Symphony Orchestra, 1977–78; Detroit Public Library, Music, Art, and Literature Department, Detroit, Michigan; call number: R789 D48.

2. Antal Dorati, Notes on Seven Decades, rev. ed. (Detroit: Wayne State University Press, 1981), 196.

3. *Gramophone,* November, 2014.

4. *Star Tribune,* Minneapolis, January 7, 2007.

5. Dorati biographical sources: *New York Times*, November 15, 1988; "Dorati, Antal," *The Scribner Encyclopedia of American Lives*, vol. 2: 1986–90, ed. Kenneth T. Jackson, Karen Markoe, and Arnold Markoe (New York: Charles Scribner's Sons, 1999), 256–58; "Antal Dorati," *Encyclopedia of World Biography*, vol. 32 (Detroit: Gale), 2012.

6. *American Scholar,* Summer 2013, 93.

7. Programs, Detroit Symphony Orchestra, 1977–78; Detroit Public Library, Music, Art, and Literature Department, Detroit, Michigan; call number: R789 D48.

8. *Detroit Free Press,* November 4, 1977.

9. *Windsor Star,* November 3, 1977.

10. *New York Times,* November 4, 1977.

11. Programs, Detroit Symphony Orchestra, 1977–78; Detroit Public Library, Music, Art, and Literature Department, Detroit, Michigan; call number: R789 D48.

12. Dorati, 336–37.

13. Ibid., 338.

14. Ibid.

15. *High Fidelity,* September 1979.

16. *Stereo Review,* August 1984.

17. *Gramophone,* February 1984.

18. *American Record Guide,* September–October 1996.

19. *Stereo Review,* April 1986.

20. Liner notes, Bartok, Miraculous Mandarin: Music for Stings, Percussion, and Celesta, London/Decca recording, 1985.

21. Programs, Detroit Symphony Orchestra, 1978–79; Detroit Public Library, Music, Art, and Literature Department, Detroit, Michigan; call number: R789 D48.

22. Ibid.

23. Dorati, 343.

24. *Detroit Free Press,* April 27, 1979.

25. *New York Times,* April 29, 1979.

26. *Washington Post,* April 30, 1979.

27. Programs, Detroit Symphony Orchestra, 1979–80; Detroit Public Library, Music, Art, and Literature Department, Detroit, Michigan; call number: R789 D48.

28. Reprinted in: Programs, Detroit Symphony Orchestra, 1979–80; Detroit Public Library, Music, Art, and Literature Department, Detroit, Michigan; call number: R789 D48.

29. Ibid.

30. Dorati, 344.

31. The Detroit Symphony Orchestra Collection, Box 6, Folder 26, Walter P. Reuther Library, Archives of Labor and Urban Affairs, Wayne State University.

32. Programs, Detroit Symphony Orchestra, 1979–80; Detroit Public Library, Music, Art, and Literature Department, Detroit, Michigan; call number: R789 D48.

33. The Detroit Symphony Orchestra Collection, Box 6, Folder 26, Walter P. Reuther Library, Archives of Labor and Urban Affairs, Wayne State University.

34. Woodford, 225; *New York Times,* September 12, 1980.

35. The Detroit Symphony Orchestra Collection, Box 6, Folder 26, Walter P. Reuther Library, Archives of Labor and Urban Affairs, Wayne State University.

36. *New York Times,* September 12, 1980.

37. *Detroit News,* September, 23, 1984.

38. Ibid.

39. Programs, Detroit Symphony Orchestra, 1980–81; Detroit Public Library, Music, Art, and Literature Department, Detroit, Michigan; call number: R789 D48.

40. Ibid.

41. *Baker's Biographical Dictionary of Musicians* (New York: Schirmer, 2001); *Encyclopedia Judaica* (New York: Macmillan, 2007).

42. *New York Times,* December 16, 1982.

43. Ibid.

44. Ibid.

45. Ibid.

46. Ibid.

47. *New York Times,* December 22, 1982

48. *New York Times,* April 14, 1985.

49. Ibid.; *Baker's Biographical Dictionary of Musicians* (New York: Schirmer, 2001).

50. *New York Times,* November 30, 1983.

51. *High Fidelity,* February 1985.

52. *Detroit News,* September 23, 1984.

53. Ibid.

54. *New York Times,* April 14, 1985.

55. *High Fidelity,* February 1985.

56. Ibid.

57. *New York Times,* April 14, 1985.

58. Ibid.; *Detroit News,* September 23, 1984.

59. *New York Times,* April 21, 1985.

60. PR Newswire, October 10, 1985.

61. *New York Times,* October 20, 1985.

62. Programs, Detroit Symphony Orchestra, 1985–86, Detroit Public Library, Music, Art, and Literature Department, Detroit, Michigan; call number: R789 D48.

63. *New York Times,* March 2, 1987.

64. Ibid.

65. *New York Times,* September 24, 1987.

66. *New York Times,* November 11, 1987.

67. Ibid.

68. *New York Times,* December 15, 1987.

69. *Globe and Mail,* November 14, 1987.

70. *Globe and Mail,* May 3, 1988.

71. PR Newswire, February 7, 1989.

72. *Times,* February 14, 1989.

73. PR Newswire, February 9, 1989.

74. PR Newswire, January 31, 1989.

75. *New Republic,* March 27, 1989.

76. PR Newswire, February 19, 1989.

77. *New York Times,* March 5, 1989.

78. Ibid.

79. Ibid.

80. *Chicago Tribune,* March 8, 1989.

81. *New York Times,* March 5, 1989.

82. Ibid.

83. Ibid.

84. *American Record Guide,* January–February 1993.

## CHAPTER NINE

1. *New York Times,* November 4, 1991.

2. *Detroit Free Press,* May 22, 2005.

3. *Stereo Review,* September 1990.

4. *New York Times,* April 8, 1979.

5. Ibid.

6. Ibid.

7. Ibid.

8. *New York Times,* February 22, 1980.

9. *Baker's Biographical Dictionary of Musicians* (New York: Schirmer, 2001).

10. *New York Times,* October 6, 1986.

11. *New York Times,* April 20, 1986.

12. *New York Times,* January 18, 1990.

13. *Stereo Review,* September 1990.

14. Ibid.

15. Programs, Detroit Symphony Orchestra, 1990–91; Detroit Public Library, Music, Art, and Literature Department, Detroit, Michigan; call number: R789 D48.

16. *New York Times,* November 4, 1991.

17. *New York Times,* October 27, 1991.

18. *New York Times,* November 4, 1991.

19. http://www.phil.frb.org/research-and-data/publications/business-review/1990/brja90dw.pdf.

20. Woodford, *This Is Detroit,* 234.

21. *New York Times,* November 4, 1991.

22. Ibid.

23. *New York Times,* November 6, 1991.

24. Ibid.

25. *American Record Guide,* January–February 1993.

26. Ibid.

27. *Stereo Review,* April 1992.

28. *American Record Guide,* January–February 1993.

29. Ibid.

30. Ibid.

31. *American Record Guide,* November–December 1993.

32. *American Record Guide,* November–December 1994.

33. Ibid.

34. Ibid.

35. *New York Times,* May 25, 1994.

36. *Detroit News,* June 2, 2005.

37. Ibid.

38. *Detroit Free Press,* May 22, 2005.

39. *The Scotsman,* May 12, 1999.

40. *Detroit News,* June 2, 2005.

41. Ibid.

42. Ibid.

43. *Detroit Free Press,* May 22, 2005.

44. *Denver Post,* July 14, 1996.

45. Table 23, "Michigan—Race and Hispanic Origin for Selected Large Cities and Other Places: Earliest Census to 1990," United States Census Bureau.

46. *Encyclopedia of African-American Music,* vol. 3 (New York: Greenwood, 2011).

47. *American Visions,* April–May 1994.

48. *The News & Record,* September 26, 1999.

49. http://www.sphinxmusic.org/index.

50. Ibid.

51. *Billboard,* April 13, 2002.

52. *American Record Guide,* July–August 1995.

53. *American Record Guide,* January–February 1996.

54. *New York Times,* January 22, 1996.

55. PR Newswire, March 26, 1996.

56. Woodford, 237–39.

57. Ibid.

58. PR Newswire, March 26, 1996.

59. PR Newswire, September 30, 1997.

60. Ibid.

61. Ibid.

62. PR Newswire, April 17, 1998.

63. Ibid.

64. Ibid.

65. Ibid.

66. *Birmingham Post,* April 29, 1998.

67. Ibid.

68. Ibid.

69. *Times,* May 1, 1998.

70. *Birmingham Post,* May 4, 1998.

71. *The Guardian,* May 5, 1998.

72. *The Age,* June 11, 1998.

73. M2 Presswire, October 22, 1998.

74. PR Newswire, November 12, 1998.

75. *Crain's Detroit Business,* May 15, 2000.

76. Ibid.

77. Ibid.

78. Ibid.

79. *Detroit Free Press,* January 20, 2000.

80. Ibid.

81. Ibid.

82. Press release, Guardian Industries, September 9, 2000.

83. Ibid.

84. *The Palm Beach Post,* January 19, 2001.

85. *Scotland on Sunday,* July 15, 2001; *Detroit Free Press,* August 21, 2001.

86. *Detroit Free Press,* August 21, 2001.

87. *Detroit Free Press,* October 1, 2001.

88. *Detroit Free Press,* October 8, 2001.

89. *Detroit Free Press,* October 17, 2001.

90. *Detroit News,* November 25, 2001.

91. *Musical America,* May 3, 2003.

92. *Detroit News,* October 6, 2003.

93. Ibid.

94. *Detroit Free Press,* December 26, 2004.

95. *Detroit News,* June 2, 2005.

96. Ibid.

97. Ibid.

98. Ibid.

99. *American Record Guide,* September–October 2005.

100. *Detroit News,* June 2, 2005.


**CHAPTER TEN**

1. *New York Times,* April 10, 2011.

2. *Crain's Detroit Business,* September 12, 2005.

3. *Detroit Free Press,* June 2, 2007.

4. *Crain's Detroit Business,* October 15, 2007.

5. *Detroit Free Press,* October 8, 2007.

6. *Baker's Biographical Dictionary of Musicians* (New York: Schirmer, 2001); *Contemporary Musicians* (Farmington Hills: Gale, 2003).

7. *Detroit Free Press,* December 14, 2007.

8. *Detroit Free Press,* November 26, 2008.

9. http://www.macrotrends.net/1358/dow-jones-industrial-average-last-10-years.

10. http://www.treasury.gov/connect/blog/Documents/FinancialCrisis5Yr_vFINAL.pdf; Bloomberg, September 14, 2012.

11. http://www.treasury.gov/connect/blog/Documents/FinancialCrisis5Yr_vFINAL.pdf; Bureau of Labor Statistics: http://data.bls.gov/timeseries/LNS140000.

12. *Crain's Detroit Business*, December 5, 2011.

13. *Detroit Free Press,* November 26, 2008.

14. *American Record Guide,* May–June 2009.

15. Ibid.

16. *American Record Guide,* May–June 2009.

17. *India Currents,* October 26, 2009.

18. *New York Times,* November 16, 2009.

19. *Crain's Detroit Business,* December 5, 2011.

20. *Detroit Free Press,* March 18, 2010.

21. Ibid.

22. *Detroit Free Press,* March 28, 2010.

23. Ibid.

24. *Time,* July 5, 2010.

25. *Detroit Free Press,* August 24, 2010; *New York Times,* August 29, 2010.

26. *Detroit Free Press,* August 24, 2010.

27. Ibid.

28. Ibid.

29. *Detroit News,* August 28, 2010.

30. *Detroit Free Press,* August 29, 2010.

31. *Detroit Free Press,* October 4, 2010.
32. *New York Times,* October 3, 2010.
33. *Detroit Free Press,* October 4, 2010.
34. *Detroit News,* September 30, 2010.
35. *Detroit Free Press,* October 1, 2010.
36. *Detroit Free Press,* October 7, 2010.
37. *Guardian,* November 20, 2010.
38. Ibid.
39. http://www.npr.org/blogs/therecord/2010/11/05/131107706/without-an-angel-donor-the-detroit-symphony-orchestra-could-go-dark.
40. http://www.detroitsymphonymusicians.org/archives-2010-11/where-we-stand-list/december-2010/.
41. *New York Times,* November 6, 1996.
42. http://www.adaptistration.com/blog/2011/01/21/chicago-symphony-musicians-leaflet-for-detroit/.
43. *New York Times,* February 21, 2011.
44. *Detroit Free Press,* February 22, 2011.
45. *Detroit Free Press,* March 1, 2011.
46. http://www.adaptistration.com/blog/tag/detroit-symphony-orchestra/.
47. *New York Times,* April 9, 2011.
48. *New York Times,* April 10, 2011.
49. *Detroit Free Press,* April 12, 2011.
50. *New York Times,* April 10, 2011.
51. http://www.detroitsymphonymusicians.org/archives-2010-11/press-room/may-2011/.
52. http://www.adaptistration.com/blog/2011/05/26/reading-between-the-lines-in-detroit/.
53. *Detroit Free Press,* September 18, 2011.
54. *Crain's Detroit Business,* December 17, 2012.
55. *Detroit Free Press,* January 5, 2012.
56. *Crain's Detroit Business,* December 17, 2012.
57. *Detroit Free Press,* January 22, 2012.
58. *New York Times,* May 13, 2013.
59. Ibid.
60. *Gramophone,* July 2013.
61. *American Record Guide,* January–February 2014.
62. *New York Times,* December 11, 2013.
63. *Crain's Detroit Business,* January 15, 2014.
64. *New York Times,* March 21, 2014.
65. www.dso.org.
66. *New York Times,* August 8, 2014.
67. www.dso.org.
68. *New York Times,* November 12, 2014.
69. www.dso.org.
70. *Crain's Detroit Business,* December 15, 2014.
71. *Detroit Free Press,* November 11, 2014.
72. *New York Times,* June 16, 2013.

# Appendix:
## Detroit Symphony Orchestra Personnel
## 1906–2015

## VIOLIN

Adams, Emily Mutter: 1st, *1938–42, 1943–49, 1951–63. See also* E. M. Austin

Altschuler, Eugene: 1st, 1954–59

Andreasen, Adolph: 1st, 1914–15, 1915–18

Applegate, Geoffrey: 2nd, 1981–83; 1st, 1983–86; Pr 2nd, 1986–2011

Arbeitman, Haim: 2nd, 1954–55

Austin, Carl: 2nd, 1944–45

Austin, Emily Mutter: 1st, 1962–76. *See also* E. M. Adams

Babst, August: 1st, 1922–23, 1924–33

Baraniecki, A.: 1st, 1919–20

Barnes, Robert: 2nd, 1961–66

Barrett, James D.: 2nd, 1926–27; Asst Pr 2nd, 1927–34; 1st, 1934–38; Pr 2nd, 1938–39; 1st, 1939–42, 1943–45; Assoc Con (2nd chair), 1945–49

Bartlett, Larry: 2nd, 1972–81

Basham, Glenn: 2nd, 1980–81; 1st, 1981–82

Bayer, Conrad: 1st, 1914–16

Bemus, Lloyd: 1st, 1916–18

Benavie, Samuel: 2nd, 1934–37; Asst Pr 2nd, 1937–42

Bengtsson, Roy: 2nd, 1952–54, 1963–95

Biase, Paul Pasquale: 2nd, 1944–46

Bistritzky, Zinovi (Sam): 1st, 1932–42, 1946–49; Asst Conc (2nd chair), 1951–52; Asst Conc (3rd chair), 1952–72. *See also* Personnel Manager

Blaaha, W.: 2nd, 1918–19

Blesch, Frank: 1st, 1906

Boell, Edwin: 2nd, 1906

Boesen, Jack: 2nd, 1943–45; 1st, 1945–49, 1951–79

Boisvert, Emmanuelle: Concertmaster, 1989–2011

Bourbonnais, James: 2nd, 1943–44; 1st, 1945–46, 1951–73

Breyen: 2nd, 2/26/1914

Briglia, Pasquale: 1st, 1906, 2/26/1914, 1914–18

Brueckner, Herman: 1st, 1906; Asst Conc (2nd chair), 2/26/1914, 1914–16; Sec 1st, 1916–18

Caplan, Z.: 1st, 1920–21; 2nd, 1921–24

Carey, Burt: 2nd, 1938–42; 1st, 1943–46

Cassie, James: 1st, 2/26/1914. *See also* Viola

Chase, Karl W.: 1st, 1920–42, 1943–49. *See also* Personnel Manager

Colman, Sidney: 1st, 1951–59

Courtois, Jean P.: 2nd, 1921–42, 1943–49

Cramer, Ernest: 2nd, 1952–69

Crispin, John W.: 1st, 1916–17; 2nd, 1917–18, 1943–49, 1951–66. *See also* **Librarian**

Crocker, Sarah: 1st, 2007–08

Crocov, David H.: 1st, 1918–24

Culp, Sigmund: 1st, 1921–22

Currier, F. S.: 2nd, 1919–31

Cyncynates, Ricardo: 2nd, 1985–88

Dagnar, Walter: 2nd, 1915–16

D'Aiuto, Christopher: 2nd, 1952–53

Danielyan, Lilit: 2nd, 1999–2011

D'Antonio, Franklyn: 1st, 1977–81

Davis, C. W.: 2nd, 1917–18

Davis, W.: 2nd, 1929–30

Dayne, A.: 1st, 1916–17; 2nd, 1917–18; Asst Pr 2nd, 1918–19

De Palma, Otto: 2nd, 1944–49

Deslippe, Marguerite: 2nd, 1982–85; 1st, 1985–86; Deslippe-Andrews: 1986–88; Deslippe: 1988–94; Deslippe-Dene: 1994–2010; Deslippe: 2011–

De Stephano, Michael: 1st, 1916–18; 2nd, 1921–23; 1st, 1923–24

De Tomasi, Americo: 2nd, 1915–17

Di Bello, Gina: 2nd, 2005–06, 1st, 2007–08

Di Natale, J.: 1st, 1920–21

Divinoff, I. (Miss) : 1st, 1918–20

Downs, Lillian: 2nd, 1965–1976. *See also* L. Fenstermacher

Downs, Thomas: 2nd, 1965–2001

Duitman, Elayna: 2nd, 2001–10

Edley, Morris: 2nd, 1966–68

Elkind, Jacob: 2nd, 1921–22. *See also* **Viola**

Endres, Hubert: Asst Pr 2nd, 1919–21; Pr 2nd, 1921–42, 1943–48

Epstein, Samuel E.: 2nd, 1928–42, 1943–44, 1946–49

Erkkila, Unto: 1st, 1951–56

Eschmann: 1st, 2/26/1914

Everett, Charles: 1st, 1966–67; Asst Conc (4th chair), 1967–69

Fabris, P.: 1st, 1927–31

Faeder, Arthur: 2nd, 1915–18

Fafard, Joseph L.: 2nd, 1967–68

Farnham, A.: 2nd, 1927–28; 1st, 1928–31. *See also* **Keyboard**

Feiler, H.: 1st 1918–19; 2nd, 1920–21

Fenstermacher, Lillian: 2nd, 1976–2000. *See also* L. Downs

Ferentino, L.: 2nd, 1918–19

Fischer, Ronald: 1st, 1981–83; 2nd, 1983–93; Sabbatical, 1994; 2nd, 1995–

Francis, Derek: 1st, 1965–98

Friedenzohn, Elias: 1st, 1965–66; 2nd, 1966–72; Acting Asst Conc, 1972–73; 1st, 1973–2013

Garagusi, Nicholas: 1st, 1920–21, 1923–24, 1926–27, 1944–45, 1951–59; 2nd, 1959–64

Geerts, J.: 2nd, 1918–19

Gerstel, Alan: 1st, 1973–2004

Gewirtz, J.: 1st, 1919–20

Gingold, Josef: Concertmaster, 1944–47

Gluck, Joseph: 1st, 1963–71

Goldman, Joseph: Asst Conc (3rd chair), 1974–88; (2nd chair), 1988–89; (3rd chair), 1989–2000; Sec 1st, 2000–2012

Goldman, Laurie Landers: 1st, 1997–2003; Sabbatical, 2003–04; 1st, 2004–. *See also* L. Landers

Goldsmith, Kenneth: 2nd, 1958–59; 1st, 1959–60

Goldstein, Herman: 1st, 1920–24

Gorner, Joseph: 1st, 1920–33

Granover, Hyman: 1st, 1914–17

Green: 1st, 2/26/1914

Griffen, Beatrice: 1st, 1932–34

Groff, Raphael: 1st, 1919–33

Grossman, Arthur: 2nd, 1943–45; 1st, 1948–49

Gruenberg, Maurice: 1st, 1919–20

Haapaniemi, Will: 2nd, 2014–

Halfmann, Virginia: 1st, 1965–72

Halprin, O.: 2nd, 1944–46

Han, Hae Jeong Heidi: 2nd, 2014–

Hancock, Frank E.: 1st, 1920–42, 1943–49, 1951–64

Hancock, LeRoy: 2nd, 1919–42, 1943–48; Asst Pr 2nd, 1948–49; Sec 2nd, 1951–59

Harris, Graham: 1st, 1918–20

Haug, Henry: 2nd, 1906, 2/26/1914

Hebert, A.: 2nd, 1916–17

Hellmann, Leo: 2nd, 1921–38

Heyde, Erhard: 1st, 1922–28; 2nd, 1928–33

Hochberg, Morris: 1st, 1943–48; Asst Conc (4th chair), 1952–66

Hughes, Alfred W.: 2nd, 1926–27, 1928–34; Asst Pr 2nd, 1934–37; Sec 2nd, 1937–42, 1944–45

Hughes, John: Assoc Conc (2nd chair), 1989–2002; Sec 1st, 2002–03

Hullinger, Inez: 2nd, 1960–61; 1st, 1961–66

Hung, Yien: 2nd, 1984–93

Hunneman, E. G.: 1st, 1917–19

Hutton, Ward: 2nd, 1914–16

Hwangbo, Sheryl: 2nd, 2013–

Iatzko, Lenore: 2nd, 1980–83; 1st, 1982–84; 2nd, 1984–87. See also L. Sjoberg

Igelmann, Otis: 2nd, 1924–26; 1st, 1926–39; Asst Conc, 1939–42, 1943–45

Inoue, Masuki: 2nd, 1966–67

Jackson, George L.: 1st, 1932–42, 1943–49; 1st, 1951–62

Jin, Hui: 2nd, 2000–2007

Joerin, Fred: Pr 2nd, 2/26/1914, 1914–16; 1st, 1916–17; Pr 2nd, 1917–18; 2nd, 1918–26

Kaloyanides, Kimberly: 1st, 1997–2000. See also K. Kennedy

Kaplan, David: 2nd, 1916–17, 1919–21, 1922–28, 1944–49, 1951–66

Karl, Harold: 2nd, 1952–54

Karr, Josef: 1st, 1922–42

Katz, I.: 2nd, 1920–28

Kaufman, Malvern J.: 1st, 1966–68; 2nd, 1968–75; 1st, 1975–95; Extended Leave,

1995–97; 1st, 1997–2001

Kennedy, Kimberly A. Kaloyanides: 1st, 1999–2003; Assoc Conc (2nd chair), 2003–11; Acting Conc 2012–13; Assoc Conc (2nd chair) 2013–. See also K. Kaloyanides

Kershaw, Clarence: 1st, 1915–16

Kesner, Edouard: Pr 2nd, 1951–85; Sec 2nd, 1985–86

Kilb, Oliver: 2nd, 1918–42, 1943–49

King, William Grafing: Concertmaster, 2/26/1914, 1914–19; Asst Conc (2nd chair), 1919–39; 1st, 1939–42, 1943–46

Klaus, Rachel Harding: 1st, 2013–

Klein, Herold R.: 2nd, 1964–66, 1968–71

Kleiner, Gustave: 1st, 1923–38; 2nd, 1938–42; Asst Pr 2nd, 1943–48; Pr 2nd, 1946–49; Sec 2nd, 1951–58; Asst Pr 2nd, 1958–59; Sec 2nd, 1959–64

Knudsen, Ronald: 1st, 1959–63, 1964–65

Knudson, Margaret: 2nd, 1968–70. See also M. Tundo

Kohon, I.: 1st, 1918–19

Kolar, Victor: 1st, 1919–21; 1st + Asst Cond, 1921–23 [Asst Cond, 1921–25; Assoc Cond, 1925–40; Cond, 1940–42]

Kosloski, Gary: 1st, 1974–75

Kottler, Louis: 2nd, 1938–42

Kreiner, Edward: 1st, 1915–16

Krejci, Edgar C.: 2nd, 1945–46

Kugel, B.: 2nd, 1927–29

Kuskin, Samuel: 1st, 1921–22

Landers, Laurie: 1st, 1991–92; Acting Asst Conc (4th chair), 1992–95; Sec 1st, 1995–98. See also L. Goldman

Laudenslager, Harold: 2nd, 1951–71

Lebensohn, Henry: 2nd, 1914–17

Leib, Max: 2nd, 1943–44; 1st, 1944–46

Lieberman, H.: 2nd, 1928–30

Llinas, Emilio: 2nd, 1964–65; Asst Pr 2nd, 1965–68

Lucker, Henry: 1st, 2/26/14, 1914–16. See also Viola

Maddox, Walter: 2nd, 1964–99

Maebe, Arthur: 1st, 1931–32, 1933–42, 1943–45

Malone, Adam: 2nd, 1951–54

Mancini, Albert: 2nd, 1923–33, 1934–36, 1937–42, 1943–45. *See also* **Trumpet**

Manouelian, Varty: 1st, 1998–2005

March, Wilbert: 2nd, 1946–49

Margitza, Richard: 2nd, 1956–64; 1st, 1964–95

Mark, Samuel: 2nd, 1953–54

Matheys, Henri: 1st, 1917–19

Mei, Ni: 2nd, 2006; 1st 2007–08

Meltzer, M.: 2nd, 1917–19

Mendelssohn, P.: 2nd, 1920–21

Micklin, H.: 2nd, 1919–20

Miller, Kenneth: 2nd, 1952–53, 1954–55

Mischakoff, Mischa: Concertmaster, 1952–68

Mishkind, Abraham: 1st, 1959–63

Mishkind, Elaine: 2nd, 1959–63

Mo, Hong-Yi: 2nd, 2009–

Molchan, Dennis: 2nd, 1966–68

Mortchikian, Bogos: 1st, 1968–72; Acting Assoc Conc (2nd chair), 1972–73; Assoc Conc (2nd chair), 1973–88; Sec 1st, 1988–2006

Murphy, Robert: 2nd, 1973–2013; Sabbatical First Half of 2013–14; 2014–15

Musicus, D. B.: 2nd, 1916–17

Napolitano, Camillo: 1st, 1906

Noland, Keylor: 2nd, 1955–56; 1st, 1956–59

Nosco, Henri: Concertmaster, 1951–52; Asst Conc (2nd chair), 1952–56

Novak, Sofia: 2nd, 1981–82; Novak-Tsoglin: 2nd, 1982–83

Nuttycombe, Wilbert: 1st, 1951–55

Ollstein, Samuel: 1st, 1918–20

Ourada, Ann Alicia: 2nd, 1980–83; 1st, 1983–85. *See also* A. Strubler

Paioff, M.: 1st, 1920–21

Park, Eun: 2nd, 2005–06; 1st, 2007–

Paul, E.: 2nd, 1920–22

Pavese: 2nd, 2/26/1914

Peterson, Francis: 2nd, 1948–49

Peterson, Gordon: 2nd, 1968–72; 1st, 1972–74; Asst Conc (4th chair), 1974–90

Petremont, Charles: 1st, 1964–65

Phillips, Paul: 1st, 1972–80

Plank, G.: 2nd, 1916–21

Polah, A.: 1st, 1918–19

Polant, Victor: 1st, 1919–23, 1924–26, 1927–33

Postle, Glenn: 1st, 2/26/1914, 1914–17

Preuss, Frank: Asst Conc (4th chair), 1970–72; Assoc Conc (2nd chair), 1972–1972

Primo, Umberto: 2nd, 1948–49, 1951–56

Rachlevsky, Mischa:1st, 1977–84

Reitz, Henry G: 1st, 1906

Rene, K.: 1st, 1924–27

Resnick, Felix: 2nd, 1943–49, 1951–53; 1st, 1953–54; 2nd, 1954–68; Asst Pr 2nd, 1968–92; Leave of Absence, 1992–93; Sec 2nd, 1993–2008

Reynolds, H. W., Jr.: 2nd, 1917–18

Robbins, Jacob: 2nd, 1985–91

Roberts, Richard: Asst Conc (3rd chair), 1973–74

Roeder, Charles F.: 2nd, 1914–18

Ronmark, Adrienne: 2nd, 2008–09; 1st 2009–

Rosen, Jerome: Assoc Conc (2nd chair), 1968–72

Rowe, Laura: Asst Conc (4th chair), 1995–2000; (3rd chair), 2000–2004; (4th chair), 2004–11; Sec 1st, 2011–13. *See also* Laura Soto

Rubenstein, Irwin: 1st, 1917–18

Saam, Frank: 1st, 1951–58

Saar, Joseph: 2nd, 2/26/1914, 1914–16; Asst Pr 2nd, 1916–17; Sec 2nd, 1917–18

Sakarellos, Alexandros: 2nd, 2014–

Saslav, Isidor: 2nd, 1955–58; 1st, 1959–61

Saxby, N. E.: 2nd, 1918–20

Schapiro, Stanislaw: 1st, 1924–42, 1943–49, 1951–53

Schauer, Charles: 2nd, 1906

Scheffer, A.: 2nd, 1916–17

Schiller, Leo: 2nd, 2/26/1914, 1914–16

Schkolnik, Ilya: Concertmaster, 1919–42, 1943–44

Score, Alvin: 2nd, 1960–2013

Seigel, Harvey: Asst Pr 2nd, 1951–58; 1st, 1958–60

Seiniger, Samuel:1st, 1917–19

Shapiro, Meyer: 2nd, 1944–46

Shen, Yin: 2nd, 2005–07

Shiller, Ralph: 1st, 1962–74

Shtrum, Haim: 2nd, 1968–72

Siegel, Henry W.: 1st, 1936–42, 1943–45

Silberman, B.: 1st, 1919–20

Sist, Clark: 2nd, 1955–59; Asst Pr 2nd, 1959–65

Sjoberg, Lenore: 2nd, 1987–2000 (sabbatical first half of 1999–2000), 2000–2010. *See also* L. Iatzko

Skobel, J.: 2nd, 1919–20. *See also* **Viola; Trumpet**

Smith, Bruce: 2nd, 1975–2014

Smith, Linda Snedden: 2nd, 1967–68; 1st, 1968–2010

Sommer: 1st, 2/26/1914

Song, Yoonshin: Concertmaster, 2012–

Soto, Laura: 1st, 2014–

Spiegel, William: 2nd, 1906

Staples, Beatriz Budinszky: 1st, 1964–2014

Staples, Gordon B.: Asst Conc (2nd chair), 1956–68; Concertmaster 1968–89; Conc Emeritus, 1989–90

Staples, Gregory: 2nd, 1999–2008, 1st 2009–

Stepniewski, Adam: 2nd, 1991–92; Acting Asst Pr 2nd, 1992–94; Asst Pr 2nd, 1994–2013; Acting Pr 2nd, 2014–

Striplin, Joseph: 2nd, 1972–

Strubler, Ann Ourada: 1st, 1984–2010. *See also* A. Ourada

Stulman, Elya: 2nd, 1927–28, 1930–42, 1943–49, 1951–56

Sturm, Bernard: Pr 2nd, 1918–21; Asst Pr 2nd, 1921–27; Sec 2nd, 1927–38

Sturm, Carl: 2nd, 1944–49

Sutherland, George A.: 2nd, 1917–18

Szitas, Gabriel: 1st, 1945–59; 1960–71; 1974–75; 2nd, 1975–84

Szmulewicz, Stanislaw: 1st, 1919–34; Pr 2nd, 1934–38; 1st, 1938–42, 1943–48

Tak, Edward: 1st, 1919–20

Tanau, Marian: 2nd, 1995–

Tessari, Bertolo: 1st, 1920–38; 2nd, 1938–42

Thiede, A.: 1st, 1918–20

Thorpe, John: 1st, 1914–17

Toth, LeAnn: 2nd, 1972–75; 1st, 1975–2012

Treger, Charles: 1st, 1951–54

Tundo, Margaret: 2nd, 1970–80; 1st, 1980–2005. *See also* M. Knudson

Urso, Santo: 2nd, 1938–42, 1943–44; 1st, 1944–49; 2nd Asst Conc (3rd chair), 1951–52; Sec 1st, 1952–66; Asst Conc (4th chair), 1966–67; Sec 1st, 1967–84

Vallance, Fred G.: 2nd, 2/26/1914, 1914–16; Pr 2nd, 1916–17; Sec 2nd, 1917–18

Von Myhr, Erik: 1st, 1918–20

Voudry, L. J.: 2nd, 1920–21

Wade, Arthur: 2nd, 2/26/1914, 1914–15

Wang, I-Fu: 2nd, 1979–80; 1st, 1980–81

Wang, Jiamin: 1st, 2013–

Waring, James: 2nd, 1953–99. *See also* **Trombone**

Warn, Charles: 1st, 2/26/1914, 1914–16

Warner, Maurice: 1st, 1920–26, 1936–42

Weil.: 2nd, 2/26/1914

Weiler, N.: 2nd, 1919–20; 1920–21

Weiner, M.: 1st, 1943–45

Werner, Edward: Asst Pr 2nd, 2/26/1914, 1914–16; 1st, 1916–17

Wey, Jennifer: Asst Conc, 2013–

White, George F.: 2nd, 1915–16; 1st, 1917–18; 2nd, 1918–19

Wiley, E. R.: 1st, 1917–18

Wilkinson, Herbert: 2nd, 1906

Williams, Carl: 2nd, 1956–59

Willing, Robert: 1st, 1906

Winietzki, J.: 1st, 1920–22

Wolff, L.: Asst Conc (2nd chair), 1918–19

Woolley, Stacey: 2nd, 1983–84; 1st, 1984–89

Wu, Hai-Xin: 2nd, 1995–2004; Asst Conc (3rd chair), 2004–11; Acting Assoc Conc, 2011–12; Asst Conc, 2012–

Yanover, Jules: 2nd, 1945–46; 1st, 1946–49; 2nd, 1951–52

Yost, Gaylord: 2nd, 1906

Yunck, William: Concertmaster, 1906

Zaplatynsky, Andrew: Asst Conc (4th chair), 1973–74

Zhang, Jing: 2nd, 2013–

Zhou, Mingzhao: 2nd, 2014–

Zomora, Florence: Asst Pr 2nd, 1958–59; Sec 2nd, 1959–60; 1st, 1960–61

Zonas, Nicholas: 2nd, 1946–49, 1951–57; 1st, 1961–90

### VIOLA

Abramowitz, S.: 1916–17

Amato, Guyton: 1943–48; Asst Pr, 1948–49, 1951–69

Barnes, Darrel: 1962–65

Barnes, Robert: 1966–67

Barragan, Jean: 1922–23

Bialy, Gregor: 1919–22

Bloquelle, Hugo: 1906

Blumenau, Walter: 1920–42, 1943–49, 1951–64

Cassie, James: 1906, Pr, 1914–18. *See also* **Violin**

Coade, Caroline: 1996–2013; Acting Asst Pr, 2013–

Coffey, Valbert P.: 1919–20; Asst Pr, 1920–28; Pr, 1928–34; Asst Pr, 1936–42. *See also* **Keyboard**

Compton, Catherine: 1973–2000; Sabbatical, 2000–2001; 2001–14

Culver, Robert: 1965–66

Eastes, William: Pr, 1918–20

Elkind, Jacob: 1920–21, 1922–25, 1937–42, 1943–49. *See also* **Violin**

Ernst, M.: 1917–18

Evans, C.: 1919–20

Evich, Walter: 1952–98

Fenstermacher, LeRoy: 1967–96

Gilbo, Demott: Asst Pr, 2/26/1914, 1914–16

Gordon, Nathan: Pr, 1958–85

Hollman, Hart: 1973–

Holtz, Deborah: 1967–68

Hubicki, Taras: 1943–49, 1951–73

Humphreys, Mitchell H.: 1928–42, 1943–49, 1951–59

Ireland, David: 1952–73; Asst Pr, 1973–85; Acting Pr, 1985–87; Sec, 1986–2000

Israel, Theodore: Pr, 1955–56

Jeffers, Darryl: 1982–94

Keintz, Mark: 2/26/1914, 1914–17

Kolodkin, Herman: Pr, 1920–23, 1925–28

Krost, Ben: 1934–39

Lane, Lee: 1965–66

Laraby-Goldwasser, Erina: 2005–07

Lepske, J.: Asst Pr, 1918–19

Levine, Abraham: 1944–45

Lifschey, Samuel: Pr, 1923–24

Lionti, Vincent J.: 1983–87

Lowery-Garcia, Shanda: 2001–03; Lowery: 2003–06; Lowery-Sachs: 2006

Lubalin, Harry: 1918–19

Lucker, Henry: 1918–19. *See also* **Violin**

McCaw, Henry: 1914–16

Megantz, Samuel: 2/26/1914, 1914–17

Mellow, Glenn: 1980–

Mischakoff, Anne: 1968–72

Mishnaevski, Alexander: Pr, 1986–2013, Pr Emeritus 2013–

Pachook, S.: 1922–23

Patti, Anton: 1946–49, 1951–53, 1962–82

Peiffer, William: 1948–49, 1951–52

Poole, Valter: 1927–42; Asst Pr, 1943–48; Pr, 1948–49. *See also* **Keyboard; Conductor**

Porbe, Philip A.: 1964–85; Acting Asst Pr, 1985–87; Sec, 1986–2000

Preucil, William: Pr, 1956–58

Rabung, Otto: 1906, 2/26/1914, 1914–17

Rudolph, Theresa: 2001–06

Salis, Jean: 1920–22

Schnerer, Gary: 1965–2000

Schwartz, David: Pr, 1951–53

Shaevsky, T.: 1944–45

Shapiro, Meyer: 1946–49, 1951–69;
	Asst Pr, 1969–73. *See also* **Violin**

Sheldon, E. M.: 1917–30

Silver, Paul: 1980–81

Simonel, Emile: 1951–62

Singer, Joseph: 1927–33. *See also* **Horn**

Skobel, J.: 1917–19. *See also*; **Trumpet**

Smith, Barrett: 1960–62

Speil, Emil: 2/26/1914

Speil, Ernst: Pr, 2/26/1914

Staszewski, Eugenia: 1943–49, 1951–86

Stilman, S.: 1921–22

Storch, E.: Asst Pr, 1916–17

Su, Han: 2007–

Thal, Max: 1919–34; Asst Pr, 1934–36; Sec,
	1936–42, 1943–46

Van Valkenburg, James: 1986–87; Asst Pr,
	1987–2013; Acting Pr 2013–

Venturini, L.: 1920–21

Volk, F.: Asst Pr, 1917–18; Sec, 1918–19

Wade, Arthur: 1914–18; Sec, 1918–22,
	1924–42, 1943–46

Wallfisch, Ernst: Pr, 1953–55

Waselowich, Nicholas: 1952–54

Werner, Hans: Asst Pr, 1919–20

Wilcynski, John: 2/26/1914, 1914–17

Wilkinson, Herbert E.: 1916–17

Wittman, Florian: 1921–22, 1923–24;
	Pr, 1924–25; Sec, 1925–28; Asst Pr,
	1928–34; Pr, 1934–42, 1943–48

Wollerman, Frank: 1906

Zhang, Manchin: 1994–95, 1995–2005

Zheng, Han: 2001–

Zsiga, John: 1952–65

## CELLO

Abbas, Philipp: Pr, 1918–25

Abel, F. L.: Asst Pr, 2/26/1914, 1914–15

Amster, Richard: 1964–65

Andrews, Clinton: 1973–74

Andries, Henry A. I.: 1906

Argiewicz, Bernard T.: 1920–22, 1928–30;
	Asst Pr, 1930–33; Sec, 1933–37; Asst Pr,
	1937–39; Sec, 1939–42, 1943–47

Babini, Italo: 1959–60; Pr, 1960–97

Babini, Susan: 1975–76 (from 5/28/76),
	1976–77. *See also* S. Richter; S. Weaver

Bachmann, Arthur: 1928–42, 1945–48;
	Asst Pr, 1948–49; Sec, 1951–72. *See also*
	**Keyboard**

Baskin, Karen: 1974 (Shaffer by 11/21/74).
	*See also* K. Shaffer

Beaume, Gilbert L.: 1928–29; 1934–42,
	1943–45

Becker, Jacob: 1944–49, 1959–66

Bergman, Robert A.: 1989–

Besrodney, Boris: 1921–22

Bianchi, I.: 1920–21

Borsody, E.: 1927–29

Brannand, Charles: 1952–55

Broeder, Fredrick: 1918–28

Budson, David: 1966–68

Burjo, Clarenz C.: 1914–17

Butler, Jeffrey: 1985–86

Butler, Timothy: 1978–80

Chanteaux, Marcy: 1978–79; Asst Pr,
	1979–97; Acting Pr, 1997–2003; Asst Pr,
	2002–10; On Leave, 2011–12. *See also*
	M. Schweickhardt

Curry, Ralph: 1977–78

Dayne, F.: 1914–18

de Maine, Robert: Pr, 2002–13

de Veritch, Nina: 1968–70

Di Fiore, Mario: 1961–2011

Dressel, Hans: 1906

Fayroian, Debra: 1977–95; Sabbatical,
	1995–96; 1996–2006. *See also*
	D. Hillman

Fickett, Barbara: 1967–83. *See also*
	B. Hassan

Findlay, C. K.: 1920–24

Forstot, J.: 1944–45

Frederiksen, S.: 1919–20

Gatwood, Carole: 1981–2012

Geary, Frank: 2/26/1914, 1914–18

Gelzayd, Mitchell: 1943–45, 1951–52

Gennari, Elio: 1953–54

Graham, William: 1956–79

Guenther, Herman: 1929–42

Gusikoff, B.: 1918–20

Hall, Raymond J.: 1923–32; Asst Pr, 1932–36; Sec, 1936–42, 1943–49, 1951–61. *See also* Personnel Manager

Hall, Russell A.: 1943–49, 1951–66

Hassan, Barbara Hall: 1983–2010. *See also* B. Fickett

Hillman, Debra: 1975–77. *See also* D. Fayroian

Himmer, Hans: 1922–32, 1932–33

Hollander, E.: 1917–18; 1922–23

Holskin, Jacob: 2/26/1914, 1914–15; Asst Pr, 1915–18; Sec, 1920–42, 1943–49, 1951–59

Horvath, William: 1958–73

Jelinek, Jerome: 1951–53

Kapke, A.: 1918–20

Kapler, Jacob: 2/26/1914, 1914–18

Ketchum, L. B.: 1915–16

Kim, Dahae: Asst Pr, 2013–

Komarovsky, C.: 1922–28

Korkigian, Edward: 1952–80

LeDoux, David: 2012–

Levine, David: 1965–66, 1972–86

Markiewicz, Thaddeus: 1943–46; Asst Pr, 1946–48, 1951–79

Marsh, Douglas: 1948–49, 1951–59

McCafferty, Peter: 2012–

McKay, Haden: 1983–

Miquelle, Georges: Pr, 1925–42, 1943–49, 1951–54

Motto, Luigi: 1906, Pr, 2/26/1914, 1914–18

Nast, Ludwig M.: 1919–32, 1932–33

Newkirk, Robert: 1955–56

O'Riordan, Una: 2007–

Olefsky, Paul: Pr, 1954–60

Parker, Dennis: 1986–88

Pilawski, Frank: 1920–21

Pleier, L.: 1919–20

Plumm, I.: 1915–17

Plunkett, Kevin: 1980–82

Richter, Susan: 1966–67. *See also* S. Weaver; S. Babini

Saltzman, David: 1978–88

Schon, Gerald A.: 1917–18, 1922–42, 1943–47

Schwab, Leroy: 1919–28

Schwarzmann, Jasha: 1924–28; Asst Pr, 1928–30, 1936–42, 1943–44; Asst Pr, 1944–45; Assoc Solo, 1945–46

Schweickhardt, Marcy: 1974–78. *See also* M. Chanteaux;

Shaffer, Karen: 1974–75. *See also* K. Baskin

Simpson: 2/26/1914

Skoenneman, A.: 1918–19

Steiner, Ferenz J.: 1917–19

Steinke, Bruno: 1921–22

Stolarchyk, Peter: 1966–67

Sturm, Julius: Asst Pr, 1918–28; Sec, 1928–29, 1948–49

Thies, P.: 1918–20

Thurman, John: 1970–97; Acting Asst Pr, 1997–2003; Sec, 2003–07; 3rd ch 2008–11

Weaver, Susan: 1966–76. *See also* S. Richter; S. Babini

Wilde, A.: 1920–21

Wingert, Paul: 1980–

## BASS

Agnesy, Karl: Asst Pr, 1919–20; Pr, 1920–22

Badalamenti, Carlo: 1915–19

Baer, Charles: 1944–49, 1951–68

Benner, Raymond: Asst Pr, 1962–85; Sec, 1985–88

Bodwin, Linton: 1973–

Braunsdorf, Eugene W.: 1921–31; Asst Pr, 1931–42, 1943–49. *See also* **Librarian**

Brohan, Gaston: 1919–20; Asst Pr, 1920–28; Pr, 1928–42, 1943–49; Sec, 1951–53; Asst Pr, 1953–59; Sec, 1959–64

Brown, Christopher: 1972–74

Brown, Kevin: Pr, 2014–

Carbone, John: 1967–68

Casertani, A.: Asst Pr, 1917–19

Cerny, E. G.: 1918–21

Couchoud, Emile: 1928–29; Asst Pr, 1929–30; Sec, 1930–32, 1932–36, 1937–38

Culp, B.: 1918–19

Edwards, Stephen: 1972–

Elkind, Sol: Pr, 1919–20, 1922–27; Sec, 1927–42, 1943–45

Ernst, Roman J.: 1927–28

Farias, Dalmiro: 2/26/1914, 1914–15; Asst Pr, 1915–16

Flowerman, Martin: 1966–67

Gladstone, Robert: Pr, 1966–2003

Goeldner, Charles: 2/26/1914, 1914–15; Pr, 1915–16

Green, S.: 1920–21

Greenberg, Henry: 1924–27

Haines, Carl: 1914–15, 1915–16; Asst Pr, 1916–17; Sec, 1920–21

Haines, Herbert: 1914–15, 1915–17

Hanna, Alexander: Pr, 2008–12

Hardmann, Walter: 1943–49; Asst Pr, 1951–52; Sec, 1952–72. *See also* **Tuba**

Hutchinson: Marshall Larry: 1983–

Ilku, Julius: 1960–71

Jamitz, Reuben: Asst Pr, 1952–53

Janowsky, Maxim: 1964-2012

Kalsow, Fritz: 1906

Kazakevich, Joseph: 1952–57

Kourkly, George: 1921–23

Krausse, Joseph: Pr, 1927–28

Lacey, Alex: 1944–49, 1951–52

La Mantia, P.: 1917–18

Lermonth, John: 2/26/1914, 1914–16

Luck, Arthur: 1919–42, 1943–49, 1951–52. *See also* **Percussion; Librarian**

Lumm, Arnold: 1944–45

Maier, W. C.: 1917–18

Mathews, John: 1953–59

Moeller, Adam: Pr, 2/26/1914, 1914–15; Sec 1915–16; Pr, 1916–18

Molina, Stephen: 1976–85; Asst Pr,

1985–2003, 2014-; Acting Pr, 2003–08; Asst Pr, 2008–12; Acting Pr, 2012–15

Monohan, Thomas, Jr.: 1964–66

Mott, E.: 1917–18

Norton, William: 1914–15, 1915–17

Palecek, James: 1938–42

Pennington, Donald: 1968–94

Peters, Lynn: 1970–72

Pitchersky, Meyer: 1928–36

Querengaesser, K.: Pr, 1918–19

Rahmig, P.: 1923–24

Reeser, Frank: 1937–42, 1943–49, 1951–61

Richko, Steven M.: 1944–45

Rifel, Craig: 1980–2014

Robinson, Richard: 1989–2012

Satur, J.: 1916–17

Sayor, D.: 1918–27

Schremser, Emil: Asst Pr, 2/26/1914, 1914–15

Shinkevich, T.: 1944–45

Sinco, Frank: 1951–76

Sklar, Philip: 1918–28, 1936–37

Sroboda, J.: 1920–21

Steger, Albert: 1951–82

Tinnette, Nicholas: 1906

Van de Graaf, John: 1928–30; Asst Pr, 1930–31; Sec, 1931–37; Pr, 1951–66; Sec, 1966–70

Vopatek, F.: 1917–19

Wulf, John H.: 1919–42, 1943–49

Wurtzler, Bela: 1957–59; Asst Pr, 1959–62

Zimberoff, Nathan: 1938–42, 1943–44

### HARP

Bartlett, Mary: 2nd, 1943–48

Burr-Brand, Helen (Mrs.): 2nd, 1917–22

Caratelli, Ann: Pr, 1948–49

Carter, Winifred (Mrs.): 2nd, 1923–33; Pr, 1933–38

Clark, Ruth Dean: 2nd, 1963–65. *See also* R. Janes

Crosby, Carole: 2nd, 1965–76; Co-Pr, 1976–80

Davis, Andrew: Pr, 1915–16

Dell Aquila, Joseph: Pr, 1931–33

Druzinsky, Edward: Pr, 1952–57

Gelfius, Henriette: Harrietta, 2nd, 1921–23

Ilku, Elyze Yockey: Pr, 1968–76; Co-Pr, 1976–77; Pr, 1980–88. *See also* E. Yockey

Janes, Ruth Dean: 2nd, 1951–52, 1958–63. *See also* R. D. Clark

Krokos, Eugenia: 2nd, 1937–38; Pr, 1938–42, 1943–48; 2nd, 1948–49. *See also* E. Kuhnle

Kuhnle, Eugenia: Pr, 1951–52; 2nd, 1952–56. *See also* E. Krokos

Masri-Fletcher, Patricia: Pr, 1988–

Ostrowska, Miss Djina: Pr,1918–31

Pavese, Carl C.: 2nd, 1915–16; Pr, 1916–18

Wagner, Rebecca Lewis: 2nd, 1960–61

Wurtzler, Aristed: Pr, 1957–58

Yockey, Elyze: Pr, 1958–68. *See also* E. Ilku

## FLUTE

Barone, Clement: 4th + picc, 1959–62; 3rd + picc, 1962–70; 4th + picc, 1970–91

Ben-Meir, Shaul: 2nd, 1967–88; Leave of Absence, 1988–89; 2nd, 1989–97

Briglia, Nicholas: 1906

Buck, David: Pr, 2012–

Caratelli, Sebastian: Pr, 1947–49

Cerny, R.: Alt 1st, 1922–23

Coppola, Carmine: Pr, 1937–42

Culp, Simon; 3rd + picc, 1918–19; 4th + picc, 1920–21; 3rd, 1921–22

Dikeman, Philip: Asst Pr, 1992–2009; Acting Pr, 2009–11

Fayer, Anton: Pr, 1920–21

Forsythe, Gordon D.: 3rd + picc, 2/26/1914, 1914–15

Gelfius, Justus: Pr, 1922–23

Gilman, Irvin: 2nd 1956–67; Asst Pr, 1967–68

Grenier, Noble: 3rd or 4th, 1915–16

Hadricka, M.: 2nd + 2nd picc, 1922–27; 3rd + picc, 1927–28

Kaplan, Boris: 3rd + picc, 1916–17

Klenner, Adolph: 1906

Kouloukis, Nicholas: Pr, 1918–19

Krueger, Otto E.: 3rd + picc, 1914–16; 2nd, 1916–19; 3rd + picc, 1919–21; picc, 1921–22; 3rd + picc, 1922–27; Pr, 1943–47; 2nd, 1951–56

Lennig, C. Edwin: 3rd + picc, 1926–27; 2nd, 1928–42; 2nd, 1943–49

Monroe, Ervin: Pr, 1968–2008

North, Charles K.: Pr, 1919–20; Co-Pr or 2nd, 1920–22

Packard, R. H.: 2nd, 1917–18

Parsons, Ralph H.: 3rd + picc, 1917–18

Patchett, Denton: 3rd + picc, 1916–17

Patrick, Robert: Asst Pr, 1968–91

Pellerite, James: Pr, 1951–56

Phares, Hale: 4th + picc, 1943–49

Schleede, Waldo E.: 2nd, 2/26/1914, 1914–15; 4th + 2nd picc, 1917–18

Seel, Robert E.: 2nd, 1919–20

Smith, W. C. L.: Pr, 2/26/1914, 1914–16

Sparrow, Sharon Wood: 2nd, 1997–2007; Pr, 2008–09; 2009–2011; Acting Pr, 2011–12; Acting Asst Pr, 2012–14; Asst Pr, 2014–

Teal, Larry: 3rd, 1951–62

Tipton, Albert: Pr, 1956–68

Viggiano, Vincent: 2nd, 1914–16; Pr, 1916–18

Witteborg, August: 2nd + 2nd picc, 1927–28; 3rd + picc, 1928–33; Pr, 1933–34; 3rd + picc, 1934–42; 3rd + picc, 1943–47; 3rd, 1947–49; 4th + picc, 1951–59

Wummer, John: Co-Pr, 1923–24; Pr, 1925–37

Yeschke, Theo: Pr, 1921–22

Zentner, Miles: Asst Pr, 1965–67

Zook, Jeffery: 4th + picc, 1992–

## OBOE

Abbott, Sidney W.: Pr, 2/26/1914

Baker, Donald: Pr, 1973–2014

Barnard, Jay: 2nd, 2/26/1914, 1914–16; 4th, 1917–18

Baskin, Theodore: Asst Pr, 1973–75

Bastian, Walter: 4th, 1943–44

Bottesini, Mario: Pr, 1918–19

Byrne, Thomas J.: 2nd, + EH, 1918–19;
2nd + 2nd EH, 1919–21; 2nd, 1921–22;
2nd + 2nd EH, 1922–25; 2nd, 1925–27;
2nd + 2nd EH, 1927–34; 2nd, 1934–42

Corne, R.: Pr, 1929–30

Cowart, Robert: 4th + EH, 1965–73

De Busscher, Albert: Pr, 1918–19

Fonteyne, J.: Pr, 1919–20

Fosnaugh, Monica: 4th + EH, 2012–

Gerhardt, Paul: 3rd + EH, 1919–20

Guilhot, Richard: 3rd + EH, 1925–33

Hall, Harold: 3rd, 1946–49, 1951–64;
3rd + EH, 1964–65; 3rd, 1965–69;
2nd, 1969–73; 5th, 1973–77

Heron, Shelley: 2nd, 1985–96;
Sabbatical, 1996–97 (1st half only);
2nd, 1997–2014,

Hutcheson, D.: 4th, 1944–45; 3rd,
1945–46

Kelemen. Frank: 3rd + 4th, 1918–19;
3rd + EH, 1936–38

Krauter, Paul: 2nd + EH, 1916–17;
3rd + EH, 1917–18

Labiner, Steven: 4th + EH, 1973–75

Long, Harold: 3rd, 1943–44; 3rd + EH,
1944–45

Lubin, Carl: 1906

Lukatsky, Joseph: 4th + EH, 1951–52

Mariotti, Arno: Pr, 1952–73

Minsker, John: 3rd + EH, 1934–36

Odmark, Ronald: 4th + 2nd EH, 1946–49;
Asst, 1951–73; 2nd, 1973–79; 5th,
1979–82

Pirie, Samuel, Jr.: 3rd + EH, 2/26/1914;
Pr, 1914–15; Pr, 1915–18; 3rd, 1920–21

Rey, A.: 3rd + EH, 1922–25

Snow, John: 2nd, 1979–85

Sorton, Robert: Asst Pr, 1975–88

Vaillant, Jules: Pr, 1920–22

Van Der Velpen, Dr. A.: 3rd + EH,
1914–16; 2nd + EH, 1916–17

Van Emmerik, Dirk P. W.: 4th + EH,
1920–21; 3rd + EH, 1921–22; Pr, 1922–
29, 1930–32; Pr + EH, 1932–33; Pr +
EH, 1933–34; Pr, 1934–42, 1943–49

Ventura, Brian: Asst Pr 1988–

Wardrop, Laré: 3rd + EH, 1938–42; 2nd,
1943–45; 2nd + EH, 1945–49; Pr,
1951–52; 4th + EH, 1952–65

Womble, Treva: 4th + EH, 1975–2009

**CLARINET**

Arey, Rufus M.: Pr, 1919–23

Cornelsen, Douglas: 2nd, 1970–2012

Couf, Herbert: Pr, 1952–56

Davis, Emery: 3rd + bcl, 1954–56

De Caprio, A.: 2nd, 1924–25

Forlani, H.: 3rd, 1923–24

Fossenkemper, Marius E.: 2nd, 1922–24,
1925–31; Pr, 1931–42, 1943–49,
1951–52

Green, Oliver: 4th + bcl, 1948–49, 1956–
2006. *See also* **Personnel Manager**

Griss, William: 2nd, 1943–49, 1951–70

Hammond: 3rd, 2/26/1914, 1914–15

Herrick, William: 4th + 2nd bcl, 1920–21;
3rd + bcl, 1921–23; 4th + bcl, 1923–24;
3rd + bcl, 1924–42

Jacobson, Harry: 1906

Krejci, Charles: 2nd, 2/26/1914, 1914–15,
1915–18; 3rd, 1918–19

Liberson, Laurence: Asst Pr + E♭ cl, 1981-

Long, Claude: 3rd + bcl, 1914–16

Luckerman, Alfred G.: 3rd, 2/ 26/1914;
1915–16; 3rd, 1916–17

Luconi, Alberto: Pr, 1923–26

Melidon, Vincert: 4th + E♭ cl, 1951–56;
Pr + E♭ cl, 1956–57; 3rd + E♭ cl, 1957–66;
Asst Pr + E♭ cl, 1966–69

Mentkowski, A.: Pr, 1918–19; 2nd,
1919–22

Oien, Theodore: Pr, 1988–2014

Orme, Shannon: 4th + bcl, 2008–

Rosen, Bernard: 4th, 1943–46; 4th + E♭ cl,
1946–48; 3rd + E♭ cl, 1948–49; 3rd + bcl,
1951–54

Sand, Albert: Pr, 1926–28; 2nd, 1931–40
Schaller, Paul: Pr, 1957–87. *See also* **Personnel Manager**
Schmidt, R.: Pr, 1928–31
Schroeder, Carl: 2nd + bcl, 1918–19; 3rd + bcl, 1919–21. *See also* **Librarian**
Schweickhardt, Brian: Asst Pr + E♭ cl, 1969–81
Skiano, Ralph: Pr, 2014–
Teal, Lawrence: 3rd + bcl, 1943–48
Van der Velpen, Dr. Arthur: 1906
Votruba, William: 3rd + bcl, 1915–16; 4th + bcl, 1916–17; 3rd + bcl, 1917–18
Waha, Rudolph: 2nd, 1940–42
Weiland, Paul: Pr, 2/26/1914, 1914–18
Wolff, Philip: 3rd, 1921–22; E♭ cl, 1925–26

### BASSOON
Austin, Philip: 2nd, 1972–81
Barris, Robert: 2nd, 1966–69
Basson, Stephen: Asst Pr, 1965–69
Bindemann, Albert: 1906
Cooper, Hugh: 4th, 1946–47; 3rd, 1947–49; 2nd, 1951–64
Del Busto, Angel: Pr, 1943–46
Ferris, Kirkland: 2nd, 1982–84
Ganson, Paul: Asst Pr, 1969–2002; On Sabbatical, 2002–03; Asst Pr, 2003–04
Hammond: 3rd, 2/26/1914, 1914–15
Kaplan, William: 2nd, 1964–66
King, Victoria: 2nd, 1984–
Kohon, Markus: 3rd + cb, 1918–19
Krejci, John V.: Pr, 2/26/1914, 1914–18; 2nd, 1918–19; 4th, 1920–21
Kropula, Hjalmar: 2nd, 1914–17
Krueger, Richard: 2nd, 1932–38
Kruse, William: 2nd, 1943–49
Lewis, Dr. Sol M.: 4th, 1943–46
Lindsey, Lyell: 3rd + cb, 1962–66; 4th + cb, 1966–92
Logue, Eugene: 4th + cb, 1947–49
Loomis, Allen: 3rd, 1915–17
Luck, Andrew: 2nd, 1938–42
Ma, Michael Ke: Asst Pr, 2005–

Meerloo, Samuel: Pr, 1918–19
Mosbach, Joseph H.: Pr, 1919–42
Pezzi, Vincent: 2nd, 1919–33
Pfeuffer, Robert: 4th + cb, 1951–58; 3rd + cb, 1956–62
Ragland, Larold: 2nd, 1969–72
Sato, Atsuko: 2nd, 1981–82
Schoen, C.: 3rd, 1916–17; 2nd, 1917–18
Schon, Gerald A.: 4th, 1922–29; 3rd + cb, 1929–42, 1943–47
Schon, John: 3rd + cb, 1919–28
Schoon, Marcus: 4th + cb, 1992–
Schroeder, Robert: 3rd, 1951–58
Sharrow, Leonard: Pr, 1946–47
Sirard, Charles: Pr, 1947–49, 1951–74
Van Sycle, George: 1906; 2nd, 2/26/1914, 1914–15
Williams, Robert: Pr, 1974–

### SAXOPHONE
Holomb, J. W.: 1916–17

### HORN
Abbott, Mark: Asst Pr, 1982–2001; Utility, 2001–
Alcott, Harry: 4th, 1917–18
Alonge, Raymond: Pr, 1951–56
Alvey, Merle M.: 3rd, 1943–48
Andruschkewitsch, Alexander: Asst Pr, 1924–29
Bacon, Thomas: Asst Pr, 1968–73
Balaam, Frank: 4th, 1946–49
Barnes, Ernestine: 6th (Utility), 1944–45; Asst Pr, 1945–47
Berndt, Otto: Pr, 1923–24
Brown, William: 6th (Utility), 1948–49; 2nd, 1951–52; 3rd, 1956–58
Brunnemer, Robert: Asst Pr, 1962–63
Burns, Robert G.: 2nd, 2/26/1914, 1914–15
Carabella, John: 6th (Utility), 1959–60
Darling, Williard: 1947–48; 2nd, 1948–49; 4th, 1951–57; 2nd, 1957–59; 4th, 1959–2003

Evans, Theodore: Asst Pr, 1944–45; 2nd, 1945–48; 4th, 1948–49; 3rd, 1951–54; 2nd, 1954–55

Everson, David: 6th (Utility), 1999–2001; Asst Pr, 2001–

Fries, Robert: 3rd, 1959–61; Pr, 1961–63

Gleich, Adolph: 1906

Graul, Charles: 3rd, 2/26/1914; 2nd, 1914–16

Greer, Lowell: Asst Pr, 1973–78

Grunow, William: 2nd, 1915–18

Hellstein, Francis J.: Asst Pr, 1934–36; Pr, 1936–37; Asst Pr, 1937–42, 1943–44; Pr, 1944–47

Hilmer, Heinrich: 3rd, 1928–37

Hinshaw, William: Pr, 1943–44

Hornstein, Harry: 4th, 1918–19

Hudish, Benjamin: 2nd, 1918–19

Huebner, Ernst: 4th, 1919–46

Jaenicke, Bruno: Pr, 1919–22

Johnson, Sune: Asst Pr, 1936–37; 3rd, 1937–42

Karoub, Carl: 4th, 1958–59

Kennedy, Bryan: 2nd, 1982–95, 1998–

Kenny Thomas: 3rd, 1958–59

Krehbiel, Arthur: Pr, 1963–72

Macdonald, Walter: Asst Pr, 1929–30

Mackey, Richard: 2nd, 1952–54

Mann, Gustav E.: 1906; 4th, 2/26/1914, 1914–17

Masarie, Jack: Asst Pr, 1966–68

McWilliam, Fergus: 2nd, 1979–82

Miersch, Erwin: 2nd, 1919–21, 1926–27, 1927–36

Patterson, Lucius: Pr, 1947–49; 3rd, 1952–56

Pelletier, Alphonse: 3rd, 1926–28

Pituch, Karl: Pr, 2000–

Replogle, Steven: 6th (Utility), 1997–99

Resch, Alfred: 2nd, 1921–27

Roth, Donald: 2nd, 1955–58

Sabatini, William: Pr, 1956–61

Sansone, Lorenzo: Pr, 1918–19

Sauve, Edward: Asst Pr, 1961–66; 3rd, 1966–81

Schultz, Kenneth M.: 2nd, 1937–42, 1943–45; 4th, 1947–48; Asst Pr, 1948–49

Seder, Theodore A.: Pr, 1937–39

Singer, Joseph: 6th (Utility), 1930–33

Slootzky, Bany: Pr, 2/26/1914; Pr, 1914–16; 3rd, 1916–17

Stagliano, James Albert: 5th, 1919–21; Alt Pr, 1921–22; Asst Pr, 1922–24; Pr, 1924–30; Asst Pr, 1930–34; Pr, 1934–42

Stango, Emilio: 3rd, 1915–16 (to 1/14/16); Pr, 1915–16 (from 1/14/16), 1916–17; 3rd, 1917–18; 6th, 1920–21; 7th, 1944–45

Stevens, Dorothy: Asst Pr, 1951–58

Stimm, George A.: Pr, 1917–18; 3rd, 1918–26; 2nd, 1936–37; 8th, 1944–45

Strong, Scott: 3rd 2014–

Tryon, Denise: 4th, 2003–09

Unsworth, Adam: 2nd, 1995–98

Vernon, Keith: Asst Pr, 1958–61; 3rd, 1961–66; Asst Pr (6th, Utility), 1966–73; Asst Pr, 1973–74; 6th (Utility), 1974–95

Wade, Eugene: Pr, 1972–2000

Wagner, Corbin: Asst Pr, 1979–82; 3rd, 1982–2013

Weaver, Charles: 2nd, 1959–79; (7th, utility), 1979–80. *See also* **Librarian**

Yarbrough, Johanna: 4th 2012–

Yegudkin, Arkady: Pr, 1922–23

## TRUMPET

Anderson, Stephen: Asst Pr, 1992–2010; Acting Pr, 2010–12; Asst Pr, 2013–

Basse, Herman: 3rd, 1919–20

Belknap, Alvin: Asst Pr, 1958–91

Benge, Elden: Pr, 1928–33

Bryant, Willard: 1906

Carroll, John: 4th, 1977–79

Di Blasi, Francesco: 4th, 1951–53; 3rd, 1953–59

Dietzel, W.: Pr, 1922–23

Eberly, Hunter: Pr, 2013–

Edwards, C. E.: 3rd, 1917–18; 4th + 2nd piston, 1920–21

Fenimore, Howard: 1st, 1934–36

Good, Kevin: 4th, 1979–80; 2nd, 1980–

Green, Donald: Pr, 1975–82

Haas, Donald: 4th, 1953–73

Heim, Gustav F.: Pr, 1920–21

Henkle, L.: Pr, 1943–44

Hull, Walter: 4th, 1915–17

Jewell, Ralph: 4th, 1943–44

Kaderabek, Frank: Pr, 1966–75

Kearney, A. E.: 3rd + 1st piston, 1920–23

LaRose, Louis: 4th, 1944–45

Lower, F.: 3rd, 1923–29; 3rd + 1st piston, 1923–28

Lucas, William: 4th, 1988–

Lubin, Solomon: 1st, 1918–26

Mancini, Albert: 4th + 2nd piston, 1923–28; 3rd + 1st piston, 1928–31; 3rd, 1931–32; Pr, 1932–33?; Pr, 1933–34; 3rd, 1934–36; Pr, 1936–37; 3rd, 1937–42, 1943–45. *See also* **Violin**

Mathie, Gordon: Asst Pr, 1951–53

Miller, Samuel: Pr, 1921–22

O'Hara, Floyd: Pr Cornet (3rd), 2/26/1914; 3rd, 1914–16; 2nd, 1916–18; 3rd, 1918–19; 2nd, 1919–42, 1943–44; 3rd, 1944–46; 4th, 1946–49

Parcells, Ramón: Pr, 1982–2010

Roberts: 2nd Cornet, 2/26/1914

Schmeisser, Otto: Pr, 1926–28; 3rd, 1936–37

Schultz, Donald: 2nd, 1946–49

Sipley, R. A.: 2nd, 2/26/1914, 1914–16; 3rd, 1916–17; 4th, 1917–18

Skobel, J.: 4th, 1919–20. *See also* **Violin; Viola**

Smith, Gordon: 2nd, 1945–46; 3rd, 1946–49; 2nd, 1951–80; 4th, 1980–87

Smith, Leonard B.; Pr, 1937–42

Tamburini, James: Pr, 1944–49, 1951–66

Van Amburgh, Earl N.: Pr, 2/26/1914, 1914–18; 2nd, 1918–19; 4th, 1921–22; 4th + 2nd piston, 1922–23, 1928–31; 4th, 1931–33

Weitzel, Leonard: 1906

Wennerberg, K.: 2nd, 1944–45

## TROMBONE

Addison, William A.: 3rd (bass), 2/26/1914, 1914–22

Casimiro, Lionel: Pr, 1951–53; 4th, 1953–54

Chase, Allen: 4th, 1952–53; Pr, 1953–68

Eder, F.: Pr, 1924–25

Eschrig, Fred: 2nd, 1932–44

Farmer, Clifton: 2nd, 1946–49

Ferentz, John Sr.: 3rd (bass), 1922–23

Gurin, Nathaniel: 3rd (Asst Pr), 1978–89; Acting Pr, 1989–97; Asst Pr, 1997–2014

Hawes, Randall: 4th (bass), 1985–86, 1986–90; 3rd (bass), 1990–

Hayden, Harry: 3rd (bass), 1943–45

Janes, Elmer: 3rd (bass), 1945–49, 1951–78; 4th (bass), 1978–81. *See also* **Librarian**

Jones, Robert: Pr, 1944–49

Klaber, Thomas: 4th (bass), 1980–81, 1981–85

Kuhn, David: 1906

Lilleback, Walter D.: Pr, 1925–29

Nabokin, P.: 3rd (bass), 1923–24

Nagelvoort, Barnard: 1906

Rivera, Carlos B.: Pr, 1943–44; 2nd, 1944–46

Simons, Gardell: Pr, 1937–38

Skrzynski, Joseph: 2nd, 1951–97

Smith, Dennis: Pr, 1966–71

Smith, Max: Pr, 2/26/1914, 1914–24; 2nd, 1924–33

Stoll, Fred C.: 3rd (bass), 1924–25

Thompkins, Kenneth: Pr, 1997–

Turner, Raymond: Pr, 1971–90

Van Amburgh, Frank L.: 1906; 2nd, 2/26/14, 1914–24; 3rd (bass), 1925–42. *See also* **Personnel Manager**

Waring, James: 4th Asst Pr, 1959–67.
*See also* **Violin**

Warms, Gerhard: Pr, 1929–42

## TUBA

Hamburg, George: Pr, 1918–20
Hardmann, Walter: 2nd, 1944–48. *See also*
  **Bass**
Jacobs, Wesley: Pr, 1970–2008
La Gasse, Oscar: Pr, 1943–49, 1951–70
Nulty, Dennis: Pr, 2009–
Reeves, E.: Pr, 1916–18
Till, Otto: Pr, 2/26/1914, 1914–17
Webster, William V.: Pr, 1920–42

## TIMPANI

Bauch, Daniel: Asst Pr, 2006–09. *See also*
  **Percussion**
Becher, Richard: Pr, 1921–22
Epp, Jeremy: Pr, 2014–
Harris, Milton: Pr, 1951–53
Jones, Brian: Pr, 1998–99, 1999–2011
Manzer, Lawrence W.: Pr, 1919–42,
  1943–49
Martin, J. C.: 2nd, 1920–21
Paine, Frederick S.: Pr, 1918–19; 2nd (Asst
  Pr), 1922–42 [Asst Manager, 1931–39].
  *See also* **Percussion; Librarian**
Pangborn, Robert: 2nd (Asst Pr), 1973–
  2009. *See also* **Percussion**
Parks, George: Pr, 2/26/1914, 1914–15.
  *See also* **Percussion**
Rabbio, Salvatore: Pr, 1958–99
Tomlinson, Benjamin S.: 1906; Pr, 1914–
  18. *See also* **Percussion**

## PERCUSSION

Bauch, Daniel: 2006–08; Acting Asst Pr,
  2009. *See also* **Timpani**
Becker, Joseph: Pr, 2012–
Carter, H. L.: 2/26/1914, 1914–15,
  1916–17
Cooper, Arthur E.: 1915–34; Pr, 1934–42,
  1943–49, 1951–64

Cooper, Charles F.:1917–42, 1943–49,
  1951–64
Ding, Ian: Asst Pr, 2002–09; Acting Pr,
  2009–10; Asst Pr, 2010–11
Fickett, Norman: Asst Pr, 1965–2002
Ledingham, Jack: 1943–48, 1951–68.
  *See also* **Librarian**
Link, C. E.: Pr, 1918–19; 3rd, 1919–20;
  2nd, 1920–21. *See also*
Luck, Arthur: Pr, 1923–37, 1938–42,
  1944–45, 1952–64. *See also*
Makowski, Raymond: 1963–94
Martin, J. C.: Pr, 1920–21. *See also* **Timpani**
Nissly, Jacob: Pr, 2010–11
Paine, Frederick S.: 1914–16; Pr, 1916–18,
  1919–20, 1921–22; Pr, 1922–42. *See also*
  **Timpani; Librarian**
Pangborn, Robert: Pr, 1964–2008; Sec,
  2009. *See also* **Timpani**
Parks, George: Pr, 1914–16. *See also* **Timpani**
Pichardo-Rosenthal, Andres: Asst Pr, 2014–
Tomlinson, Benjamin S.: Pr, 2/26/1914,
  1914–15. *See also* **Timpani**
Tundo, Sam: 1968–2006
Vair, Harold: 1937–39
Wohl, Adolph A.: 1918–19

## KEYBOARD

Bachmann, Arthur: Celeste, 1951–72.
  *See also* **Cello**
Coffey, Valbert P.: Celeste, 1920–28; Organ,
  1939–42. *See also* **Viola**
Farnham, A.: Celeste, 1928–29; Celeste +
  2nd Piano, 1929–31. *See also* **Violin**
Ferguson, Ray: Organ, 1979–80; Keyboard,
  1982–84
Hill, Ellwood W.: Organ, 1961–62
Kilby, Muriel: Keyboard, 1977–80 (Out
  Part Season); 1980–81 (Return Part
  Season), 1982–84
Kottler, Mischa: Piano 2, 1952–53; Piano
  Pr, 1953–70
Lungershausen, Alice: Harpsichord,
  1966–73

Mannebach, Margaret: Piano Pr, 1929–42, 1943–48

Marriott, Frederick: Organ, 1964–73

Poole, Valter: Celeste, 1931–33; Celeste + 2nd Piano, 1934–37; Celeste, 1937–49. *See also* **Viola; Conductor**

Roeckelein, Richard: Organ, 1958–60

Schweickhardt, Marcy: Piano Pr, 1970–74. *See also* **Cello**

Sweeny III, John S.: Piano 2, 1947–48; Piano Pr, 1948–49, 1951–53


## LIBRARIAN

Allen, Ethan: Asst, 2005–

Braunsdorf, Eugene: Asst, 1931–42. *See also* **Bass**

Brigman, Merle A.: Asst, 1920–22 [Asst Manager, 1925–27]

Crispin, John: Asst, 1966–68. *See also* **Violin**

Hermann, E. C.: Pr, 1918–19; Asst, 1919–20

Janes, Elmer: Asst, 1973–81. *See also* **Trombone**

Kaufman, Malvern: Asst, 1971–73. *See also* **Violin**

Ledingham, Jack: Asst, 1968–71. *See also* **Percussion**

Link, C. E.: Pr, 1920–21. *See also* **Percussion**

Luck, Arthur: Pr, 1921–42, 1943–49, 1951–64. *See also* **Percussion; Bass**

Mann, Gustav E.: Pr, 2/26/1914, 1914–16; Pr, 1916–18. *See also* **Horn**

Olivia, Robert: Asst, 2002–03; Pr, 2003–04

Paine, Frederick S.: Payne, Asst, 1922–24, 1924–31 [Asst Manager, 1931–39]. *See also* **Timpani; Percussion**

Schroeder, Carl: Asst, 1918–19; Pr, 1919–21. *See also* **Clarinet**

Steger, Albert: Pr, 1964–82. *See also* **Bass**

Stiles, Robert: Asst, 2002–03; Acting Pr, 2002–03; Asst, 2003–04; Pr, 2004–

Sturm, Julius: Pr, 1920–21

Weaver, Charles: Asst, 1980–98. *See also* **Horn**

Yoffe, Elkhonon: Head, 1982–2003


## PERSONNEL MANAGER

Bistritzky, Zinovi: PM, 1961–71; Co-PM, 1971–72

Chase, Karl: PM, 1948–49. *See also* **Violin**

Green, Oliver: Asst PM, 1972–73; PM, 1973–93. *See also* **Clarinet**

Hall, Raymond J.: PM, 1943–48, 1951–61. *See also* **Cello**

Hansinger, Nicholas: Asst PM, 2002–08

McGillivray, Michael J.: PM, 1994–95; Personnel and Operations Manager, 1995–97

Molina, Stephen: Asst PM, 1983–90; Assoc PM, 1990–93; Acting PM, 1993–95; Assoc PM, 1995–97; Acting PM, 1997–98; PM, 1996–2015. *See also* **Bass**

Rochon, Heather Hart: Asst PM, 2011–15, PM, 2015–

Schaller, Paul: Asst PM, 1970–71; Co-PM, 1971–72. *See also* **Clarinet**

Van Amburgh, Frank L.: PM, 1929–42. *See also* **Trombone**


## STAFF CONDUCTORS

Abrams, Teddy: Asst, 2012–14

Bertini, Gary: Music Advisor, 1981–83

Ceccato, Aldo: Music Director, 1973–77

Dorati, Antal: Music Director, 1977–81; Laureate, 1981–89

Dunner, Leslie: Asst, 1988–90; Assoc, 1990–95; Resident, 1995–99

Ehrling, Sixten: Music Director, 1963–73

Freeman, Paul: in Residence, 1970–79

Freudigman, Eric: Dir of Choruses, 1986–93

Gabrilowitsch, Ossip: Music Director, 1918–36

Gales, Weston: 1915–18

Fischer-Dieskau, Martin: Fellow, 1978–79

Ghione, Franco: 1938–40

Greenberg, Philip: Apprentice, 1974–76; Asst, 1976–78

Gross, Murray: Fellow, 1980–82

Herbig, Gunther: Music Director, 1984–90

Hetu, Pierre: Asst, 1970–73

Järvi, Neeme: Music Director, 1990–2005;
Music Director Emeritus, 2005–

Jean, Kenneth: Asst, 1978–82; in Residence,
1982–85

Kolar, Victor: 1936–37, 1940–42; Asst,
1922–25; Assoc, 1925–36, 1938–40

Krajewski, Michael: Fellow, 1979–80; Asst,
1982–85

Krueger, Karl: Music Director, 1943–48

Paray, Paul: Music Director, 1951–62;
Emeritus, 1963–69

Poole, Walter: Asst, 1944–48, 1951–70;
Pops, 1970–71

Shui, Lan: Asst, 1995–97

Slatkin, Leonard: Music Director, 2008–

Stein, Stephen: Exxon/Arts Endowment,
1986–87; Resident, 1988–90

Wang, Ya-Hui: Asst, 1997–99

Wilkins, Thomas: Resident, 2000–2010

# Index

Page numbers in *italics* refer to images.

Orchestra Place, 208–10, 213–15, 225
Osnos, Max, 86
Oundjian, Peter, 227, 230

Page, Clarence, 189
Paradise Theater, 78
Paray, Paul: background of, 113–16; compositions of, 127–28; as conductor, 109, 112–13, 116–17; and Detroiters, 131–32; Ehrling on, 141; with Elisabeth Schwartzkopf, 133; as guest conductor, 132; labor relations under, 131; and Mercury recordings, 117–25; retirement of, 135–37; and United Nations concert, 130–31; and Worcester Music Festival, 129–30
Parsons, Anne, 227, 231, 236, 237, 239, 245
Paterson, Murray, 71, 77, 80, 81, 82
Perlea, Jonel, 112, 113
Perlman, Itzhak, 215–17
permanent orchestras, 18–19
permanent touring fund, 217
Peters, Roberta, 128
Pettitt, Stephen, 218–19
Philadelphia Orchestra, 129
Philharmonica Hungarica, 164
phonographs, 42
Pilkington, Ed, 239
Pincus, Bernard and Marilyn, 214
Pituch, Karl, 237, 252
Poole, Valter, 95, 98, 109, 116, 149–50

racial diversity, 188–90, 205–7, 249–50
Rackham Symphony Choir, 125, 127
radio broadcasts: under Dorati, 167; Ford Sunday Evening Hour, 67–68, 72–73, 74, 83–84, 86–87; under Gabrilowitsch, 56, 62; under Järvi, 199; "Music for Michigan" series, 99–100; "Symphony of the Americas" broadcasts, 95
recession, 156–57
recordings: under Dorati, 168–70, 172; under Järvi, 196–97, 200–202, 206–7;

under Krueger, 95, 99; under Paray, 117–25, 135–36; under Slatkin, 233, 248–50
record players, 42
Reichhold, Henry: ambitions of, for DSO, 93–95; background of, 91; DSO membership campaign of, 93; moves DSO to Music Hall, 97–98, 99; and Twilight Summer Concert Series, 101; and Women's Association, 159
Reiner, Fritz, 72
Reitelman, Sandra, 242
Remick, Anna Thomson, 40
Remick, Jerome Jr., 107
Remick, Jerome Sr., 39–40, 42
Renaissance Center, 168
Resnick, Felix, 124
reverberation, 53
Richard, Father Gabriel, 1–2, 253
Robertson, Leroy, 102
Robinson, Richard, 188, 189
Rockwell, John, 155, 182, 195
Romney, George, 148
Rose, Leonard, 144–45
Russel, John R., 18, 24–25

Sabata, Victor de, 112, 113, 153
St. Matthew Passion (Bach), 60–63
Samaroff, Olga, 48, 54
Sam's Cut-Rate, 86, 89, 93
Save Orchestra Hall initiative, 151
"Save the Symphony" campaign, 83
Schalk, Franz, 92
Schkolnik, Ilya, 39, 48, 95
Schlagobers (Strauss), 208
Schnabel, Artur, 56
Schonberg, Harold C., 129, 143, 146–47, 153
Schubert Festival, 171
Schurmann, Hans, 173
Scriabin, Alexander, 32–33
Segerstam, Leif, 217–18
Semple, Robert, 141, 152, 157, 160, 170, 175